PRINCESS MARGARET AND THE CURSE

PRINCESS MARGARET AND THE CURSE

AN INQUIRY INTO A ROYAL LIFE

MERYLE SECREST

Skyhorse Publishing, Inc.

Copyright © 2025 by Meryle Secrest

All rights reserved. No part of this book may be reproduced in any manner without the express written consent of the publisher, except in the case of brief excerpts in critical reviews or articles. All inquiries should be addressed to Skyhorse Publishing, 307 West 36th Street, 11th Floor, New York, NY 10018.

Skyhorse Publishing books may be purchased in bulk at special discounts for sales promotion, corporate gifts, fund-raising, or educational purposes. Special editions can also be created to specifications. For details, contact the Special Sales Department, Skyhorse Publishing, 307 West 36th Street, 11th Floor, New York, NY 10018 or info@skyhorsepublishing.com.

Skyhorse® and Skyhorse Publishing® are registered trademarks of Skyhorse Publishing, Inc.®, a Delaware corporation.

Visit our website at www.skyhorsepublishing.com.

Please follow our publisher Tony Lyons on Instagram @tonylyonsisuncertain

10 9 8 7 6 5 4 3 2 1

Library of Congress Cataloging-in-Publication Data is available on file.

Cover design by Kai Texel
Cover photograph by Getty Images

Print ISBN: 978-1-5107-8256-3
Ebook ISBN: 978-1-5107-8552-6

Printed in the United States of America

". . . I wanted change and excitement and to shoot off in all directions myself, like the colored arrows from a Fourth of July rocket."
—Sylvia Plath, *The Bell Jar*

"Life is indeed dangerous . . . but the essence of it is not a battle. It is unmanageable because it is a romance, and its essence is romantic beauty."
—E. M. Forster, *Howards End*

Contents

Chapter 1	Pomp and Circumstance	1
Chapter 2	The Ghosts of Glamis	9
Chapter 3	Too Strict: Too Lax	27
Chapter 4	Odd Girl Out	37
Chapter 5	The Glass Curtain	55
Chapter 6	The King Will Never Leave	77
Chapter 7	A Pawn in the Game	103
Chapter 8	Margaret Learns to Lie	143
Chapter 9	Everybody Likes Him	161
Chapter 10	Her Special Island	183
Chapter 11	A Slipper on the Lawn	199
Chapter 12	Portrait of a Lady	221
Chapter 13	Dr. Kenneth Jones	241
Chapter 14	Arrows of Desire	261
Endnotes		281

PRINCESS MARGARET
AND THE CURSE

CHAPTER 1

POMP AND CIRCUMSTANCE

"Sword and buckler by thy side,/Rest on the shore
of battle-tide,/Which, like the ever-hungry sea/
Roars round this Isle;"
—Basil Hood, *Merrie England,* 1902

EVERYWHERE THE LITTLE GIRL LOOKS, she is swept up and enveloped in a fanfaronade of red. This is a red of fathomless depths, a red of omnipotence and splendor, as sumptuous as velvet, as intense as lightning, as glowing as banked fires. It appears in sweeping, flaring cloaks and unmanageable trains, in livery lavishly trimmed with gold braids, on the seats one sits on; it arrives in huge hats, gloves, on armrests and stools. It is omnipresent, eclipsing blues and golds, this triumphant symphony of color. Even above her head, it is hanging and swaying from heights so distant she cannot see them, mute, multicolored witnesses to the splendor of celebration that day of May 12, 1937. For her name is Margaret Rose, she is not yet seven years old, and she is waiting to see her father and mother being crowned King and Queen in Westminster Abbey.

From her booster seat in the royal box, she watches, her chin propped on the edge of a wall, as masses of soldiers arrive in their red jackets, their helmets sporting long, curling white feathers, and take up their positions, standing row on row up and down the aisles, silent as stones. Noble ladies appear in their gowns of sinuous white satins and sweeping skirts, designed to display heavy ropes of pearls and diamonds that sway and sparkle with each rustling step. She is sitting next to her big sister, Elizabeth, now eleven, as well as their formidable and imposing grandmother, Queen Mary, and the Princess Royal. Vast throngs keep arriving—it is recorded that the Abbey's audience that day was eight thousand people. To the constant movement and murmuring inside is added peals of bells outside and a thundering organ. One can hardly hear oneself think. Margaret is too absorbed, too wide-eyed to talk. She has already seen her parents in full regalia. Papa is wearing a loose blue tunic, breeches, and white hose, but you can't see them because everything is covered up by his Robe of State. There is a big ermine cape up around his ears and down over his hands. It also has a red velvet train so very long that Papa cannot move until six pages behind him pick it up and carry it as he walks. Mama has the same kind of robe but smaller, and it doesn't really wrap her up, so you see more of her white dress underneath and all her best jewelry as well.

Margaret and her sister have matching dresses in the same kind of creamy silk trimmed with lace. The short sleeves are very puffy—the latest fashion—and Papa, who supervised the dress himself, wanted to see lots of little gold bows going down the front all the way from the neckline to the hem. Then Margaret found out that Elizabeth was getting a train, and she wasn't. So, she cried a lot, and Papa changed his mind. It was fun to swirl around and watch the train try to catch up. The best part, though, were the shoes. Would Crawfie (her governess, Marion Crawford) like to see them, she asked shyly. Crawfie would, and Margaret Rose lifted her skirt to reveal an expanse of sunburned leg, a pair of socks, and the prettiest, daintiest shoes in the world, all made of silver. For once, she, a nonstop chatterer, was too awed to say a word.[1]

Edgar, the first English king, had been crowned a thousand years before, in 973, in the old Roman town of Bath in the West of England. In those days, a small monastic church occupied the spot on which a proper abbey would eventually be built in the fourteenth century (it is still there). Perhaps it was the monks who set the pattern for what would become a part political and civil, part religious affirmation of God's anointing of his chosen one. For the next thousand years kings never wavered from the wonderful delusion that they had been divinely ordained to rule. There were some gentle jokes along the way. One of the stories told about King Canute is that he decided to test his omnipotent authority by going down to the seashore and commanding the waves to stop. He was awfully annoyed when they didn't.

There was another, rather large issue to contend with. However convinced they might feel, British kings faced a patchwork of warring principalities with their own ambitions and spheres of influence, and were always at war. Families who would eventually acquire great stature and influence evolved from those who had supported certain monarchs in their eternal battles to punish warring tribes and establish larger spheres of influence in the process. The rewards could be substantial: land, fortunes, even castles, names, and legendary influence. The more possessions you acquired, the more important you were, leading to the inevitable emphasis on dress as a status symbol and instant display of wealth, not to mention precedence in the pecking order. To the medieval mind, there were three estates. The lowest was that of the peasant in the fields. Second came the nobleman with his power and influence; the first estate was reserved for the clergy, being closest to God.

The nobly born did have a responsible role to play in the natural order of things, to defend the other two estates and "maintain justice and order."[2] If attacked, the owner must be prepared to defend the other two estates by sheltering and feeding them inside his castle or walled city. He was their defender, their savior, and to take on this noble task was required of the sons in the great families. Protecting the weak, righting wrongs, guarding the realm with sword and buckler always at the ready: This was his destiny. His high moral purpose.

Curiously enough, to this day, young men in the royal family usually go into the services, often the army or navy, and, until very recently, royal courtiers were recruited from the military. Old traditions die hard.

Over the centuries, the sword itself became symbolic, not of aggression but magical transformation—a force for good. The tales surrounding King Arthur are a case in point. Arthur, who receives his own sword named Excalibur through supernatural means, and who may or may not have actually existed, has survived in the popular imagination for eons, along with his Knights of the Round Table, Galahad, Guinevere, and Merlin, in poetry and art. The story in all its artful forms has even survived "Monty Python and Holy Grail," an irresistible spoof that has done no particular harm to the original, which survives in many forms.

One of them is art. The nineteenth century Pre-Raphaelites took up the legend with particular enthusiasm, leaving some marvelous paintings behind them. There is "Beguiling of Merlin," for instance, the "Wedding of St. George," and the "Lady of Shalott." Sir Edward Coley, in particular, imagined scenes which he depicted with the meticulousness of stained glass. The artist Edward Burne-Jones wrote that, for him, "a painting was a beautiful romantic dream of something that never was, never will be . . . in a land no one can define or remember, only desire."

As for the sword itself, Tennyson wrote that moonlight "ran forth and sparkled keen with frost against the hilt/For all the haft twinkled with diamond sparks/Myriads of topaz-lights, and jacinth work/Of subtlest jewelry. . . ."[3]

Such thoughts come to mind upon visiting the collection of crown jewels on display in the Tower of London. One enters a dark, theatrical space, with exhibits spotlit at murky intervals. The first to arrive out of the gloom are three swords hanging in the air as if magically suspended. By far the most interesting is the Sword of State, dated 1678, which was commissioned by Charles II and is, along with the two others, carried in front of the monarch whenever he or she enters Parliament, as has been the case since the reign of Richard the Lionheart in 1189.

This particular sword could double for a real-life Excalibur. Its scabbard—decorated by silver tracery of such delicacy one cannot believe it was made by a mortal hand—is encrusted with jewels and made of solid gold. Its artful suspension in mid-air seems poised, as all the objects are, between the real and the fantastical, as if Cocteau had been called to repeat, with his uncanny sleight of hand, the wizardry he used to such effect in "La Belle et le Bete." One improbable object of staggering beauty follows another; the ornamental flask, or ampula, carved out of gold with an eagle's head that holds the holy oil, or the Imperial Mantle, whose heavy golden folds are ornamented with roses, thistles, and shamrocks.

Finally, one arrives at the cabinet of crowns and the special crown itself, belonging to King Edward, which, at the moment when it crowns the monarch, releases a fanfare of trumpets and yet another peal of bells. Then the roar of "God save the King" echoes in the great cathedral as the nobles, in unison, place the coronets on their own heads.

This particular day, May 12, 1937, had further significance. Everybody knew by then that a different king was supposed to have been crowned that day, not George VI but his oldest brother David, the future Edward VIII. Their father, George V, had died in 1935, and David, as the oldest of four boys, naturally succeeded him. But then, what was viewed as a tremendous scandal was leaked by the foreign press.

It turned out that David, while Duke of Windsor, had fallen in love with Wallis Warfield Simpson, an American charmer from Baltimore, who was already divorced, not once, but twice. The Church of England did not recognize divorce in those days. Once was bad enough, but two times—! And not even English.

In the middle of it all, Edward VIII had had enough, causing yet more gasps of horror by saying he did not want to be King or Emperor if he could not have the woman he loved and make her his Queen. A century before, he might have shot himself. Instead, he abdicated, left his family, his throne, his crown, and his kingdom and went into exile in France. It was the biggest scandal that ever was. But there it was, a coronation date and no King. Bertie had to save the day.

Bertie, otherwise known as the Duke of York, was a slim, good-looking younger brother with sensitivity and a natural reluctance intensified by his being left-handed. Forced to use his right, he developed a debilitating stammer. He and his beautiful Scottish wife were ensconced in a handsome, but not large, town house on Piccadilly, where they lived in relative obscurity and might occasionally be photographed taking Elizabeth and Margaret Rose for picnics, walks, or on horseback in the adjacent St. James's Park. Being forced to become King was almost more than he could bear. In court circles he was referred to as "poor old Bertie." How was he ever going to live up to the job?

Bertie was right to panic, because the realm he was about to inherit was vast. Measured by actual area, the British Empire, when considered in terms not only of its dominions, but also such factors as its colonies, protectorates, and mandates, was the largest empire in history and for one hundred years the foremost global power. By 1913, it comprised 412 million people, almost a quarter of the world's population at the time and a similar percentage of the world's land mass. It was axiomatic that the sun never set on the British Empire. Of Africa, it was also said that one could travel from the Mediterranean to the Cape of Good Hope without leaving British soil. Britain was unchallenged as the predominant naval power. Children at school were shown on a map that all the pink parts were British, and there was a lot to be proud of. "Rule Britannia!" Land of hope and glory indeed.

The historian Alan Allport observed, "In 1939 the folds of the Union Jack smacked smartly against flagstaffs all the way from the Eastern Mediterranean to Brisbane, from the Great Rift Valley to the Yucatan Peninsula . . . Albert Frederick Arthur George Windsor was not only the world's greatest Christian king, but also the world's greatest Hindu king, Sikh king, and Muslim king."[4] There is no record of what George VI was thinking that day, but something can be discerned from his stiff and careful movements and frozen expression as the crown descended with its awful weight on his head. Long live the King!

Elizabeth and Margaret Rose were too excited to be frightened of anything, but they faced an endurance test of their own. Their usual wake-up call came at 7:30 a.m. However, on this day of all days, a band outside their window woke them up at five, and quite soon after breakfast a delegation of dressers descended to make sure that not a hair was out of place, the coronets went on the right way round, their nails were clean, their dresses ironed, all the bows and ribbons had been tied, and the final effect was flawless. Two hours later, they were escorted to one of the palace's many horse-and-carriage affairs for the two-mile drive to Westminster Abbey, accompanied by Queen Mary and the Princess Royal.

This particular coach was called the Glass Coach and was usually reserved for brides on their way to their wedding. In 1923, their mother had taken it on her journey to the Abbey to marry their father; in years to come Princess Anne would do the same, and so would Lady Diana Spencer. None of the carriages had springs but only leather straps, so occupants had to smile and wave bravely while being tossed around like corks on an ocean, even at a walking pace. The Glass Coach was considered better than most, but not by much. Elizabeth noted in her diary that it was "very jolty."

Even though coronations—who does what when, and with which hand—are ruthlessly rehearsed, under the pressure of performance, anything can happen and usually does. In his book, *Coronation*, the historian Hugo Vickers records that the ceremony for Queen Victoria almost self-destructed. First, the eighty-seven-year-old Lord Rolle stumbled and actually rolled down the steps. Then, by mistake, the Bishop of Bath and Wells turned over two pages of the service at once and confused everybody. The young Queen finally turned to the Dean of Westminster and said, "Pray tell me what I am to do, for they don't know."

George VI and his wife, who was being crowned as well, were hardly any better off, as *Coronation* also records. First, Dr. Christopher Foxley-Norris, the Dean of Westminster, whose solemn duty it was to carry the crown, also stumbled and fell down some steps. The precious object, thoughtfully attached to its royal pillow by some stout ribbons, trembled alarmingly but stayed in place. The befuddled Dean did less harmful damage, giving the wrong regalia in the wrong order to the wrong peer, although no doubt the enormous audience was none the wiser.

As the moment finally arrived when the crown descends on the King's head and the nobles crown themselves, Elizabeth and Margaret Rose, up on their balcony overlooking the proceedings, managed to do the same. But then Margaret couldn't remember where the front of hers was. She took it off, looked at it doubtfully, gave up and stuck it back on at a distinctly rakish angle. Curiously enough, so did the Archbishop of Canterbury, in the act of crowning the King. He, too, kept turning the object doubtfully. The King had problems of his own. At a certain moment in the proceedings, he must stand, but he couldn't because one of the supporting Bishops had a foot firmly planted on his train.

"I had to tell him to get off it pretty sharply, as I nearly fell down," the King said later.[5] It was that kind of a day.

If such gaffes were noticed by the foreign press, they were not recorded. However, next day the *New York Times* had a headline story about the little Princess Margaret Rose who was not "acting as a princess should" and clearly bored as the hours ticked by. First, she began to wriggle a lot. Instead of sitting upright with hands neatly folded, she started to loll about, showing desperate signs of looking for something to do, picking up the program and putting it down again. Why couldn't she sit still and not fidget?

Then she put out a finger and tried to play "Inky Dinky Spider" up and down her sister's arm, giggling away. Elizabeth, a model of correct behavior, pretended to ignore her. Then she frowned. When disapproval had no effect, she gave her sister a nudge. That didn't work either. Then, horror of horrors, Margaret Rose opened her mouth and yawned—as it looked right into the Archbishop of Canterbury's face. All this was minutely documented for readers of the *New York Times*.[6,7] Less remarked on by the press, the Marquess of Donegall fell asleep. The even more august Duke of Marlborough, who was fumbling with his coronet, somehow released an unsuspected shower of chocolates, which cascaded all over the carpet.[8]

Elizabeth's diary conceded that the ceremony did seem to be awfully long, especially the prayers at the end. Turning yet another page, she found the work "Finis" just as her statuesque grandmother, Queen Mary, did. They looked at each other conspiratorially and smiled. Once back in the Palace, there were endless photo sessions to be endured. Then they had to appear on the balcony with Mama and Papa, smile, and wave as packed crowds surged and cheered below. The royal party came and went for hours and hours. The last appearance was close to midnight. Elizabeth confided in her diary that she stood so much her legs ached.

Dingy London neighborhoods had been decorated with bunting, flags, and gay paper streamers for community parties that went on all over the city. Elsewhere in London, the great buildings were splendidly lit up: Buckingham Palace, Westminster Abbey, Hampton Court, Windsor Castle, and even, for the first time in nine hundred years, the Tower of London.

As for the procession itself, representatives of the Empire came from parts as far distant as Australia to march in the long, winding procession that was headed by the superb golden coach of 1762, thirteen feet high and weighing four tons. Eight horses are required to pull the carriage in their red harnesses, accompanied by coachmen, postillions, and equerries attired in elaborate scarlet and gold uniforms and sporting on their sleeves the royal emblem with its motto, "*Honi soit qui mal y pense.*" More than twenty-five thousand policemen and soldiers lined the royal routes—so many, it was joked, that if war had been declared that day, the King couldn't have mustered an army.

But the real stars on the street were the vast crowds, variously estimated at from 100,000 to 500,000 and then as many as one million people—who made sacrifices of time, money and endured hours of misery in their determination to be part of this great, once-in-a-lifetime event. Not only was it the most widely publicized coronation, but it was the first to be heard on radio and the first to be televised, even if only a very few people in 1937 owned TV sets. *The New York Times* reported, "Regiment after regiment passes the small, brightly lit screen. We can see the kilts swinging, the bayonets gleaming, the stirrups and spurs of the horsemen. . . ."[9]

As the endless parade swung by, the crowds swayed and cheered. Some people had slept in parks to be the first, as dawn broke, to rush and claim the choicest spots on the edge of the sidewalk. Others, with the means to book one of the expensive reserved seats, nevertheless came early. Bigger enclosures for standing room cost less, and were also competed for vigorously in the early morning hours. The newspapers reported "most of the spectators had stood for eight to fifteen hours by the time the procession arrived. They paid a heavy price, fainting in the thousands. . . ." Others, in the formal morning wear of silk top hats and morning coats, were part of the general free for all, usually clutching sandwiches and umbrellas. Rain was forecast and arrived on time, turning into a downpour around three o'clock. People held newspapers over their heads or tried vainly to wrap them around their skirts and shoes. Those who brought umbrellas were pelted with soggy balls of newsprint by latecomers who found their views blocked by forests of umbrellas.

Still, the tone was remarkably good-natured, even jolly. To add to the misery, bus drivers of the huge fleet of double-deckers that normally plied the center were on strike. They wanted shorter hours; understandably, since in the days before traffic exhaust was considered a health hazard, the long-suffering bus drivers were getting ill. The prime minister begged them to call off their strike just for one special day. They refused. The vast crowds arriving in special trains, walking across the bridges, or fighting their way in and out of the tube stations, took that in good humor, too. Taxis were the only solution for the elite peers in their ermine capes and velvet trains, but not, of course, to be easily had. The last exhausted visitor, after a wait of four or five hours, left the Abbey in a cab at nine that night.[10]

As for the new King and Queen, one imagines them finally peeling off their gloves and fixed smiles around midnight and collapsing into bed. What a day! Somehow, they had survived, but it took superhuman patience and stamina. As the Queen remarked sadly, "We aren't supposed to be human."[11]

Chapter 2

The Ghosts of Glamis

> "Glamis thou art, and Cawdor; and shalt be/What
> thou art promised: yet do I fear thy nature . . ."
> —*Macbeth*, ACT 1, Scene V

From afar, Glamis Castle, surrounded by level lawns in a superb setting in the county of Angus, Scotland, could not seem a more ideal setting for the birth of a princess. There, Princess Margaret Rose of York, second daughter of the Duke and Duchess of York, was born on August 21, 1930. For over eight hundred years Glamis has been standing in its verdant setting—fourteen thousand acres of parks, streams, and gardens—fashioned from red sandstone mellowed to a pinkish gray. The effect is a charming disorganization of design, massive without seeming so and amazingly intact despite the odds against it. Its huge central keep, turreted towers, scattered flocks of windows, and crenelated roofline give it the ethereal air of a chateau in the French Loire valley.

One thinks of the romantic ideal as described by Alain-Fournier in his novel, *The Grand Meaulnes*. His hero, Meaulnes, is a teenager who wanders away from his small village and finds himself lost in a wood. Suddenly, he comes upon a chateau full of children. They have organized a *fête champêtre* and wear costumes reminiscent of Watteau's paintings. All the doors are open. So are the windows, and children in their silk dresses and doublets and hose are beckoning towards him. He enters and meets the most beautiful girl, perhaps a princess. Alain-Fournier continues the story of their grownup love affair. But this is secondary to that magical moment between childhood and young manhood when he finds his adolescent ideal in a chateau. The book was published in 1913, and its author died on the battlefields of World War I one year later. But his book became a classic of French literature and has twice been made into a film.

To catch sight of Glamis at a distance is to conjure up similar visions. But these vanish slowly once the visitor enters a mysterious building whose tempestuous history is all too real. True, the reception rooms are pleasant enough, if a bit too reminiscent of Edwardian ideas of coziness rather than elegance. Or even the statelier seventeenth- and eighteenth-century rooms that follow, with their coved and stucco plasterwork ceilings and remarkable stained-glass windows. The further the visitor is allowed to explore, the more surface domesticity peels away to reveal the crude and undeniable truth: lethal spears strung along bare stone walls.

Here are coats of armor, underground storerooms, dungeons, abandoned kitchens, stopped up wells and all the detritus of centuries. The outer walls are so massive, sixteen feet thick in some places, that actual rooms were carved out of them and small windows hewed out of the stone, partly explaining the higgledy-piggledy look on the outside. The impression of disorderly, almost-deranged living for centuries is intensified by the warren of corridors that have penetrated the thick walls, leading somewhere or nowhere, perhaps to a secret chamber or, more likely, a walled-up dead end.

Sir Walter Scott, who spent a night there in 1790, described a persistent feeling of dread as he was conducted by flickering candlelight up narrow, dark and winding stone staircases, their steep, irregular treads worn into hollows from centuries of wear.

He wrote, "(A)s I heard door after door shut, after my conductor had retired, I began to consider myself as too far from the living and somewhat too near to the dead."

One of the castle's many persistent legends is that this was where Duncan, King of Scotland, was murdered by Macbeth, as depicted in Shakespeare's play. There is even a hall named after Duncan. This cannot possibly be true, because the historical figures involved predate the castle by three hundred years (eleventh vs. fourteenth centuries). If the reference is to Shakespeare's play of 1606, it is not one to celebrate either.

Problems began with the first performance, when the actor playing Lady Macbeth became ill, and the playwright, in the days when men played women's parts, had to take over the role. That set in motion a bizarre series of accidents that have afflicted performances to the present day, including actual deaths on stage—actors falling off the stage, or actual daggers being substituted for pretend ones. During a Royal Shakespeare Company performance in 1937, the brilliant young actor Laurence Olivier's career almost came to an end when a stage weight fell without warning and missed him by inches. In theatrical circles, it is referred to superstitiously as "The Scottish Play."

Then there are stories that might, or might not, be true. One of them better documented than most, involves a Monster—a vile, misshapen creature kept hidden in a secret chamber.

Curiously enough, he was not insane—Jane Eyre's famous novel includes the baleful presence of a mad wife kept locked away in an attic, the Victorian solution for hiding inconvenient relatives—just too frightful to be let loose. One person described him as "a human toad."

Such a rumor, that an actual Monster was hidden somewhere in the castle, seems to have arisen during the nineteenth century and was investigated recently by Mike Dash, a writer for *Smithsonian Magazine*.[1] Dash concluded that, despite repeated denials, too many people seem to have stumbled on the person himself to be discounted. For, as Claude Bowes-Lyon, 13th Earl of Strathmore (1824–1904) is reported to have said, "If you could even guess the nature of this castle's secret, you would get down on your knees and thank God it was not yours."[2]

Persistent ghosts also appear from time to time down through the centuries, usually benign figures who turn up when least expected. One of those most often seen, it would appear, was the wife of a titled owner. She and her young son were falsely charged with having conspired to poison the King, James V, in 1537. Both were tried for treason and convicted. She was burned at the stake. (Her son, being too young for such a fate, was imprisoned instead, and survived.) The lady liked to wear gray and can sometimes show up in the middle of the morning. This happened one day to Rose, the future Countess Granville, sister to Elizabeth Bowes-Lyons, the future Queen Mother. The castle has its own small chapel where Rose would play the organ for family services. One morning she entered it to practice some hymns and found someone already sitting there, she thought in prayer. It was a lady in a gray outfit. So as not to interrupt her, Rose waited politely at the entrance. When no one came out, she became exasperated and went in to take a look. The figure, of course, had disappeared.

Elizabeth Bowes-Lyons, always called Lizzie, was born on September 4, 1900, and such apparent reminders of a brutal past had been taken in their stride by the large and boisterous family—ten children—of the 14th Earl of Strathmore, Claude Bowes-Lyon, and his wife Cecilia. Once upon a time, a hapless neighboring family, the Lindsays, in flight from some sort of baronial feud, arrived at Glamis, begging for protection. Instead, they were conducted to one of the castle's hidden chambers, walled up, and left to starve to death. By the time Lizzie's generation had arrived, what agonies took place there were long forgotten, and it was just the room with skulls in it.

The only chamber no one wanted to sleep in apparently was Earl Patrick's room, renamed from its former inhabitant, the family's private hangman. At one time, the Lyons actually employed a hangman of their own, although how often his services were required is not recorded. You could not put children to bed there because they would wake up screaming. One guest, Arthur Lowther, later Lord Ullswater, something of a daredevil, said he wanted to sleep in it. All went well until he woke up in the middle of the night and began to walk around. Suddenly, the floor collapsed under his feet. The sleeper below awoke to find a pair of legs protruding from his ceiling.

Such was the historical legacy of Elizabeth Angela Marguerite Bowes-Lyon, direct descendant of all the other Bowes-Lyons who had called the castle home since it was presented as a gift to Sir John Lyon in 1372 by Robert the Bruce. A less likely descendant of that haunted and tempestuous group would be hard to find. Photographs show her as the most appealing of little girls. When she was just four years old, we find her posing protectively with her little brother David, aged two, in beautifully smocked overblouses. One arm cradles her brother's neck while a gentle hand restrains his arm. David, so encircled, a loved child, looks into the distance, his curls in golden profusion on his forehead. There is a clear family resemblance in the deeply set eyes, rosebud mouths, and chubby cheeks.

The last two in a long line, they were inseparable. One of their favorite games was to cover themselves in white sheets, giggling and hiding in a dark corner, then jump out at passers- by, who would pretend to be scared. Another was dressing up in costumes. Once Lizzie was nine and beginning to take dancing lessons, she would wear a long, old-fashioned gown of heavy silk or satin, crisscrossed with ribbons at the bodice, descending to the ankles and spaced at intervals with bobbles, just like a Jester's outfit.

As the last girl in the family, Lizzie was even less likely to be subjected to any great expectation except, perhaps, a brilliant marriage, and there, looks and etiquette were all that was needed. Why, after all, should her pretty little self be tormented with facts and figures when it was so much more important that she be kept happy and busy, with lots of friends and out in the open air? Once she had children of her own, she would be grateful for that kind of childhood. It was rather a matter of "Be good, sweet maid, and let who will be clever," a maxim that would have some consequences when the time came to educate her daughter Margaret.

Lizzie's way of turning her head had the disarming, vulnerable look that one saw at intervals after she grew up. There was something very affecting about that look, her ability to seem perfectly delighted wherever she went, her genuine interest and natural self-assurance. She was irresistible. Certainly, the Duke of York, second son of George V, thought so. More than just first impressions were involved. There was also something very down to earth about this girl. She could put on heavy boots and tramp the moors without worrying about her clothes or her hair or how far it was. During the 1914–1918 war, Glamis became a hospital for the wounded, and she threw herself into this new situation, playing cricket along with those well enough to convalesce, her long hair flying.[3]

In September 1916, a shooting party took place and Lizzie and her mother were alone in the castle with their military patients. In the early evening, one of the soldiers happened to look up at the tower ninety feet above his head and saw smoke coming from under the roof. The castle was on fire. While waiting for three fire brigades to arrive, Lizzie and the maids began frantically applying buckets of water. Two village fire brigades arrived within minutes, but their equipment could not throw water high enough to attack the blaze. Fortunately, the third arrival could and soon had the fire under control. But then a cold-water storage tank in the attic suddenly gave way, and a torrent of water began pouring down the main staircase.

By then, enough neighbors had arrived to help that Lizzie could rapidly organize them into a group to sweep the water down over the stairs and out of the house. But still more willing hands were needed to move furniture, carpets, and precious objects out of reception rooms. She was a marvel of tireless organization and quick thinking, and the dangers were averted, as everyone realized. Her mother wrote, ". . . poor darling she was quite worn out after & ached all over for days." She was just sixteen.[4]

Along with neighbors and staff, soldiers who were well enough to walk helped the family. A considerable amount of good will had been built up by the young Elizabeth in particular, who was frequently filling in for the nurses, arriving in the wards with gifts of cigarettes and tobacco, and writing letters home. She was always ready to make a fourth at cards—whist was the usual game—even if she couldn't get the hang of it.[5] Along with her ability to rise to the occasion, she had a sense of fun. She once dressed up as a maid and conducted a tour for a group of visitors. She received several tips with a curtsey, for her surprisingly detailed commentary.[6]

Kenneth Clark, who would become Surveyor of the King's Pictures, took to her at once. So did the Duke of York, who saw her as a being apart, an ideal girl, contrasting her shining qualities with his ineptness; he said, "I am only a very ordinary person when people let me be."[7] It would be fairer and truer to conclude, as Janet Flanner did, that he was duty-bound by rank and work as his mother, Queen Mary, and, therefore, difficult to talk to. Bertie's determined effort to persuade Elizabeth to become his duchess is well known. Finally, after the third proposal, she consented. They were married in 1923, and thus she became the Duchess of York.

In any discussion of the Bowes-Lyon family, a reference is usually made to the fact that they were "hard drinkers." Patterns of behavior tend to be repeated in families down through the generations, and within the British Isles, the Scots have an unrivaled reputation for their fondness for, and consumption of, a strong drink. The Bowes-Lyons also had the ability to "hold" their liquor, as if this showed strength of character, and not to keep up with everyone was proof of lack of inner worth. A couple of months after becoming pregnant with their first-born in 1925, the Duchess wrote to her husband, ". . . the sight of wine simply turns me up! Isn't it extraordinary! It will be a tragedy if I never recover my drinking powers."[8] She sounded almost distraught.

Kenneth Clark, the distinguished art historian, museum official, scholar, and TV personality, who was no stranger to alcoholism in his own family, was disturbed to find in the 1930s, when they became friends, that the little Queen started drinking at 11:30 in the morning. He consoled himself by adding that she only drank Dubonnet before lunch. Perhaps that was true then. But years later, as we know from first-hand testimony, it became two parts Dubonnet to one part gin, and by the time lunch was served "she was feeling no pain," as the expression went, facing life in a benevolent haze.

Major Colin Burgess, who took care of her in later years, said that a well-spiked Dubonnet would be followed every day by wine for lunch, with perhaps a glass of port afterwards. Six o'clock, "the magic hour," she called it, would bring about two martinis, followed by pink champagne during the meal. In the years when she was resident at Clarence House in Westminster, a guest for afternoon tea would be presented with a tray of gin and tonics to keep him going before the meal was brought in on a tray. After the substantial tea with lots of cakes, and a suitable interval, a tray of whisky and sodas would discreetly appear. It would seem that royalty's benevolent hospitality floated on a sea of libations.

And not just the family itself. Something called the Windsor Wets, a congenial group in and outside the royal enclave, was devoted to games, cards, and the single-minded effort of drinking until one was, in the native argo, "thoroughly soaked." The young Duchess was known for her fondness for such when Margaret was born because, barely a year later, she was invited to become the club's patroness (in 1931). She accepted. She wrote, "from half pint to Jeroboam, let us go forward together . . ." It was all in good fun, but it masked as inner insecurity on her part. When this Scottish girl, who had spent her life in a remote castle, was suddenly catapulted into one of the world's most prominent roles, constantly on display, photographed day and night, even she, who was ready for almost everything, quailed at the prospect. She could not face it. She once said, "I couldn't get through all my engagements without a little something."[9]

As has been noted, the new mother could not bear the taste of wine and, plausibly, never regained it during the pregnancy (in 1925) of her first-born, the future Elizabeth II. The only way to judge is that the young Elizabeth does not exhibit any of the special problems seen in children laboring under the particular handicaps of a child with fetal alcohol syndrome. In any case, no doctor is likely to have warned her mother not to drink. Prevailing medical opinion had it that the placenta protected the growing baby from alcohol's effects, even if it became clear that something was going wrong. Awareness did not come for the next four decades, until a doctor in France and two pediatricians in the US wrote similar papers on the dangers of alcohol at any stage. They were right. This happened in the 1970s, some forty plus years after the births of Elizabeth and Margaret.

It was nobody's fault except the doctors. One wonders what the medical conclusion was when two daughters of John "Jock" Bowes-Lyon, older brother of the Duchess, and his wife Fenella had two daughters, Nerissa (1919) and Katherine (1926), who were severely disabled?

By a strange coincidence, "Jock's" wife Fenella had a sister named Harriet, who married a military man, Major Henry Neville. They proceeded to have seven children. Three more of their daughters—Idonea (1912), Rosemary (1914), and Ethelreda (1922)—were similarly affected and placed in the same institution, the Royal Earlswood, the same year (1941). They, too, could not talk and had the mental age of six.

The details of Margaret's birth were also unknown and have only recently come to light. This could have been for security reasons but also seems to have been a lingering consequence of the Victorian prudery that kept women's lower limbs well covered, when the glimpse of an ankle was tantamount to a sexual invitation.

At the time, the public also wasn't aware that the Duchess had a C-Section. In those days, the surgery, called a "high vertical," was exactly that, making such a radical solution equally dangerous to the mother and the baby. The procedure was a last resort if the baby was about to arrive feet first, or any other way besides the head first that nature intended. This method, standard for centuries, was, however, increasingly questioned. New alternatives were being put forth. That same year, in 1926, a doctor in Glasgow had pioneered an operation that called for a much smaller incision—lower down and horizontal—with less danger to the mother and the baby and a faster, safer recovery.

If the attending surgeons knew of this new technique, one assumes that they were not about to experiment on a royal person. Elizabeth later hinted in her letters that her recovery had been long and painful. By the time Margaret was due, a second Caesarian was out of the question. The baby's arrival was expected between August 6 and 12. As August 6 arrived, the special correspondent for the *Baltimore Sun* reported that J. R. Clynes, home secretary, left London in a hurry. His presence would be needed at Glamis, not only to sign all the official papers, but in a quirk of history stemming from the days when it was easy to switch babies and substitute infant imposters, he had to be in the room at the actual event to ensure this did not happen. (The custom was eventually dropped.) His arrival was duly noted by royal watchers of comings and goings as proof that the baby would shortly arrive.

As it happened, it didn't, and since it was to be a natural birth, everyone had to wait. Mr. Clynes was obliged to loaf around for another two weeks. Similarly, Sir Henry John Forbes Simson, honorary consulting surgeon at the West London hospital, and principal member of the team who had delivered Elizabeth, took up a protracted residence near Glamis to await the event.

The pregnant mama wrote to Queen Mary, "I wish Mr. Clynes had waited until he was sent for, but he would not do that, and here they are all waiting & hovering like vultures! I shall be glad when they are all gone."[10]

To add to her exasperation, tour buses were arriving to clutter up the village streets, circumnavigate the castle itself, park edge to edge at the locked gates, and unload their sightseers, presumably with cameras and binoculars at the ready. There was not much to see; young Elizabeth was on her pony, the Duke was bound to be on a shoot, and the mother-to-be buried somewhere inside the castle.[11] Finding nothing much to photograph, visitors climbed up the nearby Hunter's Hill, where great bonfires were always lit to signal great events, from wars, murders, or the arrival of a new prince. All was in readiness; a vast pile of rushwood was already built, covered with a tarpaulin, ready to be lit the minute that news arrived that the probable prince (or princess—since in those days nobody knew ahead) made his debut. Finding nothing to buy in the way of souvenirs, visitors made off with so much souvenir rushwood that the villagers had to post guards.[12]

All Britain was on edge, or so the *Baltimore Sun*'s foreign correspondent reported. Everyone, in Scotland in particular, was hoping for a boy. He would be the first heir to the throne born north of the Tweed for many years.

Finally, on August 21, the hoped-for labor pains began to arrive at about 3:30 in the afternoon. As luck would have it, the great day was experiencing a gale, with thunder, lightning, heavy winds, and violent, lashing rain. Wind soughed in the chimneys and buffeted the ancient roofs with their tiles and turrets, turned umbrellas inside out, sent leaves flying, and branches cracking. Rain turned the lawns into swamps and lashed at the old windows. All the power lines into the castle went down, which meant that Glamis Castle, not for the first time, was again out of touch with the outside world.

Something had to be done. As cars tore through the villages of Forfar and Glamis, windows flew up in the village, and front doors opened to watch the sudden roar of sleek black cars flying past. The word went out, shouting the news down the street, "The lassie's got her bairn." The manager of a local movie house, in the middle of showing a film, put a message on the screen, and the film's excited patrons rushed "pell-mell into the wet streets."[13]

The power lines were restored at last, barely minutes before a baby, weighing six-and-a-half pounds, was safely delivered at 9:30 that evening. A new relay of messengers on motor bikes was dispatched to drive the 380 miles to London and deliver the official messages to be posted at Buckingham Palace and elsewhere. Meanwhile, the news was being relayed by telegram, telephone, and telex around the Empire: A CHILD IS BORN. Tomorrow the waiting beacon would be lit and answered by blinking lights from the distant hills. The Earl of Strathmore's estate would breach two huge barrels of ale for the foresters, plowmen, and house servants and tankards passed around to drink to the health of mother and baby. As flames from the bonfire reached two hundred feet into the air, a highland band piped reels for the crowds of celebrants. In London, the next day, on a warm summer afternoon, the Royal Horse Artillery fired a forty-one-gun salute to honor the new Princess, and crowds in Hyde Park stood smartly to attention. The same salute at the Tower of London brought similar crowds to attention. Then the bells of Westminster Abbey began to peel.[14] The news was out. It was not a boy.

The source of all the commotion had been passed over to a nurse, and her mother was resting comfortably in bed, no doubt with a fire burning. The room had always been hers, simple and sparely furnished, with a four-poster bed, heavy gold hangings, a dressing table, desk, and a few chairs. From her windows, Lizzie could look out over the sweeping lawns and distant hills. Bertie, by contrast, was lodged in a small, dark room at the end of a long stone corridor, its circular windows about the size of ships' portholes. Elizabeth was in London staying with her grandparents, and the baby had a nursery suite of her own in another part of Glamis.

Nurse Beevers, "Nanny B," took baby Margaret from her mother's arms and whisked her away to her own quarters, one presumably supplied with its own staff, supplies, and rocking chairs. One does not know how the baby was fed. Hugo Vickers, the author of a biography of the Queen Mother, thinks it unlikely that she was breastfed. In those days childbirth was seen as a confinement followed by a long convalescence in bed. Letters of the Duchess make it clear that she took full advantage of the idea. In any case, breastfed babies need to be nursed every two hours around the clock, and the apparent distance between the baby's own suite and mother's bedroom argues against it.

Professional nannies would be conversant with the infant formulas on the market. Nanny B, the daughter of a carpenter, took midwife courses and became a temporary maternity nanny to some prominent society families. After the family moved back to London, the girls were put in care of Clara Cooper Knight, known as "Alah," who had been their mother's nanny. Alah was daughter of a tenant farmer on the Strathmore's Hertford estate and is described as "kind but firm."[15]

The birth only took six hours. In contrast to the trauma of young Elizabeth's arrival, this one was almost easy. "My darling Mama," Lizzie wrote to Queen Mary a week later, "I am feeling so much better than last time." She would be back on her feet soon. The new arrival "is nice & round & neat . . ." She was obviously pleased, if not ecstatic.[16] After some back and forth—she liked the name of Anne—Margaret was decided upon, being a good old Scottish name, and Rose was added.

If Lizzie and her husband had chosen a name for a boy, she does not mention it. If she was disappointed, this was not surprising, because she must have known how important it was for her countrymen to have a possible King in line for the throne. It couldn't be helped. Margaret would be Margaret Rose throughout her childhood; the second name was discontinued at some vague future date.

In the years following the Great War, the Duchess of York had become the personification of all that was admired in young womanhood. Her resourcefulness and sturdy independence have been cited, along with her down-to-earth ability to tramp across the moors in sensible shoes. The British Liberal

Party politician and journalist Philip Whitwell Wilson, commenting on her growing popularity, observed she was the direct opposite of what one usually thinks of as a duchess: "In New Zealand she waded waist deep in the Tongariro River to land a rainbow trout... Hoping for big game in Africa, she learned to use a rifle." At home in the drawing room, she played the piano and liked to sing; she read the classics and spoke several languages.

Unlike her mother-in-law and the queens before her, the Duchess did not wear the formal toques that marked them both as regal consorts. She followed the latest fashions of the short, flippy skirts and straight up-and-down silhouettes, along with the sleek, trim hairstyles and cloche hats of the period. When she went on tour, her wardrobe could fit into two trunks rather than the vast equipage deemed necessary for a queen on her way somewhere.

"In her hat and fur cloak, the Duchess of York looks as everyone is trying to look," Wilson wrote.

A modernist through and through, she had her green bedroom carpet at the White Lodge in Richmond Park redyed a daring black. She replaced the drab gray living room upholstery for a jolly yellow and red and, for the kitchen, banished labor-intensive items and bought the latest labor-saving ones—from America.

Her initiatives, friendliness, positive outlook on life, and ability to disarm were winning friends everywhere. When she arrived one day to play a solo game of golf at St. Andrews, her car was mobbed. But perhaps her greatest triumph so far was her surprising success in winning the approval of Queen Mary and King George V, her in-laws. Her tact was already pronounced, but what was not sufficiently appreciated, perhaps, was her ability to deflect criticism. Wilson cites her triumph concerning a bas-relief that aroused the rage that simmered just below the surface of King George V's demeanor. In this case his anger was directed at A. G. Walker, a noted sculptor, who had made the elementary mistake of carving a bas-relief of baby Elizabeth in her mother's arms, which was about to be exhibited at Burlington House. King George raged and fulminated. One does not know whether he called it a national disgrace, but no doubt that was the inference. How could he? The King wanted the offending article banished if not (one guesses) smashed to smithereens.

Then the duchess went to see it. "Lizzie," as she still liked to be called, flashed one of her most disarming smiles at her father-in-law. She thought the plaque looked just lovely. The King, for whom she could do no wrong, melted.[17]

For the fact was that both grandparents were delighted with their newborn—they would be just as pleased when Margaret made her appearance four years later—in contrast to their curious lack of interest in the well-being of their four sons when they became parents themselves. Their extravagant attentions to the first little girl would be turned, in the same way, when the second came along. In the case of Elizabeth, there was a particular reason for their hovering because they served as surrogate parents for several months. When Elizabeth was only a few months old, the Duke and Duchess of York made a state visit to Australia and were gone for six months.

Once Elizabeth was left in her care, Queen Mary sprang into action. She took to popping in and out of the nursery several times a day instead of waiting, in time-honored protocol, for the baby to be brought to her. (Twice a day.) She read books about childcare and declared that bringing up babies, or learning how, was a hobby of hers. Even George V was paying attention to baby Elizabeth, who arrived every day while he was having breakfast and was usually allowed to fondle his beard. If he was in a good humor. And he usually was.[18]

Then the great day arrived: Elizabeth produced her first tooth. The news went out around the world and made headlines.[19] When the King found out, he dispatched footmen far and wide and personally ran to the Queen to tell her the news. She, of course, knew already, but pretended to be surprised. (Elizabeth had recently begun to teethe on her pearl necklace.) Suitably warned of her husband's astonishing new interest—he was, after all, the father of five sons and a daughter, whose daily development he (presumably) took in stride—the Queen resolved to flash the news of the baby's first word "across the ether" as well.[20]

After frequent bouts of babysitting, and whenever the grandparents were required to return Elizabeth to her parents, George V took it very hard. As if in expiation for all those years of barking at his sons, the monarch had at last allowed himself a heartrending expression of feeling. He had gone exploring his vast palatial domain and figured out that once the leaves had dropped from the trees in Green Park, he could just see the windows of the Piccadilly house where she was growing up. He must see her every day, he determined. It was essential to his health and well-being. So, his granddaughter was required to stand at the right window at the same time every day and wave. She must have been visible only with a first-rate set of binoculars.

"There she is!" her besotted grandfather would shout. He would wave back.[21]

For the fact was that she might one day become Queen and Empress. Given the immutable rules of secession, the first in line was Elizabeth's Uncle David, the Prince of Wales. Her father came second, and, as the first child to arrive, she came third. This was close enough for the sentries guarding the gates of Buckingham Palace as she came and went with a nurse in a royal motor car, usually clutching a favorite toy. She was smartly saluted every time. And when Mummy and Daddy finally came back from their trip to Australia in June of 1927, protocol had it that she was the one in residence at Buckingham Palace and would therefore be "receiving" them.[22] The dispatch continued that, despite her teething problems, Elizabeth had taken up her social duties and entertained her first playwright, Sir Barrie, and been chucked under the chin by that intrepid aviator, Col. Lindbergh. On her fourth birthday in April 1930, a few months before her sister was born, Elizabeth could be glimpsed in the Palace courtyard as vast holiday crowds behind the railings strained to catch sight of her, watching the Palace guards. She was "a little figure in primrose yellow."[23] As she walked across the quadrangle, the crowd began to cheer wildly and rushed at the police on duty. So great was the crush that both the Norman and St. George's gates had to be closed.[24] Then the little girl gave a little wave and the crowd roared.

She did not try her curtsey that day, or they might have screamed even louder. She had just learned how to do it and had been trying it out all over the Palace. There was something so artless and charming about a footman finding himself flustered by a little girl curtseying at him. One can imagine the scene as he regains his poise, makes a compliment, and the little girl rushes off to try someone else.

While Mummy was at Glamis having her baby, the grandparents were, as usual, spoiling little Elizabeth rotten and putting off once more the moment when their darling would have to go home. A few letters from the little girl to her mummy have survived. She is trying so hard to say the right things, and sends lots of love to Mummy and Mummy's baby, too. Then she goes walking in the rain and splashes about in the puddles.[25] She is trying to be so good and, having graduated from a cot to a proper bed, is being "very quiet in it."[26] One sees a glimpse of the long and arduous process by which a little girl turns into the one who does everything right.

Soon thereafter, she was to go to Glamis to be reunited with Mummy and Daddy and meet her new sister. A friend, staying in the castle, wrote, "That wonderful child Elizabeth is very excited," thinking at first that the baby was some sort of special doll. But when the baby wriggled, gurgled, and opened her eyes, she was ecstatic.

"She then took each of the three Doctors by the hand & said, 'I want to introduce you to my baby sister.'"[27] A full-length article about her in 1936 would declare Elizabeth "The Most Important Little Girl in the World."[28]

The fact that Margaret's status was foredoomed to be eclipsed by her sister's goes back a very long way—to the moment of birth, in fact.

A month or so after her birth, the issue of baptism came up: it would need to be in Scotland. There was a move to bring the Archbishop of Canterbury,

Cosmo Lang, up for the occasion. This intensely irritated her mother. After all, the Duchess wrote to Queen Mary, "the little angel's" arrival was hardly of any great importance. The Prince of Wales, heir apparent, was bound to marry and have some lovely children and heaven knows how many other people would be ahead of Margaret in the line of succession.[29]

So why were people fussing about her? If anyone might become Queen, it would be Elizabeth. There is a story about that. When Elizabeth was only three, she was in the drawing room with Mummy one day when someone came to announce that a visitor wanted to see the Duchess. The little girl coolly replied that Mummy could not see her. She must go away. Mummy stepped in, just in time. Was it some inner awareness of her future role, or the special way she was being treated, or both?

Writing to the Archbishop in September 1930, the Duchess reiterated her view that her baby girl was "very nice." She added, "I am glad to say that she has got large blue eyes and a will of iron, which is all the requirement that a lady needed."[30] All she had to do was disguise her will, and use her eyes.

Official photographers took a few pictures of baby Margaret as an infant and then began in earnest once she passed her second birthday. These are instructive. Photographers of the period used soft focus, sepia tones, and blurred outlines so as to present their subjects discreetly and with a flattering look that tended to create bland, unrevealing, totemlike figures. This, of course, was ideal for the royal family and surprisingly popular; they might end up as postcard inserts in cigarette packs. It is something of a surprise, almost a shock, to find photographs of a toddler surmounting such obstacles. This is the case of a portrait by Frederick Thurston & Son of Luton, art publishers to their Majesties in 1932, which became a postcard and published often enough for copies to turn up, moderately priced, in miscellaneous ephemera in the flea markets up and down Notting Hill Gate.

Margaret is seated barefoot on a wide windowsill in the home of her grandparents, the Earl and Countess of Strathmore. She is smiling, her golden curls in a soft frame around her face, very much at ease. What one is drawn to is the piercing intensity of her eyes. They dance and sparkle, full of fun; they seem almost incandescent. In other words, apparently, normal in every feature.

When, in 2022, the Scottish government published a guide to "Fetal Alcohol Spectrum Disorder," it emphasized that there were so many factors to consider that making this kind of diagnosis was difficult. If the mother drank early in the pregnancy—sometimes before she knew she *was* pregnant—a child's facial features, which are already being formed, are affected in certain recognizable ways. These include eyes set wide apart, a flattened bridge to the nose, and the same kinds of peculiarities around the mouth. But a child can look perfectly normal and continues to be affected by damage to the brain, nervous system, bone structure, and everything else, since alcohol continues to wreak its havoc for the full nine months. Such handicaps develop as stunted growth, an inability to deal with feelings, irritability, temper tantrums over something as minor as holding a pencil. And that problems can begin to show up when the baby is only a few weeks old.

The same paper has estimated that as many as 172,000 people in Scotland may be affected.

"It is the most overlooked neurodevelopmental condition in Scotland," they claim.

Similar reports in U.S. journals make the same point. The condition is thought to be "remarkably common." In 2018, Dr. Michael Charness, a neurobiologist then at Harvard Medical School, wrote: "it was disturbing that the problem had not received the attention it deserved. As a result, not enough is known how various structures in the body are damaged, including the brain, or when; only that they are."

When Queen Elizabeth II celebrated her seventieth year on the throne in February 2022, a fascinating group of home movies, never seen before, gave the viewer a glimpse not only of the Queen herself, but her sister Margaret at a very early age, then perhaps two or three. Elizabeth is walking in a garden, headed towards the camera. Somewhere in the background is a tiny figure in a white dress, completely absorbed in the business of putting one foot in front of the other, trailing her sister with all the fierce determination of her small person. Arriving finally beside her sister, she is bursting with excitement. She lets out a crow of triumph, almost a scream of pleasure. To hear such a sound from one so young is, simultaneously, a clue of the formidable personality-to-be, and unsettling.

When Marion Crawford became governess to the two princesses in 1932, Elizabeth had just turned six, and Margaret was two. "Crawfie," as she came to be called, had already heard the rumor that there was something wrong with Margaret. It was said she was "deaf and dumb."[31] Nowadays, parents looking for children to adopt always want to know whether a particular baby's mother drank, because the worse the problem is, the sooner they show up in the baby. It is also well known that the more the infant needs help, the more difficult it can be to provide.

Jodee Kulp, an author who dedicated her life to raising awareness of fetal alcohol syndrome, adopted Liz, her future daughter, at aged five months. She discovered an immediate problem as soon as she tried to pick up the baby: the child stiffened, became "as flat as a board," and started to wail. After much trial and error, the only way to calm the child was to hold it next to her skin, bundled up against something very soft. The same issue took constant rocking, singing, massages, and warm baths. The next big issue was that she needed constant feeding around the clock, every two hours or less. It took a relay of three adult caregivers.[32]

In Margaret's case we do not know what it took to get her fed and asleep, but the fact that she was always being carried by Nurse Alah suggests this was the only way to calm her. The rumor "deaf and dumb" is obviously untrue but could have come about because the baby was not responding.

Queen Mary has been judged somewhat harshly by posterity for not lifting a finger to prevent the brutal upbringing of hers and George V's sons. All changes in a flash where these two granddaughters are concerned. She declares that she is studying child development and acting in other grandmotherly ways by having the girls stay with them. During one of those visits to Sandringham when Margaret is visiting, Mary finds that the girl is "a great pickle." The little girl insists on annoying Papa. How? She is fascinated by his beard. She wants to play with it, and, going along with the game, he pretends to be hurt, and she laughs. Why? It is just part of the game.[33] How naughty of this little girl, now two-and-a-half, to laugh when he cries, looking at him with "wicked eyes."[34] She must be very bad. How any grownups with small children of their own can take Queen Mary's conclusions at face value is hard to imagine.

Nevertheless, the word is out. Margaret is incorrigible and naughty. It is all the fault of her parents who spoil her. William Shawcross, the Queen Mother's official biographer, describes Margaret, then aged ten, as "mischievous and provocative."[35] He returns later to the same theme, "bright, beautiful, mercurial, and willful."[36] She has a "naughty winsomeness."[37] The die has been cast. Everyone understands that her older sister is a model of good behavior—obedient, stable, and self-controlled. Margaret is spoiled, flighty, and out of control. She has a wicked streak. Seemingly, it all began when she, only a toddler, derived pleasure from hurting Papa.

It is tempting to speculate that the "she is bad" theory is not quite what the grownups around her with positions to maintain might have thought behind the scenes. After all, the fates of five little girls in the Bowes-Lyon family had been banishment. This was not quite so easy with a royal baby, announced with such fanfare just a couple of years before. The solution was at hand: She was to be labeled perverse and difficult (after all, she looked quite pretty) and leave it at that. Bad behavior can easily be put down to negligence on the part of the governess and spoiling by parents. She was like that, and they were doing the best they could with a kid who was born difficult. "Naughty" became a code word perhaps. Everyone in a tight inner circle knew that she actually had another sort of problem, but "we don't know what it is." If they did think this way, it was kept a secret.

Studies in print describe the day-by-day development of children with fetal alcohol syndrome. They vary greatly, from mildly impaired to severe. Whether the damage affects just the facial features, or a whole galaxy of other problems, is being studied, but without knowing exactly when the pregnant mother drank or even how much, such studies have to be tentative. Nobody wants to put a double-blind study in motion. The case of Liz Kulp, the little girl similarly affected, was severe. She was so affected that for the first six months of her life she would actually scream if anyone tried to touch her. It took many months before this tortured infant could look her caretaker in the eye. In fact, a relay of helpers was needed to feed her around the clock, while dealing with her projectile vomiting and hours of listening to her crying.

The parallels in Margaret's case are significant. Liz Kulp, who tells her own story in *The Best I Can Be*, when faced with learning to read, could not deal with it. She said the letters "danced on the page." One of Margaret's tutors said she was "the most difficult child she ever had to teach."[38] Both of them struggled to learn to write. Liz Kulp lacked the fine muscle control needed to hold a pen. The same problem dogged Margaret, who ended up wrapping a fist around her pen, as can be seen in photos signing her name when she was in her thirties. A large correspondence of Margaret's handwriting in the Royal Archives, all letters to Queen Mary, show how she struggled to master this art, beginning with agonizingly careful letters from age seven and for the next four or five years until lines would no longer be needed to stop the letters from dancing.

Both responded instantly to music and showed natural gifts. Liz Kulp explained that her ears were "eating the music and putting it into her tummy." She began learning to play the harp when she was seven.[39] As for Margaret, there is the famous story that she was being carried when, hearing a tune she knew, she started humming it and was almost dropped in surprise by the astonished adult. It was a tune from *The Merry Widow*, and she was just a year old. Before long, she was picking up other melodies and playing them on the piano. At some point, it was suggested she learn to read music, but she objected that since she was playing them anyway, why bother?

Liz invented stories all the time and had a hard time separating fact from fiction; her mother despaired of teaching her the difference.

"We have been shocked many times by the incredible tall tales flowing . . . from the mouth of someone who (supposedly) had a limited imagination."[40]

Crawford makes a similar point about Margaret's vivid, and sometimes "appalling" dreams, about "green horses, wild elephant stampedes, talking cats . . . that went into two or three installments."[41]

Liz was a chatterbox. So was Margaret. Liz's mother said, "Whatever popped into her mind flowed out of her mouth."[42] It took a while before her mother understood that the endless stream literally reflected everything she was thinking; the little girl eventually learnt how to think without needing to speak it. The same could probably be said of Margaret.

Liz was a biter. The first time it happened, the toddler fastened on her mother's chin and refused to let go; she had to be pried off. Margaret preferred hands and left marks to prove it.[43]

Both little girls had lightning switches of mood. Margaret could switch from smiles and kisses in a flash and was suddenly in a rage. Liz once explained to her mother that the mood was like a current that began at her feet, then traveled up her knees and into her head. After that, she had no control; she could not stop herself.[44]

The kind of person exposed before birth to alcohol, Kulp wrote, had poor impulse control, had "limited cause-and-effect reasoning, memory issues, and difficulty understanding abstract ideas." Such a person "has trouble with money, time and math, gets easily frustrated, and is decidedly volatile."[45] What was lacking, as Jane Austen would have said, was prudence. More or less since the eighteenth century it had been a point of pride never to reveal feelings at all. If one suffered, it was in silence. This translates as the well-known "British reserve," or having "a stiff upper lip." Such codes of conduct applied to society at large. But those with the most to lose, meaning face plus status, adhered to it with the most rigor. Since the Royal Family was seen as the exemplar of all that constituted the British ideal, along with their great status came cruel emotional demands.

They had to be perfect, more than human, since they represented an ideal. They were locked, as it were, into the most luxurious of prisons masking their feelings "more rigorously than . . . necessary for ordinary people," the Infanta Eulalia, daughter of Isabella of Spain, observed.

"Most princesses I know are reduced by this inexorable discipline to non-entities whose mouths are twisted in an eternal smile."[46]

Her Royal Highness made this prescient observation in *Court Life from Within*, published in 1915, fifteen years before Princess Margaret was born.

CHAPTER 3

TOO STRICT: TOO LAX

> "What lingers from the parent's individual past,
> unresolved or incomplete, often becomes part
> of her or his irrational parenting."
> —Virginia Satir

THE NEWS IN OCTOBER 1930 was succinct. The baby Princess Margaret Rose had arrived in London on the overnight train from Scotland after a journey of 350 miles in a special compartment with her parents, sister, and nanny. The train arrived fifteen minutes ahead that morning, hoping to evade a crowd. But as they appeared on the platform, people rushed towards them anyway, craning for a glimpse of the baby. She was securely camouflaged under a capacious shawl of white wool. The family was whisked off to their Piccadilly mansion by motorcar. A single, laconic paragraph.[1]

Such telegrammatic communiqués would have been quite understood by readers of the London dailies, which, before TV and digital news, along with BBC radio, were the sole sources of information in Britain in the early twentieth century. The proprietors of the big London papers that went all over Britain specialized in such decorous self-censorship as befits the family of a possible heir to the throne, who might one day—one never knew—become the emperor of dominions on which the sun never set. It was just good business to want to shield such persons from any news that might give them distress, or even mild embarrassment. The public should be told only what they needed to know, something "warm, comfortable and reassuring."[2] Newspapers in New York and elsewhere on the East Coast could print what they liked, but access to those sources of information were a week away by ocean liner (no big airlines in those days), and so they didn't matter. Here at home, the royal family was "untouchable."

An interesting case in point involves the tragedy that befell one of the brilliant figures of the age: Charles A. Lindbergh. As everyone knew, Col. Lindbergh was the intrepid American pilot who had, in January 1927, made the astonishing flight of 3,600 miles solo from New York to Paris. It took him 33½ hours, and his reception, when he finally landed on solid ground, was tumultuous. He was, after all, the first to succeed. His audacity and endurance captured imaginations around the world. It has already been noted that in the absence of her parents, baby Elizabeth herself had already received the colonel in Buckingham Palace. Once George V and Queen Mary heard the news, they extended a second invitation to the hero and awarded him a rare honor, the Air Force Cross, a few months later. Elizabeth, now up and walking, gravely shook his hand. He gave her a pat on the cheek.[3]

So, Lindbergh's link with royalty was already established. They would have been as appalled as everyone else to learn in 1932 that his son Chester, not yet two years old, had been snatched from his bed in Lindbergh's home in Hopewell, New Jersey, on March 1, 1932. The ransom demanded was $50,000. But by the time it was paid, the baby had been murdered.

Two years passed before Richard "Bruno" Hauptmann, a thirty-four-year-old carpenter and German immigrant, was found and arrested. His trial eventually took place in January 1935. He was convicted and finally electrocuted in the spring of 1936. In effect, the kidnapping, hunt for the murderer, and eventual fate dominated the press internationally for four years.

That same month the warning letters started for the Duke and Duchess of York, informing them that "their two baby royal princesses, and particularly Elizabeth, were in danger of being kidnapped." When the Lindbergh kidnapping was first reported, the parents discussed further protections for their children with Scotland Yard. They were told not to worry; "ordinary arrangements were sufficient to protect them." But the Yard suggested that a trip to the West Country to visit their grandmother, the Countess of Strathmore, should be postponed, and "it might be advisable to keep the princesses indoors for a couple of days."[4]

This particular threat against the lives of two princesses does not seem to have been reported elsewhere—the author can find no reference to it in newspaper archives or biographies. Neither can another such report be found of a threat two years later, which was at least published in the United Kingdom in the summer of 1934. *The Sunday Express* reported that the girls, on holiday at Glamis, were cloistered behind bolted and double-locked gates, guarded by armed men. The wooded avenues leading to the castle were patrolled day and night.[5] Two days later, on August 20, an "unqualified denial," presumably from the Palace, dismissed the idea that the lives of the princesses were in danger. If they had not been seen in the village, that was because they were in quarantine. There was an outbreak of scarlet fever in the area. Why it should be necessary to double-lock them inside the castle with armed men was not explained. Anxious protectiveness was bound to increase and monitoring, from the minute to the second.

The point of view most often expressed nowadays is that the little girls led normal lives—or lives consistent with their aristocratic counterparts. This idea does not bear much examination. To begin with, they were on public display almost from birth with crowds prepared to rush at them en masse, as was seen when the four-year-old Elizabeth walked out of Buckingham Palace to watch the palace guards perform, something that would send most children screaming for their mothers. They were vulnerable any time they left the doors of their house to be taken somewhere, or get in a car, or ride a pony or play in the park, despite the detective from Scotland Yard who shadowed them discreetly. It was normal, on occasion, to lock gates behind them and have guards posted outside their nursery. And for several years, they were living on the sidewalk of one of the most heavily traveled and internationally famous streets in London: Piccadilly.

The curious name of Piccadilly has been variously explained. But it seems to have been derived from "piccadill," a kind of stiffening fabric considered essential for collars and much else in the making of elaborately shaped women's skirts, for instance, from about the sixteenth century on. Known for such artifice, a successful tailor, Robert Baker, was consulted far and wide, and he set up shop in what is now named after his principal trade. Piccadilly Circus was created in the nineteenth century to connect the brand-new shopping avenue called Regent Street with the city's major theaters along Shaftsbury Avenue.

After World War II, when gasoline, or petrol, was no longer rationed, the onslaught of the private car began. All kinds of solutions were going to remedy that. One of them involved a wholesale clearance of everything that stood in the way of a greatly enlarged traffic circle and with a double-decker solution for pedestrians above. The project failed, not because of the folly of the idea, but it was agreed there still wasn't enough room for traffic.

Piccadilly Circus, in its original outlines, has become a pedestrian playground again, is an Underground stop, and elderly ladies selling flowers can still be found under the statue of Eros, that métier celebrated by George Bernard Shaw in his play *Pygmalion*.

Walking west, one encounters a kind of residential area that was very much the provenance of rich men in the 1930s. A photograph of this part of Piccadilly on a foggy evening in 1932 shows vastly bigger sidewalks, illumined with the latest in bright streetlights, very little traffic, and rows of enormous stone townhouses, one after the other, leading to Wellington Arch. If a buyer positions himself with care, there are a few choice dwellings that have Hyde Park on one side and Green Park on the other, with a fine view of the Arch as well. A great many of them did. The same photograph records Lord Rothschild in bowler hat, sporting a cane, "wrapped in his greatcoat and silence," as Dickens once described it, about to enter the gates of his own private paradise.

The Piccadilly home of Princess Margaret and her family for the first seven years of her life, at Number 145, disappeared one night in October of 1940, though not by design. Early in the London blitz, a high-explosive bomb landed just behind it and reduced it to rubble. By then the King had been crowned, they were in residence at Buckingham Palace and their daughters had been moved to safer quarters at Windsor. A caretaker, his wife, and their child were found in the wreckage; the available evidence suggests they did not survive. The site has now been taken over by a hotel, the Intercontinental London Park Lane, which boasts of its regal, rather too literal, foundations.

The house seems to have acquired a reputation for being ordinary, if not shabby, since its disappearance. One cannot tell one way or another from the few black-and-white pictures of interiors that survive. From the written descriptions it sounds quite capacious, even grand. The dining room, if indeed it seated thirty comfortably, had to be spacious. The staircase is described as elegant and was hung with tapestries from Brussels. There are references to occasional tables containing fine bronzes, of lacquer screens, and evidence of porcelains and antique silver. There was room for a library. There was also a ballroom. The staircase itself was particularly well lit because of a large glass rooftop dome and a circular landing. Apparently, that was just right for Elizabeth's collection of toy horses. And there were twenty-five bedrooms.

Accounts are silent on the perpetual problem of how to shoehorn enough bathrooms (or even, any) into an eighteenth-century mansion. One is accustomed to seeing, in period films, guests staying at country houses queuing up to take baths (showers were unknown) in the one facility on their particular floor. One of Ngaio Marsh's most successful plots hinges on the notion of a murderer taking a bath when he, in fact, is somewhere else stabbing somebody. In Dorothy Sayers' *The Nine Tailers*, disaster strikes when a guest insists she can safely stow away her priceless necklace hidden in a chamber pot. But this was London, the date was 1930, and even provincial cities like Bath were building public housing with bathrooms in them. Although, it was said that once the poor were rehoused in such palatial quarters, they had to be instructed about not using the tubs for coal storage, but for washing themselves in them, since they had never seen them before. Surely the little princesses had their own bathroom by then and did not, as is also suggested, have to resort to nineteenth-century Victorian basins with matching china water jugs.

One is surprised to find a family of four people, even if they entertained a great deal, needing all those bedrooms. But it seems they employed a large staff of twenty-one, most of whom slept *in situ*. There was a housekeeper, a butler, an under-butler, three housemaids, a cook, three kitchen maids, two footmen, a ladies' maid, a valet, a telephone operator, and a night watchman. There was a nanny and governess as well.

In addition to the surplus of bedrooms, the two little girls had two nurseries, one for day and one for night. Still, they needed a place to play outside. Happily, behind the house was one of those hidden gems in London, a small private park for the express consolation of those who inhabited the deserts of stone, brick, and concrete that surrounded them on four sides. This particular oasis, Hamilton Place, could only be entered with a key, which made it relatively safe from vandals. However, it was fenced, as was customary, by iron railings, which offered no protection from prying eyes. Whenever the little girls went to play with the prams, their bicycles, their balls and teddy bears, the word would go out, and, as if by magic, there would be a ring of gawkers: yet another audience. Perhaps it was then that Elizabeth learned the first rule of defense: refusing to see people one did not want to meet. She soon perfected the narrowed-eyes look, the one that goes right past you. For Margaret, four years her junior, it took longer.[6]

Elevation to the throne, and all that it meant in terms of power, prestige, and influence, had been fought—sometimes to the death—for centuries. So, it is not particularly surprising that, when the Duke and Duchess of Kent's daughter Victoria turned out to be the unexpected heir apparent, her mother connived, first of all to secure her daughter's position, and then become regent instead. Jane Ridley, the future Edward VII biographer, wrote that the Duchess turned her considerable energies to this single aim with the assistance of her comptroller, secret lover Sir John Conroy, to help bring this about.

Sir John, an unscrupulous Irish officer, well understood that Victoria could legally become Queen as soon as she reached her eighteenth birthday, which would come on May 24, 1837. She would succeed William IV, who was ailing. If the King would oblige them by dying before then, the Duchess could take charge immediately, since Victoria was still a few years under age. If he clung to life, as they devoutly hoped he would not, Victoria must be stopped by fair means or foul. Professor Ridley wrote, "No Gothic novelist could have invented a villain blacker than Conroy. He terrified Victoria with tales of plans to poison her . . ."

Then she contracted typhoid at the age of sixteen, which was a stroke of luck they had not anticipated. In her weakened state, Conroy stood over her, waving a document for signature that would give him the position of private secretary and demanding she sign it. She courageously refused. Both of them resorted to similar stratagems, shadowing her every movement, almost by the minute and attempting to break her spirit. The King, who was in sympathy with the young girl and aware of her mother's treachery, held out until Victoria could become Queen. He died a month later.

By the time Albert Edward, the future Edward VII, their first son and second child, was born, Queen Victoria had contracted an idyllic marriage with Albert of Saxe-Coburg-Gotha, a handsome, brilliant, but obscure German prince. The baby was named for his father, but the rejoicing appears to have stopped there. By that strange and sad alchemy that causes girls who hate their mothers to become mothers who hate their children, Victoria recoiled from the new heir-apparent with repugnance. Babies were "more like little plants," she said, capable of "that terrible froglike action." He was ugly. She feared he was backward.

Her entourage of nurses and tutors dutifully echoed the royal opinion. The pressure was on to reform the small boy whose only sin was to have been born a prince. Not surprisingly, given the impossible demands made upon him, the prince was a slow learner. The only solution was longer and longer time at lessons, from eight in the morning until six at night. He was obstinately refusing to learn, so he was punished. When the student hid under his desk and screamed with frustration, he was whipped. The vindictive mother added insult to injury in later years by blaming the son she had refused to love for the death of her husband. A courtier later explained to Harold Nicolson, "The House of Hanover, like ducks, make bad parents. They trample on their young." Edward's son, Bertie, later said, with justice, "I had no boyhood."

As for George V, Edward VII's son and Margaret and Elizabeth's grandfather, the older he became, the more benevolent, as has been noted. He must have astonished his entourage by insisting he must see the small Elizabeth every single day or, "his health would suffer." Time was running out, and regrets for what cannot be undone tend to rise to the surface and become a haunting sense of lost opportunities.

Like many other male members of the House of Windsor, George V had been sent to naval college and subsequently joined the Royal Navy. Philip Ziegler explained that its officers were recruited largely from the gentry or aristocracy, because the navy offered "less opportunities for debauchery," and inculcated virtues thought desirable for a king, i.e., "sobriety, self-reliance, punctuality, a respect for authority, and an instinct to conform." Harold Nicolson, whose biography of the king is a model of tact, felt obliged to write that, "In seeking to instill into his children his own ideals of duty and obedience, he was frequently pragmatic and sometimes harsh." He was impatient, quick-tempered, and shouted a lot. George V also said, reportedly, "My father was frightened of his mother; I was frightened of my father, and I am damned well going to see to it that my children are frightened of me."

Sharp, sudden angers—as Kenneth Rose, another of George V's biographers wrote—can be taken in stride by a loved child. What is harder to bear is what Rose, writing in 1983, called "chaff," but might nowadays be known as teasing and ridiculing, something that the King used on friends and foes alike, and particularly as put-downs on his sons and daughter. When his first-born son Edward (always known as David in the family) wanted to know where his baby brother Henry had come from, his father jovially explained that the baby had flown through an open window on wings, a variation on the old "stork brought him" routine. What, David wanted to know, happened to the wings? "Oh," his father explained airily, "they were cut off." As Rose noted, Victorians brought up their children without the help of psychologists.

One may safely assume that the future George VI, born in 1895 just a year after his brother David, Prince of Wales, was subjected to an extra special dose of this kind of badinage. He had a built-in flaw, as it was considered in those days. He was left-handed. As late as 1935, some forty years later, to be left-handed was not only cause for concern but ridicule. This writer's own grandfather used the fact of my being "skiffy-handed" to have a good laugh at my expense. Teachers at elementary schools would repeatedly place the pencil in the proper hand of five-year-old's, unless, by chance, they had already learned to write. Being obliged to switch hands was the frequent cause of stammering, a point that even the exemplary film *The King's Speech*, about George VI's consequent affliction, did not see fit to mention.

As for Queen Mary, she is described as excruciatingly shy and emotionally unavailable as a mother. She did not understand her children's needs, and apparently did not want to understand them. Perhaps she was as afraid of her husband's sharp tongue as her children and deferred to him in a helpless kind of way. He must know what to do. He was the father of these children, but after all, he was their king as well. So she reasoned.

In her study of the reasons why Edward VIII abdicated, Frances Davidson has described the result of the Queen's frozen inability to step in and help her children. She has described how they were in the care of an incompetent nanny with a sadistic streak. The nanny adored young David and was jealously competitive with his mother. When due to present the youngster to Queen Mary, the nanny would secretly pinch him so that, as the baby was handed over, he started to cry. He was, of course, immediately returned to the nanny, and his mother was none the wiser. As for Bertie, he was completely ignored, and so badly fed that he developed stomach trouble. As he grew, he began to develop knock knees and obliged to wear painful braces to correct them. In those days, the cause was believed to be congenital; it is now believed it is most often rickets, stemming from a poor diet seriously deficient in Vitamin D. By the time Bertie was three years old, he was stammering. This, too, was explained away (as late as 1974) as the result of a "nervous condition."

Queen Mary, always called May by her friend Mabell, Countess of Airlie, said, "The tragedy was that neither (she nor her husband) had any understanding of a child's mind." Of his father's constant strictness and bullying, David wrote, "I have often felt that despite his undoubted affection for all of us, my father preferred children in the abstract." As for Bertie, the perpetual stammerer, whose affliction always seemed worse when his father appeared, nobody knew what to do about it. His father, exasperated, would shout, "Get it out! Get it out!" and complained about him constantly to his friends. George V's solution was to poke fun at his expense, "mimicking him and laughing at him." Margot Asquith, wife of the Liberal Prime Minister, told the King finally that if he went on being so horrid to his children, he would drive them to drink." Whether this criticism had a salutary effect is not known.

Given a demanding and ridiculing father, an emotionally frozen mother, and an indifferent education, the future George VI grew up in the shadow of his more gifted brother. Interestingly enough, he was a fine sportsman, and, like his father, a first-class shot. He developed what might have been once called "an inferiority complex." But his frequent protestations that he was just an "ordinary sort of bloke," masked a real and genuine hatred of the role he was forced to assume as a prince. He did not want to be hemmed around all his life by obligations and restrictions. He wanted to be ordinary. How wonderful to be free, to go where you wanted when you wanted, to marry the girl you loved, to be happy, away from the public eye. If he only could.

Nowadays, no sensible couple who can afford it would think of hiring a farmer's daughter with no training to take charge of their small children, let alone a child with an important future ahead of him or her, such as becoming the king or queen of an empire. Not only did she and others like her from the "lower orders" take charge, but she gained immediate status, because "nanny's word was law." She had her own wing in a separate part of the house, often described as being behind a green baize door. She had her own nursemaids and could even overrule the family cook on the important issue of children's menus. She was given the power to nurture or destroy the well-being of somebody else's children. This was the universal practice, more or less, until the end of World War II.

Nowadays, those with the means to hire a nanny expect them to be college educated. Norland College in Bath, founded in 1892, gives a three-year course on everything a competent nanny needs to know. The college's philosophy is based on the theories of Friedrich Froebel (1782–1852), an early specialist in child development. Froebel advanced the then-hypothetical idea that children were not blank slates to be written on, but that each had a budding gift, which it was a teacher's challenge to discover and encourage. To that end, a child needed to be given the blank building materials—paper, chalks, clay, paint, beads to thread, and more—to experiment with. One famous example of such a way of discovering talent was the felicitous decision to give the young Frank Lloyd Wright a set of wooden building blocks—and his mother had studied Froebel's ideas. This concept, now well accepted, was once considered almost sacrilegious.

Norland students are trained in psychological development, including how to deal with stubbornness, temper tantrums, eating disorders, and a host of other issues many parents spend a lifetime learning. The nanny cannot shout at the child. She cannot slap it, let alone spank it. By the end of the course, she has learnt how to counter a potential kidnapping and is trained in taekwondo, the art of self-defense, by a black-belt expert. Successful completion of such a course commands a big salary.

The old system, which was still in place when Margaret came along, had the biggest of many flaws: a nanny was still a servant and served at the pleasure of her employers. Ultimately, what she did with her charges in the sanctity of her wing did not matter. What did matter was that when they were brought to visit their parent for five minutes once or twice a day, they were washed, brushed, wearing clean pressed clothes, and in a reasonably good humor. That was all. That was the problem. Finally, her tenure was bound to be brief, because the little boy in particular had probably been signed up for a boarding school somewhere at the age of seven or eight, and she would be out of a job. Again.

It is astonishing that despite the fact that this custom was full of pitfalls, it continued from its first flowering in the Middle Ages—when children were treated as little adults—until it petered out a relatively short time ago. One hates admitting to the sneaking suspicion that it continued on because many wealthy parents did not want to know what was going on behind the green baize door. For every dear old nanny tucked away in a wing of a great house, whom her former charge always goes to visit, as in *Brideshead Revisited*, there are countless examples of the horrors inflicted on those who eventually write about them, like Sir Compton Mackenzie, or the miseries inflicted on Lord George Curson, as described by his biographer, Kenneth Rose. These and many other examples are cited in Jonathan Gathorne-Hardy in his book, *The Rise and Fall of the British Nanny*, published in 1972.

A more recent example is the poignant memoir of Lady Anne Glenconner, *Lady in Waiting*, her autobiography published in 2020. Born Lady Anne Coke in 1932, she would become the lady-in-waiting and dear friend of Princess Margaret. She was only seven when World War II began, and when her parents left for Egypt, Anne and her five-year-old sister were put in charge of a governess, a Miss Bonner, for three years. Lady Glenconner wrote, "She was fairly all right with my sister, but really cruel to me. Every night, whatever I had done, however well I had behaved, she would punish me by tying my hands to the back of the bed, and leaving me like that all night." When asked about that, she said, "Even to think about it made me physically sick."

How did she survive?

"You just got on with it," she said. It was right up there with "stiff upper lip." Children attacked by sadists, with no recourse, had to bear abuse in silence.

Such traumatic events sometimes have lifelong consequences. In Lady Glenconner's case, it caused a permanent emotional scar and perhaps a lingering belief that being shabbily treated had to be borne because she did not deserve any better. She married an immensely wealthy, charming, and unpredictable man, who could behave irresponsibly, one might even believe maliciously. They were married for fifty-four years, and he left his sizable fortune to his former manservant. She and their children were penniless.

"And to do it to our children . . . I despaired. Going against everything, my mother had always taught me, I let emotion take over and I screamed and screamed and screamed into the pitch-black night."[7]

CHAPTER 4

ODD GIRL OUT[1]

MARION CRAWFORD IS AN OVERLOOKED but extremely interesting figure and a reliable witness to the developing characters of the little princesses whose lives she would observe on a daily basis for the next sixteen years (1931–1947). She is the one person whose views in any way coincide with a contemporary understanding of child behavior. There is a reason for this.

During her course work at Moray House Training College in Edinburgh, her studies took her into the poorer parts of that big industrial city in Scotland.

"Here I saw a great deal of poverty and had to (deal) with children who were not very bright because they were undernourished. I . . . became fired with a crusading spirit. I wanted to do something about the misery and unhappiness I saw all around me. I wanted desperately to help . . ."[2] Teaching, she vowed, would be her life's work.

The merest chance led her to a summer position with a prominent family in Dunfermline, which in turn led to a post teaching the small daughter of Lady Rose Leweston-Gower. Rose, née Bowes-Lyon, introduced her to her younger sister, the Duchess of York, who was looking for a governess for Elizabeth, now five years old, and the one-year-old Margaret. Two weeks later, "Crawfie," as she came to be known, was hired.

What she might have thought of the horrific demands made upon young princes by their parents and tutors in the early part of the twentieth century is not recorded. She might have known more about the ideal Victorian gentleman, as epitomized by the Duke of Westminster, a gent, scholar, and widely praised benefactor. As has been noted, princesses were in a somewhat different historical category, being traded back and forth like pedigreed mounts for their assets, usually land or money, and sometimes both.

On the surface, it seemed as if nothing was left for a modern-day princess to do than marry for social status and begin having children (boys preferred) as soon as possible to secure the family's succession. However, comments made in the late 1920s that followed the marriage of the new Duchess of York reveal that what was required was perhaps less obvious but equally exacting. Dear Lizzie was, after all, the daughter of an Earl, and in addition was greeted on her wedding day by her new father-in-law, George V, as "Your Royal Highness." Nevertheless, in the ultimate scheme of things, she was of lesser status.

Writing in the *New York Times* in the summer of 1928, Philip Whitwell Wilson (1875–1956), a journalist and MP for the British Liberal Party, said that her marriage was "delicate" because of Queen Victoria's "strongly held" belief that the reigning house should "stand alone." Wilson continued, "If the Duke of Argyle married the Princess Louise, he would be accepted as the Queen's son-in-law, but his relatives would not be included."

The present King George V and Queen Mary had taken a slightly more tolerant view, but nevertheless the new duchess was faced with the same kind of dilemma "(since) there can be no deviation from the inexorable laws of precedence. At court . . . Elizabeth's own brother cannot come within speaking distance of his sister." There was no denying that the Bowes-Lyon family included a cousin who committed suicide after he was jilted and the illegitimate child of another family member who worked as a shop girl.

The duchess herself almost forgot, moments after her marriage, that she was supposed to curtsey to her new in-laws as she and her husband passed them by. Wilson concluded, "To succeed as a princess, you must know the exact limits of your position, fill that position, but never transgress the limits."[3]

Once Margaret had escaped from the baby carriage and was placed into the care, for at least part of the day, of the young governess, life improved fast for the small princess. Most vintage photographs of the period are not dated, but have clues of their own, depending on the little girl's expression. Margaret being carried around or pushed around in a pram, a captive of her nanny's fears, never shows her smiling, and she often seems to be frowning. Once she is transformed into an adorable, curly-haired toddler, it is because she is standing and holding on tight to her sister's hand, smiling from ear to ear.

For Margaret was a special child, not just because she was born in an ancient Scottish castle full of legendary associations, and in the middle of a thunderstorm. If she did not actually fly through the window, as her grandfather laughingly explained to one of his children, neither was she likely to adapt to fit somebody else's expectations about whom she, as a princess, would become.

From the beginning, she was herself. It would take a playwright, perhaps that cozy insider, the great James Barrie himself, to perceive the true nature of this bright, funny, outgoing, and hovering little sprite, his own Tinker Bell, devoted, magical companion of Peter Pan. Wait—why not a female incarnation of Peter Pan himself, as imagined by Arthur Rackham? The temptation to find resemblances between the two personalities is hard to resist. She was, after all, perfectly proportioned in every respect but small-boned for a girl—and on the stage Peter is always played by a woman. The resemblances were clear enough, in her free-spiritedness, her boldness, gift for fun, her independence, and impish qualities. She could easily become the leader of a band of lost boys who had fallen out of their perambulators (rather than climbed out) and ended up in Neverland—the world for children who never grow up.

No one quite knew what to do with this careless, self-absorbed, generous, loving, and imperious personality, full of mischief and fun, who was not easy to predict and was never going to yield to the barking commands and arbitrary demands that passed for discipline in the House of Windsor. Only her father, perhaps, and close friends, were going to experience the vulnerable, tender, yearning side of this particular little girl, who would come to see the world around her as a battleground. One thinks of Tinker Bell on the stage, asking generations of child audiences, "Clap if you believe in me," and the audience that always applauds.

In short, she was a natural performer. People remarked upon her astonishing ear for music—melodies most often cited come from Lehar's "Merry Widow," and her early love of singing in a small, clear voice. They refer to her uncanny ability to mimic others, done with such humor and timing that she would have her listeners collapsing with laughter. Her idea of livening up a party, when she was four years old, was to crawl under the table and make a perfect nuisance of herself by tickling everybody's ankles.

Her favorite person in all the world was Daddy. After finishing her own meal in the nursery, she would be taken down to visit her parents, who were now having their meal. She would climb up onto Daddy's lap and ask for the same treat every time, i.e., a glass of soda water she called "windy water." The Duke would exclaim, as he always did, "You can't possibly like it!" and she would solemnly reply that she did because it tickled her nose.

Papa might have had a special reason to be solicitous of his second daughter. Her unacknowledged disability had destroyed the fine muscles in the hand that allow one to write, in an age when letters were always written by hand, unless they were for business and typed (in which case they were usually impersonal). Perhaps she was left-handed, as her father had been, and forced to write with her right hand. Perhaps she had been right-handed, as most people are, and lost the capacity as a consequence of fetal alcohol syndrome. It would not have mattered. She still could not write clearly, as letters to her "Darling Grannie" clearly show. At seven years old, her letter of thanks for a toy teapot was as labored as that of a child of five.

She never improved. A photo of her signing a visitor's book when she was in her twenties showed that her whole fist is wrapped around the pen in the manner of a leftie who has been forced to use her right hand. Only someone who has been through it can appreciate the effort involved.

This disability was not generally known, and the bias goes back for centuries. Even in the 1930s, a child who wrote with her fist in the Royal Family would have been considered handicapped. The emphasis was on getting him or her to look as normal as possible. In this particular case, an empire was at stake.

Her mother tells the story that when Margaret was five years old, she delivered a somewhat disconcerting piece of news. Writing to Queen Mary, the Duchess said, "Margaret Rose came to me today, & after looking at me very affectionately, & giving me a sweet kiss, said, 'Mummy darling, I really do believe that I love Papa much more than I do you.'" Her mother added, "I felt very small."[4]

Marion Crawford, who seldom saw her at first, called Margaret Rose an "enchanting, doll-like creature," and "the baby everyone loves at sight."[5] As she grew older, she loved to have stories told to her and usually wanted the same story over and over again. One of her favorites was "The Little Red Hen." She knew it by heart and would be indignant if Crawfie missed a paragraph and make her repeat the passage.

"It had to go exactly the same way every time."[6]

Then Crawfie would tell them stories from her own childhood, growing up in the Scottish countryside and the animals she had as pets.

Both princesses were fascinated by other children. A poignant photograph exists of a new little girl standing between the two of them with a puzzled look, while Elizabeth is doing her best to coax the child to talk, full of smiles, bending towards her with both hands tucked between her knees. Making friends with strangers was discouraged, and the two were thrown back on each other's company most of the time. Crawfie did her best to introduce them to the modern world outside the airless confines of their own cloistered existence. She took them for a ride on the top of a double-decker bus and then introduced them to a train trip on the London Underground. They had never been on an elevator before and clung to her in fright the first time they tried it. In such cases, they were always followed at discreet intervals by bodyguards.[7]

Occasionally, greatly daring, Crawfie would quietly slip them outside the confines of Hamilton Gardens and into the limitless vistas of Hyde Park, surprisingly, without being discovered for the most part. That was especially exciting, with its tame flocks of swans and pelicans, and its groups of boys and girls floating their toy flotillas on the lakes. Kensington Gardens is close by, so perhaps they even passed beneath the fourteen-foot statue of Peter Pan himself. There he was, towering above them, headstrong, free as the air, the spirit of childhood itself, ready for new adventures.

Almost the first thing Crawfie did in her efforts to expand their horizons was teach them some new games. They played Cowboys and Indians among the bushes. This was a special treat, because in the days when coal was the only source of heat, black dust drifted down among the tulips and cherry trees, stifling everything with its smothering blanket of dirt. Being dirty was something quite new, and they took to it with enthusiasm.

The boisterous Bowes-Lyon family had always been known for its odd repertoire of games. One of their twists on an old standby was Hide and Seek, which the future George VI also liked to take part in. In this version, the emphasis is not on the last person to be found (the winner) but on the last person to find anyone (the loser). During his morning break, the duke was often on the scene. Crawfie said he was "The fastest runner I ever knew." She continued, "I can still see him putting on an immense spurt round the statue of Byron, which stood in the gardens . . . and came in very handy for us as 'home.'"[8]

There was another Bowes-Lyon game called "Are you there Moriarty?" which their cousin, Margaret Rhodes, described as involving a lot of quite important grownups lying around on the floor and being beaten on the head with cushions and rolled up batons made out of newspaper. She never could understand what that one was about.[9]

Family traditions die hard, and perhaps no one in that old and distinguished family remembered what the title meant any more. One can trace, as well, the remnants of emotional patterns back through the Windsor generations and evidence of familiar ways of reacting, not just in King George VI's own past, but his unconscious compulsion to repeat them in the unhappy present.

What is not well known is that this stammering prince, who was held up to frequent ridicule by his father, turned out to have expressed the same tendency to explode with rage that his father did, and over trifles. Or perhaps it was not a trifle but one provocation too many, and he was goaded into what he would have considered overdue outrage. On the surface, his small family seemed to overlook the storms.

"Oh, that," Lady Glenconner remarked. "Margaret learnt how to deal with him when she was four."[10]

What was sadder and sadder, as Kenneth Rose wrote, was the "embarrassing chaff itself."

In the case of his children, such badinage might hit hard and even leave "emotional scars." Habitual use of ridicule to control children (perhaps including name-calling?) certainly bothered his wife, who had witnessed her husband doing the same thing to Elizabeth and Margaret once too often.

Curiously, she seems never to have brought the issue up at the time, when it might have done some good. But that she did object was discovered in her archives on a piece of paper. She wrote, "Be very careful not to ridicule your children or laugh at them. When they say funny things, it was usually innocent."

She also wanted him to stop shouting at their children. Did he not remember how miserable he felt when his own father yelled at him? How his love for this parent was stifled and died? She continued, "None of his sons are his friends, because he is not understanding & helpful . . ."

When it comes to disciplining children, it is always easier to see someone else's mistakes than one's own. His wife had her own way of showing displeasure—often over trifles—that was just as counter-productive. While the king raged and fumed over some servant's errors to the Palace Steward, Mr. Ainslie, treating it as the latter's fault even when it wasn't, the queen was likely to smolder. She, as the folk song goes, who "smiled not for one, but she smiles on us all," could shut up like an oyster at the least infraction. F. J. Corbitt recalled that, once when sending out invitations, he omitted to include the name of a former housemaid. The Queen sent around a member of her personal staff to deliver a strong rebuke, and the next time he passed her by, her face had turned to stone.[11]

Last but not least was the family's use of practical jokes. George VI apparently continued the tradition of making others the butt of jokes that may well have been played on him. Marion Crawford recalled that in the summer of 1939 they stayed near the popular seaside resort of Eastbourne, taking full advantage of this "unexpected spell of freedom." She loved everything about Eastbourne's sandy shore, except for the fact that it seemed infested by millions of bright green, wriggly worms. These were *Symsagittifera Roscoffensis*, tiny creatures about the size of a pencil tip, part plant, part animal, that swarmed together and rotated in masses on the sand. They were easy enough to find because of their Dayglo color and were utterly repulsive.

One day at Eastbourne her employer, by now King, handed her a present, or so he said. It was in a matchbox. All unsuspecting, Crawfie opened the box to discover a disgusting, writhing interior of Dayglo green. She must have cried out and thrown it on the ground. Hardly the kind of present one expects to get from a King—but what a laugh! How easy it was to get even with someone by making them the butt of a joke. Perhaps that gave this nine-year-old an idea? In the future, she used the idea with enthusiasm.

In their final halcyon days before they moved into the Palace, the little princesses lived in a house just like everybody else with a number on the door and its own bell push. Nothing fancy.

There is a distinctly nostalgic tone to the way Marion Crawford describes the pleasant routine of their lives in those days. It was delightful to take walks with the dogs in the nearby parks—unnoticed by anyone—in blessed anonymity. In the mind's eye, perhaps it is always afternoon on a sunny day. The girls wear cotton dresses and the parents similarly casual wear, comfortable and forgettable. Even if Mummy and the girls show evidence of resident hairdressers in the smooth undulations of waves and perfected curls, the occasion is relaxed, casual, and self-absorbed.

Crawfie was at pains to record how much time the Duke and Duchess took with their children on a daily basis, certainly much more than high-born parents did with their own in the far-off 1930s. There was a daily, well-established routine. After their nursery tea at five, Elizabeth and Margaret Rose would join their parents for lengthy card games of rummy and something called "racing demon" where the goal was to be the first to get all your cards. After an hour or so, it was bath time, and their parents shortly joined them.

"Hilarious sounds of splashing could be heard coming from the bathroom, to be followed by energetic pillow fights in the bedroom."[12]

Once the girls were tucked in bed—each one munching on an apple—the Duke and Duchess dined together quietly and then sat by the fire and talked or read until lights out at midnight. They rarely dined out or had visitors. The person who came most often was Uncle David, Prince of Wales, who liked to appear in time for tea and card games afterwards with the girls, usually "Snap" or "Happy Families." He bought Elizabeth several of the A. A. Milne books for children, and they memorized the poems. Their favorite was, predictably enough, "Changing Guard at Buckingham Palace."[13]

During their frequent weekends at the Royal Lodge in Windsor, charades was one of their favorite games, and Margaret joined in with a will. When it was your turn, you had to pretend to be someone else, and the others had to guess who it was. Margaret won hands down. She was so accurate and so funny that she "kept us in fits of laughter" as she fastened on character traits that both revealed and parodied the person in question.

Like many other fetal alcohol syndrome children, she had an imaginary playmate, a certain Cousin Halifax (no relation to anybody). He came in handy as the reason for all sorts of things, including homework undone, jobs forgotten, or perceived bad behavior on her part.

"I was busy with Cousin Halifax," she would say grandly, as if that explained everything, with a sideways glance at Crawfie to see whether her governess would swallow that one.

She had a quick temper and would "take a whack" at someone when provoked—her sister presumably. But at the same time, she had such a winning personality, what Crawfie called "a gay, bouncing way with her," that it was hard to stay angry. She would give you a sidelong look, then want to "kiss and make up," with "all forgiven and forgotten."[14]

Their father, whose deprived childhood had led, in his case, to an aversion to being physically close to anyone, could not resist her. Crawfie wrote that Margaret could penetrate that reserve with a disarming warmth and eagerness. She would wind her arms around his neck, settle into the crook of his arm, and look at him such adoration that, Crawfie wrote, "she brought joy into his life."[15] She seemed able to invoke loving responses from even unresponsive adults, wrote the psychiatrist Dennis Friedman in his psychological study of the Royal Family, *Inheritance*. If her behavior was manipulative and her charm seductive, this was "a sad reflection on her parents and governesses."[16] They wanted her as a screwball and cutup—very well, she would become one. Elizabeth Longford recounts how Margaret was once dressed up as an angel for a children's fancy dress party. Her mother remarked with some amusement that she did not look very angelic. "'That's all right,' replied Margaret. 'I'll be a Holy Terror.'"[17]

Elizabeth, quiet and reserved, was less demonstrative, but just as much affected by this outgoing personality who was always ready for fun. But as she got older, there was a distinct shift in attitude: Margaret became less of a playmate and more of the little girl with annoying problems. Such a show of exasperation masked other feelings, perhaps, that Margaret was just too demanding, too much of a show-off. Or perhaps the biggest reason was, as Elizabeth complained, "Margaret always wants what I want." Crawfie wrote that she could still hear Margaret's "pretty dear little voice" calling, "'Wait for me, Lilibet . . . Wait for me!'"[18]

The coronation of George VI in 1937 catapulted Margaret Rose from being the problem daughter of a relatively obscure prince into national prominence at the age of seven. She was suddenly subjected to pressures and expectations from all directions. Nobody knew what was wrong with her. In addition, the move to Buckingham Palace was now bringing them into the aegis of a cadre of highly trained, upper-class group of professionals whose status, ultimately, depended on theirs and the future importance of a royal family of flawless reputation and continual aplomb.

Instead of a comfortable rowhouse on the edge of a busy thoroughfare, "We Four," as Papa fondly called them, were about to be scattered in the far reaches of a building so monstrous that just going through and exploring its rooms, stairs, underground cellars, and secret alcoves might take a lifetime. For Buckingham Palace, originally bought by George III in 1761 as a modest family home for his wife, Queen Charlotte, would be much enlarged sixty-five years later by a successor, George IV, into an early version of the immense palace it would become.

Although photographs only show a single façade, in fact, the Palace is a quadrangle sitting on thirty-nine acres and containing its own park and three-acre lake, as well as the guest quarters one would expect and the multiple offices needed to administer the King's affairs. It famously contains 775 rooms. These include 52 royal and guest bedrooms, another 200 bedrooms for staff, 78 bathrooms, 92 offices and 19 glorious staterooms, including a throne room. The whole edifice is linked by infinities of corridors, and its extensive basements similarly complicated with stairs, passageways, and cellars.

The Tyburn River continues to run somewhere underneath, but history teaches us that in London this is to be expected. The website for the Palace claims that an astonishing number of people, perhaps fifty thousand a year, visit the Palace as guests in a normal year. Still, most of her majesty's subjects know it only through film and photographs.

The Palace also includes a resident ghost or two. One is said to belong to a monk who died in his cell—there was a monastery on the same spot in the distant past. The other is a certain Major John Gwynne, private secretary to Edward VII, who shot himself in his Palace office. He had just divorced his wife, and the resulting scandal was too much for him to live down. Staff members have claimed over the decades that they have heard a single gunshot coming from the office in which the disgraced major died.

It could well have happened. The story is too good to resist. The problem is that a lengthy search to discover evidence that this happened has been unable to uncover any part of it, or him, and a Major Gwynne was not private secretary to King Edward VII during his reign of 1901–1910. The only issue about which there can be no doubt is the certain ruin that would follow if, during that particular decade, some couple of social status was foolish enough to undertake a divorce, and certain to be held up for public censure in all the papers. It is possible that someone, perhaps a friend, name disguised, agreed to be named co-respondent in a divorce suit in which the King was actually involved, since his many affairs with married women were general knowledge. And that influential friends made sure that the King's name never appeared in the newspapers. The noise of a single gunshot people claim to have heard is intriguing. What if someone really did?

Although the girls were sad to leave home "like children all over the world," Crawfie wrote, they were excited about moving into a palace.[19] The new King and Queen were not, however, and argued fruitlessly to stay where they were. Marion Crawford did not look forward to the move either. The size was intimidating, for a start, and full of hidden dangers and inconveniences. The rooms looked exquisite enough. Before she and the children moved in, she was invited for tea in the Belgian suite, on the surface looking like a stage set, all done up in pink and gold. She saw a pretty little chair in the same colors, so she sat down. It had a cane seat, hidden from immediate view by a cushion, that had not been repaired since Victoria's day. She sat, it split apart, and down she went.[20]

Something similar happened the first night she was ushered into the bedroom that was to be hers. When the maid came to pull back the curtains, everything—heavy brass rods, pelmets, curtains and all—came down with a crash, just missing their heads. One did not expect the light switch that turned the lights on and off in the room to be halfway down the hall. You never knew who you would meet outside the bedroom door on your way to the bathroom. It might be the postman (the Palace had its own post office) or a fleet of messengers. It was like living in a village. Or a museum.

The unexpected was the rule. For instance, the whole Palace was overrun with mice.

There was even a Vermin Man who did nothing but give full-time attention to them, even though he never seemed to make any difference. Once Crawfie found a very large mouse (or maybe it was a rat?) sitting with composure on one of her towels and ran to a postman passing by to dispatch it. He put down his bag of letters and kindly obliged.[21]

If the dwelling places people inhabit can be considered for their propensity to encourage family intimacy or inhibit it, this was no place in which to live at all. As Crawfie explained, it was a cross between a hotel and an office building.

It also felt like a village, since people were constantly coming and going, and the distances were considerable. Mummy and Papa were now in their own suite, quite a walk away from the nursery wing. There were no more morning romps, and lunches had to be planned well in advance, because the King and Queen were always busy. Even getting to the garden outside meant a five-minute walk down endless halls and passageways.

The nursery wing had a sizeable staff—chamber maids coming and going, footmen to fetch and carry, and the princesses had maids of their own to minister to their whims as well as their wardrobes. Margaret and Robina Macdonald, born in a small, bleak village in the Scottish Highlands, were two sisters who began as royal chambermaids and after years of exemplary service, were promoted to take exclusive care of Elizabeth and Margaret respectively. They arrived at the point of becoming confidantes, too, and the attention of the press. In 1961, when her mistress was all grown up, Robina (or Bobo), who remained in Princess Margaret's service, was offered $150,000 by a newspaper, not identified, to spill the beans on her lady. It was indignantly refused. They are often seen in the background and not always named, these conservatively dressed, trim and close-mouthed sisters who knew so much and never said a word.[22]

In such an atmosphere, resistance to any change came slowly in the Palace; tradition and custom were all. That extended to the way meals were delivered. Crawfie explained that the kitchen was far away, at the Buckingham Palace road end. The nursery wing, however, was at the other end of the building, the Constitution Hill end. Getting a meal meant going up and down stone steps and along corridors almost half a mile away. Food was always cold by the time it arrived at the nursery wing, at which point hot plates had been thoughtfully provided to warm them back up again. That there might be a simpler way of doing things had not, it seemed, occurred to anyone. On one of their interminable walks Lilibet remarked dryly, "People here need bicycles."[23]

Sometime during his quarter century as King and Emperor (1910–1936), George V, in expressing his thanks to one of his departing private secretaries, wrote, "Thank you for teaching me how to be King." This was probably the literal truth. In a million practical ways, the King's private secretary was an indispensable figure and a man (it was always a man) who held the office together. First of all, he was usually retained for a certain period while a new monarch learned the ropes.

A private secretary knew from experience what a king did, how it was done, when it should happen and where, whose advice to take and whose to avoid, and how the king presented himself to the world down to the fine details of which outfit plus which medals. Or not. The secretary also knew what the king could say at any particular time, and what he could not do. The list was always growing. The private secretary was indispensable and therefore a towering presence in the Palace at any given moment.

In all practical respects, he was the force that regulated and administered a vast empire; the liaison between the King and his government, the church and the armed forces. He was the person you had to get on your side if you wanted to reach the great man himself. Little wonder that George V, under such daily and remorseless schooling, became known for doing the same thing in the same way at the same moment and exacted equal precision from others, down to the second. That was what it took to be a king. It also had practical advantages. Depending on the minute and the second, in a building as sprawling as Buckingham Palace, you always knew what the King was doing and where to find him.

To become the King's private secretary was not, surprisingly, very well paid. But the prestige was enormous, and there were extra perks, like a handsome grace-and-favor mansion for instance, control of a sizeable staff, and daily access to great men in every walk of life. One could be sure of a medal at the end of it, and perhaps a title if one did not have one already. One's satisfaction would be that, in an uncertain world, one had done one's bit to keep the monarchy alive and thriving, added one's own modest postscript to the history of England, and protected the status quo—in one's own small way.

Until quite recently, it was customary for courtiers to come from generation after generation from the same family. In *The Decline and Fall of the British Aristocracy*, David Cannadine traces at some length the fortunes of the various families involved and attitudes towards Queen Victoria's court.[24] At one period it was generally thought the great monarch had gathered "drones and flunkies" around her, and nepotism was rife.

Views were modified after Sir Henry Ponsonby, as newly appointed private secretary, brought about a number of reforms. New faces appeared to serve the growing family of the royal children, notably Victoria's, Edward VII's, and George VI's. Nevertheless, many of the old families were well represented and relatives of the sovereigns. People like Lord Nigel Claud Hamilton were seen at court for over 30 years, and he became treasurer to Queen Mary. The Marquess of Lincolnshire, friend of successive sovereigns, had a younger brother, Sir William Carington, who joined the court in 1880 and also served for over 30 years before dying in 1914. Such careers were not uncommon. That of Sir Alec Hardinge's was, Cannadine wrote, especially noteworthy for its longevity and influence. Born of a patrician background but without much income, Sir Alec, described by Harold Macmillan as "supercilious, without a spark of imagination," was showered with royal favors by succeeding monarchs. Plum appointments continued, along with special favors to his son who served George V, Edward VII, and George VI. His daughter married into the Lord Chamberlain's office.

Yet more important was the career of Sir Alan "Tommy" Lascelles, who would figure prominently in preventing Edward VIII's ("Uncle David's") marriage to a divorcée. But more of that later. Lascelles, the grandson of the fourth Earl of Harewood, was educated at Marlborough and Trinity College, Oxford, went hunting and shooting with all the best families, continued as aide-de-camp to his brother-in-law, the Governor of Bombay, and married the Viceroy of India, Lord Chelmsford's daughter.

Lascelles continued to gain favor as assistant private secretary to George V, continued as private secretary to George VI and stayed on for another year in the same role to Queen Elizabeth. A cousin married George V's only daughter, "A connection that can hardly have done Lascelle's own career prospects any harm," Cannadine observed.

Yet one more family often mentioned for its service to the Crown was that of Sir Henry Ponsonby, whose prominence as private secretary in 1870 was facilitated by the fact that his predecessor was his wife's uncle. Their son, Frederick, became treasurer of the household; another branch of the same family was a comptroller to the Lord Chamberlin and one of his grandsons was secretary to the Queen of Norway. One could cite similar examples of royal favor to members in the Airlie and Colville families.

The rewards were often generous. Sir Alex Hardinge was ensconced in a residence in St. James's that had forty-five rooms. He was also given the use of the Winchester Tower at Windsor and another house on the Balmoral Estate. Those in favor would be covered in stars and ribbons, and at least one Ponsonby became a peer. Those courtiers favored by the Crown, this "aristocratic monopoly," tended to be obscurantist and reactionary to a man. They were, Sir Lionel Cust wrote in 1930, "saturated in regal officialdom, besotted with hierarchy, order and precedence, and obsessed with 'all the paraphernalia and etiquette of a court.'"[25] Almost all of them were born during the reign of Queen Victoria, and acutely aware, as was Sir Alan Lascelles, who had a reputation of being curt, of their privileged backgrounds. They were also aware, as Cannadine wrote, that the order, hierarchy, rank and title they once took as their due now survived "unchallenged and intact only within the hallowed precincts of . . . Buckingham Palace."

Such attitudes were reflected, not only in privileges granted and withheld, but the actual uniforms the Palace servants wore in 1932 when F. J. Corbitt first arrived at the Palace to join the Comptroller of Supply staff. For instance, upper servants were smartly dressed in stiff white shirts with high collars, white ties, and dark blue tailcoats lined with silk, their gilt buttons bearing the royal initials. Under servants, however, wore scarlet coats embroidered in gold and black gold-embroidered waistcoats. Those in command usually did not wear such liveries but black frock coats with high collars and impeccably creased trousers.

When George VI arrived, he took a keen, almost obsessive interest in such matters, especially once Britain was at war with Germany. He decided to redesign their costumes along the lines of Civil Defense uniforms. Instead of frock coats, he wanted a battledress blouse top secured at the waist with a strap and buckle and bearing a large "GR VI" emblem on the left- hand pocket. He wanted epaulet cords on both shoulders and more gilt buttons bearing his initials. The King was particularly fussy about the back view; trousers should be sharply pressed and not bag at the seats. Such regalia not only denoted status, or lack of it, but ensured that the right people had privileges, which kept out those who were not entitled.

Take the dining rooms, for instance. Each group had its own dining room, suitably decorated, the silverware and plate, glasses, tables, and menu precisely graded to reflect status, or the lack of it. The Royal Family came first, of course. They had the grandest room and adjoining bathrooms. Next came the skilled workers, accountants, clerks, and the like, who enjoyed similarly lavish, leisurely, and superior fare in the Officials' Mess. Third in line were the upper servants, who dined quite handsomely in the Steward's Room and were waited on by other servants further down the social scale. Last of all were those who ate in the Servants' Hall, where the food was plain, but there was usually plenty of it. Nobody went without in those days when, Corbitt noted, there were usually three or four courses and money was no object.

"It is a complete social pyramid in itself at Buckingham Palace, and here, if nowhere else the . . . lines are rigidly drawn," he wrote in 1932. "It is absolutely forbidden for a servant, for instance, from the Steward's Room to go into the Officials' Mess except on special occasions . . ."

Everyone learned what to say and what not to say if by chance you ran across the King himself, although Corbitt, who was in Buckingham Palace every day, did not meet him for a year. His respect, loyalty, and admiration for those he served shines through every page of his remarkable book, *My Twenty Years in Buckingham Palace*.[26] Only once or twice does he allow a joke to slip through. This one was about two courtiers whose spheres of influence overlapped so precisely that it was the source of constant antagonism between them. Once, when a minor repair was needed, neither could decide who had the authority to command, so the repair was never made.

If Buckingham Palace, by its size alone, exerted a kind of impersonal formality on its inhabitants, the indication is that they all began to feel a chilling in the atmosphere as soon as they moved in. Crawfie observed that, however much their parents wanted Elizabeth and Margaret to feel they were "part of the community," it was extremely difficult to achieve.

"A glass curtain seems to come down between you and the outer world, between the hard realities of life and those who dwell in a court."

It really could not be done.[27] To begin with, there is the sudden exalted status, not just of their parents but the daughters themselves. Writing to Elizabeth at Sandringham, the Queen addressed her letter to "Her Royal Highness."[28]

Was the seven-year-old Margaret a Royal Highness, too? Well, yes, she also had the same elevated status, but for her, living in a palace had a new set of problems; she and her sister were no longer in the same boat, sharing the same closeness, wearing the same clothes, and being taken everywhere together. Perhaps her temper tantrum when she discovered that she would be wearing a different dress than Elizabeth, with a shorter train, during Papa's coronation, was Margaret's realization that she was becoming less important. The question is valid because her great grandfather had reacted in just the same way.

The Prince of Wales, Albert Edward, also known as "Bertie" to his family, had the misfortune to be born soon after Victoria, Princess Royale, namesake of the queen. The little girl, always called Vicky, was a phenomenon. By the time she was three, she could speak French and could already read.[29] At the age of four, she was learning Latin and—this hardly seems possible—reading Gibbon's *Decline and Fall of the Roman Empire*. She read Shakespeare for relaxation. Of course she did.

What was needed was another genius to measure up. That was not Bertie. He was a nice normal boy, which, in that family, could only be regarded with the deepest misgivings. He was ridiculously slow at learning French. He was three years old already and only had a few words. Six months went by, and he still would not do his lessons. He threw his books about and sat under the table. His parents believed that he had a learning disability. What his parents could not understand, his biographer wrote, was that their expectations were monstrous and that what they saw as "naughtiness" was any child's normal reaction to impossible demands. His attention-seeking behavior was also to be expected from a child who finds himself clearly overshadowed.[30]

If Vicky was a marvel, so in her own way was Elizabeth. If asked to do impossible things, given her age, like sitting motionless for an hour (her reward was a cookie), Elizabeth did it. As ever more "oughts and shoulds" arrived, Elizabeth famously tried to do everything perfectly. Crawfie wrote, "It was very touching to see how hard she tried to do what she felt was expected of her."[31] But then the governess began to worry that she was almost too good, almost too tidy. She would hop out of bed several times a night to get her clothes arranged just so and her shoes placed exactly on the floor. This was worrying. The solution was ridicule. That was typical and probably as good as any other in this case. In one hilarious session, Margaret exercised her talent for teasing and mimicking, and they "laughed her out of this."[32]

On another occasion, Lilibet showed that even she had her limits. Margaret and Elizabeth were also learning to speak French, though not perhaps before they were three. They had a French teacher whose idea of rapid instruction was copying long lists of verbs. One day Crawfie heard some ominous noises coming from the school room. Mademoiselle was screaming about something. In the days when all school children used pen and ink, Elizabeth had picked up her large, ornamental silver inkpot full of ink and emptied it on her own head. She sat there impassively, while Mademoiselle no doubt gave vent to "Ah non, ce n'est pas vrai," "Hélas!" "Au secours!" and similar expressions of alarm. The ink trickled all over Elizabeth's face and neck and into her lap, streaking her golden curls a deep blue. No doubt that particularly mind-numbing lesson in memorization had come to an end.[33]

By the time she was ten years old, Elizabeth's future was being confidently predicted by newspapers and magazines on both sides of the Atlantic; she was destined to bring about a second Renaissance, a new Elizabethan golden age. She had become, according to the *New York Times* in 1936, "The Most Important Little Girl in the World."[34] Clair Price wrote, "There cannot be any doubt of the high destiny that looms above Elizabeth's golden curls."

The writing was on the wall. Hospital wards, hand-painted china, and boxes of chocolates had been named for her. The Princess Elizabeth March was in the repertory of all the military bands. Her picture had appeared on Canadian postage stamps. "Princess Elizabeth Land" was named for her in Antarctica. She stood in effigy in Madame Tussaud's. She was receiving so many letters she was about to get her own secretary.

All this fame and glory came with a price. Since, as a Queen, she would have to learn to stand for hours, she took all her lessons standing. She was not allowed to read newspapers but, presumably, was informed on what was good for her once a week when Crawfie read her a digest of the week's events. Once a week, taking lunch with her parents, she was required to do the whole thing in French.

There were compensations. She had her own pony, stabled at the Royal Lodge, and her very own dolls' house. This was a gift from the Welsh people, scaled at two-thirds normal size and complete in every detail for the "Queen of English childhood," it was said. She had a bicycle and her own electric car with her own coat of arms on the door, in which she could tear around the grounds of Windsor Castle at the dangerous speed of five miles an hour. All of this must be a consolation for all the things she must pretend to do. For instance, she could never be tired, even if she wanted to. She could never speak her mind, even if stuck with the world's most crashing bore, and she had to keep on smiling. In short, she was learning the hard lessons of what it would mean to be a princess of the realm, let alone a queen. That was the price for being so special and different. That was living behind a glass curtain.

As for her sister, the one who declared she was "always going to be naughty," what she was learning behind the façade of Buckingham Palace can be implied by the way she behaved once they were both in their own nursery wing. That crawling around under a dinner table and tickling people's feet—could that be the behavior of a little girl who was out of control. What about the little girl who liked to hide behind heavy drawing room curtains, then jump out and say "Boo!" Was that so very bad, when her mother and uncle used to do the same thing all the time at Glamis, when they were children? One could go on.

Even the "I'm being naughty now," seemed harmless, such as the time when she dunked her cookie into her tea and then, grinning at her guests, tells them her mother told her not to.[35] What about the time when, in Africa, she obliged to listen to a native African chief give an interminable lecture, she had giggled when he lost his place? Did that really call for being sent to her room? There were a few occasions that looked a bit like getting even, it is true, as when she put tapioca into Elizabeth's bath and salt in her tea.[36]

But most of Margaret's exploits, the ones that are cited nowadays to prove how "bad" she was, have fallen into the kinds of things people with a hidden disability will do just to be noticed. When she rowed out into out into the middle of a pond and refused to come back, it looked like sheer naughtiness to parents. Or, with her Girl Guide teacher in tow, and again in a boat at Windsor, she pulled the plug in the bottom.[37] No harm was done then either, but it meant the teacher had to wade ashore, skirts held high, and she was quite cross about it. Then she, the little rascal, had a good laugh at her teacher's expense.[38]

There were other ways to carve out a space for oneself. Margaret seized on the opportunities the Girl Guide movement represented and competed for the merit badges everyone was eligible to take. History has not recorded exactly what they were, only that she won them all. She and her sister both studied the piano, but while Elizabeth was only mildly interested, Margaret finally applied herself with zest. She was a natural athlete, common with fetal alcohol syndrome children. She took swimming lessons and won the Children's Challenge Cup at the Bath Club in London. And when they both took painting lessons, Margaret was the one who created a comic strip character, called Pinkle-Ponkle. He mostly flew about in the air like Peter Pan. But when he came back to earth, he ate worm sandwiches with caterpillar jam.[39] No playwright could have done better.

J. M. Barrie and Margaret understood each other from the start. Barrie remembers being invited to one of her birthday teas at Glamis and sat beside her. He was at work on his last play, "The Boy David" (1936), about the Biblical figure, King Saul, and Goliath, now seldom performed. Barrie recalled there was a pile of presents on the table, but she had picked one out and given it the place of honor by her plate. He asked, "as one astounded," "Is that really your very own?" Her reply interested him so much that he used it in his play and even paid her a token sum for every time it was spoken, one assumes as an incentive.

What she did, he wrote, was put her special present between them both. Then she said grandly, "It's yours. *And* mine."[40]

Chapter 5

The Glass Curtain

"Why can't I try on different lives, like dresses, to see which one fits best and is more becoming?"
—Sylvia Plath, *The Unabridged Journals of Sylvia Plath*

To leave an attentive and loving atmosphere and move into an enormous building that imposed not just formidable distance but a strait jacket on behavior would have been unsettling at any age, and particularly this little girl with her hidden disability. At home, she and her sister had always been treated alike. They ran freely in and out of each parent's rooms, read the same books, had the same governess and nurse, lived in the same quarters, and ate the same food. They were not, as was the custom in well-born households, shown to their parents for five minutes a day, and forgotten for the rest of it. Their mother, one of a boisterous group of ten, was given wide latitude and showed early independence of mind. Their father made it his business to ensure they both had the loving concern that had been so markedly lacking in his own upbringing. He liked to say, "Elizabeth is my pride, and Margaret is my joy." The girls were not prepared for such a radical cooling of the emotional atmosphere and the major upheaval of the move itself. But then, nobody was.

Under the watchful eye of Crawfie, they had been coached in good manners and knew how to behave when their parents were inspecting the troops or opening something and took them along. (Stand quietly behind them and don't put your hands in your pockets.) There had always been time reserved in their day to work off high spirits; their parents made sure of that.

Inside Buckingham Palace, there was a new level of control at work they could not have imagined. An aristocratic network of command centers was peopled by "all those awe-inspiring men in livery, who seemed so proud and disdainful of outsiders," F. J. Corbitt wrote,[1] looming over them in their red, white, and gilt splendor. Little princesses must sit up straight in their chairs—no slouching, wriggling, or biting their nails—which they both did for quite a while. They had to sit here, stand there, not dawdle, never giggle, always fold their napkin the right way when finished with it, and curtsey and bow their heads to their own parents. The rules were excruciating; the way you picked up a teacup, for instance, or walked down a flight of stairs without holding the banister, or never used certain words ("Pardon?", for instance), or even thought anything not stamped and sealed by the thought police. There were ever so many ways to control how you behaved and what you did without knowing it.

Who knew where all the rules came from? Schools of manners were just as rigid as those controlling the court of Louis XIV in the seventeenth century, perhaps worse. As was noted, "courtiers lived under the despotic surveillance of the king, and upon their good behavior, their deference and their observance of etiquette their whole careers depended."

If the king was displeased, he passed you by without a word, his eyes glazed, and nobody else knew you either. On the other hand, a kind word and a smile from the man on high, and your days were embroidered with flattery. "At Versailles, and the courts all over Europe which imitated it—everything was done to make it very clear who was superior to whom; and of course, each time anyone was being polite it was simultaneously acknowledging rank and demonstrating who stood where."

In the decade before World War II, F. J. Corbitt's memoir, *My Twenty Years in Buckingham Palace*, is instructive in its explanation of such graded spheres of influence. Perhaps maids in the royal nursery cleaning out the royal fireplaces no longer had to stand up and curtsey every time the royal baby went by in his bassinette. But the Lord Chamberlain, chief officer of the court, still led the royal procession on state occasions by walking backwards, as had been done since time immemorial.[2] Precedence was immutable, and when Prince Philip married Princess Elizabeth, he still walked a deferential two steps behind her, no doubt measured by the inch. It was Precedence again, "that despot ne'er o'erthrown." Elizabeth, "The Most Important Little Girl in the World," bore it all with heroic patience. Margaret was mutinous.

After the abdication of Uncle David and her father's Coronation, Margaret was second in line to the throne, a position she held for the next decade. That ended once Elizabeth married Philip, Papa died in 1952, and their first-born, Charles, became Prince of Wales. Now he was the next in line, as his children would be. Elizabeth also had three more children. Every time another royal prince or princess was born, Margaret slid back another place in the increasing line of those next in the queue. By the time all these nieces and nephews grew up and had children of their own, Margaret had slid from second to twenty-fourth in line. In all the Coronation photographs of 1937, she is standing below her parents and next to her sister. By the time she is grown up and has a husband and children of her own, she is sitting far to the left at the end of the row. One more chair and she would have disappeared altogether.

As her dynastic importance dwindled and disappeared, Margaret may be forgiven for clutching her remaining titles around her, rather the way an elderly woman might cling to the raddled remnants of what was once a splendid cloak. The title of "Her Royal Highness" remained her own; no one could take that away from her. As for the second reference, which was Ma'am, it had to be pronounced just right, that is to say, to rhyme with "ham" and not Ma'am as in "calm." A whole lunch party might spend a bemused hour marveling on the intricacies of how HRH must be addressed. And, of course, she was never to be called by her Christian name, not by anybody. Or maybe one or two. Her famous look would send the temperature in the room down several degrees if you got it wrong. "Well, at least," she would say, "I am a king's daughter and a queen's sister." There was that.

The rule that everyone in the Palace must know exactly where the King and Queen were at all times took hold during the reign of George V as a practical necessity in a building containing hundreds of rooms. The dear King had learnt his drill so well that courtiers, it was said, could set their watches by not only where he was, but where he was going and with whom. Once he had left this world and was joined by George VI, that modest and easily persuaded person, Margaret's papa, bent his mind in the directions most desired, i.e., to follow everyone else's advice. George VI was a terrific shot and played doubles at Wimbledon. He liked to design medals and actually *did* design uniforms for the troops, making it a rule that the pants did not bag at the seat. He was, as it turned out, brave, resourceful, and much-loved during World War II for many reasons. So was his Queen.

As for their daughters, they were set adrift in this vast mausoleum where clusters of rooms took single-minded concentration, not to mention time, just to find. Princess Elizabeth, who never complained about anything, darkly said once that "they ought" to issue bicycles to its inhabitants. Being so far away from parents and governesses made the girls prey to servants who were allowed by custom to take over, adding immeasurably to the list of "oughts and shoulds" to which the girls were now subjected. It is a safe guess which girl took the brunt of all the "don'ts." Elizabeth, by then, had become almost too good to be real. Wasn't she adorable, after she had learnt to curtsey, as she went looking for more servants to curtsey in front of, racing down the corridors? What a splendid example she set, jumping out of bed four or five times a night, so she could be sure her slippers were lined up the correct millimeters apart? And how about her impish sister who had given many a nurse the slip and had to be held firmly by the hand at all times or she would disappear down a rabbit hole? And who nobody could teach how to write? When asked what ambition he had for the girls, George VI answered gruffly that he would be happy if Margaret could write a readable letter. Perhaps Crawfie alone knew how often Margaret's fits of giggles could become screams of frustration, from the requirement of perfect behavior at all times and places, no matter what.

So, we return to the rare description of another little girl with the same disability, but with the benefit of a more enlightened upbringing in a book, *The Best I Can Be*.[3] It charts the slow progress of Liz Kulp, with additions by her mother Jodee Kulp, who adopted her. Liz, whose birth mother was a hopeless alcoholic, was more severely damaged, but offers clues to the same kinds of issues she and the princess shared.

For instance, Liz had special problems with reading and writing because letters danced on the page whenever she tried to pin them down. Because of her brain damage, she lacked the fine muscle control that it takes for the rest of us to write. Whether she was left- or right-handed is not clear, but she still needed guidelines until she was seven and always had a funny way of holding a pen with her whole fist, as photographs show.

The princess might have also heard fluorescent lights in department stores buzzing that gave Liz Kulp a headache and "made the world dance." The only way to control her screaming fits of sheer frustration was to take her to a quiet area and calm her down—what to others would have looked like "spoiling." These fits, in Liz's case, went on for years and might last as long as two hours, on the floor, kicking and snarling. She slowly learned to tell herself "Stop. Focus. Control."[4] Like the princess, Liz loved music and asked for music lessons. That was the most soothing of all.

The Kulp family, at least, knew what was wrong. There was no such knowledge available when Princess Margaret was growing up. She was willful, rebellious, spoilt, fill in the blanks. Add in the low status of princesses, whose lives were dictated by men and whose wishes counted for nothing, and the miracle is they did not file her away and forget her in some conveniently obscure institution. As it was, they could freely express their exasperation and be sure of a sympathetic response. A courtier told the biographer Sarah Bradford that Margaret was "a wicked little girl." He would have liked to give her "a hell of a slap."[5] Her sister at age twelve took to expressing grown-up concerns.

"Whatever are we going to do about Margaret?"

Given what we know about behavior, deportment, and excruciating rules about sitting down, standing up, eating, and everything else, not to mention the layers of precedence (how others were greeted and what you said, or didn't), the fading days of Empire before World War II must have been particularly difficult for Margaret. The comment by a royal courtier in Buckingham Palace that the young princess, aged only seven or eight, was "a wicked little girl"[6] says it all. Any spirited youngster would rebel, let alone someone with a hidden mental handicap who cannot be expected to live up to such demands. As Diane Malbin, author and leading expert who founded the Fetal Alcohol Syndrome/Drug Effects Clinic in Portland, Oregon, delicately expressed it in her book about fetal alcohol spectrum disorders: any "chronic poor fit" between the child and his or her environment makes for defensive behaviors. Margaret had them all. She became rigid and argumentative. She began acting out, and her attempts to run away and hide became more and more frequent. She was also defiant. She said more than once, in effect, "All right then, you'll see how bad I can be."[7]

What reactions followed this kind of outburst are clear enough to guess. As one general is said to have remarked in answer to a question: "We know what the Queen's views are. She doesn't have any views."[8] High time this wicked little girl learned to obey. For her own good, of course.

Share and share alike. That was how Margaret had been brought up, and she was sure this must be the right way. J. M. Barrie, who adored this sparkling little girl, intuitively understood her. Her reactions towards children less fortunate than she and Elizabeth were instinctively generous, and Crawfie had probably told them often enough about the starving children she had seen on the back streets in Edinburgh. The knowledge that there could be children with nothing to eat and nowhere to sleep horrified them. At the same time, the idea of being able to play on the streets was a startling idea, quite romantic, and even enviable to girls who had never enjoyed the modest pleasures of playing hopscotch on the pavement, jumping on a double-decker bus, or buying a penn'orth of peppermint balls in a sweet shop. But then, suppose you didn't have any money? What if you got cold or ill? What if you were always hungry?

Barrie told the girls about how such children ended up in the hospital and how nurses gave up their own beds so a sick child could sleep. Yes, he said, their lives were very hard. But sometimes they could also be "uproariously funny."

After World War II, one occasionally met, in Pratt's Hotel in Bath, a small scuttling figure carrying a tray, washing floors, cleaning and vacuuming, or delivering your breakfast with an apologetic smile, as if prepared for a compliment or a curse. Her name was Louie Stride, and she would not have found anything funny about her life as a little girl starving on the streets.

Happily, we know quite a bit about that life, because she left a rare record of her upbringing in one of the prettiest West Country towns—the most complete eighteenth-century town in Europe before the second World War. It is also a town with extensive Roman baths and has many royal associations going back to the sixteenth and seventeenth centuries, as the names of its streets, terraces and crescents constantly bear witness: Queen's Square, the Royal Crescent, the King's Circus, the Royal Mineral Water Hospital, Coronation Avenue, and Victoria Park, among them. All the "quality" visited Bath at some point, and famous men and women lived there, from William Pitt to Sheridan, Shelley, Gainsborough, and Richard Brinsley Sheridan. Jane Austen, though she did not care much for Bath, has made it famous again. It is an elegant, high society sort of place, and so the idea of it having any poor people is hard to believe. But there were many at the beginning of the twentieth century.

In *Britain at Bay*, Alan Allport wrote that Britain in the 1930s remained a country of staggering want and inequality. Two-thirds of income earners brought in a weekly wage of less than two pounds, ten shillings—an amount that was barely half the minimum considered necessary for a family of four to live decently. More than a million families were too poor to pay rent for proper housing with electricity, running water, and an indoor toilet.[9] In a country as rich as England, there were people everywhere living in damp, decrepit, vermin-infested rooms, and their children were being fed on bread, margarine, potatoes, and sugared tea, with corned beef occasionally thrown in, according to George Orwell in his landmark study, *The Road to Wigan Pier*. In the years before and after the Great Depression, things only got worse. What could happen to a town supported by a single industry was a case in point. In 1936, Palmer's Shipyard, which employed almost everyone in Jarrow, was forced to close and threw hundreds of men out of work. As a result, two hundred of its unemployed set out to march on London some three hundred miles to the south.

The then-Duchess of York visited the town that summer. She wrote of driving through "a horrible scene of desolation," past "large crowds of emaciated, ragged, unhappy people." It made her cry. Surely someone could help them somehow?[10] Their plight, and their heroic march, softened no hearts once they reached Whitehall. It was taken for granted that the gulf between the classes was inevitable and immutable. Photographers of the day took note. In 1937, someone found two boys waiting to enter Lord's Cricket Ground for the match between Eton and Harrow. They were wearing top hats, ties, waistcoats, and nicely tailored black suits. Some grubby looking local lads are saying something rude, and the boys in top hats are pretending not to notice. In fact, as Louie Stride wrote, hungry children on the street were beneath anyone's notice.

Louie Stride's mother was a prostitute, with a small income on the side cleaning shops for sixpence an hour. Somehow this never added up to food for her four-year-old daughter, except "sporadic meals of bread and tea." So, Louie was always hungry and "would do anything for food."[11] She went to school at that age and would steal food from the younger children. She remembers grabbing a piece of bread from a baby and running into a lavatory to eat it. Her surprisingly vivid and detailed memory is not about life in Bath, or the children she met, or how she was treated, for the most part, but primarily what it took to find bread on the streets. Just bread. Milk as well, if she was lucky. First, she went around the cafes and restaurants in the early morning, whatever the weather, looking for scraps in the gutter—"it was surprising what you could find"—knocking on doors for stale bread. She knew all the best places and so did a crowd of ragamuffins with the same idea, begging to be fed.

If that didn't work, as a last resource you would make the trek to Manvers Street, where there was a bakery, and take a pillow case with you. For three pence you might get a whole bag full of leavings, and every once in a while, someone would take pity on you and, with a wink, give you a nice fresh bun just out of the oven. Oh, the smell! And what a feast on the way home! And so she ran wild on the streets by day and was "locked in at night."[12]

In retrospect, it is difficult to understand how a child like Louie, in stained and dirty clothes, her head shaved because of persistent lice, often barefoot, could be in such desperate straights and not be noticed. One has a shadowy impression of an alcoholic, feckless, but well-meaning mother, who periodically tries to do better and is still pretty enough, or flirtatious enough, to find an occasional protector to pay the rent for favors granted.

Louie herself, growing up fast on the streets, learned about money soon enough and began to steal from her mother so that there would be something left for food at the end of the week—which there often wasn't. In such cases, she would show up for school on Mondays and then faint because she had not eaten for two days.

At first, she was given water to drink. But after the same thing happened several Mondays in a row, it occurred to some of her teachers that maybe she was hungry. One of them left to buy milk and a bun.

"Well, the way I grabbed the bun and wolfed it down told them all."

Every day from then on, she was provided with hot milk and Virol—a nutritious, sticky brown syrup made of malt, sugar and vitamins—and also given dinner in a restaurant beside the Abbey. She stopped fainting after that.[13]

The great thing about life, as Louie learned fast, was to have a man about the house. Any man. She found this out after one of their "moonlight flits," which happened when the rent was past due and they skipped to the next town. It happened often enough, and Louie knew the drill. They would hire a large hand cart—they could be had by the hour—and load everything they possessed into it, which usually wasn't much. Then they would wait in darkness for the right moment, sit Louie on top, and off they went to the next stop, which, since Bath was in a valley surrounded by hills, could be a formidable undertaking.

In this case the next refuge was in Holloway—one of the oldest streets, until the bombings of Bath, contained remnants of sixteenth-century buildings—a rough, working-class neighborhood and a steep climb up from the river. There her mother had rented a room in a tiny cottage behind a sweet shop, and they finally got some sleep. Next morning, the street was in an uproar. All the women in the neighborhood were screaming outside their door, yelling at her mother and trying to hit her. She was a "Scarlet Woman," coming to live among decent people, with a Bastard as well.

"They weren't going to tolerate that and they didn't."[14]

What hurt most was being called "a Bastard." It was mean and unfair. But then she noticed that if you had a man in evidence, you were left alone. Even if he was not married to your mother. Respectability was everything.

Curiously enough, this same rough justice—the all-important existence of the man in the house—was just as true at the opposite end of the social spectrum. Young debutantes were being groomed, trained, for a single goal in life: marriage and respectability, and the sooner the better. In *Lady in Waiting*, Lady Glenconner explained, "For girls of my background, the point of being a debutante was to be introduced to a generation of eligible men, with the intention of marrying one as soon as possible. Girls didn't have the freedom to shack up with a single boyfriend to test them out, and if we did, we only got as far as the heavy petting stage."[15]

Finding the acceptable man was crucial, and this meant a constant round of dances and weekend parties, the goal of which was mutual introductions—the more, the better. In 1950, Anne Glenconner was just eighteen, two years behind her dear friend Margaret, so the same circumstances applied. In those days, eighteen was hardly too young. The reality was that many older boys had just died in World War II; as for their surviving counterparts, they were serving two years of compulsory military service. So, the competition was fierce among available suitors.

No one quite wanted to say that while falling in love was desirable, it was not necessary. What was necessary was to marry someone very presentable, if possible; the first born, if possible; with land, money, and social status. What had been true since the Middle Ages was that a girl took on the status of the man she was marrying, moving higher ". . . to correspond with the social rank of her husband."[16] Then, since divorce was very difficult and usually impossible, she might later contract a liaison of a more tempestuous nature, so long as she was discreet about it.

Money and status came first. So, a girl had to learn how to flirt, how to charm, how to dress, how to please future in-laws, and, if possible, take on an enormous household and be prepared for a fast engagement by the time she was nineteen. A big society wedding at twenty-one and she was set up for life. Lady Glenconner remarked that if you had not pulled off this major feat by the time you were twenty-four, you were on the shelf. She herself married, at the late stage of twenty-three, a madly handsome and formidably rich man, Colin Tennant. Rather too late, she found out about insane tempers and decidedly unorthodox sexual tastes—but it was too late.

A similar fate awaited Pamela Harriman, an Englishwoman with the right background who would eventually marry Averell Harriman, a distinguished American diplomat, a former U.S. Ambassador, former Governor of New York, and businessman. She herself would serve as an ambassador, well known for her wit, charm, and as a hostess with a unique sense of style and taste. Her first marriage, in 1939, was to Randolph Churchill, son of the great Prime Minister, who had every virtue except charm and an alarming tendency to make drunken marriage proposals. Legend has it that he was in a similar state when he proposed to Pamela and was accepted. Who could turn down Sir Winston, the great Prime Minister, as a father-in-law? Marrying the right man was traditional, and she was set on a long path that ultimately led to fame and fortune, if by a circuitous route.

Pamela Harriman told an interviewer in 1997, "It is almost incredible to people I work with today to realize I was born in a world where a woman was totally controlled by men. I mean, you got married and there was kind of no alternative. The boys were allowed to go off to school. The girls were kept at home . . ." in a kind of purdah until they married.[17]

For a thousand years at least, fairy tale heroines have always been princesses. "Once upon a time," as stories began since time immemorial, such stories have contained wicked stepmothers, dragons and ogres and hobgoblins, but the heroine will always be a princess. Even Cinderella, some think the oldest story of all—coming, as folklorists Peter and Iona Opie have argued, from China—is not the waif who marries the rich man. She is properly a princess herself, disguised as a little barefooted scullery-maid, sitting by a fire. Her superior status, artlessly betraying a regal attitude towards life itself, can be discerned only by the right person—a prince, for instance. She will have to endure many trials and reversals of fortune, but all will end happily because she is a princess.

Take, for instance, one of Hans Christian Andersen's stories, "The Princess and the Pea," which tells of a prince who travels "the whole world" looking for a princess who is "real." But she has to have a certain something that he cannot quite define. And every time, no matter how beautiful and apparently eligible the candidate was, there was always something that "did not seem quite right."

He returned to his father's castle exhausted and very sad. Then one night a sudden thunderstorm woke him up. The clouds clashed and roared, the heavens released blinding curtains of rain, and just as things could not get any worse, there came a great knocking at the town gate. The King went down to see who it was. It turned out to be the saddest, wettest, most bedraggled girl he had ever seen. Her hair dripped lankly around her ears and trickled to her shoulders. Her eyelashes were so wet she could barely see. Little rivulets cascaded out of her ears. Her dress clung to her legs, and she squelched as she walked. Who could she be? Well, she said, she had heard he was looking for a princess. She was the real thing.

The Queen took her in, hung up all her clothes to dry and gave her a nightgown. She was thinking, *A real princess? We'll soon see about* that. Secretly, she put a small pea on the slats of the bed where the strange girl was going to sleep. Then she heaped it with twenty mattresses and twenty more eiderdowns. The princess went to bed.

Next morning, she was asked how she had slept.

"Oh, abominably badly!" she said.

She tossed and turned all night because there was large hard lump in the bed somewhere, and she was black and blue.

Such delicacy of feeling meant only one thing. So, she and the prince married and lived happily ever after. And that, the great author explained, is how you tell a princess.

A princess might, of course, be traveling in disguise although a short visit down through the centuries has not come up with princesses pretending to be homeless and penniless when they are not. In fact, a new study of five daughters of King Edward I in the thirteenth century, *Daughters of Chivalry*, reveals that they were better placed to lead independent lives than their counterparts are nowadays.

The study by the accomplished medieval scholar Kelcey Wilson-Lee comes to the unexpected conclusion that they were powerful in their own right. They were well-educated, could marry for love, took over the management of castles, and, if necessary, could raise their own companies of "men-at-arms." For example, after daughter Joanna's husband died, she not only chose her second husband, in defiance of her father's wishes, but married him. Another daughter, Mary, shunted off to a nunnery to get rid of her when she was six, made prudent use of her connections to travel freely, and acquired desirable real estate and a small fortune as well, spending it on some very expensive gold jewelry. Women could be regents, become alliance brokers and even patrons. They could do almost as much as their brothers.

As in a fairy story, such women did not get divorced. As a practical matter this was difficult and, in any case, very expensive. The sensible alternative was separate castles, assuming that you had one to spare. There was no particular social censure involved, at least not then. But, a curious thing seems to have happened over the centuries. By the time Queen Victoria ascended the throne in the 1850s, being a married woman was tantamount to giving everything she was to her husband. In law, he and she were one, but the snag was that he had assumed her very existence into himself, and she was nothing. If she had money when she was married, that became his. If she worked for a living, that was his, too. Whatever her body produced, i.e. children, were his. She existed to please him, and if it turned out she had made a ghastly mistake and he beat her, she was stuck with him. He could play around, but she couldn't. And so on. It was a terribly bad idea to walk away from a bad marriage, and what the law could not do to make her see the error of her ways, society conspired to impose. Even Louie, growing up on the streets of Bath, had figured it out in her childish wisdom. Any man was better than none.

As John Mortimer notes in his first volume of autobiography, *Clinging to the Wreckage*: "The past is like a collection of photographs: some are familiar and on constant display, others need searching for in dusty drawers. Some have faded entirely, and some have been taken so amateurishly and on a day so dark that the subjects are seen like ghosts in a high wind and are impossible to identify."[18]

From today's perspective, it is difficult to see how the Victorians, those intrepid men who climbed mountains, penetrated wildernesses without end, and established actual countries, could have been so blind to the desperately needed reforms at home. The ghosts in a high wind, in their epoch, were all the women who tried to live up to manly expectations; who were "angels in the house;" who bore all, accepted all, and left the world in quiet anonymity. How perfect was that ideal? Not very, obviously—no more than Queen Victoria herself, who spent her widowhood creating a deity from dimming memories of her Albert, adoring him at the same moment that she rejected his children.

The story about the centuries-long fight of women for equal status has been well told. For this narrative it is enough to know that by 1930 or thereabouts, they had finally won the vote (1928) and the then Prime Minister Stanley Baldwin could say in a speech to his all-male members of Parliament that "Women will have with *us* the fullest rights. The ground and justification for the old agitation is gone."[19] The legality was one thing; reality was another. For women during that period, nothing much had changed. Women were still being barred from well-paying careers, expected to arrive at their weddings as virgins and cheerfully give up their own jobs, particularly during the Depression, on the theory that married men with families to support had the greater claim.

Enter Uncle David, Prince of Wales and future Edward VIII. If his father had been all that was expected of him by the mandarins at court; that is to say, ruled by duty, uxorious, affable, punctual, impeccably attired and never having a single thought of his own, his heir was the opposite. The new king, now forty-one years old, not only was different, but one gets the feeling that he absolutely did it on purpose, rather like the adolescent who is old enough to smoke and is about to do everything else as well. One of the curious facts of history is that he is never called the "Rebel King"—the epithet applied to his niece Margaret almost as soon as she was born. It is hard to see why. He was even more of a rebel than she was, and his refusal to do what was expected of him caused a national crisis. The fact is that, even as king, or perhaps especially because now he *was* the King, he refused any longer to live up to others' expectations. He was going to be himself. So there. That would never do.

In his book, *The Decline and Fall of the British Aristocracy*, David Cannadine explores the degrees by which an intricate network of peers that had intermingled with, and upheld the rights of, royalty, was losing its influence following the first World War. Such new trends came from America. Hostesses like Elsa Maxwell, Laura Corrigan, Nancy Astor, Emerald Cunard, and Henry "Chips"

Channon replaced the traditional elite that had exerted exclusive power as a class. Besides, generations of their young heirs had been slaughtered in the trenches. Their attitudes and ideals "perished with them."[20]

Now the "Bright Young Things" dominated society. So did "gossip columns, night clubs, cocktails, shorter skirts, and dancing . . . Members of the peerage married (and divorced) more plebianly than ever before." The Prince of Wales disliked his father's friends and was intrigued by this younger crowd of newcomers with their fresh, relaxed attitudes, their sense of fun, and their penchant for flirtations, in or out of marriage. One of his early conquests was Thelma Furness, daughter of an American diplomat and wife of the first Viscount Furness, chairman of a shipping company. She was the twin sister of Gloria Vanderbilt and a sometime movie star, all of which would have sounded exotically unfamiliar to her star-struck lover. They had something like a two-year affair when, in 1931, she made the mistake of introducing David to an even more fascinating companion, and her best friend, the equally married Mrs. Wallis Warfield Simpson. Chips Channon, who met her at lunch in the winter of 1934, found her "a nice, quiet, well-bred mouse of a woman with large, startled eyes and a huge mole."[21] He was to revise that opinion later. Before too long, Thelma Furness had been dropped, and the lady from Baltimore, with her large, startled eyes, became the prince's constant companion.

F. J. Corbitt has left a telling description of what changed once the new king arrived. The old days of knowing where the king was at any given moment were gone forever. For instance, during George V's reign, all of Buckingham Palace was aware that Tuesday was stamp day, this week and every week. At fourteen minutes past ten in the morning, the king would appear in the Grand Hall, immaculately dressed and probably, like the White Rabbit, looking anxiously at his watch . . . "Oh my ears and whiskers . . ." How could he possibly be thirteen seconds late? He would disappear to the salon in which his vast and valuable collection of postage stamps was kept. He would spend the whole day there. Even lunch and tea must be delivered to that room. And if you were an equerry, you had better have a jolly good reason for interrupting, or your ears would burn with epithets, used and polished to a high luster since the king's days in the British Navy.[22]

Fast forward to his successor, Edward VIII, equally natty in appearance but quite unpredictable. He might intend to eat lunch on the dot of 1:15 p.m. but not get around to it until half past two.[23] His staff never knew what he would do and when, which presented a brand-new set of problems, although he was full of apologies when this was explained to him, and always promised to reform. He usually had insomnia, so he never wanted to go to bed either. As a bachelor, "it was nothing unusual for him to come back . . . at one, two or three in the morning, bringing a party of half a dozen gay friends with him."[24] The bell would ring, sandwiches would be ordered, drinks would be served—he only wanted a pot of tea for himself—and one imagines him falling into bed as a new day dawned.

The diaries of Tommy Lascelles, in this connection, make fascinating reading. The courtier who was to cause so much trouble for him on the issue of divorce—both for the Prince of Wales and the Princess Margaret—was a curious blend of open, resourceful admiration and ruthless, unyielding ideas about how the royals should behave. He had entered Buckingham Palace as private secretary to the Prince of Wales in 1920 and left his service in protest, in 1927. Unfortunately for the prince, Tommy was enormously popular and influential and would cause no end of trouble in the years to come, in or out of office. He wrote later that he began his service with affection and admiration. But admiration turned to dislike, he wrote, because "his unbridled pursuit of Wine and Women, and of whatever selfish whim occupied him at the moment, was going rapidly to the devil . . ."[25] He was no longer fit for office. Tommy could not help himself from hoping that the prince, who liked to ride point-to-point, would fall off his horse and break his neck.[26]

It is difficult nowadays to imagine the kind of upheaval that hit the nation when, shortly after his arrival, the American press leaked the story that Edward VIII intended to marry a twice-divorced American, Mrs. Wallis Warfield Simpson of Baltimore. As a little girl growing up in Bath in those days, I clearly remember the headlines in the papers and universal expressions of shock. An American lady, the Queen? Surely he must be joking? Nobody knew where Baltimore was. And divorced *twice*? The Church of England did not recognize divorce even once, so to be divorced twice must be very bad.

Many authors since have tried to unravel the mystery of why Edward VIII would have chosen such an unsuitable person. *A King's Story*, his autobiography written just after World War II (1947), is interesting for its lack of special pleading. In fact, its tone is noncommittal, but in the context of what was already known about his upbringing—his extraordinarily unfeeling, ungiving mother and a father who ranted at his sons as if they were all naval cadets—one can see why their son wanted someone who was more emotionally accessible and even why she had to be someone who had been married. In newspaper dispatches, the impression is given that the two had scarcely met, but, in fact, she had been his constant companion for several years.

Then there was the issue of just how much pressure he was willing to accept in order to do what everybody—the church, the politicians, the courtiers, the aristocracy—thought he ought. All that pomp and circumstance, the golden carriage, the coronation robes, the courtiers walking backwards—what did it mean anymore? As Jeremy Paxman commented in *On Royalty*, none of the royal families of Europe had anything remotely resembling authority or power. They had become like the "pipsqueak" principalities of Monaco or Lichtenstein, "fancy-dress fodder for magazines which survive by telling us things we did not need to know about people we have hardly heard of . . ."[27] All his life, the new king had been hedged around by don'ts and oughts. Now they were even telling him whom he could marry. It was too much. When he stepped down, he made it very clear that Wallis, the one person he loved more than life itself, was the reason. When he remarked that his brother would make a better king than he would, he meant it. Chips Channon, the American outsider, observed, "it is the aristocracy which still rules England, although nobody seems to believe it."[28]

Years later, James Pope-Hennessy, who was writing the official life of Queen Mary, visited the Duke and Duchess of Windsor, as they were now titled. In 1957 they were living in exile in a country house outside Paris, "Le Moulin des Tuileries." He found the Duke "Less small than I had been led to believe . . . a well-proportioned human being." Just then he had been working in the garden, and his tobacco-colored hair was blown out in tufts on either side of his head. He was looking "crumple-faced and wild, like Shaw's Dauphin." But once he emerged from a makeover by his valet, the Duke became "very silken and natty . . . he has his father's eyes, and some, I fancy, of his mannerisms." Pope-Hennessy was agreeably surprised to find him "exceedingly intelligent, original, liberal-minded, and . . . one of the most considerate men I have ever met . . . Like the Duchess, he is perhaps too open and trusting towards others."

The house was almost too perfect in its American showcase kind of way, and as for the guest's bedroom, every contingency had been provided for, including various kinds of notepaper, nail files, and fruit. The hostess's ensemble matched the décor in flawlessness. Here she was, smiling, full of enormous goodwill, quite frank and speaking with a pronounced Southern accent. To look at her was to marvel.

"She is flat and angular and could have been designed for a medieval playing card. The shoulders are small and high; the head very, very large, almost monumental; the expression either anticipatory . . . or appreciative . . ." Her sense of goodwill was infectious, and the only moment a shadow crossed her face was when the subject turned to the Queen Mother, the reason for his visit, after all. Then a kind of "facial contortion," became "very unpleasant to behold."[29]

As for the Queen Mother, that enigmatic, upright, and unsmiling figure whose galaxy of titles included those of Princess, Duchess, Queen Consort, and Empress of India, her niggling adherence to precedence and protocol and her complete ability, it would seem, to mask her feelings, were noted even while she was alive. She had devoted "the total of her energy and conscience to not being herself." This was the conclusion of Janet Flanner, the superb American diarist whose weekly letters from Paris and London, published by the *New Yorker*, were models of sharp observation. One of the best profiles ever published about the Queen Mother is contained in *London Was Yesterday, 1934–1939*, in which Flanner spends quite a bit of time investigating the love-hate relationship between the British idea of the monarchy and its spasmodic confrontations. They came, incidentally, at a significant time of change in her subject's life.[30]

Victoria Mary, always called May, was born in Kensington Palace, London, in May of 1867. She was the daughter of Prince Francis, Duke of Teck, and Princess Mary Adelaide, granddaughter of King George III. Princess Mary, or May, was the oldest of four children, and only girl in the family—her father was a gambler, which made income tight if nonexistent—and the little girl seems to have been pressed into service taking care of her three younger brothers: Adelphus (b. 1868), Francis (1870), and Alexander (1874). Such a heavy adult role at too early an age seldom works well for anybody. Perhaps this had something to do with a sensitive child's withdrawal, as anecdotal evidence indicates, resulting in an adolescent solution of hiding one's feelings in self-defense. She became a silent, watchful girl, facing life with more equanimity than she probably felt.

This minor member of the British royal family, nevertheless, caught the eye of Queen Victoria, who decided to cultivate her. Such a statuesque, composed girl, whose generous outlines and tiny waist had been designed by fate for Victorian clothes, seemed to have a natural poise. It is said that Elizabeth exactly resembled her at a certain age. Margaret certainly inherited her hourglass figure and took particular pride in her tiny waistline. The Queen decided Mary of Teck was just right for Prince Albert Victor, Duke of Clarence, oldest son of the Prince of Wales, when she was twenty-four years old. All seemed to be going well, and hardly was the engagement announced when the Prince fell ill and succumbed to an epidemic of influenza. He then died. Nothing daunted, and after a decent interval, Queen Victoria tried again. A new engagement, to Albert's brother George. First, there was a girl, Mary. Then, one after another, four rambunctious boys. Oh no, not again! Perhaps May's patience was at an end. At any rate, she was an inattentive, uncaring mother.

When she died in 1953 at the age of eighty-six, the Duke of Windsor wrote to his wife: "My sadness was mixed with incredulity that any mother could have been so hard and cruel towards her eldest son [himself] for so many years, and yet so demanding at the end without relenting a scrap. I'm afraid the fluids in her veins have always been as icy cold as they are now in death."

Even so, and since the Duke of Windsor's unhappy childhood, a distinct lightening of the atmosphere had taken place in Buckingham Palace. His mother's resident bully—"I always have to remember," she once said apologetically, "that he is my king, too"—was beginning to mellow. As has been noted, the arrival of baby Elizabeth entranced George V. For the first time it occurred to his wife to open a book about child care. She grew positively possessive once she saw the effect the little girl had on her ailing husband. Not to mention his insistence that his very health depended on his waving at her every day.

A mirror change of mood was taking place in the Queen Mother, too. She who never smiled is seen in *London Was Yesterday* grinning from ear to ear, incidentally revealing teeth that needed attention. One thinks of Lady Bracknell in Wilde's "Importance of Being Earnest," speaking of a friend whose husband had recently died: "I never saw a woman so altered; she looks quite twenty years younger."

Even before this change in mood took place, the Queen Mother had always been interested in jobs for women, if not careers as well. During World War I, she was completely involved with getting a work force of women to train for men's work and was one of its principal organizers. She was surprisingly open-minded about the feminist movement, too, far ahead of her generation, seeing this as an untapped national treasure. Flanner wrote that she was in the center, "asking questions, getting answers . . . in her element."

As time went on, she, like her husband, began to add surreptitious little self-indulgences to their strict daily patterns. For her, it was a small sherry before lunch. After the meal, it became a single cigarette, straw-tipped and of Virginia tobacco. The Prince of Wales taught her to smoke. Janet Flanner concluded, "there is a story one yearns to believe that the Prince once took his mother riding on a roller coaster."[31] The possibility is irresistible.

If Margaret's grandmother secretly approved of new roles for women, her mother was surprisingly opposed. Whatever ideas she could have had as she was approaching adulthood, of blazing new trails, had vanished after marriage, replaced by something else. Persuasion, perhaps? Manipulating people, as rumors would have it? In any case, it is extremely surprising that she seemed to have a secret contempt for her own sex. It can be seen in her half-teasing, half-scornful comments to her friend, Francis d'Arcy Osbourne, 12th Duke of Leeds, that women were empty-headed creatures with nothing more pressing on their minds than new ways to do their hair. They certainly were not serious. In fact, they were incapable of it. More words to that effect.[32]

This trend in her thought was a great worry to Crawfie. In 1939 when she was thirteen, Elizabeth was given a proper tutor, the way heirs to the throne had been taught for generations. No mingling with the *hoi polloi* in a university for her. The choice was a somewhat bizarre one, as Sarah Bradford has described him in her biography of the future Queen: Henry Marten. This Provost of Eton, author of a classic school text about the history of England, had lumps of sugar in his pocket for instant energy, a curious habit of taking bites out of his handkerchief—one assumes out of desperation—and was likely to forget and address his royal pupil as "Gentlemen." Included in the classes were lectures about a famous nineteenth-century figure, Walter Bagehot, who had written the authoritative book about the English constitution and the role of the monarchy, one which was heavy going, but which Georges V and VI had managed to master. Marten had a further asset of making the past come to life.

Another tutor, Antoinette "Toni" de Bellaigue, a Belgian aristocrat who joined them in 1942, having escaped just in time from the German invasion, was a most fortunate choice. She taught French and brought into play a wider European concept of culture and civilization than the dependable Crawfie could provide. Margaret was allowed to sit in on these sessions, but not the ones given by the Provost of Eton. She, with her dragonfly intelligence and constant questions, would have benefited. She wanted to know "why not?"

Her mother was always finding reasons why not. She was needed for this or that: a new round of dentists, tailors, hairdressers, or photographers. Fresh air and happy times were more important. You are only young once, etc. Crawfie appealed to the Queen Mother, who appealed to Sir Owen Morshead, Palace Librarian. He also had little faith in the Queen's judgment, after discovering that the eighteen books she had ordered for her daughter Elizabeth were all by the humorist, P. J. Wodehouse.[33]

The Queen could not see what the fuss was about. She herself had not received a secondary education, and she had not ended up too badly. No doubt the remark was made with a roguish smile.[34] Elizabeth applied herself to Bagehot. Margaret, feeling slighted, went on asking unanswered questions.

In the spring of 1938, efforts were made to stave off what increasingly looked like World War II. At the same time, a state visit to Paris was projected for the summer. It was considered, as Janet Flanner explained, as a routine chore, awfully expensive and no doubt not very helpful, but one needed to make some sort of diplomatic gesture. To everyone's surprise, the four-day visit in July of that year turned out to be hugely, preposterously successful—the biggest public success since the Armistice of 1918.

From the opening ceremonies, which began as the royal limousine followed its stately path from the Arc de Triomphe down the Champs-Élysées to the Place de la Concorde, massive crowds, shouting and waving, followed the couple wherever they went, singing and chanting "God Save the King!" All of Paris was ablaze. Fireworks shot out in every direction from the top and bottom of the Eiffel Tower. Colored fountains played in the streets, and searchlights traced complex geometric patterns in the night sky. Famous buildings—the Crillon and the Admiralty building—were draped in cloth of gold and hung with priceless Beauvais tapestries.

The evening the couple went to the opera, they were greeted by uniformed torchbearers standing on either side of its magnificent grand staircase. Outside, its fountains, leaping into the night sky, were showered with gold dust.

"The military review at Versailles, during which fifty thousand French soldiers passed before the King, was, of course, the real point of the visit," Flanner wrote.[35] It was followed by the "grandest meal of the visiting royalties' lives," rivaling those of the old French kings in the Hall of Mirrors at Versailles. Two magnums of champagne, each bearing their dates of birth, greeted the royal visitors. They and their hundreds of guests were served Egyptian quail out of season and silver plates of food delivered by three hundred liveried footmen (each with his individually fitted white wig). Louis XIV could not have been grander.

No one sang "*Vive le roi*" any more, for obvious reasons. But the French had memorized a phonetic version of "God Saive Ze King!" and sang it with feeling.[36]

As peace began to look more and more precarious, it was "*vive le roi*" everywhere the King and Queen went in that summer of 1939. The stakes began to look higher and higher, and the need for leaders who symbolized that peace became pressing. There was something endearing about a king who hadn't wanted to be one, and whose modesty of manner showed through no matter how imposing, even dazzling, the uniforms of office that he wore.

Besides, everyone liked his wife, of modest height but so slim, with such a ravishing pink and white skin, and an almost girlish smile and wave. Canada had extended an invitation to visit, and no monarch had been there before. It seemed like the right moment. But the distances were formidable; ten days each way on an Atlantic crossing and then a grueling three-thousand-mile-plus tour by rail from the Maritime Provinces to the Pacific, and the same distance in reverse. They had also committed themselves to see Washington, DC, and be seen. The invitation of President and Mrs. Roosevelt was pressing. No British king had ever set foot in Washington either.

They left in May, encountering ice floes and fogs on the way, and dropped anchor just below Quebec at the mouth of the St. Lawrence. It was a French-speaking area, and the villages on the bank were tiny and isolated. But when the royal visitors discovered that its inhabitants were ringing church bells and lighting fires on the hills in welcome, the visit was off to a galloping start and almost buried the new arrivals with the warmth and lavishness of the welcome.

Edward T. Folliard, an ace reporter from *The Washington Post* who witnessed the arrival and only left them once they climbed back on their liner a month later, thought the King had seemed somewhat ill at ease but began to relax and enjoy himself as the weeks rolled by.

"He seems less nervous, more self-assured," he wrote on the train as the royal couple left Niagara Falls on their way to Washington. The King, at age forty-four, was slender with brown hair, blue eyes, and a friendly smile. "Like his brother, the Duke of Windsor, he is nervous and toys with his necktie. When he jammed his fingers in a train door near Winnipeg, he couldn't seem to leave the court plaster alone afterwards."

Folliard continued, "His Majesty obviously does not like stuffed shirts. He is happiest when he is around children and war veterans. He is fascinated by war medals and has broken up a dozen schedules by talking to Victoria Cross men and other veterans.

"He is a veteran himself, having served in a gun turret at the Battle of Jutland (1916). They say that he picked up more than naval lore and is a good 'cusser.'"[37]

Folliard traveled through upper New York State in a "pilot" train ahead of the royal entourage with fifty-seven other newspapermen—Americans, Canadians, French, even some Australians—a dozen photographers, telegraph men, policemen, and the like.

Behind them came the giant, crown-embossed locomotive, "the most opulent royal caravan that Washington had ever seen," Folliard wrote. Six trains, all painted royal blue and with silver and gilt decorations, pulled similarly bedecked coaches with the royal coats of arms on their doors. Two cars were reserved as bedrooms and sitting rooms for their majesties, along with a dining room, a lounge, and an official drawing room. One of the baggage cars contained a month's supply of spring water, brought from the Malvern Springs in England. Another contained three hundred pieces of royal luggage, including trunks six feet tall so as to keep the royal wardrobes in pristine condition. Such cases were simply marked "KING" and "QUEEN."

After further nonstop ceremonies to squeeze in everyone in Washington, DC, who should, or could, be included, it clearly was a relief to be whisked away by the Roosevelts to their country estate, Hyde Park, for a merciful time-out. The Queen, whose ability to smile and be delighted for a month had been tested to its utmost, wrote to Queen Mary to try to describe how hot Washington, DC, could get in June. For the modern reader: in those days, fans, blinds, and lots of iced drinks were a visitor's only weapons before the days of air conditioning. She wrote, ". . . the most stupendous heat! I really don't know how we got through those two days of continuous functions, mostly out of doors . . . I could barely breathe."[38] The last day was the best. After church, the President and the King immersed themselves in the swimming pool, and she sat, thankfully, in the shade. Later that evening, photographs were exchanged, the King gave a gold inkwell to the President and the nation, profuse thanks were made, and the royal train awaited them at the small Hyde Park stop. It was back to the real Hyde Park and some comfortable cold air.[39]

A lot had happened since they left. Their poor grandmamma's car had been hit by a truck with such vehemence it was actually turned upside down. Its passenger, now seventy-two years old, was shaken up and had hurt her eye but survived with her usual aplomb. She had thought up all kinds of excursions for her granddaughters. First, there was an exhibition at the Royal Academy in Piccadilly, not very far from where they used to live. Then a trip to the Regent's Park Zoo to commune with the penguins and elephants; a boat trip down the Thames to watch ships arriving from all over the world, and a display of gymnastics at Olympia.[40]

But what had caused the most comment by the newspapers was when they were conducted on a short trip into the Underground. A great deal was made of the fact they took third-class tickets like everybody else. Elizabeth, now thirteen, had received her first pair of silk stockings. Another headline. Perhaps the idea of sending the two girls off on a sightseeing trip to Canada and America might be rather good. All they needed were a couple of carriages. Whether either princess was ever told this idea was being considered is not clear. Margaret would have been thrilled.[41]

CHAPTER 6

THE KING WILL NEVER LEAVE

AS SOON AS WAR WAS declared in September 1939, one of the early priorities was how to get children away safely from the danger zones; London, in particular, where heavy bombing was expected. Thoughts turned to the dominions, specifically Canada, as the obvious place. They would be really safe there. On the other hand, everyone knew the Atlantic would become another war zone. Perhaps the northern routes to Halifax and Quebec would be far enough away from the U-boat patrols. An overseas evacuation agency was set up, the "Children's Overseas Reception Board" (CORB), which began singling out ships and booking children.

The first boat in service was the *Volendam* which had been plying between the Netherlands, New York, and Halifax, Nova Scotia. Operated by the Holland America Lines, the *Volendam*'s home port was Rotterdam. But as Nazi forces began to engulf much of Europe, in May of 1940, the *Volendam* left just in time and, like many other merchant ships, ended up serving the Allied cause.

The plan was to take children on board in Liverpool en route to Halifax, Nova Scotia, in a large convoy. They set off on Thursday, August 29, 1940. By August 30, they were several hundred miles off the coast of Northern Ireland and heading into the open sea, when at about 11 p.m. that evening they were attacked by a German submarine, the *U-60*, with two torpedoes. One lodged in the No. 2 hold but did not explode. The second, however, hit the No. 1

hold. The captain immediately gave the order to launch the lifeboats. In the darkness and heavy seas, everyone safely abandoned ship, with the exception of a single crew member, and were rescued by other ships in the convoy. The *Volendam* was damaged, but not seriously. It was towed back to port and, after being repaired, served as a troop transport during World War II, eventually carrying over a hundred thousand troops.[1]

Like most boats built for passenger traffic across the Atlantic, the *Volendam* traveled at a respectable speed of fifteen knots, or a bit more than seventeen miles an hour. That crossing usually took ten days, and nobody thought of going any faster. That is, until the *Queen Mary* made her spectacular debut traveling at thirty knots, or thirty-four miles an hour, and arriving in New York in four days and seven hours. That was in 1936. It took time before the idea of New York in five days became a selling point (let alone five hours on an airplane). In the meantime, most boats of that period put-putted along at a stately pace, to the great convenience of the German U-boats. The *Volendam* got away with minor damage. Others were not so lucky.

A month later, the *City of Benares*, with much the same pedigree as the *Volendam* (both were built in Glasgow), was engaged to take a new group of ninety children across the Atlantic to Quebec and Montreal. In a macabre irony of fate, some of the same children who had been rescued from the *Volendam* were signed up for the new voyage. They left Liverpool on September 13, 1940, and the passage went smoothly until the evening of September 17, four days later. The *Benares* was judged to be out of danger and set out alone into the Atlantic. But, as luck would have it, the U-boat 48 was on its trail. At about midnight, two torpedoes were fired. Both missed. Some fifteen minutes later, a third torpedo was fired and squarely hit the stern. The boat immediately began to sink.

Just how many children died is variously reported. In an article in the *Guardian* of 2010, the revised estimate is eighty-one, meaning that only nine survived.[2] Fred Steels, then aged eleven, remembered the night. The water came rushing into his cabin, and "a bunk came down on top of me." He fought his way outside, only to discover a great hole where the floor had been. Just then, a seaman grabbed him and another boy and threw them both into a lifeboat.

Derek Bech, aged nine, was traveling with his mother and two sisters. One sister made it onto a lifeboat. He, his mother, and the other sister hit the water and survived by hanging onto a tiny raft in turbulent seas.

"Some of the children were killed in the explosion," he said. "Some were trapped in their cabins, and the rest died when the lifeboats were launched incorrectly, and children just tipped into the sea.

"All I can remember were the screams and cries for help."[3] The program was immediately discontinued, and a new effort to transfer them by rail into the relative safety of the countryside began in earnest.

If a similar plan would have sent the two princesses to Canada by the same route, it was never seriously considered. There is a famous statement to this effect made by the Queen at an early stage of the war, one which her official biographer, William Shawcross, was not able to date precisely. What she said in essence was, "The children will not leave without me. I will not leave without the King. And the King will never leave."

For those who were to survive the battles on sea, land, and in the air, the terrible bombings of London that continued for two years, in an age of shortages, deprivations, anxieties, misery, loss, and horror, King George VI and Queen Elizabeth were beacons of hope and sanity. It is not too much to say that during this period, the admiration and respect of the people turned to love. Everywhere the Royal Family went in those days they were mobbed. The King, who had suffered severely from emotional insecurity and a violent stammer, found unsuspected inner strength. His wife, whose ability to rise to the occasion was marked early in her teenage years, was always by his side. Advisors suggested she appear in uniform, as her husband always did. She would have none of that.

Some of the unforgettable photographs of the war include a photograph of the Queen, with the King always in uniform by her side, stepping daintily over rubble in high-heeled shoes, hatted, gloved, wearing her best jewelry and a dress and coat ensemble trimmed with fur. They were right in the middle of it all, and they were always smiling.

Where to hide the princesses? Their safety was of even more immediate concern. The German advances took everyone by surprise. Heads of state, royal and otherwise, fled with only hours to spare before they were imprisoned. Although officially neutral, the Netherlands was about to be ground beneath the Nazi heel, taking Queen Wilhelmina, respected and influential voice throughout Europe, under it as well. She dithered, and the British had to rush in and rescue her.

After Dunkirk in 1940, it was clear to everyone that the next German objective would be the invasion of Britain. That never happened, thankfully, due to the Battle of Britain—but that is another story. It was believed that the Royal Family would be imprisoned, and the Duke and Duchess of Windsor would replace them as a kind of political window dressing. After abdicating, the Duke had been photographed being much too nice to Hitler, which hardly improved his status at home. He must be removed far, far away and be given a meaningless title that would be a sort of window dressing, too. At least, enough to neutralize him until the war ended.

He was offered, or rather, commanded, to become Governor of the Bahamas in the Caribbean in the summer of 1940, but he was being wooed by German diplomats at the same moment. He was not actually kidnapped, as is sometimes believed. It was much more subtle than that. He and his wife had passed through Spain on their way to Lisbon. What actually happened is well documented from official correspondence from both sides in William Shirer's monumental study, *The Rise and Fall of the Third Reich* (1960), and in even more detail in Andrew Lownie's book *The Traitor King*, which draws on important German archives to reveal the Duke's direct involvement in the Nazi plot. The German goal was to cajole the Duke and his wife to return to Spain. There, they would pounce.

The duke and duchess were in Lisbon awaiting the arrival of the *Excalibur*, an American liner, and planned to embark on August 1, 1940. But by then they were up to date on the matter and rebuffed the German advances. They boarded the ship not a moment too soon and arrived in Nassau two and a half weeks later. They remained there until the war ended. The Nazi plot had failed.[4]

Although there are no eye witnesses, one can guess where the princesses were hidden during the first four months of the war. The royal holdings include the ancient estate of Balmoral in Scotland, with its vast 2,500-acre holdings of rivers, woods, and fields, and includes something like 150 smaller dependencies. One of them, Birkhall, was a comparatively modest house, built in 1715, that was lent to the Duke and Duchess of York by his father as a summer place for the children. They redecorated the interiors, replanted the garden, and made frequent use of the house. Elizabeth and Margaret roamed there freely and probably knew all about the secret paths, not just the usual winding trails. It is perfectly possible that there was "a granite house in a lonely glen," hidden nearby, as a newspaper reported early in 1941. If so, it would have been well guarded.[5]

At home in Buckingham Palace, with its vast underground labyrinth of cellars and almost infinite number of places to take shelter, the King and Queen lived out the worst of the bombing. Visiting it in 1951, H. V. Morton observed in his book, *In Search of London*, that a storeroom in the basement had been converted as a bomb shelter almost as an afterthought and hardly seemed "blast proof." It would probably be useless against a direct hit. Its furnishings seemed equally casual: a couple of gilt chairs, an uncomfortable-looking sofa, a mahogany table, oil lamps, smelling salts, and some axes, presumably if the King-Emperor had to fight his way out.[6]

But when the Palace was actually hit, neither of them were anywhere near the shelter. It was eleven in the morning, the King was at work in his study, with its open windows looking directly over the inner gardens. He had an irritating eyelash in his eye, and the Queen was trying to take it out, when a bomber burst through the clouds and sent a stack of bombs—five in a row over their heads. The Queen wrote to Queen Mary, "we only had time to look foolishly at each other when the scream (of a bomb) hurtled past us and exploded with a tremendous crash in the quadrangle."[7] She continued, "I saw a great column of smoke & earth thrown up into the air, and then we all ducked like lightning into the corridor." She wrote to her sister, "I am still just as frightened of bombs and guns going off as I was at the beginning. I turn bright red, and my heart hammers. In fact, I'm a beastly coward, but I do believe that a lot of people are, so I don't mind."[8]

The Queen was soon directing first aid for injured servants and discovering that the vulnerable glass roof of the kitchen was still intact. Her French chef greeted her with a reassuring smile. There had been "*une petite quelque chose dans le coin*" but no other damage. What a miracle that the study windows just happened to be wide open. If they had been closed when the bomb fell, millions of splinters would most certainly have killed them both.

As it was, the Queen often said, "I'm glad we were bombed. Now I feel I can look the East End in the face."[9] They went straight out to the East End after lunch, an area that had been particularly badly affected. The Queen wrote, "I really felt I was . . . in a dead city, when we walked down a little empty street. All the houses evacuated, and yet through the broken windows one saw all the poor little possessions, photographs, beds, just as they were left . . ."[10] Everything was in tatters, strewn about by some malevolent hand like rags in a junkyard, broken, torn, filthy, and abandoned; mute remnants of the lives they represented.

No one was spared from such a sight, even a prominent visitor from abroad who was staying at the rarefied surroundings of No. 14 Princes Gate. He wrote to his wife that same month in 1940, "The last three nights in London have been simply hell. Last night I put on my steel helmet and went up on the roof of the Chancery and stayed up there until two o'clock . . . watching the Germans come over in relays every ten minutes and drop bombs, setting terrific fires. You could see the dome of St. Paul's silhouetted against a blazing inferno."[11]

The writer was Joseph P. Kennedy, a businessman, investor and politician, father of nine children, including: a future President, John F. Kennedy; a future senator, Edward ("Ted"); and a future U.S. Attorney General, Robert F. ("Bobby"). He had arrived in London with his wife Rose in the spring of 1938 to take up his new position as U.S. Ambassador to the Court of St. James, as it was called. His diary records that he was driven to Buckingham Palace by "scarlet-coated drivers and footmen," and after presenting his bona fides, was received by King George VI.

"I found him charming in every way," he wrote.[12]

Dinner invitations followed fast. At the first, he sat next to the Queen, who dropped her napkin. She told him to ignore it, but he reached down and presented it with a courtly flourish, which she, in turn, found most charming.

They were off to an excellent start. Many other invitations followed. They were invited for the Easter weekend in 1938, and met the princesses. Elizabeth was seated on his right at one of the meals. He learned she had just seen *Snow White and the Seven Dwarfs*, and chattered away about this Disney triumph, a huge success and the first fairy tale version of many to come. She loved to ride horseback and play games and ever so many other things.

Daddy and Mummy, as she called them, did not let them eat meals together very often, perhaps only once a week. There the rules were rigorous; everyone at table had to stop eating when they did. So Margaret ate as fast as she could in the expectation that she would be stopped soon. The Ambassador, not understanding, remarked on her good appetite. He thought the girls had wonderful manners.

After the meal, they were given a tour of the garden and shown around their Welsh playhouse. Everyone had to admire the flowers they had planted and the very neat way they hung up their tools.

"They are darlings," Kennedy remarked.[13]

At one of the dinners, seated again next to the Queen—this time she was wearing a gold dress and joking about being too fat for the chairs—she confessed a great desire to see America again soon. Although not technically at war, the Ambassador warned a trip right now might be dangerous. But, she replied, not to go would give aid and comfort to the enemy. Who was going to be bullied? Not her.

"What a woman," Kennedy wrote.[14]

It was clear she liked him, and not just for practical reasons. It appeared that the King liked him too and actually confided in Ambassador Kennedy. By then, the former would have benefitted from the series of sessions that had led him to recover from his speech impediment. He talked about that quite frankly one evening after dinner. He clearly saw a direct connection with his stammer and George V's persistent ridicule, which, he could now say, made things worse. Perhaps he, the son, could also confess that he hated him. Almost.[15]

The confession is surprising enough, but that it could be made to the American ambassador himself, said something about Kennedy's warmth of manner and disarming ability to call a spade a spade. Much as he loved England and could see the importance of supporting the war effort by a supply of armaments, the practical part of his nature dictated that Germany was winning and to enter on the British side was clearly not the smart thing to do. Although he did not mention it, not everyone in his family agreed with him, including the future president of the United States.

Before the Ambassador left England in the fall of 1940, he spent one more weekend in the royal entourage, this time at Windsor Castle, and experienced yet another bombing raid. In a letter to his wife Rose from London, he said, "If one wasn't in very good shape physically (the bombing) would unquestionably get one down sooner or later. The bomb at Windsor fell about 250 yards from the house. We were out looking at the searchlights and the anti-aircraft fire when we heard it coming and dove into the bushes. It struck with a dull thud."[16]

When the threat of invasion was uppermost and the Battle of Britain was being fought in the air, the superb refusal of the King and Queen to show whatever fears they might have felt, along with their ability to rise to the occasion, was reflected in their children's attitudes. It never seems to have occurred to Elizabeth or Margaret to wonder what might happen. They accepted their extended stay in Scotland, and when it came time to move to Windsor Castle, accepted that as well with equal equanimity, if not enthusiasm. Neither of them liked Buckingham Palace, and since their caretakers—Alah, Marion Crawford, and the Macdonald sisters—moved with them, life went on as before.

In May of 1940, two months before the Battle of Britain began, which was to decide the matter of a German invasion, they drove down the long walk into the castle. There, they would spend the next five years.

It was just getting dark, and the castle looked its worst—paintings removed, all the glass chandeliers wrapped up and removed for safekeeping, furniture draped in sheets, windows being fitted with black curtains.

Crawfie wrote "all night long ghostly figures flitted around, their feet echoing in the stone passages—ARP wardens watching for beams and chinks of light showing through the blackout."[17] They tried to joke but "most of [them] had a shiver down [their] spines and the feeling that the war had caught up with [them]." Margaret Rhodes, Queen Elizabeth's niece, who also stayed there during the war, said, "It seemed to be in a perpetual twilight."[18]

The Lancaster Tower had been fitted up with a nursery, and the princesses were used to staying there, cupboards added and bathrooms inserted into the immensely thick walls of the tower, which dated from the days of Henry VII. There were no fireplaces, and electric stoves had been installed in the bedrooms but had an uncomfortable way of refusing to work. So, the inhabitants were always chilly when not downright freezing.

A system of warning bells had been set up to wake the inhabitants if there was an air raid. One night soon after their arrival, the warning bells began to ring. Crawfie, whose bedroom was in a separate tower, threw on her new "siren suit." This was an ingenious item, brought to a high fashion by the Italian fashion designer Schiaparelli, consisting of a one-piece coverall that included wide legs, a fitted bodice, a hood, and plenty of pockets; it could be zipped up in a minute. The suit was usually made of wool but, in Crawfie's case, it was made of green velvet, and took only seconds to throw it on over her pajamas and run downstairs to the shelter.

When she got there, however, the children and Alah were nowhere to be seen. What had happened? She raced back upstairs only to find that Elizabeth and Margaret were still being coiffed and attired in a manner their nurse thought proper for young ladies. Crawfie grabbed them both and threw coats over their shoulders. They were fitted up for siren suits the next day. Then things got really bad, and they slept in the dungeons every night along with the beetles.[19]

During the period of 1940 when invasion was considered imminent, Margaret Rhodes wrote, "It was . . . called the Coats Mission because it was commanded by a high-ranking officer called Coats. A hand-picked body of officers and men from the Brigade of Guards and the Household Cavalry, equipped with armored cars, was on call twenty-four hours to take the King and Queen and their daughters to a safe house in the country should the German Threat . . . materialize."[20] She was reassured, until she discovered that, although the operation probably included the dogs, "it did not include me."[21]

There was also a tank on duty ready to shelter the royal residents whenever an air raid sounded. That was the part Princess Margaret liked best, and she threw herself into the operation with zest.

"Here it comes," she would yell, and everyone would be loaded into a rather confined space, including the dogs. Margaret insisted on being last so that she could play lookout.

On wet days, they explored the castle, always an adventure. You never knew what you would find. One time, it was the shirt Charles I was wearing the day he was executed—a bit creepy. Or the bullet that went into Nelson's heart and killed him. It might be the armor Henry VIII wore or Bonnie Prince Charlie's sword. One day, the commander of the castle arrived with several battered leather hat boxes and invited the princesses to look inside. It seemed stuffed with old newspapers. Inside the wrappings were the Crown Jewels.[22]

The period of wartime and their comparative isolation in a tower at Windsor Castle seemed, paradoxically, to have been one of the happiest times in Margaret's life. She was free at last of the soul-destroying atmosphere in Buckingham Palace, the feeling that eyes were watching for flaws every moment of the day and ready to pounce, even the servants. Or *especially* the servants. She was close by her sister and under the care of the same entourage who had been there since she was born. Crawfie had always been affectionate and loving and had too often laughed when a reprimand might have been more to the point. Perhaps one found in Windsor Castle, in those days, a distinct warming of the atmosphere—a feeling, in those terrifying times when invasion seemed imminent, that "we're all in it together" that colored the general attitude and made welcome what would have once been considered a lapse of privacy. Mollie Panter-Downes wrote that people had become positively "chummy" and strangers would knock on your apartment door and offer to share a bottle of whisky.

Then again, Windsor was only twenty miles from London, and Margaret's parents came every weekend. Life somehow continued as before, with the occasional unexpected moment—a dogfight in the skies, perhaps—that made one's life so exciting.

There were also plenty of air raids and nights of sleeping in the dungeon, which they took in stride. Their mother was more concerned.

"I am afraid Windsor is not really a good place for them," she told Queen Mary in January of 1941. "The noise of the guns is heavy, and then of course there have been so many bombs dropped . . . It is very difficult to know what . . . to do with them."

Queen Mary was a particular problem herself. In the worst of the Blitz, the Queen had moved to her country estate of Sandringham in Norfolk, a hundred miles due north of London, and near the sea. But there, she was *too* near the sea, close to what was thought might become a German landing site. She must be moved. For her part, the Queen herself was never going to leave. Never mind about her age (she had just seen her 72nd birthday). It was her duty to be seen in London.

After prolonged discussion, Queen Mary allowed herself to be talked into a move to Badminton, the seat of the Duke and Duchess of Beaufort in Gloucestershire. The huge, imposing mansion, superbly positioned on its vast estate of 52,000 acres, can be traced back to the *Domesday Book* and even contains the remains of Roman villas. However, its main building, from the seventeenth and eighteenth centuries, has Palladian additions and another kind of distinction: a game that originated there has been named for it.

Queen Mary set off one Monday in September with considerable personal effects, her own personal servants, plus the majority of her London staff as well. This consisted of sixty-five people and their families. "Quite a fleet," she wrote airily. The trip took eight and a half hours, after which she was not a bit tired and thought it had been "a lovely drive." Just what the Duchess of Beaufort thought and said when this major convoy descended on her has not been recorded. But something can be gathered from her terse remark, when, at war's end, she was asked how much of Badminton Queen Mary had made use of, she replied, "All of it."

The letters of Margaret to her grandmother, limited to the regulation thanks for lavish birthday gifts—silver rings, bracelets, and diamond-studded brooches—became informative from 1940 on, as her ability to write improved, and the war separated them. That Christmas, she wrote: "We decorated our tree for the first time. The soldiers had a ball last night, which I think they enjoyed very much," she added correctly. "We gave all the servants their presents which took a long time. Mummy, Papa and Lilibet had a funny sick feeling on Xmas Eve but it went off yesterday, although Papa still didn't feel very good. Wasn't his speech good?" she asked, a reference to the King's recent victory over a serious stammer.

By spring 1941, the daffodils and hyacinths were out, one of the Suffolk Punches had a sweet little foal and "mummy was in bed with a cold, which was a bore." Her letters begin to be punctuated with fashionable adult opinions, making one wonder how much came from her, and how much was dictated by Mummy.

In August of 1942, she was very excited about her new present, a miniature carriage made of mother of pearl, which evidently finished off a set. Unfortunately, the rest of the collection was "all packed away underground," but as soon as the war was over, she could not wait to see what it all looked like together. Now Mummy and Papa were giving her tons of jewels along with two little ornaments attached to combs to wear in her hair. Lilibet gave her books and some darling owls on a brooch.

"We have been out shooting a lot," she wrote. The weather had been "disgusting. Old Mrs. Greville came to tea with us last week. She has been very ill and has to go about in a bathchair and can only see out of one eye." It had rained a lot, which made her feel worse, Margaret added with relish. What perfectly lovely presents.[23]

In theory, at least, the Windsor regime of little heat, lots of woolies and socks, lights out, and the same food rations as everyone else, applied to them as well. To leave a room and not turn out the light was truly bad. You couldn't have more than a bit of hot water in your bath, and the king had painted a line on the side of the tub to make sure you didn't. That was right and proper.

Still, when she had her tenth birthday party in summer 1940, there were venison hors d'oeuvres, grouse, and a spectacular strawberry cake.

They were still Girl Guides, and Elizabeth, as section leader (no doubt prompted by her parents), invited a dozen girls to tea from the battered East End and introduced their two Welsh corgis, Dookie and Jane. As cups were passed around by footmen in livery, one of the guests could hardly bring herself to take a cup from the tray offered because "she was the one who did the serving."

The princesses spent their days studying history, foreign relations, cooking, sewing, piano, and languages. French had been on their agendum since childhood, and both became quite fluent. They had also been learning German, but that was hastily changed to the study of Spanish.

Every Christmas Elizabeth's father gave her a new diary, bound in handsome blue leather, her fifth, and she dutifully began her entries for 1940, illustrated with her own drawings. Scarves for fighting men were easy to knit, but when it came to knitting sweaters as well, that was quite a bit harder. Whenever they went outside, Elizabeth took her new film camera along and began to take pictures of everybody. They performed as well. On the first Christmas, for a performance of the nativity at the village hall, Elizabeth was Madonna and Margaret was an angel. They managed to get through it without forgetting any of their lines. Their mother was proud of that.[24]

Amateur theatricals were high on the list. They had both learned to tap dance, sing, play the piano, and recite poetry. They even invented a little ballet, "Apple for the Teacher," which went so well they did it twice. They were fast learning the vocabulary of wartime: gas masks, mackintoshes, fountain pens, Bisto, Ovaltine, Home Guard, permanent waves, bicycle pumps, pinafores, "Make do and Mend," and the disappearance of the familiar, bananas being one of the first to vanish. "Yes, we have no bananas." They made a song about it.

Their parents entertained in Windsor so often that numbers of distinguished guests tended to appear, often without much warning. Margaret Rhodes, the Queen's niece, who came to stay with them, almost bumped into Jan Smuts, the South African Prime Minister, one day. Margaret Rhodes remembered another occasion towards the end of the war, perhaps just before D-Day, when the King, Queen, Princesses, herself, and a friend of hers decided to have tea on a small terrace overlooking the Windsor Castle rose garden.

"A long white tablecloth swept to the ground . . . was set with a silver kettle, teapot and the usual paraphernalia."[25]

All was going well when they suddenly heard male voices, with distinctly American accents, somewhere just out of sight. The King, who was quite informally dressed, suddenly gave a start. He had completely forgotten that Dwight Eisenhower, Supreme Commander of the Allied Forces, had been invited to Windsor, and that he had promised to show him around. The Commander and his entourage would soon turn a corner, and there his host would be, having tea. Something had to be done, and fast. Where could he hide? Almost in unison, the entire party disappeared under the tablecloth, which no doubt shook if one had looked because they were laughing so hard.[26]

These were happy times, despite the war. The Queen had a kind of genius for "making life fun for their daughters and . . . guests. There was a game called 'kick the tin,' usually played after tea. All the visitors, no matter how grand, had to take part." It involved a great deal of running, climbing in and out of windows, and generally causing mayhem.

"I remember watching Sir Samuel Hoare, the Lord Privy Seal, being made to run like the devil and becoming very hot, bothered and confused," Rhodes wrote. "I try and imagine a similar holder of high office doing the same thing nowadays, and I can't. But Queen Elizabeth was very persuasive."[27] The day the then-duchess referred to Margaret Rhodes as "her third daughter," she couldn't have been happier.

On reflection, Margaret Rhodes realized that "she must have lived" in a very safe world, by which she probably meant "confined." As children, they said their prayers every night and went to church every Sunday.

"On the reverse side of the coin, we were prone to cracking disgusting lavatory jokes, but never, ever those of a sexual nature," Rhodes said. "The facts of life were a closed subject, and I was entirely innocent and genuinely wondered where babies came from."[28]

The idea that her brothers should go to prep school and then university, but not her, was another closed subject. The fact is that the class system, which still played a large role, kept upper-class girls from taking advantage of educational opportunities that were, in fact, now available for girls lower down on the social scale. For instance, girls from professional families without titles or great estates were now studying for professions that had once been closed to them. In Bath in the 1940s, for instance, at a city-run grammar school for girls, its entire faculty of twenty-seven teachers (called "mistresses") had degrees. Social prominence went only so far. Young women were expected to marry an heir (a first-born, if possible), have children to carry on a distinguished line with an ancient title, and manage a great estate. But they could not train for a career, as Princess Margaret would discover. As for her cousin

Margaret Rhodes, who was five years her senior but did not enjoy quite such brilliant opportunities: she took lessons in shorthand and typing, just in case.

Bit by bit, Britain was making it known and felt that it was fighting for its existence. Petrol (gasoline) was rationed for all but essential transport, and private motor cars were being put up on blocks for the duration. Train timetables had been cut drastically, and, far too often, there was Standing Room Only. City buses still ran, but often the last bus was at 9:30 p.m. After that, if you had not traveled on your bike, you walked home through the blackout.

Schoolgirls wore uniforms: velour hats or berets, scarves, blouses, ties, and skirts in the school colors. The universal coat for everyone was a raincoat, or mackintosh. Their mothers, who once would not be seen outside their front doors without a hat, gradually stopped wearing them and either folded a silk scarf into a triangle and tied it onto their heads or a stylish turban, if one was to be found, and tucked their hair underneath.

The solution of daytime wear for Frenchwomen during the same period was one extremely well-cut black dress—two at the most—kept interesting by a variety of different silk scarves at the neck. British women wore "a suit" most of the time, i.e., jackets with matching skirts and/or twin sets, which were sweaters with matching cardigans, topped off with a decorous pearl necklace. To buy a new suit meant one with specific government limitations. The "CC41," as it was called, governed a whole raft of consumer items, from clothes and shoes to furniture, in the cause of cutting down on raw materials. The desirable women's suit was made of wool, and its design tightly governed, right down to the number of pleats, buttons, and pockets—even seams. As the war wore on, the utility suit acquired a distinctly military air and turned groups of women, who might once have been distinguished by their colorful attire, into anonymous blurs of navy, brown, and gray. Even new shoes were regimented, from their heels to their clunky outlines. Open-toed shoes were out. The government did not like them. Suddenly, making your own dress out of a pattern was all the rage. But you had to know something about sewing and fitting, and you had to be lucky with finding the fabric.

"If" became the word that prefaced every action. You might get some fresh fish "off points," "if" you knew when it was coming in and "if" you were not too far back in the queue. Lining up for everything—getting on a bus, buying a train ticket, finding scarce food—the British became so used to have to wait for anything, that it became a running joke. First, you queued up and then you asked what you were queueing for. Certain things were gone for the duration, like paper, and if you dared ask, the reply was caustic: "Don't you know there's a war going on?"

Margaret Rhodes's memoir makes no mention of the most obvious change wrought by the war: finding enough food, which absorbed an enormous amount of energy for most working-class families. Eggs, for instance, disappeared after the Germans conquered the European continent, and as one year followed another, British rations of food continued to contract. In 1942, the meat allowance per person became four ounces a week, or a single hamburger patty.

There was something like two ounces of butter, two ounces of cheese, four ounces of bacon and ham, four ounces of margarine, two ounces of tea, and as the situation became dire, one egg a month. The German U-boats continued to sink the merchant ships crossing the Atlantic, which carried food as well as armaments and raw materials, at a frightening rate in 1942. In March of 1943 alone, 108 ships were lost.

But this situation was about to change. Two months later, the Allies began to use a new weapon which could track and attack submarines on the prowl. The bombs were launched from planes and proved to be so accurate that by May of the same year the weapon had pinpointed seventy-two submarines and sunk them. The fearsome new weapon wiped out the German fleet with such precision that as a result, the German commander withdrew his U-boats. Sometime after that, the first boxes of dried eggs and milk in great quantities, free of charge, arrived from America in British households. The Battle of the Atlantic was over.

Recent books about Princess Margaret claim that she was absurdly tiny—the word "midget" has actually been used—at a little over five feet. Her modest height is now ridiculed as if it were somehow her fault. In fact, Queen Mary used to ask her granddaughter why she had not grown taller, as if she had any control over the matter. By the time she fully appreciated her supposed shortcomings, she was acutely aware of this particular "defect," and sensitive about it.

One of the curious parallels about the lives of our previous fetal alcohol syndrome example, Liz Kulp, and Princess Margaret, whose mother's alcoholic intake can only be guessed at, is that both ended up the same height, for the fact is that the princess stopped growing, and so did Liz. In Liz Kulp's case, puberty began when she was at the age of eight with budding breasts. Sometime during the next two years, both girls did most of their growing. After menses had begun, at age ten or eleven, they might grow a further couple of inches, but that was it. We know that for Liz, who began life as a very small baby, her growth was over by the time she was ten years old. We do not know enough about Princess Margaret's puberty, but what we do know is that she stopped growing as well, and both ended up, as they went into their adolescent years, at five feet tall (or five feet one inch, depending on the source). A coincidence? Perhaps.

The princess was destined by fate to spend the rest of her life as not only a lesser being in royal eyes, but physically three or four inches shorter than the sister who would one day be queen. To be 5'4", as the future queen was, did not present any kind of handicap for her generation. It was considered a perfectly respectable height. What is surprising is how many adored movie stars were actually shorter than that, whether British or American.

Joan Crawford, for instance, was 5'3"; Bette Davis was 5'2"; Vivien Leigh, 5'3"; and Elizabeth Taylor was 5'2". In today's entertainment world, Lady Gaga is a mere 5', and Reese Witherspoon, 5'1," and their romantic leads tower over them if you look closely enough. No one calls them "midgets."

What girls and young women wore in the 1930s and 1940s is also never addressed. A photograph of Princess Elizabeth and Princess Margaret in a pony cart illustrates the issue rather well. It is the summer of 1940, Elizabeth and Margaret wear the same dress, perhaps designed by a Palace dressmaker, in a valiant attempt to make a dress for a fourteen-year-old that will somehow work for a girl with a figure and a ten-year-old who is still, more or less, a little girl. Not only does the fabric look like kitchen curtain material, but the style—portrait neckline, big white collar, puff sleeves, and tiny bows going down the front—looks gauche on Elizabeth and too young even for Margaret. This curious decision to keep them in identical outfits despite the growing difficulty went on through the war years. It appears to have stopped only once Elizabeth, now eighteen and enrolled in the Women's Auxiliary Service (ATS), was in uniform, and they dodged the issue for good.

The idea that Junior Miss might be a category all its own was taking hold in the United States. In British shops, there was nothing like it. A curious ad hoc arrangement existed, rather depending on the girl. For instance, girls leaving school at fifteen or sixteen graduated to skirts and blouses or jumpers (sweaters) and the regulation mackintoshes before trying anything as ambitious as a dress. If they wanted something for evening, they tried to make it themselves and end up, far too often, with a "loving hands at home" look. If they continued on in grammar school and sixth form, they went on wearing a blouse, tie, beret, and scarf or blazer. They just stopped wearing that shame-making pair of white ankle socks that had "kid," if not "little kid," written all over it. And walked around with bare feet inside their shoes.

The same rough rule of thumb seemed to operate in the world outside. Too old for socks?

Then, they were ready for Dior. Meantime, Princess Elizabeth acquired a special "future Queen in training" look. As she grew older, someone invented a truly ghastly hat that sat up above the hairline and made a clumsy halo around her face, as if she was being crowned in felt. Elizabeth looked perfectly delighted in it. If Margaret wanted something just like it, she did not get it.

Lucky for her.

During the war years, an interesting character appeared in their lives. She was Alathea Fitzalan Howard, elder daughter of the Viscount Fitzalan of Derwent and Joyce Langdale (who later became Countess Fitzwilliam). Isabella Naylor-Leyland, who wrote a foreword to *The Windsor Diaries*, stated that Alathea's mother came from one of the old Catholic families and premier barons of England.

"Joyce was a woman of style, taste and wit, but had little interest in children."[29]

Alathea was born in 1923—three years before Elizabeth—and her parents had separated by the time she moved in to stay in Cumberland Lodge, her grandfather's house in Windsor Great Park in January 1940.

She began to take lessons in art and dancing with the princesses and kept a meticulous diary. So, she was a daily observer of their life during the war years (1940–1945) and has drawn a fascinating portrait of her companions with the distance her age and her relatively lesser social status gave her. There was another factor. She was a member of a family that more or less ignored its children, and the princesses had parents who loved them and constantly showed it. She was on the outside, looking in.

Alathea arrived at the height of the bombing on London and Windsor, giving good cause to the Queen's worry that Windsor was not very safe either. Shortly after her arrival, air raids began to intensify. She wrote in August of 1940 that the air raid sirens went on all day, but they were mostly ignored.

"All the same, it does make the war seem curiously near to us now."

They walked over to the field by the lake to see a hole made by a bomb.

The crater was not very big. It exploded harmlessly, and Alathea picked up a bit of shrapnel.

A month later, on September 30th, the damage was more serious.

"Went to bed and slept well until 12:30 when a shattering explosion shook the house like a pack of cards."

It was the first of many time bombs, which would explode without warning. There was one in the wood behind Smith's Lawn, another right in the middle of the Lawn and a stack of others on the Long Walk. They were going to explode, but one did not know when. Sometime after it was safe, she took a tour with Grandpa to look at the results.

"The one in our wood is *vast* and uprooted a large beech tree."

Another of them went off just after she woke up at 9 a.m. She was still in bed.

"I lay in speechless horror, watching my walls *rock* violently from side to side."[30]

The worst damage came a month later, just after she went to bed. She heard two horrible whistles, "a fearful inhuman noise," coming nearer and nearer until it seemed it must hit the house. Then there was this "heartrending crash." There was a direct hit on a house further down, and someone died.[31]

For a long time after that, she joined the princesses every night in their dungeon.

Once the family learned that Alathea's broken family had essentially abandoned her and she was on her own, Queen Elizabeth folded her into the family the way she did with Margaret Rhodes. There was always room for one more. They collected numerous people for lunches and dinners, a crowd that included Tommy Lascelles, the King's assistant private secretary, whose presence at Buckingham Palace, Windsor, or Balmoral seems to have been everywhere at once. He was at the King's elbow during the day and seems to have followed him at leisure: on a picnic, for afternoon tea, beside a stream landing fish or out shooting for grouse, even playing charades after dinner. Lascelles was indefatigable.

The appearance of Lascelles on the scene when Margaret was still a child is important to know, given the major role he would one day take in preventing her from marrying—but that is for later. It is enough to know that his duties encompassed after-dinner entertainment, as happened one night when he was pressed into playing the part of a St. Bernard dog in the Swiss Alps, compete with an ice bucket slung around his neck to serve as a brand keg. It was a great bore.[32]

Lascelles had a reputation for being hard to please, which makes it all the more remarkable that he had nothing but praise for Princess Elizabeth, as leading man, and Princess Margaret as her leading lady in their performance of the pantomime *The Sleeping Beauty* at Christmas in 1942.

"I felt rather apprehensive that I should myself qualify for the title role," he wrote.

To his surprise, he enjoyed it immensely.

"Some of the scenes would have done credit to Drury Lane, and the whole thing went with a slickness and confidence that amazed me."[33]

A new pantomime the following year—*Aladdin*—received similar praise for its professional polish. He praised Margaret for her well-rehearsed and competent acting. He liked everybody, in fact.[34]

Alathea loved *The Sleeping Beauty*, too.

"It was all beautifully done," she wrote. "And Princess Margaret especially looked divine as the Good Fairy."[35]

The only thing was that Princess Elizabeth (now sixteen) looked out of place among all those children, and, "it is a pity she is always the boy."

Alathea liked Margaret right away. She found her "rather silly but very sweet."[36] She could be so funny. While she was staying at the Castle one weekend, "M. made me die with laughter by asking me if I thought L (Lilibet) and her and myself were pretty! She is an angel, that child."[37]

Or, she wrote: "Had an amusing tea in the schoolroom. Margaret was killing. After tea, we played cards again—silly amusing games."[38]

That morning they went for a walk as far as the bridge. There was a pretty stream running under it with leaves floating on it like little boats. So, they had a game about how many times they could hit the leaves by spitting on them. That was all Crawfie's idea.

"We got very giggly and silly," Alathea wrote.

Margaret kept asking Alathea if she liked her, "as if she wasn't sure!! How could one *not* like her?"[39] She was spontaneous and affectionate. ". . . we ate wild strawberries on the slopes. Margaret was very sweet and suddenly asked me to give her a kiss!"[40]

As the war droned on, Margaret left temper tantrums behind, and her behavior gradually changed course. Instead of lying on her back and kicking, moving to Windsor more or less coincided with the pleasant discovery that she could get her own back another way. She tried it at Windsor one day. It seemed one of the staff was chronically late for lunch, and everyone knew it. Margaret decided to mimic that lady's perennial behavior right down, no doubt, to the apologetic smile, the glasses that started to slip down her nose, and the invariable wobbling chair, among similar gaffes. Everyone was in on the joke and roared with laughter. No doubt Margaret was surprised and delighted at the evidence of effective public ridicule. Papa's way to get even was with practical jokes. This one was even better. But it was habit-forming, and that made it dangerous.

For Liz Kulp, the little waif with fetal alcohol syndrome whose stages of growing up are documented in print, individual letters danced about on a page, and getting them pinned down to the lines provided caused enormous effort. This may explain why the princess had so much trouble learning to write, and even her grown-up words conveyed in her letters, seem to float about on a sea of white paper. Reading would have presented the same kind of issue, and it is easy to understand why her record collection was a lot bigger than her shelves of books. Perhaps Princess Maragaret was capable of "falling on the floor in a rage, using vulgar language and shouting at people" the way Liz Kulp would do—not to mention the predictable headaches, stomachaches, and dizziness.

During the war, when the princess's companions were older and therefore in the giggly boyfriend stage, one can imagine why she would, at the age of nine or ten, want to start giggling about her own, real or imagined. The effect of puberty on similarly afflicted girls is practically unknown, although there are occasional references to its early arrival. Jodee Kulp has described the first signs of puberty on Liz, starting at about eight and the early arrival of menstruation. At nine, she was taller than most of her classmates, but by the age of eleven, she had stopped growing, which is when other girls (who have no such disability) start. Margaret's lack of height was constantly mentioned by her grandmother, as if it were her fault. She was ready for boyfriends by 1941, when she was eleven. Meanwhile her older sister, now fifteen, threatened to run away if she could not marry Philip. Margaret couldn't wait.

She was growing up, and she wasn't. She could come out with an observation about what someone at a birthday party was really thinking and surprise one with her insights. On some days, she could seem much older. Then, a day later, she might be acting like a ten-year-old, darting headlong down some steps or out of the door as if she had no idea what she was doing or where she was going.

A Washington, DC, family therapist recalled that her British aunt, Sheila Winifred Butler, occasionally took charge of Margaret's Girl Guide troop during World War II, much to her dismay. Margaret, perhaps aged twelve or thirteen, would invariably take it into her head to run off and disappear.

"She was a terror. Once when the troop was visiting a ship—it could have been a sizable sailing vessel—Margaret disappeared completely."

Butler had visions of her having fallen overboard and drowning. She was discovered some time later, hiding deep in the ship's hold. Paula Schuck, another mother who had adopted a fetal alcohol syndrome child, observed that periods of daring might be followed by her daughter's hiding in fright, as if balanced on a knife edge between recklessness and terror. She recalled that one of the problems she most feared was the way her daughter, in a crowd, would walk up to a perfect stranger—the stranger, the better—take that someone by the hand, and begin to chatter. Curiously enough, a similar behavior was described by Alathea during group walks at Windsor. In the same way, Margaret would go from one group to another, take a new hand trustingly, and start chattering away. Then she was likely to ask, "Do you love me? Do you really love me?"[41]

Elizabeth, on the other hand, never seemed to be for or against anything.

"She never suffers; therefore, she never strongly desires," Alathea wrote. "If only she could be drawn out of her shell."[42]

Bit by bit, it transpired that Elizabeth already had a "boy" or "beau"—they were sworn to secrecy—who used to visit her. Alathea wrote that "she said he's very funny,"[43] which was no great recommendation as far as Alathea was concerned because the Royals *would* keep repeating jokes they had heard on the wireless that were not very funny the first time. Presumably, she changed her mind once she met Philip—a tall, dreamily handsome youth with gold hair who was already a prince twice over, of Greece and Denmark. He was Elizabeth's second cousin, they had known each other since childhood, and she would, a few years later, become his bride and in due course give him yet a third title: Prince Philip, Duke of Edinburgh.

A moment came in 1941 when Elizabeth was fifteen, witnessed by Alathea, when her friend was not sure a marriage would ever happen. One night after supper in the nursery, Alathea and the princess went back to the latter's room, started talking, and Elizabeth showed a side Alathea had never suspected. It was not true that she never felt anything strongly enough to be upset. In that moment, she was not sure she and Philip would marry. Perhaps she would never marry anybody. She said that if she really wanted to marry someone—and if there was opposition—she would run away. She really would.

"I saw behind the outward calm and matter-of-factness into something lovable and sincere," Alathea wrote.[44] She would never forget that revealing moment. How she loved them all. The Queen, especially. "Oh, if only I had a mother like that."[45]

One of the great chroniclers of the war years, A. J. Liebling, writing for *The New Yorker*, had first visited London in the early years of the war when there was serious concern on both sides of the Atlantic that the war was already lost. Once America entered the war in 1941 and the build-up for an invasion of Europe had begun, however, Liebling returned to London. He followed in the wake of politicians, diplomats, businessmen, writers, photographers, radio commentators, performers, film stars, and swing bands who made their presence felt.

Certain Americans were already there. John Gilbert Winant, as Lynne Olson points out, came as the U.S. Ambassador before the war began and never left. He could be seen at the height of the bombing in the streets of London, asking what he could do to help. W. Averell Harriman, representing the United States on the program of Lend-Lease, was another early arrival. As head of CBS News in Europe, Edward R. Murrow set up a nightly radio program, "See It Now," that brought home to American listeners just what it was like to be bombed, reports that would make him famous.

But for most British, it was the daily arrival of American troops that had an immediate impact. Liebling wrote in 1943, "(London) was full of Americans now, and one more attracted about as much attention as an extra clam at a shore dinner."[46] He continued, "While I had been away . . . the manager of the Savoy Grille had taken over the restaurant in my old hotel on Half Moon Street, and it was now one of the busiest and noisiest pubs in London, with a British version of a swing band, no tables available on less than three days' notice, American colonels crowding out the members of refugee governments . . . and Jack, the Cockney bartender, who, during my first visit had drooped disconsolately in front of a fine assortment of whiskies, now overworked and understocked, like the wine waiter."[47]

"London had the atmosphere of a town where people are gathering for a gold rush . . . everybody felt that something good was going to begin soon. Psychologically, we had already passed to the attack."[48]

Elizabeth celebrated her eighteenth birthday in the spring of 1944 and broke precedence by becoming the first British princess to wear a uniform. She joined the ATS, became a car mechanic, and quickly rose to the rank of subaltern: in Army terms, a second lieutenant.

On the streets of London and in every provincial city, the Yanks made an impression. First of all, their uniforms were distinctive: made of a good quality fabric, nicely tailored jackets and pants. These were worn over shirts and ties. The ties were always pressed and, a few inches below the knot, tucked carefully inside the shirt as a precautionary measure. Similarly, they wore their watches with the face turned towards the body so as to protect the glass in battle. It was so distinctive and so unvarying that their many admirers wore their watches just the same way after they left. There was a medallion on their sleeves somewhere denoting which particular division they represented, always a good open question to get the conversation going. And because they wore jackets, they looked like officers to British girls, even when they weren't.

They stood out from British troops whose unvarying uniform was a blouse top with belt attached and pants of a coarse khaki wool that looked like a cheap blanket. The design impressed no one and neither did the fairly useless hats. As for the American military police, they were a breed apart after they were shipped over to keep the waiting troops in order. They were invariably very tall, well-muscled men, superbly turned out, with guns in holsters hanging from their belts and spotless white puttees into which their trouser-legs had been folded and covering their boots. Flawless white gloves and often helmets completed the outfit. They were always to be found outside a pub, curiously still, and their perfectionism and authority inspired awe, as well as a kind of menace.

They often hovered in the background, as they did in a famous cartoon by Giles. He depicts a happy, semi-coherent soldier, standing on the steps of a pub, almost disappearing under an avalanche of girls, and explaining that he cannot possibly take them all home. Perhaps some disgruntled British Tommy coined the derisive "overpaid, over-sexed, and over here." Local girls, who had not seen such an influx of young men in one place since 1939, were beside themselves. They acknowledged the wolf calls with a flirty smile on the street. They sailed out with their best dresses and lipstick from ear to ear to go dancing night after night. They went to the pictures with them, took them back to their billets and pubs, and, whenever they could, married them.

While the queen's daughter was set to learning the intricacies of spark plugs and carburetors, Dame Laura Knight had taken up her brushes to do a portrait of Ruby Loftus in a hairnet and overalls, screwing on a breech-ring. It was one of the many works commissioned by Kenneth Clark, director of the National Gallery in London, under a government scheme to put well-known artists like Knight, Paul Nash, Henry Moore, Duncan Grant, John Piper, Edward Ardizzone, and many others to work showing Britain at war. Among the subjects chosen were women who had taken over jobs once the exclusive province of men, such as work on the assembly lines, sheet metal work, assembling aircraft and making ammunition, and much else besides. American girls were trained as pilots in order to fly bombers over from holding hangars in the Midwest to Europe. Talented photographers like Margaret Bourke-White took pictures at the front. Martha Gellhorn talked her way into a war zone and filed reports from there. Women writers and photographers brought home the awful plight of families bombed out of their home and were the first to show the Nazi concentration camps. They took pictures of starving children and wounded servicemen in hospitals. They photographed the preparations for D-Day and mingled with the cheering crowds when the final moment of victory arrived: the 8th of May, 1945.

Unlike many others, Margaret's future would not be affected by the growing social realization that women could do other things besides be wives and mothers. Her natural talents leading to professions on the stage, or in music, or even cabaret—the accomplished performer she seemed destined to become—all that was barred. Her role was to obey the rules, keep her head down, perhaps add the merest fillip (in the cause of spontaneity and dash) to her routine appearances, performing such a role without question or complaint. Have children—that was a must in the cause of providing possible future heirs to the throne. Have a happy marriage—desirable, but not actually necessary. The word here was "suitable."

As for the future queen, all the demands of childhood—the pressures to be perfect, live up to others' expectations, and bury her own feelings—would be accepted in the cause of her role as a figurehead. Whatever she might learn as the years went by, observing but never interfering with politics or social trends, might one day be transformed into advice worth having, even a kind of wisdom. Meantime, she had the happiness of knowing that the man she loved, loved and supported her. Her first rebellion was to join up, despite the objections of her parents and the Palace mandarins. It might be the only time she ever did. She successfully made her point, won their praise, and this helped give her confidence. There was something tremendous ahead. Her captivating smile said it all.

The day the war ended, a former schoolgirl remembered, "we suddenly had a holiday that came out of the blue."

This schoolgirl was just fifteen, and the abrupt break in what had been years of routine left not only a liberated feeling but the impulse to wander about, sit on the grass, and absorb the immensity of what had just happened.

"I suddenly thought of going down to the river, where it is narrow and bordered with willows. I knew there was a tearoom there.

"So, we all set off. My father wore a maroon tie. My mother had a hat with blue and white feathers on it. I had just made a dress of red and white polka-dotted rayon, and I already had a blue coat. When we got there, it was just like an Impressionist painting, people boating, or sitting on the grass, having a picnic or just looking. It was the perfect day, dazzling, with a small fresh breeze, the only sound was the tinkle of spoons on cups. Everywhere the church bells were ringing."[49]

In London, Mollie Panter-Downes went for a walk that day to see how many times the same red-white-and-blue theme would come up. Sure enough, it was everywhere. There were dogs with big bows of red, white, and blue ribbons tied to their collars, people wearing paper hats, pretty rosettes sprouting from slabs of pork at the butcher's, and the same theme on bicycles and baskets. Girls in their summer dresses appeared in the grassy areas, "like flocks of twittering, gaily plumaged . . . birds" with poppies and cornflowers in their hair and ribbons tied around their waists and ankles.

There were the smallest babies, their hair sectioned and caught up in tiny little bows of the same, omnipresent ribbon. There were mothers waiting in long queues, "the string bags of the common round in one hand and the Union Jack of the glad occasion in the other. Even queues seemed tolerable that morning."

She wrote: "It was without any doubt Churchill's day. Thousands of King George's subjects wedged themselves in front of the Palace throughout the day . . . and cheering themselves hoarse when he and the Queen and their daughters appeared, but when the crowd saw Churchill, there was a deep, full-throated roar. Wherever he went, he was surrounded by people—people running, standing on tiptoe, holding up babies so that they could be told later they had seen him . . . rosy, smiling, and looking immensely happy."[50]

When Churchill joined their Majesties on the balcony at one of their many appearances that day, he left the black Homburg hat he always wore in the Bow Room, where Tommy Lascelles looked at it for a while, speculatively. When his grandchildren of the future wanted to how he had spent VE Day, what would he tell them? Well, Lascelles couldn't quite commandeer the King's crown, but Churchill's hat would do. So, he put it on. Then he similarly crowned Sir Piers "Joey" Legh, Master of the Household, and the latter's assistant, Peter Townsend.[51]

Years later, on the fiftieth anniversary of VE Day in 1995 on BBC-TV channel 1, Princess Margaret was asked whose idea it was that she and her sister should slip out of Buckingham Palace and mingle, incognito, in the vast crowds. She could not quite remember but thought it had been her parents.[52] The most complete account of that daring adventure was given by her cousin, Margaret Rhodes, who happened to be renting a flat in the Palace just then. The group, led by Princess Margaret's uncle, Sir David Bowes-Lyon, her mother's childhood playmate, numbered about sixteen and also had as escort, "a very correct Royal Navy captain."[53] Elizabeth was in her ATS uniform, and had pulled her hat well down in anticipation that she might be recognized. But then, "a Grenadier among the party positively refused to be seen in the company of another officer," however junior (she was a 2nd lieutenant) looking like that, so the future queen had to stop trying to hide.

It was early evening as they fought their way down Piccadilly as far as the Circus and then back up again to St. James's and along Green Park. Margaret was able to see the Palace's and city's magical transformation as all the lights went on after the blackout of six years. It was nine o'clock on a Tuesday night.[54]

Mollie Panter-Downes wrote, "there were cheers and 'ohs' from children who had never seen anything of that kind in their short, blacked-out lives . . .

The night was as warm as midsummer, and London, its shabbiness now hidden and its domes and remaining Wren spires warmed by lights and bonfires, was suddenly magnificent."[55] The princess said, "It was unforgettable."

As for the crowds themselves, "London had gone mad with joy," Margaret Rhodes wrote. "We could scarcely move; people were laughing and crying, screaming and shouting; and perfect strangers were kissing and hugging each other . . ."

The little group battled their way back to the Palace, struggling to push past great masses of people standing shoulder to shoulder on tiptoe and in no hurry to go anywhere. Finally, they made the railings and stood there, anonymous among thousands of others. As the crowd picked up the chant, "We want the King! We want the Queen!" they yelled happily, too.[56] Nobody recognized them.

Chapter 7

A Pawn in the Game

By the limited and highly sexualized standard of the postwar years, during which blondes like Ginger Rogers and Marilyn Monroe were the reigning beauties, the teenage Princess Margaret was likely to be dismissed as the mousy not-much. Her hair was an ordinary brown, her nose too long, she was slightly built, and very much in the background.

The spotlight was on her sister, who conveyed that special kind of radiance of a woman in love. At age twenty-one, she had weathered the year-long, quite difficult process of persuading her parents that Philip was the right man for her. After a numbing six years of war, constant scarcity, rationing, and sudden death at home and abroad, to have prevailed at last was too late for an exhausted citizenry. In London, which took the brunt of the bombing, and for the next five years, the results were still evident: boarded-up windows, crumbling walls, shrapnel-pitted stone buildings and monuments, peeling paint, and, in street after street, great gaps where homes once stood. Nature crept into the empty spaces. There was a sudden arrival of buddleias springing up everywhere and attracting all manner of butterflies, as well as a small white flower called "London Pride" that Noël Coward wrote a song about, the first signs of healing.

Now a handsome young couple had married and would inherit the kingdom quite soon—a new Elizabethan Age. Elizabeth's great future was already destined, one requiring sacrifices that she was willing to make. Somewhere in the background was Elizabeth's fifteen-year-old sister, hands behind her back, smiling faintly and ducking her head to reveal a mop of untidy hair. Their relationship had perhaps already changed, as is bound to happen when a girl of thirteen, going into womanhood, is trying to find common ground with a nine-year-old. A gap of so many years, psychologists indicate, is always difficult, particularly when one of them feels left out. It is reflected in Elizabeth's exasperated comment, "What are we going to do with Margaret?" when she is still a child herself. Or Margaret's almost desperate and lifelong attempt to keep up with her older sister, running after her and calling, "Wait for me!"

Once they reached adulthood, that had not changed much. On one occasion, when Margaret thought Elizabeth was being too personal, she snapped, "Look after your Empire and I'll look after my life."[1] The antipathy was returned. When Margaret refused to attend a fire drill at Sandringham but stayed in bed, Elizabeth reportedly said, "Let Margo burn."[2] It was a joke of course, but, the psychiatrist Dennis Friedman writes, "according to Freud, there is no such thing as a joke, and the remark might have reflected barely concealed animosity."[3]

There were also times when the teasing was not even concealed as a joke. Her grandmother's comment, "Why are you so small? Why don't you grow up?" was on a par with George V's attacks on his son for stuttering, and hurt just as much.

There was always Daddy, the person who loved her and had protected her from the beginning. But George VI, who had guided Elizabeth's education towards the role she must play, had no such ambitions for darling Margaret except, perhaps, to keep her the precious baby of the family, or at least the kid. She was his happy, silly girl, making faces and playing games, who ran to him for protection when she needed a hug. His father said once, rather grumpily, that he hoped she would be taught to write a readable letter. Margaret was the bright, heedless light in a dangerous world. For George VI, the war had tested every ounce of determination he had. And he had triumphed. But it had been at great personal cost.

And yet. There was something special about Margaret. Perhaps it was her quick responses, her ability to say just the right thing, and pass things off with a joke that disarmed a listener while acting as a kind of protection for herself. Queen Mary remarked, "She was so outrageously amusing that one can't help but encourage her." Friedman writes "That, from an early age, Margaret had to develop a seductive charm and manipulative behavior to provoke loving responses from indifferent adults, is a sad reflection on her parents and governess."[4]

Once she turned eighteen in August 1948, Margaret, in one of those sudden transformations from socks to high fashion that happened to her generation, left the nursery for an apartment of her own in Buckingham Palace. Her staff included her first lady-in-waiting, a jolly girl called Jenny Bevan, and a small staff. Her sister, married in 1947, was discreetly expecting her first child, Prince Charles, in November 1948. The spotlight was shifting to her supposed mouse of a little sister. Writers in magazines and papers were rediscovering her as a subject, along with her perfectly spaced eyes of azurian blue, her flawless skin, and luxuriant hair. She pulled together what became known as the "Margaret Set," a crowd of young aristocrats from whom the specter of war had been lifted and who were naturally celebrating with parties, dances, and elaborate dinners at the best London night clubs. With a kind of inspired taste, Margaret fastened not only on the best ideas of the Royal dressmaker Norman Hartnell but a French newcomer introduced by Odette Massigli, wife of the French Ambassador René Massigli, in the autumn of 1947. He was Christian Dior. Dior's New Look, with its nipped-in waistline and bouffant skirts, not to mention its outrageous feminine charm, was exactly right for her, and the styles she wore immediately found their way into department stores, radically scaled down, of course.

One of her coats was gored to fit a small waist, then released into a wide skirt that swung when she walked; there are numerous newspaper photos of her wearing this. The author wore a much-reduced version of the coat herself, copied in Montreal and bought in Hamilton Ontario Canada. Women might have the vote, they might drive trucks, and fly airplanes, but, in those immediate postwar years, there was nostalgic return to first priorities—courtship, marriage, family—that showed itself in the way popular songs referred to women as "Baby," men as "Daddy," and all the furs and rings men were going to give women.

On a slightly more elevated level women's magazines talked about "togetherness," raising children, and making marriages work. Undergarments, if not quite as brutal as Victorian corsets, emphasized waist, bust, and disciplined hips. Nylon hose, "uplift" bras, teetering heels, dyed blond hair, plunging necklines: all that went into the laborious construction of the "doll" look, along with Max Factor cosmetics. Thus armed, a girl went forth to do battle in the streets. It went without saying that a princess had to wear the latest fashions and look better than the best. The psychologist and novelist Nigel Balchin subsequently wrote that the princess personified "two things: she is a royal princess—and a very attractive, high-spirited young woman."[5]

Those were the days when an American picture weekly like *Look* measured a girl by her measurements. The magazine published a full-length photograph of the princess attempting to restrain her unruly skirts, in the manner of Marilyn Monroe standing over a grate. Running down beside the picture were her physical statistics: Height, 5'1"; Bust, 33½"; Waist, 21½"; Hips, 33"; Weight, 100 lbs. She missed of course; the ideal was 36"-26"-36" at the time. But, as a pinup girl, she was close enough.[6]

Princess Margaret was pursued everywhere. When she made a state visit to Italy in May 1949, she caused a traffic jam on the Grand Canal in Venice and attracted such dense and noisy crowds that even she, who had seen crowds gather since childhood, was taken aback. As a measure of their determination to record every detail of her person, it was learned that a journalist broke into her hotel room in Venice and reported that the princess wore Peggy Sage nail polish (though not the color), likes Tweed perfume by Lentheric, ("a sensuous woody floral"), and was reading one of Dorothy Sayers's mysteries, *Busman's Holiday*.[7] Its hero was another Peter—Lord Wimsey, in this case—who, according to its creator, had hair the color of straw and was not handsome at all.

For her part, she tried to record everything she saw in Italy, which took some doing because Grannie had supplied a terrifying list of all the things she had to see. By the time she got to the end, she couldn't remember any of them. In Capri, though, something happened. She doesn't say exactly what, but she devoutly hoped Grannie had not read about it, because what the papers said was "perfectly untrue."[8] Whatever it was could not have been so dreadful because her letter to Papa on the same trip does not mention it, but only how sad they were to leave the island where they did nothing but "sail and sun and drink orange juice all day."[9]

Arriving in Sorrento, the first mailbag had arrived from London. She wrote, "Imagine my (horror) when two letters in a well-known handwriting fell out. They were from that horrible woman Barbadee Meyer! Full of chat and this and that about Italy and her horrible children.

"Wasn't it all *too* much, specially as there was only one letter otherwise that I knew."[10]

In Venice, they had enormous numbers of police "who slink about . . . push people out of the way and jump in cars and make a great racket . . . They change every day and look exactly like the press, so you never know if they are going to rush at people and take their cameras away, or whether they'll produce them themselves!"[11]

A week later, she wrote him again from Florence, happy to hear the news that those "horrid old doctors" had decided he was on the mend from his leg operation.[12]

It had poured with rain ever since they arrived, but they had been wined and dined by the expatriate English crowd (probably in Fiesole), so they sat in the sun, "and it was so nice to sit peacefully and meet people. So often one finds oneself wandering through the country and not meeting a soul!" The King was now convalescing at the Royal Lodge. She was sure it would do them both "all the good in the world." He was asked to "write often, as I'll be writing every minute."[13]

By the early 1950s, Princess Margaret's photographs were on the front page of the big American magazine covers, usually photographed by Cecil Beaton. Elizabeth Taylor was also on the cover, but relegated to a small head-shot on the side. The word was out: There was a new star on the horizon.

That the princess could do what she liked and go where she liked was widely heralded in news stories. This was misleading, to say the least.[14] Had anyone ever seen the princesses riding on a bus? In a taxi? Seated second-class in a railway carriage? In fact, they always traveled in private limousines or their own dedicated railway cars. They never went out to have their hair done—hairdressers came to them—or walked their dogs in public parks. Or wrote for publication. Or gave interviews, much less provide commercial endorsements, however obliquely phrased. They were above all that.

One would never come across Princess Margaret strolling down Piccadilly, looking in shop windows. She could not leave her gilded rooms without ladies-in-waiting, a detective, and heaven knows how many others acting as buffers. Nothing much had changed since the days when ladies in crinolines who were unmarried could not entertain male visitors without a chaperone.[15]

The idea that she could marry "anyone" was equally misleading. She could not marry without the queen's consent, and, as a devout member of the Church of England, she was limited to unmarried men without past entanglements, and no Catholics need apply. The rules were enforced with great success to her uncle just before World War II, and were about to be cited again. Margaret could not even leave the United Kingdom without permission in those days. She could not vote or take part in politics, and if she had any sense, she would have no opinions at all and "disguise her will and use her eyes," as her mother said.

It was so difficult to describe what people were like in those days, as her contemporary Alice Munro, the Canadian short story writer, tried to explain in an autobiographical work, *To Reach Japan*. What was considered acceptable conversation and what not, was a tricky issue that no doubt entangled royalty even more than most.

"It would become hard to explain, later on in her life, just what was okay at the time and what was not," Munro wrote. "You might say, well, feminism was not."

Munro was born in 1931, a year after the princess.

"But then you would have to explain that feminism was not even a word people used. Then you would get all tied up saying that having any serious idea, let alone ambition . . . could be seen as suspect . . . and a political remark at an office party might have cost your husband his promotion."

People were dismissive of women when not actually being rude.

"It was a woman's shooting off her mouth that did it," Munro continued.[16]

Margaret's first major public engagement came about in October 1947 when she was given the task of launching a new liner, the *Edinburgh Castle* in Belfast. She wore a fitted beige coat with contrasting lapels and pocket trims with walking pleats and tiny bands just above the hemline; her hat was trimmed with ermine dyed brown. She wore it again for a society wedding in St. Margaret's Church in London early in 1948, and again at the opening of the Ideal Home exhibition in Glasgow in the spring of 1948. Not only did she look a picture for her debut as the launcher of big ships, but she collected a huge bouquet of flowers—just what kind they were has not been recorded. They were handed to her by the shipyard's youngest apprentice. She thought for a second, then carefully extracted a single blossom from the bouquet and tucked it into the boy's buttonhole.[17] A film director subsequently commented that "she is type-cast for the part."[18]

In a sense, the Royal Family has always been on stage—on display from the moment they are born. And, at a time when all news of the Palace was rigorously controlled, the merest deviation from the script would lead to endless hypothetical speculation about What It Could All Mean. Indeed, Princess Margaret began a new round when she offered a single peerless blossom to a young boy that day in Belfast. The lovely gesture, like something out of a fairy tale or a Pre-Raphaelite painting, caught the popular imagination. How perfect, how well-timed, and who could this person be?

Like her mother, she seemed to have an uncanny ability to rise to the occasion. Another incident found her driving past crowds of schoolchildren in a jeep and realizing they could see her better if she stood up. But when she did, her skirts began whipping in the wind, and something had to be done right away. A whispered command to a lady-in-waiting to hold them down at once did the trick. She drove on, smiling.[19] When the rumor got out that the princess, at a private party, had danced the can-can with evident relish, exposing a "froufrou" of petticoats, Godfrey Winn, one of her stoutest defenders, had some fast explaining to do.[20]

There are some interesting similarities between Princess Margaret's tastes and those of Queen Victoria. Both gravitated toward the performing arts. Her astonishing musical gift when she was less than a year old, has been recorded. Less known is her continuing ability to reproduce something she liked by ear, which made lessons on how to read music a great waste of time as far as she was concerned. Why did she need to read music when she already knew how to play it? It seems as if Queen Victoria was similarly gifted. (At the age of fifteen, she was far advanced, not just in piano but the harp as well. In 1842, the great Felix Mendelssohn was received at Buckingham Palace, and the Queen sang for him two of his own songs. He said they were performed with "charming feeling and expression.") [21]

The *New York Times* reported, "Everybody who knows Margaret . . . states without hesitation that she could not only make a living, but hit the headlines as a cabaret star . . . Margaret has a very pronounced talent, a completely individual technique which, combined with a . . . somewhat husky voice, puts her in the top class as a mimic and diseuse."[22] Her favorite number was "Baby, It's Cold Outside." This concerns a girl who has been visiting her boyfriend's apartment, and now sees it is time to leave. He is coming up with one reason after another why she should stay. It was a great Dean Martin hit in the postwar period and meant as a duet. Margaret's choice of partner is not recorded. Perhaps she sang both parts, which would have been funnier.

Another song in her repertoire was "I'm Just a Girl Who Cain't Say No," from *Oklahoma* (1943). She liked to sing this one when a Scottish minister, for instance, had been invited for tea with her mother, who would then try to stop her.[23] In fact, it was becoming harder and harder to stop Margaret from doing whatever she particularly wanted to do. The affair of the strapless evening dress, for instance: the queen prevailed, and shoulder straps were added belatedly. Most efforts failed, though, because, when it came to comic songs, somebody in the group was bound to find her funny. Including her father.

Theirs was, however, a difference in style. In her biography of George VI, Sarah Bradford supports the notion that the King's idea of a joke might not be much fun—a crawling mass of green in a matchbox, for instance. House party weekends were fated to include the guest who does not know that his half-open bedroom door is balancing several books and that his host is happily waiting for the crash. Or someone else has been targeted for an apple-pie bed, which looks perfectly innocent until you try to sleep in it. The schoolboy in him never seemed to tire of schoolboy-era jokes. Whereas his daughter's kind of fun had more to do with puncturing pompous people, at which she was adept. Or she might unnerve a new suitor by asking him why he had not yet commented on her beautiful eyes.

"Hadn't he read the papers?" she said, of course, cheekily but with the right soupçon of self-deprecation.

In those days, the princess was honing her marked gifts for keeping others at bay by the use of the deftly administered tease. She yielded to no one in her admiration for Danny Kaye and his nonstop, double-talking patter. She was beginning to be invited to supper parties honoring Kaye and was dancing with film star Douglas Fairbanks at one party in November 1948 when Kaye arrived late, "his wild hair disheveled," Chips Channon, socialite and diarist, recorded. The party was "gay and glamorous" but the princess really was "too tiny," he added with disapproval. She was becoming a tiny tyrant, who "bored and bullied everybody." She was going to get the Royal Family into trouble one day, he remarked with prescience that same year.[24] Channon continued to make fun of her particular shortcoming: her height. "The Twerp,"[25] as he called her. The Future Queen was "Lilibet" so Margaret had to be "Liliput" (with a reference to *Gulliver's Travels*).[26] It stuck, for a while.

Channon might have (but did not) make a reference to her quick wit. There is a photograph of her with Jenny Bevan sitting with her on a park bench. Margaret has said something funny, and Jenny, helpless with laughter, has collapsed into her lap. The Princess has the mingled expression of someone who cannot quite believe she is as funny as all that.

Like Queen Victoria, the princess adored the theater, and in years to come would be photographed at one command performance after another. Her first postwar experience was arranged by her sister. They sat, not in the royal box, but with two beefy officers of the guards barricading them into the stalls. Elizabeth had bought tickets for *While the Sun Shines*, a farce by Terence Rattigan concerning a young earl, his impoverished fiancée (in a navy blue WAAF uniform of the women's air force), a brash American bombardier, and a Frenchman in it somewhere. Now considered a bagatelle in a distinguished playwright's oeuvre, it was a sell-out sensation in 1945. Comedies were just the thing because audiences needed to laugh.

People were also determined to dance all night. So was Margaret. Victoria used to do the same a century before and with less justification. She wrote in her diary of May 1848, "I did not leave the ballroom till ten minutes to four!" . . . "and was in bed by half-past four—and the sun was shining." Two or three days later, she was back on the dance floor again, just as Princess Margaret had done, along with everyone else. The war, after all, was over. No doubt Margaret fell into bed at dawn with the same sense of sleepy satisfaction that her ancestor revealed. She, too, had been "very much amused."

Dances imply partners, and Margaret experienced the whirl of attention that a princess who is eligible, knowledgeable, pretty, and particularly well-placed can expect to encounter. The postwar crowd picked up and resumed the pattern to which Lady Glenconner was also subjected and writes about so feelingly. Boys as well as girls in that particular echelon of society expected it as a matter of course. That is to say, the girls of their class "came out" at nineteen, the desirable ones had found partners and were engaged a year later, and the merry-go-round of marriages took place when they were twenty-one. Margaret, with her style, charm, and wit, and her particularly desirable connections, was on the market. Astonishing numbers of candidates showed up—thirty-five of them by one count. The wonder is she had a moment to look each of them over before changing partners, on or off the dance floor. In fact, a select few began to stand out quite soon.

Perhaps the earliest was William Douglas-Home, son of the 13th Earl of Home and brother of the better-known, future Prime Minister Sir Alec Douglas-Home, and an older, sophisticated man of the world. As acting captain in the fight to drive the Germans out of Europe, when the order came to move against the port of Le Havre, Douglas-Home asked the British commander if the French citizens could first be allowed to evacuate the city but was repulsed. So, he refused to take part in the attack and was court martialed and imprisoned. Douglas-Home, besides being a man of principle, was also a prolific playwright who would eventually write more than fifty plays. It seems likely that he and Margaret met in 1947 when two of his plays were running in London. One, *Now Barabbas,* drew on his experiences in prison. The other, *The Chiltern Hundreds,* is a comedy about a would-be member of parliament, his wealthy American fiancée, and his hapless attempts to impress her with his political achievements. Bosley Crowther, drama critic of the *New York Times,* called it "a somewhat slapdash lot of fooling," but audiences liked it, and it was made into a film two years later.

Douglas-Home's friendship with the Princess, or what we know of it, appears to have been that of a mentor who discovered that her knowledge of twentieth-century literature was a perfect blank. He started her off with Christopher Isherwood. He was also eighteen years her senior, unmarried, and looking for a wife. Nothing happened, and in 1951 he married someone else.

"Sunny" Blandford, another early suitor and heir to a great estate as 11th Duke of Marlborough, often twirled Princess Margaret around the dance floor in the early days. But two months after the Princess celebrated her twenty-first birthday, he also married someone else. So that was that.

"Johnny" Dalkeith, who would become the 9th Duke of Buccleuch and a politician, was different matter. He was a Scot, they had known each other since they were children, and it is believed that George VI would have liked her to marry him. The future Duke of Buccleuch was set to inherit the largest private landed estate in the United Kingdom, covering some 280,000 acres and including six celebrated castles and palaces crammed with beautiful antique furniture, precious chinaware, silver, and priceless works of art. Born in 1923, and with a distinguished war record in the Navy, Johnny Dalkeith was as yet unmarried when his name began to be linked with that of the Princess by the ever-hopeful press.

When she knew him, Johnny Dalkeith was tall, slim, and red-haired. Even then, he had the kind of craggy, rock-hewn features that would have looked well on Mount Rushmore, with all the sterling virtues that implies. He was, like the ideal of a virtuous Victorian gentleman, at pains not to take advantage of his massive social advantages. He served modestly in the Navy, knocked around his estate in gray flannels and a sports jacket, and picked up Princess Margaret at the station in a small sports car, perhaps an MG that was all the rage in those years. With his tenants, he was unassuming, always asking for their opinions. He made friends with their children, took them for walks by the hand, and knew everyone's first names.

His enormous job called for forestry management, and he took those courses. Estate management was another necessary accomplishment, and perhaps he took the time to study all the antiques he was about to inherit, not to mention the Old Masters. He hunted, shot, and no doubt fished as well. One can expect that he had perfect manners. One can already make a good guess that the country life he offered would have suited her sister Elizabeth more than it did Margaret, and perhaps the life of a future politician's wife did not appeal much to her either. Nevertheless, around the summer of 1951, they were seen with each other frequently, and, on the occasion of her twenty-first birthday that August, Margaret was invited for the weekend. Everyone expected an announcement. Nothing happened. Two years after that, Johnny Dalkeith married a mannequin, or model, who had exhibited the clothes Norman Hartnell created. Another door had closed.[27]

Meanwhile, Johnny continued to face huge responsibilities at home and had begun a career as an MP for Parliament. Then, in 1971 while out riding, he fell—but so did his horse, who landed on top of him, paralyzing him from the chest down. For the rest of his life, he was in a wheelchair. He rose to that challenge as well, causing a sensation when he returned to the House of Commons that same year. He became a notable and much-admired spokesman for the disabled until his death in 2007 at the age of eighty-three.

On the other hand, Colin Tennant, Lord Glenconner, was the man one might want to know without getting too friendly. A whole book was needed to encompass his many contradictions: immensely wealthy, subject to expensive whims, brought up by an eccentric family, he never quite got past his childish penchant for smashing cups or hurling himself to the floor. Or his innate need to be with creative and stimulating people. Lavishly generous and parsimonious by turns, Tennant found his perfect role when he bought an uninhabited island in the Caribbean and made himself its master, as Nicholas Courtney makes clear in his masterful study *Lord of the Isle*.

When Princess Margaret knew Tennant, he was leading an adventurous troupe of thespians, most of them titled and independently wealthy, who were putting on plays for charity, more or less as a lark, with plenty of time in between for more serious pursuits like eating and drinking. Margaret, who was also taking part in the Little Theater amateur movement just then, was invited to be a director, but she was already too involved in public appearances to give it the time, so she signed on as an assistant stage director. The play, *The Frog*, was about a serial killer, played by Tennant in disguise—he chose to appear in a gas mask—and it was subsequently performed. The actors enjoyed themselves enormously. Noël Coward, asked to give a review, was appalled.

"The whole evening was one of the most fascinating exhibitions of incompetence, conceit, and bloody impertinence I have ever seen."[28] They drowned their sorrows with champagne and foie gras sandwiches until four o'clock the next morning.[29]

Several of Margaret's suitors played the role of reliable escort in those years. Chief among them was William Euan "Billy" Wallace, son of Captain Euan Wallace and Barbara, daughter of the architect Sir Edwin Lutyens.[30] Another rich playboy and socialite, Billy Wallace, receives a brief mention in the Chips Channon diaries of 1942 as "long, lovely, and languorous, with lapis eyes and a lackadaisical manner."[31] Billy was perhaps her most persistent suitor in those years, called "old Faithful" because he was always turning up. He claims to have proposed to her constantly and persistently despite her equally stubborn refusals.[32] Eventually, and in time, she repaid his persistence by saying yes, and then he responded by doing something quite outrageous. But that will come later in this story.[33]

F. J. Corbitt, author of *My Twenty Years in Buckingham Palace*, provides the answer to this saga of *La Ronde*. He writes, "I found it most amusing in those days to read . . . of the Princess's name being linked with this young man or that . . . various officers of the Guards and scions of the nobility who all of them in turn had been invited to join the Royal Party at one house of another. I have seen them all come—and go away—to wed some other lady . . . But to those of us in the background there was never any doubt whatever" as to whom the princess was in love with.[34]

The Palace had its own private cinema, and after-dinner shows were a regular feature in those early postwar years. The Royal Family saw all the new British films, and the evening always began the same way. The king and queen would arrive first and be led to their usual seats, followed by the evening's dinner guests. The princess would take her usual place. The lights would be lowered. There was always one empty seat beside her, and as the lights went down, a certain equerry would slip into it with a rug in case the princess needed it around her knees, along with an ash tray for her cigarette.

"There was a definite atmosphere of contentment between the two of them as they would settle down to watch the film," Corbitt wrote. "I always thought, 'Good luck to them.'"[35]

Then one day, Margaret's secret came out. As it happened, it was the day of her sister's Coronation: June 2, 1953. Margaret had been dressed to play a prominent part in the proceedings by Norman Hartnell. His design of a fitted bodice, short cap sleeves, and sweeping skirt was a sensation; heavy white satin was embroidered at intervals with silver and pearl rosettes, as befitted a princess whose second name was Rose. Documentary films of the event, now in color, show her walking with measured steps up the aisle in Westminster Abbey, her sumptuous train of red and white velvet flaring out behind her. Afterwards, she joined her family members on the balconies of Buckingham Palace to acknowledge the roars of the crowd greeting the new queen and her consort. By the time she and her escort had slipped away and changed into nondescript attire so as to mingle with the masses on the other side of the gates, the first reports were out to say who the mystery man was. Margaret had unmasked him in the Abbey by going to meet him and fondly, ostentatiously, flicking away a small piece of lint off his shoulder. That did it.

Peter Woolridge Townsend, a young Royal Air Force pilot, arrived in Princess Margaret's life during World War II and was destined to become a national hero as well as the unwilling cause of a royal crisis that rivaled the abdication of King Edward VIII fourteen years before, and for similar reasons. The long drawn-out and devastating consequences for Princess Margaret would be traumatic, and it is likely that she never quite recovered. Chance brought them together, and the coincidences of Time would lead to catastrophe—the aspect of their doomed love affair he would emphasize in the title of his fascinating memoir, *Time and Chance*.

The times, as it happened, were momentous enough. Britain had lost the battle of Europe that followed its entry into World War II in 1939. In short order, the British Expeditionary Force had been routed to the beaches of Dunkirk, and the daring rescue of over 300,000 troops against the odds soon followed. That amazing feat was celebrated in Britain as a kind of miracle, although Prime Minister Churchill warned his listeners at the time that wars are not won by defeats, a reminder that needed saying.

The obvious next step was for the Nazi invaders to attack the island of England itself. This was the situation in 1940 when the Luftwaffe began its bombing campaign, not only to terrorize the British themselves, but destroy the RAF in preparation for the arrival of German troops. It became known as the Battle of Britain. In that desperate battle, a cadre of highly trained fighter pilots in their Hurricanes and Spitfires played a crucial role, and Churchill would one day comment that "Never in the field of human conflict was so much owed by so many to so few." One of them would be that ace fighter pilot Peter Townsend.

As chance would have it, Townsend was tall by the standards of those days: 5'11", slim, with classic features, an arresting, boyish smile, and tousled black hair. He was the fifth in a family of seven children with family connections going back for generations in the county of Devonshire. Three of the four boys followed their father, Lt. Col. Edward Copleston Townsend, into the military and had distinguished careers; the fourth, Francis, went into the Colonial Service. Peter's sister Audrey won a scholarship to Oxford. Another sister Stephanie married Arthur Gaitskell, brother of Hugh Gaitskell, future leader of the Labour Party. These successes suggest that their mother, Gladys, had raised seven handsome, confident, and outgoing children.

This was not altogether the case. Reading between the lines, it appears that Peter was a sensitive, deeply feeling boy, easily bullied in boarding school, who developed a stammer. He later wrote he was not ready to be sent to boarding school when he was eight. Going to the prep school of Haileybury, where sadistic refinements of beatings were well advanced, was no better. He found a protector in his oldest brother Michael.

"He was a rather naughty boy with a fierce and sometimes perverse defiance of authority . . . I needed Michael and have always needed people like him; I lacked his cool courage, mine only coming with the heat of action. Michael sharpened my appetite for adventure and taught me how to handle risks," Townsend recalled in *Time and Chance*.

What might have destroyed someone with less inner strength produced a pilot of skill and daring at the moment when such qualities were in short supply. He flew, he said, "fast, hard and low."[36] His skills honed to a knife edge, he brought down the first German aircraft to crash on English soil, a Heinkel III while stationed with the RAF in Acklington early in 1940. By then, he had been promoted to flight lieutenant. He claimed two more on February 22 and April 8, 1940, and a share of a third Nazi plane in April 1940. His prowess duly noted, Townsend received a Distinguished Flying Cross (DFC) from George VI in Buckingham Palace. He also became a CVO (Commander of the Royal Victorian Order).

More "kills" followed, and six months later there was a Bar to the DFC, meaning a further award ceremony in September of 1940. The following year, after it transpired, he was personally responsible for bringing down eleven German planes, George VI awarded him another medal, the Distinguished Service Order (DSO).

"What, you again?" the monarch said, smiling.[37]

By then, he had been shot down himself. The first two times were relatively harmless but the third not quite so straightforward. It seems he was patrolling over the North Sea at dawn when he spotted a German reconnaissance plane, a Dornier. He went in for the attack, and after an exchange of fire, there was a loud explosion in the cockpit. He wrote: "My aircraft had been badly hit, but by some miracle the blinding orange-colored (flash) had not blown my guts out," so he jumped for his life.[38] Seconds later, he found himself suspended by a parachute and gently wafting his way down into the North Sea half a mile below. He was on his way home.

"But perhaps after all I never should get home, for I still had to fall into the sea, and I had no inflatable dinghy, only my 'Mae West' to keep me afloat," he continued. "I might never be picked up. 'One of our pilots is missing,' the BBC bulletin would say, leaving a last vestige of hope.

"However, in all that watery desert, there happened to be one small ship in sight . . . It was the second stroke of luck that morning. The ship was some distance away when I splashed down into the sea, but it lowered a boat, and not long afterwards I was hauled aboard."[39] His only injury was a big toe, which had to be amputated. After a peg of rum and some warmth for his shivering body, by afternoon, he was back with his squadron and flying again.[40]

After twenty months of day and night attacks, during which he flew more than three hundred operational sorties,[41] Townsend had trained himself to do without sleep but was paying the price by beginning to feel more like "a tired chicken than an avenging angel."[42] He had flown himself to a standstill.

"For fear had come to dwell within me. It had become, by day, my constant companion, my terrifying bed-fellow by night. In my thoughts and visions I saw myself crashing, over and over again, to a horrible death . . . The more I flew . . . the more fear, stark, degrading fear, possessed me . . . I found myself reacting to the smallest shudder of my aircraft, the slightest engine vibration, gripping the controls tighter and telling myself, 'This is it!'"[43]

He was close to a breakdown when he was grounded by the doctors, put on barbiturates, and in due course given a staff job at an airfield in Hunsdon Hertfordshire. He wrote that there he met Rosemary, who was living with her parents.

"She was twenty, tall and lovely—never more so than that evening we met at a local country house. I could not wait to make her my wife . . . we rushed hand-in-hand to the altar. In the ancient church of Much Hadham, we vowed—alas, all too hastily—to be one another's forever. Exactly nine months later, our first child was born."[44]

It was 1942. By then the worst was over, Hitler had turned his attentions to Russia, and Britain would never be invaded. The Battle of Britain had been won.

Realities of war for all those in the fighting, such as pilots, who faced death every day, have unpredictable consequences. Everything gets sped up and is experienced in a split second.

"Some enchanted evening/You may see a stranger/Across a crowded room."

It was like that, as Rodgers and Hammerstein framed the issue in *South Pacific*, a war film that received its first performance in 1949.

"And somehow you know . . . You must make up your mind instantly when you see the right person, because that's the way it is. Or all through life, you may dream all alone."

This kind of magical thinking had a kind of primitive logic at a time when death stretched around the globe. It came to dominate everything: songs, films, poems, plays, concerts, letters—it was in your worst nightmares.

One of the most astonishing and eloquent descriptions of love in wartime, all the more telling for its appearance as a tone poem in shades of gray, a flash of feeling in a drab room, was *Brief Encounter*. A film by Noël Coward and David Lean superimposes the lives of two conventional, well-intended people trapped in humdrum marriages against the terrifying possibilities war has suddenly made possible. Mist, a platform, an express train roaring through a station, provide the stark symbolism and, in the background, passages from Rachmaninoff's Second Piano Concerto, underline the mad, sudden, impossible hopes.

"What if . . . ?" "If only . . ."

Longing, pain, loss, misery. Suicide as the only alternative. And then nothing happens, as if nothing changed.

Or perhaps it is a simple tune, "You must remember this," that causes the anguish of a married woman who cannot release herself from the misery of what might have been with someone else, as in another extraordinary film, *Casablanca*. Or, in the case of *A Matter of Life and Death*, the issue to be explored is a Surrealist notion of what happens after death. A pilot in a damaged and burning bomber, trying to make it back to base, is talking to a sympathetic girl who is trying to get him down safely. He has no parachute, and he bails out over the ocean fully expecting to die.

But he does not die. He washes up on an English beach, and this sets alarm bells in the vast domain of the hereafter. An elegant, eighteenth-century aristocrat is sent to escort him there. But he will not go. He has fallen in love. He refuses to die.

It is a strange fact that even after the war ended, falling in love had become a concept so enmeshed with the idea of great risk, even the risk of dying, that it continued in the popular imagination for a long time. It was the price to be paid for something as overwhelmingly precious as it was rare and fleeting. A pool of light in a darkened street.

In February 1944, Townsend wrote: "Buckingham Palace, solid, square-shaped and built around an interior courtyard, is a grey, unlovely edifice. Above the steady hum of London's traffic comes, intermittently, the clatter of sentries' rifle butts on the paving and the thump of their boots as they turn about at the end of their beat."[45]

He was one of the hand-picked veterans of battle who was invited to be in attendance as equerries at the Palace in recognition, for the next three months, of their achievements. A kind of special award. First, he was briefed by Sir Piers "Joey" Legh, Master of the Household, whom he would be invited to work with soon, and then he went to meet the King.

Townsend said that he "found [himself] in the green carpeted Regency Room alone with His Majesty King George VI."

Townsend already liked him.

"[T]he humanity of the man and his striking simplicity came across unmistakably . . . And the King stammered, too. . . . I felt drawn towards him."[46]

After the interview, he was standing in the corridor chatting with Sir Piers when "two adorable girls" came along, all smiles.

"Hello Joey," they chorused, and were promptly introduced.[47]

His impression of Margaret, he would say, was the same one everyone else had at the time, of a "leggy, excitable girl with a lot to say and very little time in which to say it. She chattered endlessly in a voice far louder than the usual murmur employed by the royal family. . . ."[48] Elizabeth was then seventeen and Margaret, thirteen, at an age when giggling over young men was what young women did. They were always on the lookout, even if the men seemed much older and were wearing lots of medals.

"Our meeting was a coincidence," Townsend wrote. "But, thinking back, I would not have put it beyond the King to have buzzed them on the interphone and told them, 'If you want to see him, he's just left my study.'"[49]

Apparently, he was a special arrival even then.

As an equerry, Townsend's job description consisted of meeting and greeting guests, taking them wherever they needed to go and being generally available, a kind of lackey, albeit on an elegant scale. His tour of duty went for two weeks; then he was off for six, and presumably fully available for his wife and sons (a second son would arrive in due course). They were lodged in Adelaide Cottage, a grace-and-favour house on the Windsor Castle grounds, some twenty miles from the Palace.

He was invited for just three months. But his stay was soon extended indefinitely. It was quickly apparent that he had a kind of genius for organization. He had, after all, been in charge of an RAF squadron and had honed his gift for creating a smooth and functioning unit, which is rarer than it seems. An RAF colleague said of him: "What a lesson one man can learn from a person like that, watching the way he works with men. He never needs to be angry or tiresome, or even particularly firm. It just comes from inside him. . . . He was hero of the squadron to the ground staff."[50]

Before too long, he was working underneath Sir Piers, Master of the Household, using his skills at making things run smoothly. Then he was playing a particular role for the Royal Family as well, and being frequently invited to join the monarch shooting at Sandringham, a walk on the moors, riding with the princesses, or mixing and mingling at their parties. He was the kind of person who knows just where you will sit at dinner and make sure you are comfortable. As your dinner companion, he knew how to start a conversation, pass the salt, make a joke and—even more important—fade discreetly into the background or spring to help without needing to be told. In those postwar years when the king began to have serious medical problems, Townsend seemed to have the knack for calming and reassuring him whenever he became enraged. One of the compliments Townsend most cherished was the king's remark, "Peter, whatever would we do without you?"[51] The king is also known to have remarked that Peter was the son he never had. Everybody liked him; he was "a man of immense charm, highly intelligent and without a trace of self-importance."[52]

When the moment came to fret about Margaret, who seemed at a loss after Elizabeth married Philip in 1947, her parents turned to Peter and asked him to take her under his wing. He was, after all, fifteen years older than she was. And he had a wife and sons. They could depend on him to be tactfully aware of her rank, and when she called him Peter, to reply by calling her "Ma'am."

The fact that Margaret would always be four years younger than her sister was becoming a problem, but not in the way that might have been predicted.

With her temperament, Margaret would always want to do everything Elizabeth did. "Wait for me!" When Alathea and Elizabeth went into a huddle to giggle about boys, all of a sudden Margaret wanted to talk about boys.

When just ten years old, she was overheard to remark that the footman in the royal nursery was "frightfully handsome." By the age of fourteen, she found her way to the royal cellars and was caught in the act of trying some serious sampling. A year later, she appeared at a garden party in Edinburgh, ready for action with eyebrow pencil, mascara, powder, and the reddest of red lipstick. She was doing a methodical study of young officers in the palace guards (especially the handsome ones) and developing her ability to drop in casually whenever her sister invited them to tea. Or gave evening parties, dances especially. She was always full of fun and knew what to say. By the time she was officially ready to "come out," she had already "sneaked out."

After a lifetime of being taken everywhere together, wearing the same clothes and even the same hairstyle, Margaret can be forgiven for thinking that, when honors were being passed around, they ought to come to her as well. When, in 1947, Elizabeth was given the "freedom of the City" by the Lord Mayor of London, Margaret might have stayed home nursing her wounded feelings. Instead, Margaret suddenly appeared from a side street, and her sister had to make a last-minute appeal to her host. Margaret was fitted in.

As one of her escorts said, "She's a hell of a girl—real zing."[53]

Taking Margaret "under his wing," as a practical matter, was a disguised kind of promotion. It meant Peter would be much more involved in the planning and execution of her forays into public appearances. He is seen hovering in the background in photographs as she takes up more and more duties. For indeed, she was becoming increasingly useful to her older sister, who was absorbed in the fantastic months of preparation that went into her wedding with Prince Philip in 1947. Quite shortly after that, she was pregnant with their firstborn Charles, which inevitably meant, in those days, a discreet retirement into the background while awaiting his arrival.

Margaret and Peter's first public appearance together was the naming of the *Edinburgh Castle*, traveling to Belfast and watching as the great liner moved down the slipway and into the sea. Townsend was there on the fateful visit to Italy and was probably as frustrated as the rest of her party when they discovered the lengths the Italian press was prepared to go in pursuit of her beauty secrets—if nail polish can be included in that category.

He was there when the Royals made one of their trips to Holyroodhouse. That was the time when Princess Margaret regaled her father with a graphic description of how David Rizzio, the private secretary to Mary, Queen of Scots, was dragged screaming from his room to be put to death with daggers. She showed her father the fatal spot—with rather too much relish, Townsend thought.[54]

Townsend also accompanied her when she made her first trip abroad, representing her father, at the celebrations to mark the accession of Queen Juliana in Amsterdam in 1948. At the actual ceremony, the princess, now eighteen, was "too sweet, charming and shy, and lovely to look upon," her great aunt Alice remarked. There were further reports that, during a trip to the Rijksmuseum next day, she leaned on him and took his arm. While at the ball held following the inauguration, the princess danced with the handsome Englishman, and was "noticeably radiant."

"Without realizing it," Townsend wrote, "I was being carried a little farther from home, a little nearer to the princess."[55]

That was also the year when Peter Townsend became aware of the fragile state of King George VI's health. While they were staying at Holyroodhouse, Townsend and the king had gone for a walk up a hill behind the Palace.

"Normally, he walked with a remarkably long, steady stride, but that evening he labored and kept muttering, 'What's the matter with my blasted legs! They won't work properly!'"[56]

He had been experiencing leg cramps but, "instead of . . . doing something about it," he carried on with his heavy program and did not call the doctor for several months afterwards. It was then that he told Townsend he was suffering from arteriosclerosis and might even have to have his right leg amputated. Instead, with the help of an injection to reduce the pain and increase the supply of blood to the skin, his leg improved, and he resumed his heavy schedule.

Once Townsend was made Assistant Master of the Household, he graduated from the "gloomy equerry's room" to a green-carpeted and cozy office on the south side of the Palace, well away from the high-volume traffic on the north side, where secretaries and guests were routed every day. He called it "a little paradise."[57] So he was, if possible, in increasing contact with the Royal Family and, again, witnessed a pivotal moment in the king's decline.

It happened one evening at Balmoral, the night of Princess Margaret's twenty-first birthday party. The weather had turned wet and cold, but the king insisted on going shooting and had caught a cold. The king went to bed, but his room was directly above the main living room where the guests were shouting and singing far into the night. He rang for Peter.

"I entered his room and found him standing there, a lonely, forlorn figure. In his eyes was that glaring, distressed look which he always had when it seemed that the tribulations of the world had overcome him. Above the rhythm of the music and the dancing coming up from below, he almost shouted at me: 'Won't those bloody people ever go to bed?'"[58]

Another visit to the doctor. This time the news was somber. The king, a heavy smoker during the war years, had damaged a lung so badly that it had to be removed. The operation was performed in September 1951; it was then discovered that the other lung was also affected. He "could not be expected to live for more than two years."[59]

Sarah Bradford, George VI's biographer, wrote, "The King made tremendous efforts both physical and psychological to bring himself back to health. Not knowing he had cancer, he made himself believe that the operation had cured him."[60] He also did not know—or was not told—to stop smoking and probably went back to his deadly habit. The prediction that he would two more years to live was not to be fulfilled either.

A plan to visit Australia and New Zealand by way of Kenya was coming up but was amended over his objections. Elizabeth and Philip were substituted for the king and queen. So, at the end of January 1952, the king and queen went to the airport to see them off.

"He stood hatless in the cold wind, his eyes with the glaring look they took on moments of emotion," Bradford continued. "Whatever brave front the king put on, he knew in his heart of hearts that he was living on the edge."[61] He never saw his daughter again.

At Sandringham on February 5, the king went shooting with a large group that included gamekeepers from the neighboring estates, tenants, and police. He dined as usual with his wife and daughter, and after dinner she played the tune he always asked for, "Underneath the Spreading Chestnut Tree," and sang the words while he pantomimed them. Perhaps he did a crossword puzzle or added a few more pieces to the jigsaw puzzle that lay, unfinished, on a nearby table. Then it was "Goodnight, my dear," a kiss, and he was off to bed at 10:30 p.m. But not yet to sleep. At midnight, a watchman noticed him "fiddling with a recently fixed latch at his bedroom window." Then he finally fell asleep. When his valet, James MacDonald, went into the bedroom with his usual morning cup of tea the next day, he found that the king had died in the night. He was fifty-six years old.[62]

When Prime Minister Winston Churchill heard the news, he cried bitterly. So did many others who understood that greatness had been thrust upon George VI and that he had risen to the challenge. But none more than Princess Margaret. A friend told Bradford that to lose her father "was a terrible thing" for her. ". . . she worshipped him, and it was also the first time anything ghastly had happened to her."[63] Responding to a letter of condolence from

Lady Nancy Astor, Margaret wrote, "You know what a truly wonderful person he was, the very heart and centre of our family, and no one could have had a more loving and thoughtful father."[64]

Margaret was inconsolable. J. Bryan III wrote: "Grief made her its prey. Her appetite fell away. Her usual meager breakfast of coffee and orange juice she omitted altogether. She ate sparingly and drank nothing, not even wine. She stopped smoking. She never went out."[65] She went to bed early night after night and took sedatives.[66]

However, she and her mother had to move from Buckingham Palace, which they detested anyway, so as to make way for the new Queen, her husband, and children, into the much nicer Clarence House. This was an imposing nineteenth-century townhouse a stone's throw from Buckingham Palace and next door to St. James's Palace. It required some refurbishment, so Peter was renamed as the Queen Mother's Master of the Household and he set to work. He would be living there, too. Thank heavens for Peter.

Just when Princess Margaret fell in love with her father's former equerry is debatable. It is thought that casual companionship turned to love during a Royal three-month tour of South Africa in 1947—part by air, part by train, involving the whole family and its sizable entourage. He became her companion whenever there was time to go horseback riding on the sands, or swimming, or walks in the woods. It was documented by as reliable a chronicler as J. Bryan III, whose very detailed and lengthy description of her life, written twelve years later, takes up much of the February 1959 issue of *McCall's* magazine. According to that writer, "she fell headlong in love and stayed there."[67]

It is entirely likely that Papa had already sensed Margaret's private feelings about her handsome young equerry. She knew she could always confide in Daddy, and he would be discreet. Mummy knew that about Papa as well and did so herself. Grandma Mary, on the other hand, only wanted to know about those feelings which propriety dictated. One felt what one ought to feel, and that was that. However, her restless and quicksilver mind relished whatever was new and unexpected. So, her granddaughter sent her detailed descriptions of their trip to South Africa.

One of a series of letters came from a glorified hostel in a national park in Natal. As they drove there in two cars, "Lilibet and I were fascinated. The whole way there the road was lined by native horsemen. We had never seen so many mounted people in our lives . . . Luckily, they were not too civilized and still wore blankets, with wonderful headdresses made of tall Feathers . . ."

Arriving in Natal, there was a swimming pool to splash about in, and Basuto ponies to ride on the following morning.

"After riding, we went to a . . . native ceremony and . . . the whole population of Basutoland was a vast, silent, staring crowd, completely covering the hillside where we were. Arriving in Natal, they were split into groups and lodged in bungalows dotted on a hillside of descending levels, a kind of vast rockery." It was picturesque in a camping-out sort of way. The only problem was the constant rain and thunder (it was the spring of 1947) and no umbrellas, so whenever anyone ventured outside, they got soaking wet. Never mind. It was "great fun," she said loyally.[68]

There was, of course, no mention of a certain equerry who was, nevertheless, constantly in the background of her life, if not right in front of it. Peter Townsend was in attendance at the riotous birthday party given at Balmoral Castle to celebrate her twenty-first birthday in August 1951. This had to be one of the high moments of her life: suddenly adult and free to marry the man she loved. After the day's shoot, they went outside and she lit a torch "which was carried, running, across the lawn and through the garden and then in relays up the hill where it was used to light a huge bonfire. . . . Soon there was a blaze that would be seen for miles. Then HRH had the idea of dancing a reel, so they did it by the light of the massive fire up on the hill, in and out of the puddles. . . . It was too moving for words and we all felt rather choking by the end of the evening."[69]

Townsend's marriage had been under the undeniable strain of two people who are finally living together and belatedly discovering how little they have in common. His wife took up painting, fell in love with her instructor, and sued for divorce, which came about in December 1951, a few months after the big birthday party. In the days when "innocence" and "guilt" were the ruling factors, Townsend's wife was clearly at fault. She told Chips Channon that she had just cause because Peter was impotent, and it had taken heroic efforts to bring about the lives of their two sons—clearly mean-spirited and not even true. Channon was sympathetic and indignant. The princess was ridiculous to fall for this "sexual flop."[70] Her grim determination was making her a public spectacle. How would it all end? If only she had married Johnny Dalkeith.

One finds occasional tantalizing glimpses of people who report having seen them together, as when a guest at a Buckingham Palace garden party said that, as the last guests left, a car swerved out of the Palace.

"Inside was Margaret, looking very flushed and excited, sitting next to Townsend at the wheel. I had never seen Margaret looking so naughty, as if she were running away from something."[71]

Or the story, probably apocryphal, of a moment when Townsend, under a command from his princess, was carrying her up a flight of palace stairs when, half way up, a shoe fell off. As they laughed, the king appeared on the landing in his dressing gown. The explanations did not fool him or them either.[72]

As others have written, however, she might have not noticed him until her trip to Amsterdam in 1948. Unfortunately, the princess never wrote about her great love, and if she did so in letters, these have not been found. It could have been a gradual process for them both, one of those slowly evolving friendships that arrive at the moment when one cannot imagine life without the other.

Theirs was a complex interweaving of opposed temperaments and strong common interests. One was impulsive, outgoing; a natural performer, but heedless. The other: thoughtful and introspective, but noncommittal. Townsend developed the talent that is evident in his autobiography: a sense of time and place, a gift for narrative, and sharp portraits of colorful personalities. He was a natural writer. They both loved active sports, literature, an exchange of ideas, theater, and the arts. Each was a member of the Church of England and took their beliefs seriously. Peter had been somewhere in the background of her life since she was fourteen. She knew he was well-liked, efficient, dedicated, and discreet.

Townsend was aware of the intricacies of her temperament, i.e., her basic optimism and sudden anger, moods that could quickly knock her off balance. Her directness both unnerved and intrigued him. Her ardent longing pierced his reserves and went straight to his carefully guarded feelings. Here was someone ready and longing to love with her whole heart. She yearned for him. Her vulnerability left him breathless. At the same time, she put herself into his hands by such comments like, "When I marry, I shall need someone firm to keep me in order."[73] A photograph exists of her seated beside him in a limousine. She looks directly at the camera, with the soft, eager look of a girl in love. He, beside her, is bent forward, clearly making plans. She trusts his sense of direction, and he knows where they are going.

There is another factor: the actual timing of the love affair. It happens right after her father's death and at the same moment as her sister's accession to the throne. It is hard not to think that she was looking around for a new protector, one who would have the power to keep at bay those influential voices around the throne who had been trying to mold her into something else— someone she could never be. With her sister as queen and Peter to deflect the chorus of voices, she could be safe from their pernicious influence.

A further consideration must be mentioned. This is someone who was almost ludicrously ill-equipped for ordinary life. As a sufferer of fetal alcohol syndrome, there was no one to help her through it in the days before such handicaps were even recognized, and the kind of instruction available in those days would have been counterproductive. She had been surrounded since birth with people who ministered to her every whim. By doing so, they had prepared her to do nothing—except marry, of course. She did not know how to enter the stream of life flowing all around her. All she did know, since she was constantly shadowed by policemen and detectives wherever she went, was to be afraid of it. How much did she long to be self-reliant, and how much did she dread it? She once said, "Being a princess is all I know how to do."

Townsend, who was sent off to boarding school to sink or swim when he was eight, was delighted by her. To him, her unpredictable moods were part of her charm. He wrote about how quickly her expression would change, from "saintly, almost melancholic, composure, to hilarious, uncontrollable joy." She was as generous as she was volatile.

"She was a born *comedienne* at heart, playing the piano with ease and verve, singing in her rich supple voice the latest hits. . . . She was coquettish, sophisticated.

"But what . . . made Princess Margaret so attractive and lovable was that behind the dazzling façade, the apparent self-assurance, you could find . . . a rare softness and sincerity. She could make you bend over double with laughter; she could also touch you deeply."[74]

He wrote that they met in the red drawing room at Buckingham Palace one afternoon when everyone else was attending a ceremony at Windsor Castle. For hours, they talked about their feelings.

"She listened, without uttering a word," when he told her how much he loved her. "Then she simply said, 'That is exactly how I feel, too.'"[75]

When Elizabeth and Philip were living at Clarence House, it was configured for their use with the usual separate nursery wing for the staff of nannies, equerries, and maids. It had recently been fitted out with central heating for the first time. Now it needed to be reconfigured once more. The Queen Mother wanted the second floor as her own suite. Princess Margaret took over the third, and Peter Townsend assumed the kind of detailed, day-by-day supervision that he did so well.

For Margaret, a formal drawing room was established, along with a less formal sitting room, bedroom, and bath, plus her own kitchen and adjacent dining room. A new elevator was installed to open into the sunny drawing room, furnished with well-padded and comfortable chairs, plenty of small tables, bibelots, and the latest British, American, and Commonwealth publications. An adjacent sitting room was fitted with bookshelves for her sizable collection of books about English history, French poetry, and "romantic" novels, including a few detective stories. Cupboards were installed to house several thousand recordings, from the classics to the latest offerings from Tin Pan Alley. Her bedroom curtains were deep pink, her favorite color, and its simple décor included family photographs, three crucifixes, and paintings and statuettes of saints and angels.[76]

But the most important item was her Sheraton desk, its top inlaid with marble, and jammed with letters, papers, scissors, pencils, and pens, where she spent several hours writing letters and planning public appearances. Among them, framed in silver, was a photo of Peter Townsend. He had first moved into a small office in one of the houses adjacent to the main mansion. When this proved to be too small, he took over the huge, empty attic of the main house as his office and moved in. Quite soon he was taking his meals with the princess and the Queen Mother several times a day.

It is sometimes suggested that the Queen Mother lived under the same roof without having the least idea that the daughter and her Master of the Household were in love. This seems unlikely. She was known for her ability to mask the truth with a warm smile, no matter how she might be feeling. Just the same, given her husband's marked liking for "the son I never had," and her daughter's well-known inability to hide what she really felt, the idea that her mother did not know seems implausible. She could, of course, have pretended not to know. What seems more likely is that she knew and sympathized. She might have even hoped they would marry. She certainly did nothing to prevent it. Perhaps she sensed how much of a comfort Peter had been to Margaret when she lost her father. It is even possible that George VI also hoped for marriage for them both and said as much before he died. In any event, her attitude towards divorce was far less rigid than that of others in the court at that time.

This is clear from an incident that took place a couple of years before, in 1950, involving the second marriage of one of her nieces, oldest daughter of her brother's, John Bowes-Lyon, who had died by then. The former Anne Ferelith Bowes-Lyon had dutifully married, at age twenty, Viscount Anson, eldest son of the Earl of Lichfield; the couple had two children. The marriage did not last, and by 1938, she was a divorcée with small children. It was then that she met and fell in love with Prince Georg of Denmark, son of Prince Axel and Princess Margaretha and second cousin to George VII of England. He was acting military attaché at the Danish Embassy in London, presumably where they met.

All was set for a grand wedding in the chapel of Glamis Castle in September 1950.

European royal visitors, undismayed by the bride's previous marital alliance, were out in force; among them, the Crown Prince Olav of Norway and his daughters, the Princesses Astrid and Ragnhild; the bridegroom's parents, Princess Josephine Charlotte of Belgium and Prince Carl Bernadotte of Sweden. Canon H. G. Rorison, the chaplain to the host, the Earl of Strathmore, was to have officiated. But, at the eleventh hour, he backed out. A Danish substitute was found. He turned out to minister to an obscure church for Danish seamen in Newcastle-on-Tyne.

Margaret returned to Glamis, the place where she was born, along with her mother. In an excess of caution, one assumes, they skipped the service but attended the reception. There was some talk of the prince losing his title, but in the end, he kept it, and no one seemed unduly shocked at the presence of the British queen and her daughter. As for Princess Margaret, perhaps the message, however veiled and indirect, was that to be divorced was not as bad as all that.

By the time of Elizabeth's Coronation in 1953, Peter Townsend had known Sir Alan "Tommy" Lascelles for almost a decade—first, as one of his lowly equerries and eventually, he believed, as a friend. It is conceivable, however, that recently Lascelles began to suspect Townsend's motives. He had, after all, been with the party on the historic royal trip to South Africa in 1947 and, with his finely tuned instincts, wondered just how much the princess's interest in her constant companion was strictly disinterested. And vice versa. At Margaret's twenty-first birthday party in Balmoral, on August 21, 1951, Lascelles decided the time had come to step in.

Among those in the party was Johnny Dalkeith, whom Townsend described as "wartime sailor, red-haired, tweedy and droll."[77] He continued, "Tommy Lascelles favored Johnny (as husband for Princess Margaret)"—perhaps with reason, since Johnny's mother, the Duchess of Buccleuch, was a member of the Lascelles family.

"Tommy remarked to me, 'Dalkeith and the Princess were making sheep's eyes at each other last night at dinner,' That, as far as Tommy was concerned, apparently clinched matters."[78] If the main point of the observation was to warn off Peter, it had no effect. Sometime in 1953, Lascelles's worst fears were realized when Townsend informed him of his and Margaret's decision to marry. Townsend wrote that "Tommy remained seated, regarding me darkly while I stood before him and told him, very quietly, the facts: Princess Margaret and I were in love . . . (A)ll that Tommy could say was, 'You must be either mad or bad.' I confess I had hoped for a more helpful reaction."[79]

A Pawn in the Game

The date was Wednesday, February 18, 1953. The queen and Prince Philip were entertaining the King of Greece at dinner, and, Chips Channon wrote, they were all depressed. The princess had dropped her thunderbolt that she was engaged to the very equerry who had just opened the door to the guests. It was the Duke of Windsor crisis all over again twenty years later. There was an enormous row, and the princess took to her bed with gastric flu. The queen was stern, and the prince backed her up. The rest of the family was in despair. Channon blamed the Queen Mother for not seeing what was happening. She should have stopped it at once. "Now everyone was against her," he wrote, adding that once this was generally known, "there would be an explosion."[80]

The frantic, long, drawn-out struggle to prevent Princess Margaret from marrying a commoner will no doubt be seen by historians as one more fight in a centuries-old battle between the monarchy and the circle around them—what used to be called "the barons." Much blood was shed in such power struggles until the ultimate prize, the power of the purse, was seized by Parliament. Those who inherited the titles as king and emperor, or what was once the most powerful nation in the world and was still powerful, were vanquished.

What was left behind were empty titles and all the appurtenances of supreme power—the jewels, the castles, the ceremony and rituals, the trappings of vast wealth, and the meaningless backings away—bows and curtseys of the subjects in name only. The king himself operated in a kind of emotional twilight zone where to have any feelings at all about this historic standoff was to threaten the status quo, with who knows what revolutionary implications. Better to play along and do nothing. King George V busied himself with postage stamps. His son, George VI, became a crack shooter of game. Kings might, greatly daring, venture out into their domains once in a while, in a harmless sort of way, as when Edward VIII went down into a coal mine, or George VI played doubles in Wimbledon. Whatever their own feelings might be concerned, the Royals had to know who was really in charge. Any burst of feeling was a threat.

Edward VIII found this to be true even before he was officially crowned king. Perhaps he did not realize just how formidable an adversary he had in Lascelles, or just how contemptuous Lascelles had been when he was still the heir apparent, in his fervent hope that he would fall off a horse and kill himself. This fight over power had to do with the king's stated intention to marry a lady from Baltimore, Maryland, who had had two other husbands. Lascelles no doubt told him, without too much embroidering of the facts, that he could have Wallis Warfield Simpson as his bride, or he could have the throne, but that he could not have both. The whole muted tone of Edward VIII's memoir, *A King's Story*, has to do with his disbelief that someone else could tell him whom he could marry. To him, it sounded like the last straw. He did not put it that way, but it shines through every word. Perhaps he counted on his enormous public popularity. Perhaps he thought the aristocracy, headed by Lascelles in particular, would back off. They remained opposed. The Duke of Windsor abdicated, left England, and married the love of his life. Another battle won.

Lascelles, now in his sixties, was dealing with another issue, and a new monarch, like her uncle: new to the job, but much more malleable. This time the problem was not the queen's wishes but those of her headstrong and wayward sister. In falling for Townsend, the princess cannot have been aware of the consequences to her sister's private secretary, who held sway in the social pyramid he headed. In such a tightly graded social structure, one in which a servant faced grave consequences if he entered the dining room of someone further up the pecking order, and where one's own status is measured in millimeters, the idea that his lowly equerry might rise far beyond him by marrying a princess was not to be tolerated.

Lascelles, a gifted diarist, has been rightly celebrated for his revealing insights into the family he served. What has not been much discussed is his own reasons for taking the job in the first place. For that, one needs to revisit the matter of Churchill's hat.

On the tumultuous day in 1945 when the Allied victory over Nazi Germany was at last celebrated and the great Prime Minister Churchill joined the king and queen to wave to the crowds on the royal balcony and dropped his hat on a chair, he incidentally set in motion a gesture that possibly revealed an aspect of Lascelles's character. On the pretext of being able to tell his grandchildren what he had done, Lascelles put the black homburg on his own head. One cannot know exactly what he was thinking as the immense crowds roared their approval outside the door. But the gesture would suggest several interpretations. Of course, he admired the prime minister. Perhaps, just for that tiny second, he wanted to be prime minister. Perhaps the idea went through his head that those outside were getting all the applause, but he had engineered it all behind the scenes. He was the power behind the throne. If, instead of Churchill's hat, the king had left his crown on the chair, would Lascelles have picked it up and put it on? We will never know.

What we do know about his character is that he was jealous of his prerogatives. He sent Townsend to a job as air attaché in Brussels on such short notice that the Battle of Britain hero, let alone his diplomatic hosts, had no idea what he was supposed to do, if anything. He arrived from London in his small English Ford, laden with luggage, on July 15, just two days before Princess Margaret was due to return from a trip to Rhodesia. One newspaper, with shades of *Jane Eyre* no doubt in mind, reported the move to separate them had the "ring of Victorian melodrama." Geoffrey Fisher, the Archbishop of Canterbury, with all the authority of his office, said there was no truth to the rumor at all; it was all a newspaper "stunt." When the news of Townsend's posting reached Nairobi, the princess became ill and went to bed for two days. "That could hardly have surprised people," the paper commented.[81]

A note in the diary of Chips Channon, the indefatigable diarist who was not an admirer of Sir Alan "Tommy" Lascelles, and with reference to Buckingham Palace's notorious infestations of rats and mice, observed that in the palace, "*tous les rats sont gris*." ("In the palace, all the rats are gray.")[82]

To those following events, which rapidly meant "most newspaper readers," it became clear enough that formidable forces were trying to stop the affair. And, as important as he was, Lascelles was far from being the only one. Constant dinner parties swirled around the Abdication Crisis of 1936, when there were such "deciders" as Lord Beaverbrook; the equally formidable Esmond Harmsworth, 2nd Viscount Rothermere, a Conservative politician and owner of the *Daily Mail*; the sixth Baton Brownlow, an influential courtier; and Walter (later, Lord) Monckton, the king's solicitor. They all agreed at an all-male dinner party one night that "the marriage cannot be allowed to take place."[83] The king had to yield to the will of the courtiers and nobles in the galaxy constantly revolving and scheming at the foot of his throne. It was almost easy to pry him out of office because, as he was known to confess, he did not like being the king anyway. Now, barely twenty years later, a mere princess was raising objections; the same group rose up en masse to confront her, like Lewis Carroll's pack of cards in *Alice through the Looking Glass*. They would beat her away. It almost looked easy.

The first thing Lascelles did was to inform the queen that an obscure act of Parliament, the Royal Marriages Act of 1772, had never been repealed. The Act stipulated that, until she was twenty-five years old, Margaret would need her sister's consent to marry. Unfortunately, the queen was titular head of the Church of England, which did not recognize divorce. Therefore, she could not give her consent.

If Margaret was willing to wait until she was twenty-five, she would then only need the consent of the prime minister and his cabinet. Lascelles had already sounded out Winston Churchill whose succinct advice was, "Get rid of him." Lascelles was all for shipping Townsend off to a desert island somewhere, but this was judged too harsh, so banishment to Brussels was decided upon. Interestingly enough, the view of the princess does not seem to have been consulted, and neither was that of her sister, the queen. Had George VI still been alive, things might have been different. The story goes that once pronouncement had been made for Townsend's future—or lack of it—Lascelles made his way to Ascot, which the queen happened to be frequenting that afternoon, and told her what had been decided.

"When his story was done (the Queen) burst out, 'Why doesn't anybody *tell* me anything?'"[84]

It seemed Lascelles was always being given the role of the bearer of bad news because he was trained to show no emotion. As Lord Salisbury remarked approvingly, he was "as close as the grave."[85]

Princess Margaret waited with whatever patience she could muster—at this stage in anyone's life, two years is an eternity—to marry the love of her life. During this period, they wrote to each other constantly and made secret phone calls. In her campaign to marry Peter, she had acquired an unexpected ally. Her new lady-in-waiting, Iris Peake, fair-haired and blue-eyed, had recently taken over after Jenny Bevan resigned to get married. Iris, daughter of Lady Jane, whose father was the seventh Earl of Essex, and Osbert Peake, a barrister and Conservative MP, was seven years her senior and had faced similar hurdles. Like many other well-born aristocrats of the period, Iris Peake had spent her war years working as a clerk for M16, the British Secret Service. There she met and fell in love with one of its agents, George Blake. He was not yet the famous (or infamous) double agent he would become, but was certainly well-educated, charming and highly personable. They became engaged. But then her parents objected because he was Jewish.

In due course, Iris became enamored of another implausible charmer, Captain Oliver Dawnay, the Queen Mother's private secretary, who happened to be a married man with children. In her case, it all ended happily after Captain Dawney was free to marry, and they lived happily together for twenty-five years. But this took time, and in the interim, the lady-in-waiting was facing the same hurdles as the lady she was serving, and very ready to help in whatever way was needed. When it seemed that letters between Peter and Margaret might be being intercepted, Iris suggested that Peter use her own address in Belgravia. As for Margaret's letters, the latter would post them in a letterbox on the street.[86] No doubt she was equally helpful when the time came to arrange for a secret meeting between Margaret and Peter in the summer of 1954.

Traveling under an assumed name, that of a "Mr. Carter," Townsend flew to London in July, went straight to the bookshop in Harrods, and met Margaret, one assumes, perusing the newest best-sellers. They were bundled into a car at a side entrance and driven through the main gates of Clarence House, with no one any the wiser and particularly not the press. He wrote: "The long year of waiting, of penance and solitude, seemed to have passed in a twinkling."

They spent two hours in rapt conversation.

". . . all we knew was that, for the present, our feelings had not changed," Townsend wrote.[87]

A year later, they still planned to marry. Margaret's twenty-fifth birthday was arriving on August 21 of that year, and the queen's embargo would no longer be an issue. But the princess still needed to get the approval of Anthony Eden, who became prime minister in April 1955, and his cabinet as well. That, they reasoned with some justification, would just be a formality. Eden himself had been divorced and so had two other members of his cabinet. How could they refuse?

After the euphoria of the immediate postwar years, the Iron Curtain that Churchill had predicted descended onto Europe and the Cold War was at its height.

"Communism was entrenched throughout Europe," Derek Brown wrote in *The Guardian*.[88] "The French were being chased out of Indo-China and were engaged in a vicious civil war in Algeria; the infant state of Israel had fought off the combined might of six Arab armies, and Britain was trying to hold down insurgents in Cyprus, Kenya and Malaya."

Even more important, the new leader of Egypt, Gamal Abdul Nasser, having been elected in 1954 the year before, was in the process of seizing control of the Suez Canal, a vital shipping lane between the Middle East and Europe bringing crude oil to the nations whose economies depended upon it, Britain included. The canal was built by British and French engineers in the 1880s and, to Egyptians, represented British imperial dominance at its most aggressive.

But there was more to the issue than that. Eden had just found out, in September 1955, that there was a direct connection between Nasser's ambitions to take control of the Canal and a great power lined up behind him, i.e., the Soviet Union. Eden had just received concrete evidence that the Soviets were providing military assistance through a scheme called "the Czech arms deal."[89]

In other words, the Suez Canal affair had the potential to become a war by proxy between the great powers, a decade after World War II. The atom bomb, directed at Japan, had ended hostilities rather fast but was now a terrifying possibility for any power that wanted to unleash it because its effects would immediately be unleashed on the aggressor. It was now superseded by the hydrogen bomb, an even more appalling prospect.

Speaking on this issue at a debate in the House of Commons, Churchill said in 1954: "I said, they [members] must keep a sense of proportion. If ten million are killed in London by a hydrogen bomb, Suez will not seem of much importance to those who are left alive."[90]

Eden was nevertheless confident that America—where General Eisenhower was now president—would back him if Britain did go to war against Egypt, as looked increasingly likely. Still, he needed the political backing of the leader in the House of Lords, not only to quell fractious members of the Labour Party but his own Conservative troops as well. He was the fifth Marquess of Salisbury, whom he and his friends called "Bobbety."

A man of impeccable credentials—one of his ancestors was chief advisor to Queen Elizabeth I—he and Eden were old friends. Eden knew that, in the cause of preserving the power and prestige of empire, and one that was rapidly dwindling, he and Bobbety were united.

However, Bobbety had already put his old friend on notice that if he allowed the princess to marry a divorced commoner, he, Bobbety, would resign. It was not even a secret. Bobbety had already declared as such. He had resigned twice before over "matters of principle." Eden knew he meant it.

Eden, who had only become prime minister six months before after years of patiently waiting for Churchill to resign, had a lot to prove. A successful outcome of the Suez Canal affair was crucially important to him personally. So, it is easy to believe that the price of a political victory for him depended upon destroying the marital prospects of a princess. No one knew that at the time, least of all the couple involved.

Margaret was at the absolute peak of her popularity in those years, and the notion that someone had conspired to prevent her from marrying evoked an instinctive sympathy from the public. In May 1955, she had just returned from a trip to the West Indies when she was invited to a welcome home lunch by the Lord Mayor of London in Mansion House. A huge crowd gathered, blocking a side road, men doffing hats, and every face turned towards her like daisies to the sun when she appeared at a window. The surprising, spontaneous tribute seemed an almost overwhelming demonstration of good will.

It was not really so surprising. As Churchill had remarked, when he first heard the news (and until he changed his mind) it was really quite romantic to think the king's daughter would want to marry a dashing pilot, hero of the Battle of Britain. He thought better of that, but the average British voter did not make the hairsplitting distinctions favored by the Royal Family: that divorce was acceptable but not remarriage. All the polls by the big London dailies showed that after a terrible war the mood was "Live and let live." Why shouldn't she find a little happiness? She deserved it.

Three months later, the princess was at Balmoral for the weekend of her twenty-fifth birthday on August 21, which happened to fall on a Sunday. The day before, while Townsend was riding a chestnut mare in the Prix de Cyrano at Ostend, Margaret was at a sale to benefit Crathie Church, half a mile from Balmoral.

Townsend won his race unharmed, but as Margaret was leaving the sale, she tripped and fell full length.

She was not seriously injured, but her ankle was affected. When she went to church next morning, wearing, as befits a girl who has made the Ten Best Dressed Women list, a tight-fitting, bright pink dress with a flowered silk coat, she was limping noticeably. The officiating clergyman, in a top hat and tails, added on a spontaneous prayer for her: "Grant unto her now of Thy grace, so that she may find in Thee fulfilment of her heart's desires, that joy may be her heritage and peace her portion." At the kind words, "Princess Margaret's face flushed, and she clenched her handkerchief."[91]

That spring, every paper in Britain and the United States assumed all the obstacles had been removed and the princess and her "parfit knight" were free to marry following her twenty-fifth birthday in August 1955. The question they thought needed an answer was whether they would. In March, the big London paper, the *Daily Mirror*, tracked Townsend down in Brussels and wanted to know the answer. He hinted that the news would probably be good but begged not to be quoted.[92] A New York paper published the news that the royal chapel in St. James's Palace was being renovated for the royal marriage. The *Sunday Dispatch* in London, which supported the view that it was all a big stunt, complained "the Americans are at it again."[93] The princess was "more determined than ever" to marry, said *The People* (circulation: 500,000), the evidence for which was not provided.[94] Another paper suggested that the princess would be willing to yield on her rights to accession (she would now be third in line for the throne, behind toddler Charles and baby Anne).[95] One newspaper claimed to know that "the Queen Mother was supporting Margaret's desire to marry the officer," and another, that the Queen Mother was scouting for somewhere for the newlyweds to live in. Nobody had managed to get a quote out of the queen herself, which was not surprising, since she never commented on anything.

What was interesting was the editorial in autumn 1955 published by the *Manchester Guardian* just as speculation had reached its peak. In part, the paper observed:

"... In the first place, the months of discussion have brought out that the mass of people believe firmly that the Princess should marry whom she wants, whether noble or commoner, single man or divorced, so long as he is a British Protestant.

"There has been growing impatience with obsolete forms like the Royal Marriage Act and technicalities a spiteful king introduced to hurt his family 180 years ago . . . What nonsense it is.

"Then it has been assumed by some that the Princess' marriage with a commoner must necessarily lead to her renunciation of the succession. Why should this be? Her accession is a very remote chance . . . And even if it were not remote, would the idea of a non-royal consort be so terrible, if our democracy means anything?

"There remains the question of the attitude of the Church of England, or rather a section of the Church of England, and of the Roman Catholic Church to marriage with the innocent partner of a divorce."[96]

By this the *Guardian* referred to the practice, universal at that time, of awarding divorce to the person affected by the other partner's infidelity, as had been the case with Townsend. (His wife Rosemary had had an affair during the marriage.) Townsend was therefore blameless; the guilt fell on his ex-wife.

"On that there is only thing to be said. If we can have a Prime Minister, Cabinet ministers and judges who are 'innocent parties' we can without feeling unduly disturbed in our moral latitude to the Queen's sister."

All of this eminent good sense was being aired just at the moment when the couple in question were finally about to reunite. The princess, her eyes dancing, was glimpsed in the car that was delivering her to Clarence House after an overnight train trip from Balmoral on Thursday, October 13. If there was a particularly joyful look in her eye, the professional watchers missed it. However, there was no mistaking the body language as Townsend, arriving from Brussels the same day in his small green Renault. As reporters looked on smilingly, he took both hands off the wheel, his face beaming. Then he, too, disappeared inside Clarence House.

On Friday, October 14, Townsend was to be found in Lowndes Square, outside the house of the Marquess of Abergavenny, and walked through the usual jostling mob of reporters, photographers and well-wishers, carrying two books and a leather riding jacket. He was going away for the weekend and would not say where. But the *New York Times* knew. He and she were spending the weekend at Allenby Hall—the country home of Margaret's cousin, Mrs. John Lycett Wills and her husband, which was not far from Windsor Castle, where the Queen Mother was staying for the weekend.[97]

By then the usual mob of journalists and photographers followed them as far as they could but were barred from closer access by heavy gates and guards. Nevertheless, they received bulletins of a sort from the Wills's seven-year-old daughter.

"Margaret drank champagne with mummy and Peter for some time before dinner," she said. "They were all laughing and seemed very happy."[98]

There was also a one-paragraph report from the *New York Daily News* that added substantially to this comment. It appears this was a special dinner, one to celebrate the engagement of Margaret and Peter. He gave her a diamond ring. The article added that the princess would not wear the ring publicly until after her engagement was officially announced.[99]

The next day—Saturday, October 15—the heavy gates of Allenby Hall swung open, and a royal car flashed past. In it was Captain Oliver Dawnay, one of the Queen Mother's equerries.

Twenty minutes passed, and the same car raced back out, heading in the direction of Windsor Castle. It seemed that the courtier had brought some disturbing news.[100]

There were new requirements being imposed upon the princess if she intended to marry Group Captain Townsend. First of all, she must give up her rights to accession, for herself and her children. Second, she must give up her title; she could no longer be addressed as "Her Royal Highness." She could no longer live in a grace-and-favor mansion. She could no longer expect a yearly income from the public purse. She could not be married in church, and she would have to live abroad, time not yet specified. The hasty arrival of the royal vehicle and the equerry from the Queen Mother's household appeared to indicate that the Queen Mother knew about the terms being imposed and wanted to warn her daughter.

In the daily press reports that follow the drama during that fateful month of 1955, there is a reference to the princess's willingness to step down from her position as heir to the throne (she was third in line at that point, behind young Charles and baby Anne, so the possibility was already remote). But not, it would seem, the full list of prohibitions—loss of status and income—that were spelled out for her that day. These were presumably to act as a disincentive and satisfy the objections of Lord Salisbury, that presence behind the scenes whose every whim had to be granted for fear he might suddenly bolt.

The larger irony, seldom mentioned, had to do with the Church of England's opposition to divorce in the first place,[101] particularly since the church itself came into existence some hundreds of years before when a British king (Henry VIII) could not get a legal divorce from the Pope in Rome. The ground seemed to have shifted quite remarkably in the intervening years. Now the issue was not so much the importance of a male heir, although this had been a factor in the opposition to Edward VIII's choice of a woman who could not have children, but a Royal Family's need for impeccable respectability. One occasionally had to upset a few people—an unmarried princess, for instance. Her private wants counted for little in this scenario. Here was a girl who had all the men in the world after her. And she had just had her own Rolls Royce built to her specifications. What more did she want? She should shut up.

Behind the scenes, the prime minister had to stop Bobbety from resigning—again—by presenting the princess with what must have looked like miserable terms out of a desire to punish her. And that was what she would lose in marrying Peter: title, status, money, even her country as well. Perhaps her family would turn their backs on her, much as they had done with Uncle David, refusing to have her in the house, much less call her a daughter. All this, one assumes, was Eden's way of placating Bobbety, whose shadow hovered over this whole sad episode. And he must have been placated, because he did not resign. Would any princess accept banishment, figuratively or literally? How could anyone, even a hero who had helped stop the German invasion, make up for what she would lose? The situation was equally desperate from Eden's point of view: another vital link of empire was about to be destroyed. The princess must be stopped—even her fiancé saw that. It was sad, but everyone had to make sacrifices. Even if the lady in question had no idea what else was at stake.

What is missing from this picture is what Princess Margaret felt when she received the news. Her official biographer, Christopher Warwick, tried to draw her out on this point when he interviewed her for his book, published in 2002. She refused to talk about it.

"It's over and done with," she said.[102]

Naturally, their letters were the best insights into what both thought and felt. This would then have become clear, since they wrote to each other almost every day for two years, and particularly the communications between them during the month of October. Townsend's letters to her are in the Royal Archives and closed until 2030.

As for Margaret's letters to him, these have probably been destroyed. There are two explanations for this. The first, from him, was that he threw them all away.

"I was in the middle of the African veldt, miles from anywhere, when I took out a pile of letters and . . . tore them up and threw them to the winds . . ."[103] According to newspaper accounts, that is not how it happened. They report that in April of 1958, Townsend, his son Giles, sixteen, and Hugo, twelve, had stopped off in Paris to spend the night in a Left Bank hotel. It was the end of a three-week tour of France and Spain, as well as a visit to the Brussels World's Fair. Next day, Captain Townsend planned to escort his sons back to their British boarding schools.

Townsend made the elementary mistake of leaving most of their luggage in the car. In those days, if one had a private car, even if locked, it was automatically targeted on the Paris streets, and opening it was child's play. Inside were two cameras, two suitcases, $1,000 in travelers' checks and currency, and other personal items. All vanished by morning, including a large envelope containing some important business papers. He seemed particularly concerned about those, and the word got around that they must be letters from the princess. Townsend denied it at the time, but this now seems likely.

Also included in the theft was his personal diary. Considered useless, it had been tossed onto the sidewalk, where some kind soul found it and turned it in to the police. Perhaps a large manila envelope, full of letters in English, did not seem worth anything either and ended up in the Seine.[104]

Princess Margaret's letters might have provided some clues to that October 17, 1955, when she discovered just what marrying Peter involved. But one photograph in particular is almost as good. It shows her in a car, lips slightly parted, eyes staring blankly ahead, in shock and despair.

What is also missing is what Eden planned to do if, despite every argument that was being made to deter her, Margaret declared that she was going to marry Townsend anyway. This is the subject discussed in a secret file that was placed in the National Archives at the time and only released 50 years later, after her death in 2002.[105] The file, in the form of cryptic notes and incomplete drafts of letters, most of them by the prime minister himself and some in his neat hand, nevertheless establishes the surprising information that the government would make handsome concessions if she insisted on marrying. Not only would the princess *not* lose her title or position, but she would continue to have access to the public purse. Of course, she would not have to leave the country.

This astonishing piece of news, to the effect that she would be showered with benefits if she went ahead with her fool plan, is testimony to the game of high stakes being played here. When she wrote to him asking if the government would step down on its requirement that she leave the country, for instance, he would not answer that. She had to make a formal request to her sister first. It was a thoroughly treacherous response. She only knew that she had an enormous amount to lose if she said she was going to marry—status, income, maybe even her right to live in England. The penalties were harsh. That was all she knew. Eden's refusal to say what all the options were until she chose, demonstrates first of all, the answer many wanted, including Salisbury, and the way she was being cynically manipulated. The public statement she made on October 31, 1955, to the effect that she would not marry, surprised everyone and especially the newspapers and magazines which, to judge from the reports, were not aware of what she had to lose. In fact, they had been confidently expecting that she *would* marry, for months. The huge and glassy *Life* magazine, which was published that same day, ran a headline at top right saying that she would and then had to pull the edition for a rewrite, no doubt at vast expense, replacing it with something innocuous. Meanwhile, the secret file vanished and stayed under wraps for the next fifty years.

Townsend saw the issue clearly. His immediate reaction was to leave the scene at once, cut his ties with Brussels and embark on a tour around the world—getting as far away physically as he wanted to be, mentally and emotionally. He said later, "I was made to look ridiculous. For two years I couldn't breathe. I hadn't the courage to open a newspaper."[106] His autobiography, *Time and Chance*, published almost twenty-five years later, in which he reviewed all that had happened that fateful month of October 1955, proves that he never knew anything about the secret offer.

At her death in September 2022, Queen Elizabeth was praised not only for her steadfast service, but, it was said, for her wise counsel to the many prime ministers who came and went during her long reign. If it was true later, it was not the case in the early years. She would have been counseled by Lascelles, to the effect that she had to avoid political choices at all costs, even when her own sister's happiness was concerned. When Eden explained to her that Salisbury's opposition to the marriage was the main stumbling block, and how desperately he, Eden, needed his support over a war with Egypt, that was politics, and she had to stand back.

Eden was too much a politician not to realize that his own popularity was directly connected with Margaret's. Poll after poll, huge majorities wanted her to marry the man she loved. Very well. If she was willing to give it all up for Peter, Eden would change his tune. Her love had survived the test. Now, hey presto, they could marry in Westminster Abbey after all. She could keep her title, her funds, and her privileges. All was forgiven. Eden was working on this secret offer behind the scenes, even as he publicly espoused the other. The moment she made her announcement on October 31, 1955, the secret file was buried in the Royal Archives for decades; it did not appear until 2004, two years after her death. They were concealing a vast conspiracy that included Buckingham Palace and the queen that, one believes, ruined the life of a princess. The conspiracy swept Queen Elizabeth II into its bitter path as a major player. Without knowing it, a treacherous, sordid little game was being played, with Margaret and Peter as pawns.

Salisbury's determination to stop Princess Margaret from marrying Peter had many strange consequences. After Egyptians seized the Suez Canal, Anthony Eden, Churchill's stalwart backer throughout World War II and now Britain's new prime minister, received the votes he needed from both houses of Parliament to declare war against Egypt. Joined by Israel and France, he promptly sent troops in 1956. Powerful voices—notably Russia, the United States, and the United Nations—forced an end to the fight in favor of a political solution.

Eden, after years of patient waiting, lost political face and was forced to resign from office after less than two years (April 1955–January 1957). His career was at an end.

On the home front, Peter Townsend, prevented from marrying Princess Margaret, went on to a happy marriage and more children with a young woman who looked just like her. Princess Margaret, prevented from marrying Peter, needed to save face and did so by marrying a talented photographer, as she later admitted, on the rebound. It was fated to end badly. The relationship between the queen and her sister was going to be tarnished when the princess rightly suspected the queen had something to do with the result.

What the so-called scandal did do was gradually remove the stigma of divorce itself so that future royal generations could marry and divorce without losing face. Not to mention losing their titles and much else.

The chances are that she did find out something after she had made her great renunciation, and it was too late. What would she feel then? Ill with rage because her sister, somehow, had not smuggled out three words of advice, "Just say *yes*"?

Would she feel betrayed?

Sometime afterwards Lascelles loftily told a friend, "Ever since the breach with Townsend (the Princess) has become selfish and hard and wild." Peter had been her lover, her solace, her defender and, most of all, her escape from the stifling world she was trapped in. Now he had fled, and there was no one else.

All of a sudden, she seemed to have turned against her sister. In her dealings with the queen, a friend said, she had become "informal to the point of coarseness." At a picnic in Balmoral, Margaret threw a dishcloth into her sister's face in a fury.[107] The princess believed that Lascelles was the one who had ruined her life and refused to speak to him. She was wrong.

Chapter 8

Margaret Learns to Lie

"Sigh out a lamentable tale of things,/Done long
ago, and ill done."
—John Ford, *The Lover's Melancholy*

For someone who had, by the conventions of her social milieu, become an old maid at age twenty-six—never mind about having this disastrous state of affairs forced upon her—the princess seemed remarkably unaffected in the days and weeks that followed. Despite her high position, a daughter of the king had been defeated by obligations and expectations that essentially left her defenseless against the ingenious stratagems and outright falsehoods used against her.

Yet, unlike Violetta, Verdi's heroine in *La Traviata* (a title which can be translated as "the one who goes astray"), she did not follow the conventions of what she ought to do next. After nobly spurning her own devoted lover, Violetta had the good sense to get ill, go offstage, and die. Princess Margaret perversely refused to do likewise. A few days later, she was out dancing with new partners. She laughed and sang into the small hours. She wore diamonds and tiaras and drove the press mad with frustration.

At her first big appearance since her public October renunciation, a full-dress affair in the Palace for seven hundred diplomats that November 1955, the princess was radiant in a spectacular evening gown of pink and white satin embroidered with roses.[1] The press looked in vain for the fatal flaw, the faint smile and the ducked head. Instead, as she pirouetted between a fashion show, yet one more charity tea, a variety show, a nightclub performance by Lena Horne and, at the circus in December, she "threw back her pretty head and laughed out loud."[2] Whatever could be wrong with her?

At Clarence House, there might be a comfortable physical distance between the Queen Mother and her daughter, but little emotional separation. Properly speaking, Princess Margaret had not left home and probably never would. Daughters who go to boarding school, university, and then apply for jobs or begin careers, have started on the fitful, largely unconscious, necessary testing of their own strengths that ushers in adulthood. Even princes were allowed to fight it out in boarding schools and subjected to the indignities of a lowly sailor's duties. Princesses stayed at home until they "came out" and were expected to find new roles as chatelaines of lucrative aristocratic estates as fast as possible.

Mummy was always around and knew what to do in the self-preservative job of eking out her own private space by constructing a fake one for public consumption. Cecil Beaton, who photographed the Queen Mother repeatedly, knew she had a mask but discovered, in one of their meetings in 1970, that she was capable of showing the person behind it.

"She talked about a bad dream she couldn't get rid of, how she was afraid of always being late," he wrote, and went on to give some saucy imitations of old generals playing cards. She was adorable.[3]

No doubt she had drilled her daughters about punctuality and correct attire. But her invariable gift was a smile and how much it could convey. Beaton also wrote, "I have never seen . . . such a marvelous regard as came from those incredibly bright eyes . . . (with their) look of interest and compassion."

The Queen Mother always entered a room with a smile of anticipation wherever she went. Much as she had stepped daintily over the ruins during the London Blitz, looking composed and smiling in her high heels and pearls, no one knew what an effort it was privately, or how scared she really was.

Her bright, sensitive daughter, a born performer, had begun to assume the same confident smile in her public appearances in a show of unity that did not always reflect what was happening behind the scenes. Take the issue of marrying Peter, for instance. They argued bitterly. In August 1955, after reaching her twenty-fifth birthday, Princess Margaret apologized for "having blown up at intervals" over her mother's objections.[4] Her mother explained an "agony of mind" along with all the practical problems that would surround such an unorthodox choice. Perhaps Margaret knew that Mummy had sought the advice of Lascelles when the subject came up two years before, which cannot have made her very happy.[5]

The Queen Mother's agony of mind, as she expressed it, can be imagined easily enough. Peter Townsend was the Royal Family's special favorite, the recipient of their particular affection. George VI had even called him "the son I never had." However, the example of her husband's brother, fifteen years before, had put into stark relief the awful fate that befell a member of the Royal Family who married the wrong person. Everybody knew what the remedy was, when a great man fell in love and if divorce meant ruin. He carried on a loving friendship behind the scenes. Even their wives were allowed this time-worn solution—discreetly of course. Why couldn't Margaret do the same? No one could prevent her from seeing Peter. Discreetly, of course. Smiling took care of rumors and gossip, if you were clever.

So, the princess moved on, and her smiles were quite genuine. One newspaper announced, "Princess Trills of Lizzie's Kills." She went around with a new escort, Lord Plunkett—handsome, younger, and unattached. She was maintaining "a merry pace," said another. The papers dusted off, again, the idea of Billy Wallace as the Secret Chosen One. There was even a confident prediction she would marry the Prince Bertil of Sweden. (He had made the classic mistake of welcoming her to his country.) But then the prince, with remarkable speed and asperity, made it known he had no plan to do any such thing. (The princess said nothing.) Another dead end.[6]

Peter Townsend's memoir, *Time and Chance,* reveals him as a writer of considerable natural gifts, including one for vivid portraits of character and, at the same time, a reluctance to express his own feelings. In the case of the long-drawn-out agony of attempting to marry a princess, he was in a particularly awkward position. According to protocol, he could not ask her in the ordinary way. She had to ask him. This barrier appears to have led to a reluctance even to reveal his own passionate longing for such a union. He appeared to feel that propriety required him to do nothing and say nothing, in case he might appear rash and vulgar and further reduce his chances. In any event, as a servant of the Crown, it did not matter what he thought or felt. He had no status. Authority held the cards—as he discovered when he was banished to Brussels in 1953, more or less on 24 hours' notice. What if he had to leave England permanently?

The press either didn't know, or didn't care. They peppered him with the same question, and for days and days he had to reply with the same noncommittal responses. They were relentless. They dropped out of trees and popped up out of ditches.[7] He had to force himself to be polite long after he began to feel desperate, hounded, persecuted. The fact that he could say nothing didn't mean that he was not secretly concerned about the odds against them. Not only was the princess being presented with punishing terms, but Lord Salisbury, the celebrated and influential Leader of the House of Lords and close friend of the Royal Family, had vowed to step down if they married. Townsend suspected that Salisbury's political support was crucial to the prime minister at that particular moment. He had already guessed the truth. What Townsend was apparently never to learn was the existence of the Secret Offer.

Even if he did learn about it belatedly, one wonders if he was too exhausted to care. He wrote that the "trial by public ordeal"[8] and the "crushing weight of world opinion" brought him close to the breaking point.[9] He wrote, "The story was ended; the book was closed."[10] There remained "only the glow, once shared, of tenderness, constancy and singleness of heart."[11] That was his verdict in 1979, but it was not quite as simple as that.

Perhaps as a natural result of being so hemmed in, once freed, physically and emotionally, Peter decided to go around the world. He had it all worked out. Norman Barrymaine, a personal friend and author of *The Peter Townsend Story* (published in 1958), wrote that the sudden decision had been calculated down to the last decimal point. Townsend would visit sixty countries in eighty weeks, a total of sixty thousand miles. Since he had decided to do much of it by road, he needed just the right kind of car. That, for the adventurers of the time, could only be the Land Rover.

The 1950s and 1960s were the golden years for this off-road, four-wheel drive car, the English version of an American station wagon, the kind of car one could subject to all kinds of off-road hazards and would refuse to break down. It had been launched by the Rover Company at their factory in the small town of Solihull in Warwickshire in 1947. The car, reliable as it was, was bound to break down somewhere. Could he possibly join the assembly line for a week? He was happy to work as an unpaid mechanic. That way, he could learn the intricacies of design and what might be expected from its engine after taking such a beating. It was the middle of July 1956.[12] The news made a three-paragraph item at the bottom of a column—a "filler."

There was another, larger article five days later in the *Sunday Express*, one of Lord Beaverbrook's personal fiefdoms. It seems the Viscount Hambleden, owner of the British bookstore chain of WK Smith, known all over the British Isles, also owner of a storied estate in the Thames Valley, was having a house party that weekend of July 14–15. He and his wife's estate in the Chilterns was not far from Henley-on-Thames. It included a manor house, once a hiding place for Charles I during the Civil War, forty-four houses and cottages, village shops, and the indispensable pub. Princess Margaret was one of the guests. Townsend was back in England, so it followed that he must also be in hiding there somewhere. When asked, the hostess politely declined to say. Reporters knew enough not to bother trying to waylay the gentleman himself. They descended en masse on his mother, who had been known to give artless answers. This time that door shut with a bang.[13]

The princess was, of course, protected from this kind of harassment by the hovering of her detectives. Still, she was vulnerable to the daily papers, baying for blood or, at the very least, a scratch or two as they launched speculations that could be blown up to support three-column headlines. Even the subject herself, if she was Royal, had only to yawn, be photographed with a long, elegant cigarette holder in public, or kick off her shoes in a cinema to guarantee an extra fifteen-thousand circulation for a big London daily. Safe inside their towers, the pursued might have been entertaining the idea that, since the press would print anything, perhaps that eagerness could be turned to advantage. Just how cleverly you could do that was not worked out until a later arrival, the princess who turned heads and touched hearts a few decades later. Getting even, somehow, was what you did in those days, turned into a kind of parlor game when Princess Margaret was growing up. How soon would she try it? It meant knowing when to hint, when to tease, when to deny with dignity, and when to engage the help of trustworthy friends with good journalistic connections. What fun it was to launch a rumor that she knew was not quite a lie, but not the truth either. Then watch the dailies to see which one was the first to bite.

We have a clear portrait of her day in the interregnum following the Great Renunciation and before her decision to marry Antony Armstrong-Jones. This account was from someone who saw her daily. In fact, he was living at Clarence House. He was her valet, David John Payne, who had, like everyone else who was part of the Royal Household, signed an agreement not to describe his stay or anything he heard. This blanket rule had already been broken by Marion Crawford, with serious consequences to her, and others would eventually follow. Payne was stopped by a court order from publishing his memoir, *My Life with Princess Margaret*, in the United Kingdom and is not mentioned in indexes or quoted by royal biographers in that country. There was no such hurdle to the book's publication in the United States. A somewhat awkwardly abridged version appeared in *Good Housekeeping* of May 1961. Gold Medal books published the complete text in paperback. It is now considered rare and priced accordingly.

The day Payne went to apply for the job as the Princess's personal valet, his potential employer was presented with a tall (6'1"), well-built twenty-eight-year-old with the kind of bearing that makes itself felt after six years in the Royal Marines. However, Payne was in such a state of nerves he was sure she was bound to notice, and only had a brief impression of a small figure wearing a pink and white cotton dress, her dark hair "brushed into a bouffant style," and the distinct smell of some unidentifiable perfume. Despite his inner conviction that his chances of any job were about nil, there were a lot of reasons to want someone just like him. A former Marine might well act as a bodyguard if necessary—if there was a fire, for instance, or an intruder had been discovered. In fact, someone who could pick her up and carry her might well have been the first thing she thought of. She would take him. He couldn't believe his luck.

Even when he was given a tiny, not very appealing bedroom and received the bad news that his nocturnal companions would be her three pet dogs, Payne kept pinching himself. How could he, the son of a country bricklayer, have ended up here? There must be a mistake.

He describes Princess Margaret's day, beginning with breakfast in bed. That took two people. Payne would pick up a tray from some distant kitchen—these were always far away—and arrive at her door promptly at nine. A trolley was stationed in the corridor outside her bedroom. Payne would deposit her fastidious morning repast on it: tea in a china cup and a bowl of fresh fruit, usually a mix of bananas, grapes, oranges, and/or peaches, depending on the season.

At that point, he wrote, Ruby Gordon, Margaret's personal maid, would take charge. He wrote: "Mrs. Gordon—without waiting to knock—threw open the door . . . wheeled the trolley in, and drove it up to the bed." Then she would pull back the curtains and tidy up the room by picking up yesterday's dress and underwear, stockings here and there, and anything else she found.

Yesterday's shoes and the omnipresent cigarette lighter and holder went to Payne. With much meticulous scrubbing and polishing, the shoes must be returned to mint condition. The same attention had to be paid to the lighter. As for the holder, that took pipe cleaners and white methylated spirits. The sitting room was also on the agenda: dusting, replacing the water of the many displays of fresh flowers, and, in particular, removing used glasses from the drinks tray and bringing up the daily pitcher of fresh orange juice.

Then it was time for him to collect the mail, pick up her itinerary for the day's events, and do errands. He had about finished by eleven. The princess, having read all the papers, listened to the radio, and written letters, was ready for her bath. But not, one imagines, without a fond look at her collection of three photographs, grouped on a small table, of Peter Townsend.

Then, throwing off her "luxurious pink silk eiderdown," the princess would walk over her wall-to-wall carpeting and into her similarly equipped bathroom, on the theory, no doubt, that marble would be too frigid for the royal bare feet. The room's walls were tiled and equipped with much shelving for perfumes, miscellaneous equipment, and the cosmetics (that her valet was at pains to explain) she applied herself. She also arranged her own hairdo, unless it was a very special occasion requiring the ministrations of an expert.

While taking her bath, she kept up a running conversation with Ruby in the bedroom.

Ruby was one of the two Scottish sisters who had been hired as nursery maids and quickly made themselves indispensable. Each was now in charge of the queen and Princess Margaret respectively. Ruby was Margaret's dresser, meaning she was responsible for whatever outfits the princess wore that day, from hat to heels. She still looked after her every need. She was also the only one allowed to use the Princess's name. "Come along, Margaret," she would say briskly if her charge had an appointment that morning. "Time to get up." And if, as often happened, the princess went to bed late the night before, there would be a weak protest.

Ruby was also in earshot for the daily bath.

"Ruby, you have forgotten my bath salts." Or, "Ruby, what dress are you putting out for me today?"

The princess was remarkably helpless about little things. There was soap in her eye, and Ruby was needed immediately. Ruby would hurry in.[14]

All day long, the dogs were everywhere.[15] Keeping them walked, fed, and groomed was one of Payne's responsibilities. With one exception. This was a King Charles Spaniel named Roly, whom the princess bathed herself. A sullen and protesting Roly would be hauled off into the royal bathroom periodically to lose his doggie smell—or else. His mistress would be all ready for him, a skimpy pinafore not much protection over her usual immaculate attire. There would be a jug of perfumed soap at the ready. Then, with Payne's help, the protesting Roly would be lowered into the bathtub. The Princess would go at him with a will, scrubbing his coat with her fingernails until he was a mass of writhing soapsuds. By the time he emerged, everything was soaked, including his mistress. But it was all in good fun. Roly stopped minding once warm air was applied by a hair dryer, while his mistress gently combed out the knots with a comb. As she flicked his curls into place, she was crooning, "Pretty Roly. There's a lovely dog, isn't he . . . ?"[16]

We know from Hans Christian Andersen and his succinct portrait of a princess trying to get a good night's sleep that the way to pick her out from the crowd is by her perfectionism. As well as her irritation—not to say exasperation—with all those around her who fail her exacting standards. Payne records other examples of just how exacting a truly grand princess can turn out to be. On weekends, the princess, who was a tireless hostess, liked to entertain guests at the Royal Lodge, which had a swimming pool. This item became a particular cause for complaint, because the ground staff just plain weren't doing their job. It was always dirty, or so she claimed. One weekend, the princess had had enough. Payne was instructed to summon the gardeners responsible for the pool. Her expression of "pained outrage" said it all. They were in for it. He happened to be at the pool himself, arranging a tray of drinks, so he lingered to see what was going on. The two men on duty duly arrived.

"'Look at that," Margaret said, pointing at the pool. "Filthy. Take a look."

The unfortunate two peered over the water's edge and could distinctly see two autumn leaves floating on its pristine surface. What did they intend to do about it? The two men apologized profusely, removed the offending objects, and slunk away. Not enough! The next thing he knew, Payne's mistress, like an avenging angel, attacked the pool's waterline with a long-handled scrubbing brush with almost superhuman zeal to make sure it was quite, quite clean.[17]

On yet another occasion, she decided that something was very wrong with an immaculately trimmed hedge separating the rose garden from the lawn. In this case, it was not lacking in hygiene. She found fault with the design itself. Someone had set things up so that one could not easily go from the rose garden on one side to the lawn on the other. It was a bore to walk all around the hedge. She had a solution.

On the time-honored theory that if you want something done right, do it yourself, she rummaged around in the tool shed and its orderly rows of implements until she found a nice big, sharp set of shears. The shed subsequently looked, one gardener reported, "as if a tornado had hit it."[18] Then she went to work to make a hole in the hedge. It took quite a long time. According to the gardener, she "snipped and hacked, chopped and pulled at the hedge until she was calf-deep in a pile of severed branches. She worked away with . . . fierce concentration" and finally stepped back to admire her work. There it was, a magnificent hole. So convenient. One could now saunter between the two areas with no trouble at all. She retired justified, no doubt like some forest nymph, bedecked with twigs and leaves.

If one was spending one's every waking hour at the service of a particularly fierce and determined little person, one learned to sense her moods well in advance. Not that this, it turned out, was very difficult. Each morning at the same hour, with clockwork regularity (shades of George V) Payne's mistress, fully dressed and coiffed, would step out of the elevator in the main corridor. It was her valet's job to be there as the doors opened. As a rule, she smiled and greeted him pleasantly, wishing him good morning.

"What was the weather going to be like today?"

There was usually some special instruction for him. So he would follow along behind as she made for her sitting room. All would be well.

On the other hand, "[his] heart would sink if she stepped briskly out of the elevator, her head held high, glanced at me with a slight lift of an eyebrow, but not a word before marching along to the sitting room. . . . On really black days she hurried to her room and gave the door a resounding slam."[19] Those were the days when he knew, without being told, that a bottle of vodka should be added to the drinks tray along with the orange juice.

At lunch, in the right mood and with enough encouragement, she could "entertain the whole room" with devastating leers and winks, mercilessly recording the manners and expressions of the crashing bores, usually called Colonel Blimps, with whom she had had to deal at the latest dreary function. Everyone knew exactly what kind of hangers-on had pushed themselves forward; it was a running joke. The Queen Mother would murmur, "Oh, Margaret, really!" and exchange meaningful smiles with the others at her table.[20] As Queen Mary used to say, "One could not help laughing."

Few studies exist to help one understand what happens to a bright-minded girl who discovers she has been born a princess. One can only guess at what might have happened to Margaret, once she grew up. Pressures and counter-pressures came at her from all directions. To begin with, there is the absolute deference, and later obedience, accorded to her from the moment her eyes open. Her every wish is a command, even when she has soap in her eye and doesn't know how to get it out. Someone fetches and carries, brings food and removes it, dresses and undresses her, hovers over her and follows her discreetly wherever she goes.

Once outside the palace, someone has to physically prevent the screaming multitudes from surging at her, fighting to break free and touch her as she flashes by in her golden coach. She is a being apart. Once upon a time, a lesser being "taking liberties" by addressing her by her first name might have ended up in the Tower of London. Now, to do so would result in a freezing look and another kind of banishment.

On the other hand, here is someone whose every act, even her every thought, has been preordained since childhood. She lives and breathes, holds herself and moves, according to the perverse whims of others. For the rest of her life, she walks and talks in obedience to conventions that go back for centuries. She can never be good, or good enough. No wonder she goes around asking strangers, "Do you love me?" Even after she spends several years begging and pleading for the right to marry a man who, by all accounts, is an impeccable choice and a national hero. He has a fatal flaw and there is no hope. She cannot even show how much such a loss has cost her. Smile, smile, smile. No wonder, then, that she is in a rage when servants are less than perfect, and with unreasonable demands when she finds two leaves floating in a pool.

A girl who has no chance to become her own person has to find devious methods. She discovers that the perfect way to get even is to hone her sense of the ridiculous. One is reminded of Alice in Wonderland at the end of a long series of setbacks. Finally, she is in a courtroom being judged by some perfectly ridiculous people. She responds with "Who cares about you? You are nothing but a pack of cards!" Her tormentors turn into cardboard, fly up in the air, and she is free at last. Getting even is her lifeline. No wonder she is so good at it.

Among the paths Princess Margaret was barred from taking was a career in the theater, even though she was a born performer. She had a career of sorts, by way of compensation, performing at private dine-and-dance parties. These were given by some highly placed hostesses, among them the Duchess of Marlborough, the Countess of Mountbatten, the Duchess of Devonshire, among many others.

The guest lists were submitted for the approval of the princess—usually no more than fifteen or sixteen. Approval once given, the princess would require a grand piano, a room with bath and dressing room, plus rooms for her maid and chauffeur. There must also be a phonograph on hand.

Then the day would come. There would be a wonderful dinner, followed by the once-in- a-lifetime experience of listening to the princess sing and accompany herself at the piano. By then, her tongue-in-cheek humor was already well-known and keenly anticipated. We know about at least one of these parties in June 1958 because it was described by Eddy Gilmore, who had the rare privilege of being one of the guests, even if he was not exactly in the inner circle at Buckingham Palace. He had made his name as a journalist during World War II when he pulled off the impossible feat of interviewing Stalin, for which he received a Pulitzer Prize. He had subsequently met and married a Russian ballerina. Their efforts to leave Moscow, which were unsuccessful until Stalin died in 1953, subsequently became *Never Let Me Go*, a film starring Clark Gable and Gene Tierney. It made them both celebrities.[21]

The star, Gilmore wrote, silenced conversation with "a very adult blue chord." First came a spiritual, as the pianist hummed the harmony. She then launched into her version of a wonderfully sad Russian folk song.

"*A magaluchne, moi pulozhenie, moi vasnotchky*" Princess Margaret sang. "*Lelikrshnie, ovat ne meduzhelsky*," she continued, sending a roguish smile at the Gilmores. One debutante gasped in admiration: "She even speaks Russian!"

On and on the princess went, making convincing noises in languages she did not speak, to the growing delight of her audiences. She ended with a sly imitation of a British singer, whose efforts to imitate an American accent had not been well received. It was all in very good fun. But all too soon, there were no more encores. It was time to dance. Somebody turned on the phonograph and the princess took to the dance floor, no doubt doing a pretty passable imitation of The Twist.

A close observer of the London *charivari*, as *Punch* used to call it, would naturally have an eye for a good picture. Princess Margaret had taught herself to take black-and-white and color photographs with a French 35-millimeter camera and a "Japanese reflex." With characteristic determination, she had amassed a shelf-full of handsome albums, meticulously dated and labeled, and would spend hours rearranging them, according to Payne. Most were of the Royal Family, babies, children, and her dogs, along with the many guests who came and went at their country estates in Windsor, Sandringham, and Balmoral. There were so many times when the princess had gone out for walks with the dogs, a scarf tied around her head and a camera in hand, quite unrecognized. She would return with new rolls to be developed, and John would be dispatched to have the photos developed at a camera shop. Then, once Tony Armstrong-Jones came into her life, the film would go for service to his basement flat on Pimlico Road.

The princess and her valet shared a love of the theater and would exchange views once they had both seen the same show. In the 1950s, a new group of young intellectuals from the working class had arisen, almost spontaneously. They were the "Angry Young Men." These writers, poets, and playwrights shared the same antagonisms against what, for centuries, had constituted the ruling class and were challenging its privileges, rules, customs, and devastating assumptions. In *Look Back in Anger* (1956), John Osborne, with his working-class hero, set the mutinous tone of the debate, as did John Braine's novel *Room at the Top*" (1957), Alan Sillitoe, Arnold Wesker, and Kingsley Amis in his novel, *Lucky Jim*. These "vigorously realistic dramas of contemporary life" were something quite unexpected and swept out the tired, predictable plots of the middle class, set in dated drawing rooms. Everyone was talking about them.

One day in February of 1958, Cecil Beaton, stricken with a bad cold, nevertheless rose from his sick bed when the princess invited him to lunch to tell him about having sat for the sculptor Jacob Epstein, who was working on a bust of her. She described the result, in her usual mocking terms, as having "google eyes," a hooked nose, and "cadaverous" cheeks. Then the conversation moved to the subject, as Beaton wrote in his diary, of Angry Young Men. She commented, "I like Angry Young Men. They're not nearly angry enough. If they're angry, I'm furious!"[22]

Unfortunately, playwrights like Osborne had assumptions of their own that were particularly misogynistic. One of the exceptions on the London stage at that time was *A Taste of Honey* (1958), whose heroine Jo was from a working-class family in Lancashire. The play was considered remarkable, not only because its author Shelagh Delaney was only nineteen, but because its heroine was "not so much a rebel, but a revolutionary," one reviewer observed. Perhaps the same could be said for Margaret behind her glass curtain. Did she also say at that period that she "wanted to marry an angry man"?

If she was at home in the evening, she usually had her nose in a book, although just what she liked to read is not described. Payne has provided a description of a typical evening: ". . . she propped herself up on the settee with plenty of cushions, drinks and cigarets [sic] near at hand." Dinner was served on a tray at eight, at which point, "she would move to one of the coffee tables in the sitting room and, fork in hand American style, go on reading whatever it was, usually a paperback novel, propped up on the table." After dinner, she usually kicked off her shoes and lay on the settee listening to Frank Sinatra records and lazily waving her cigarette holder in time to the music.

One evening, Payne found her in a typical attitude, half asleep, her head pillowed on two pink brocade cushions and her dark hair forming a fan around her face.

"I stood there for a few seconds, inwardly moved by the sight of this sleeping beauty."[23]

He left, having forgotten what he came in for. There could be no doubt about it. He was smitten.

There was another time, summoned to the pool, when he found her waiting for him. She was wearing the briefest of yellow bikinis and with a towel slung loosely over a shoulder, that concealed nothing. She had just come out of the water and her body was glistening.

"Little droplets of water trickled down around her arms and legs."

He stood there and stared, transfixed. Convention required that a lady, caught unawares, would have snatched up a coverall to conceal her near-nakedness at a moment like this. "His" princess, posing and pirouetting, was wearing a reckless, provocative smile. No amount of caution, or outright scandalized objections, would have saved her from this flirtatious disregard for the particular delicacy of her position or make her realize how easily this kind of behavior could be misunderstood. But then she never seemed to know danger when she saw it. Not because she refused to see it. But because she *could* not.

In August 1957, Princess Margaret went to Balmoral along with the rest of her family to celebrate another birthday. The papers marked this occasion predictably, as it had all the others. But this time, there seemed to be considerable handwringing over the idea that she was still single. *The Evening Standard*, also owned by Lord Beaverbrook, was taken particularly seriously, because it was well known that the paper reflected his views. Nevertheless, it took a certain kind of impertinence to assume, as the paper did, that every single girl felt the same way. That is to say, that she had only three more years before arriving at the big "Three-O"—the end of any hope of a happy marriage to anybody. After all, the authors continued, by then the single girl would be two years past the age when, in France, she officially became a spinster. A girl—any girl—lived by her looks, and when those were fading . . . The paper went on enumerating the reasons why even a princess should be worried. It had to be clear to her that the field was narrowing every year as more and more eligible men were snapped up. Anyway, once she was thirty, she would be so set in her ways, and her opinions so emphatic, that nobody would want her.[24] She had better, in vulgar parlance, "Get a move on."

The princess, no doubt in happy ignorance of her blighted future, puttered around in a kilt and "wellies," took long walks, went riding, and took ever more photos for her family albums at the inevitable picnics. But, as in any fairy story, a possible solution to her predicament was about to present itself, on her birthday. That morning, there was a knock at the gates of Balmoral, that storied estate in the tiny town of Ballater, a remote part of Scotland. The guards went to find out who it was. They were met by Jean Baptiste Guerraz, a forty-four-year-old French hotel manager. And he was a bachelor! Speaking in perfect English, the handsome stranger politely sought an immediate audience with the Queen Mother. Why would he want to do *that*?

In some surprise, he replied, "Isn't it the custom in Britain to see a girl's father or mother before asking her to marry you?" The guards, equally surprised, asked, "What girl would that be?" Princess Margaret, of course.

In any proper fairytale, readers would soon find out that the Queen Mother had been watching the whole exchange from behind a screen. As the guards were about to march the handsome stranger away, the Queen Mother would intervene, invite him to tea, and feed him lots of honey and cakes. For his part, the suitor, in his immaculate velvet and silks, would enchant Mummy and her lovely daughter so much that the marriage would have taken place practically on the spot. A happy ending, right there.

At this point, reality asserts itself. The suitor never got as far as the front door. In fact, he was loaded into a Jeep, or something like it, and driven fifty miles to Aberdeen. There, he was kindly treated, given a meal and a bed for the night—at the local jail. The next day, he was escorted to a boat and sent back to France. The lady in question probably never knew of his existence.[25]

Although John Payne does not mention it, "his" princess took up her royal duties with every appearance of conscientiousness and zeal. One afternoon as he was coming down the corridor, he could clearly hear her voice behind her sitting room door. He opened the door and found his mistress walking slowly up and down the middle of the room, reading aloud from the sheaf of notes she was carrying. In a clear voice, she addressed the room, congratulating it on the new addition to ". . . its hospital." She ended with, "It now gives me great pleasure to declare this building open."

She turned to him with a bright smile and asked what he thought. He approved as a matter of course. She was still frowning and hesitant. After a moment's hesitation, she scratched something out and tried new. "*Now* I have great pleasure in declaring . . ." Happy at last, she put the speech back on her desk. She was ready for the next day.

Princess Margaret was in demand. To everyone's surprise, she had a knack for making an event out of something usually plodding and predictable, like planting a tree, opening a new bridge, or bringing some sense of occasion to opening yet another hospital wing. Much as she had, on impulse, put a flower into the buttonhole of a youngster who had handed her a bouquet, she had a way of upending formalities by doing something unexpected. People liked her. The reaction was not lost on the queen and her husband, who thought she was ready to go solo on important trips to East Africa and Canada in 1956 and 1958.

Feeling she had something important to do—representing the British Crown overseas—brought out the best in her. She approached the matters at hand as seriously as she had executed her previous duties, and set out with a will on the quite difficult work of conveying happy expectation wherever she went, while managing to insert a surprise or two along the way. For instance, after opening a new bridge over a lake in British Columbia in the summer of 1958, she was supposed to be driven a few hundred yards to unveil a couple of plaques. It was a lovely day, the walk beside the lake looked very delightful, so why not walk? To the consternation of her guards, she proceeded to do just that. While admiring crowds cheered and applauded, she ambled along. Nothing terrible happened, and she made her point. People worried too much.[26]

A couple of weeks later, the princess was about to make a speech on the steps of Toronto's City Hall when she noticed someone trying to work his way through the crowd. It was a young man, bare to the waist, in filthy work pants, with four missing front teeth. Arriving at the front row, he stood there with a large toothless grin. The princess, who had been watching his successful progress, gave him a big wink of approval.[27]

What might have unnerved some people tended to demonstrate unsuspected strengths of fast-thinking and resourcefulness in her. It happened on the same Canadian trip. She was being given a ride in a stagecoach pulled by two elderly cart horses. All went well until the horses, spooked by a sudden sound, reared up and plunged forward. As the doorless, ancient stagecoach rocked and hurtled down the street, the princess located a metal brace and held on grimly. Some fast thinking kept her in her seat, and the driver finally brought the horses to a standstill five blocks later. She descended, perfectly composed. She could have fallen to her death, but she was smiling.[28]

She was unnerved only once. The princess's African tour was a case in point. It included Kenya, and this was a problem because the then-British protectorate had been subject to uprisings since the 1920s, when colonial immigrants, attracted to its rich soils, had begun to invade and forcibly take possession by fair means or foul. The question was still not settled after World War II, and a three-year battle (1953–1956) had just established an uneasy truce.

The princess arrived in Nairobi and had barely been installed in a hotel when the news came through. The leader of the Mau Mau—an organization that had been fighting to get the British out of Kenya for thirty-five years—had been found at last. It had taken three years to capture Dedan Kimathi, an almost mythical figure who had slipped out of every net and seemed invisible despite massive efforts to waylay him. The day she arrived in Nairobi, Kimathi had been spotted in the bushes beside a trail some hundred miles distant in the Aberdare mountains, wearing leopard skins and not much else. The policeman who spotted him fired and wounded him in the thigh. He was now in custody. As the princess arrived, she actually saw some "weary African soldiers . . . trekking back from the Aberdares and steel-helmeted police at their posts along the side of the road."[29] It was all a bit too much, even for her. Pleading exhaustion, she took the next day off.

The press was always ready to pounce at the least opportunity. When, at a native rally in Tanganyika, she was introduced to Peter Townsend's younger brother Francis, who was District Commissioner for the Arusha region, all pencils were poised. But nothing much was to be gained by a smile from him and a "Very pleased to meet you," smile of reply from her.[30] What was not generally known was that the princess and Peter Townsend were still in contact. It is believed that Ruby Gordon was posting her mistress's letters and collecting Townsend's at her home address, a tactic that had worked before.

The automatic assumption was that it would be a scandal if the two ever met again. But in fact, it seems true that Princess Margaret was "putting into operation a long-term plan to bring Peter Townsend back to Britain so that he can serve as her faithful friend and unofficial counsellor," the *Baltimore Sun* reported.[31] No one seriously thought the much-maligned couple could be prevented from meeting again, however much the press might try to inject some shock value into that possibility. What no one realized was that the fall of Eden's plan to keep the Suez British had changed the atmosphere very much for the better, as far as the princess was concerned.

In the fall of 1956, British and French troops landed to repulse the Egyptians but were forced by international pressures, mostly from the United States, to withdraw a week later. It was a colossal and humiliating failure on Eden's part. Early in 1957, he resigned as prime minister after a tenure of only twenty-one months—the shortest on record. Later that year, there was a report that the princess had begged the queen, with tears in her eyes, to allow her and Townsend to marry. Again, she was refused.[32]

Margaret was back in London; Peter was still traveling and about to reach South America. He said that they were never going to marry or marry anyone else either; he was sick of England and much else. An indication of his exasperation can be guessed at the day the Japanese freighter on which he was traveling docked at the port of La Guaira, Venezuela. He was still in his cabin and breakfast had just been served, when a photographer burst into his room, camera at the ready. Almost instantaneously, Townsend, at the end of his patience, threw everything at him: fried eggs, fried potatoes, rolls, butter, jelly, and plate. No doubt he made a mess of the camera.[33]

His biographer John Barrymaine, who was watching the drama unfold, even as he was writing an account of it, met Peter in Algeria in the spring of 1958. The man he met was "very different from the one I had bidden farewell," he wrote.

"He was bronzed and fit; his eyes had a new alertness and there was a determination about him which I had not seen . . . since those far-off days of the Battle of Britain."[34]

He was off to Brussels and "marriage between himself and the princess was again in the air." Could he hope to arrive at Clarence House without being seen? No, he couldn't. He was going anyway. Within a matter of minutes of his arrival, huge crowds greeted him, and the afternoon paper, the *Evening Standard*, had a banner headline: THEY'RE TOGETHER AGAIN.[35]

The idea now was that they could get royal blessing for a relationship short of marriage—perfectly possible nowadays but absolutely scandalous at the time.[36] That kind of solution might have worked somehow, but was never going to work for him. Peter knew it, but whether or not Margaret did is unclear. In any event, she was due for another big tour, this time to Canada, and matters dragged on for another year. Townsend was also traveling to distant horizons. He was in San Francisco in November 1958, accompanied by his own photographer, a "Belgian girl."[37] Bit by bit, it transpired that her name was Marie-Luce Jamagne, she was just nineteen, the daughter of a rich Belgian tobacco merchant and (it was said) bore an uncanny physical resemblance to Princess Margaret.

The idea of Peter turning his attentions to a teenaged beauty must have been the most tremendous shock for Margaret, perhaps the biggest since the death of her father. How she endured the ordeal without collapsing is not known. Perhaps the two or three years of extensive travel, the endless enthusiastic crowds, the importance with which she was treated, and endless bows and curtseys had done something to boost her self-esteem. However, she was approaching thirty. Everyone in her set was probably married except her. Needling from all kinds of directions, including the papers, cannot have helped.

In any event, she told Peter that this was an amusing coincidence because she was about to get engaged, too. Would he please hold off on his announcement until she had made hers? He said he would. This version has become one of the accepted legends surrounding the life of Princess Margaret. It was a point of pride for her.

"You see," she would say, "I got in first."[38]

The only thing wrong with this story is that it cannot possibly be true.

To begin with, she could not have told Peter she was going to marry anyone else, because, at that point, she had no plans. Was there ever a letter from him? Were there even any phone calls? The account written by John Payne, who was her valet during that period, implies she knew nothing about this until the engagement was announced in the papers on October 9, 1959. He wrote that on that afternoon he happened to be passing by the policeman's lodge at the main entrance of Clarence House and caught sight of a paper announcing

Townsend's engagement: an edition that was about to be delivered to the princess herself. It was on Page One as "Stop Press."

"My first thought was to keep the papers from Margaret."

But then he realized the news would soon be everywhere, and there was no chance of shielding her from it. So, he tucked her copy under his arm and went inside. When he arrived at her rooms, he found her writing letters at her desk. As he tidied up the sitting room, "[he] watched, fascinated as she put down her pen, picked up the paper and leaned back in her chair. She was reading the stop press."

He was prepared for anything, but the sudden violence of her reaction took him aback nevertheless.

"Margaret flared into action. In one swift movement, she grabbed the paper with her left hand and hurled it with all her force across the room. It fluttered in the air and skidded onto a side table . . . still folded, curiously enough."[39] For a moment she sat bolt upright, looking blankly ahead. Then she . . . started writing again as if nothing had happened."

That evening, she donned her prettiest cocktail dress, was picked up at eight by Billy Wallace, and did not get back to Clarence House until four the next morning.

As for her engagement to Antony Armstrong-Jones, also known as Tony, that announcement was not made until four months later by the Queen Mother (February 26, 1960). By then, Peter Townsend and Marie-Luce Jamagne had been married for two months (since December 21, 1959). Princess Margaret conceded to Jonathan Aitken what was probably quite true: that she had married on the rebound. She said that, at the time, "I hadn't got any plans to marry [Tony]."[40]

CHAPTER 9

EVERYBODY LIKES HIM

"O wad some Power the giftie gie us, to see oursels
as ithers see us?"
—Robert Burns

WILLIAM GLENTON HAD A ROOM for rent. He lived in Dockland, so as to be close to his beat—he was a waterfront journalist—and had been in residence there for several years. After the ferocious bombing attacks on London during World War II, people were in desperate need of a place to live and took over storage units, abandoned coach houses, tool sheds, greenhouses—and even parts of the sprawling waterfront that had been an anathema to all right-thinking Londoners for a century.

This particular house was no prize either. It had once been the house of a sea captain, now almost buried beneath the onslaught of lorries on one side and the freighters plying great Thames on the other. Everybody knew about the desolate lives of those condemned to live there because Dickens made a point of telling them just what happened to the gangs of children running through the streets in his day. If they did not die of the contaminated water they drank or starve or die of the cold, they probably expired through some other means. As they scrounged in the mud for something to sell, they were likely to step on a nail—another sure route to misery and death. Not only was life noxious, it housed notorious gangs of thieves, cutthroats, and drug addicts. One could murder freely and often, to judge from the famous (and never solved) case of Jack the Ripper. This floating sewer would not change until the great engineering reformers of the nineteenth century persuaded the city's elders to construct the first sewers London ever had. In the 1930s, Dockland was still a massive interlocking morass of docks, warehouses, and shipyards, where a great flow of raw materials from the farthest reaches of the British Empire arrived, only to return as finished goods to be sold everywhere.

Glenton's small row house at 59 Rotherhithe Street was one of eight, miraculously intact despite heavy bombing on all sides—it had stood there for two hundred years. This forlorn remaining testament to a vanished past had recently been discovered, he wrote, by an arty crowd who had been making a stab at propping up the ancient timbers. But there was no escaping the fact that the little house stood a few feet from the river and was, therefore, subject to high tides, which would regularly invade its underpinnings and do their part to pull it down.

Rotherhithe Street was even more ancient—there were shipyards there in the time of Queen Elizabeth I—and had its own town hall until German bombs reduced it to a pile of rubble; a theater and a hospital, and it was part of the Diocese of Westminster. But its main claim to fame was that, in 1620, the Mayflower had left its docks on its way to Southampton and then across the Atlantic to America.

The previous inhabitant, an artist, had remodeled the ground floor into a large studio, now used for storage. The living quarters, sensibly enough, were upstairs on the second floor (British: first floor) where Glenton had an office, small kitchen, bathroom, and two tiny bedrooms. Also on the ground floor was a smallish room—it, too, piled with junk—that had a row of windows with a clear view up and down the river from London Bridge to Limehouse and provided the novel experience of watching ships, tugs, and barges passing by at close quarters.[1] That one was for rent.

Enter Tony Armstrong-Jones, usually dismissed slightingly in press accounts as a "society photographer." In fact, as one would say of a painting, he came with a gilt-edged provenance. His father, Ronald Armstrong-Jones, also known as Ronnie, of Welsh extraction, was a distinguished lawyer whose father was a brilliant surgeon, and whose antecedents included ship owners, a High Sheriff of Caernarvonshire, and, it is thought, King Edward I of England. His mother Anne Messel was the daughter of a wealthy banker whose ancestors included a German-Jewish banking family, originally from Darmstadt, who settled in England after the Franco-Prussian War of 1870–1871 and became Christians. The famous theatrical designer Oliver Messel was her brother; Anne herself took a meticulous interest in art, design, fashion, and décor and had the financial means to indulge her tastes. When Ronnie married Anne in 1925, her father Leonard Messel gave them a house on Eaton Terrace in Belgravia, a fabulously generous gift. Their first child Susan Mary came along two years later. Their son Antony was born on March 7, 1930—a few months ahead of his future wife.

Anne Armstrong-Jones (née Messel) was one of the great beauties of the 1930s. She was also faultlessly slim, the kind of person who can wear outrageous clothes and look right in any of them. That she was a perfect hostess goes without saying. She probably knew all about art, and with her kind of eye for the second-rate, could probably tell which often-faked Modigliani was genuine and which Dalí was an obvious fake. Superlatives falter when faced with such a being, and that made her difficult to relate to because, as we know, perfection can be hard to live with. So, perhaps it is not surprising that the marriage began to fray at the seams as early as 1931. By 1935, she was remarried, having again demonstrated her flawless taste by choosing her second husband, Michael Parsons, 6th Earl of Ross. Her reappearance in even more exalted circles led to her becoming known as "Tugboat Annie," because, it was said, "she went from peer to peer."[2]

As might be expected, Ronnie Armstrong-Jones was her temperamental opposite. She was punctual, perfectionistic, and demanding; he was easy-going and permissive, shuttling between a townhouse in Knightsbridge and the family estate, Plas Dinas in Caernarvonshire. He liked outdoor sports, shooting, and fishing; was usually late for meetings; and soon returned to another gentlemanly sport, going out with girls. He quickly remarried as well. Anne would explain crisply that no reconciliation had been possible because "Actually [Ronnie] was well-rooted in another romp by this time."[3] Frequent affairs and a tendency to make others wait for him would have predictable echoes in the life of his son Tony.

To judge from the immaculately detailed account of Tony's life by Anne de Courcy (*Snowdon*), Tony's childhood was spent being shuttled between two households. In his father's, he received affectionate, if absentminded, care. On the other hand, his mother, with her exacting demands on her own behavior and appearance, could be guaranteed to expect the same standards of her children and to be hostile to shortcomings, cool and aloof and, one supposes, abrupt and dismissive as well. During Tony's visits, she would bring out for admiration her two sons by her second husband and then belatedly remember that the boy hovering in the background was hers as well. Could it be true, as de Courcy writes, that she thought Tony was "ugly"? Anything is possible. Failed marriages can carry with them the unreasoning dislike of a mother who perceives too much of her rejected spouse in his son's features. Tony was, in due course, bundled off to a boarding school. Kenneth Rose, the well-known diarist for the *Sunday Telegraph* and biographer of George V, taught Tony briefly at Eton. He wrote in a report, "Armstrong-Jones may be good at something, but it is nothing we teach at Eton."[4]

In fact, Tony showed a precocious gift for invention. When he was only six, he not only played with submarines in his bath, he invented one. Encouraged by his uncle Oliver Messel, a prominent stage designer, he began putting together all sorts of ingenious devices. He began taking pictures. He excelled at the piano. He was a born athlete. All was going well in the summer of 1946 when, at the age of sixteen, he contracted polio. That happened five years before Dr. Jonas Salk invented a vaccine that saved millions of children from this crippling disease. Tony recovered except for a persistent limp in his left leg, which was left slightly shorter than the other. He could have been treated at home, but his mother wanted him in an infirmary, where he spent six months. His uncle often visited him, as did his sister Susan. His mother never did.[5]

William Glenton was in no particular hurry to find a tenant and especially not someone slumming it from the West End. He had seen what could happen when a smooth talker comes into the neighborhood: noisy parties every weekend, and nobody around them can sleep. He had to be sure that the person who took the room was serious-minded and quiet. Then, one Sunday afternoon the doorbell rang. Tony Armstrong-Jones had found out about the room. Here was this slight, slim man, looking far too young to be a society photographer for anybody, in his outfit of robin's egg blue jeans, suede jacket, and boots, asking to see the room.[6] Glenton's opinion began to change as the newcomer, with broad, sweeping gestures, described what could be done with these four walls and the vista from its windows. Glenton could only see a pile of junk, flaking paint, and a dirty concrete floor. But there it was, Tony had a vision and the gift for making you see what it might be like. And besides, he wanted to fix the place up for free. Glenton was convinced.[7]

"Tony arrived a fortnight later," Glenton continued, "looking like Christopher Wren about to build St. Paul's Cathedral. He marched into the house, arms full of tools, accompanied by an assistant from his studio in Pimlico Road, also fully loaded down."

The car outside had disappeared under a mountain of planed timber. Somewhere in all the equipment Tony had included a hamper of cold chicken, along with several bottles of Burgundy.[8]

"If Tony does anything, he does it in style," Glenton wrote. "And for a fearful moment I believed he was going to pull down the house."

What he had in mind just then was a long wall of cupboards, which served to hide some unsightly pipes and as a place to hide a wash basin and cooker. It also contained saucepans, cups, saucers, and numerous odds and ends. Perhaps there was room to squeeze in a few clothes hangers as well.

"For the next three days the sounds of hammering and sawing filled the house as Tony put up the floor-to-ceiling cupboard wall."

By degrees, his cotton shirt and jeans became so covered with sawdust that he took on a "mildewed look." He periodically stopped for a cigarette—the Gauloises he favored—and another swig of the Burgundy. All that remained was to finish off the newly constructed wood with a coat of beeswax—his assistant did that—while Tony went off on a thrilling quest for second-hand furniture.[9]

Glenton's account of the room's transformation is not dated, but from internal evidence it seems that Tony moved into it sometime between 1958 and 1959. This was after he took some enchanting photographs, both relaxed and flattering, of Queen Elizabeth II, Prince Philip, and their children. They were perfectly delighted with the results. Subsequently, to celebrate her twenty-ninth birthday in August 1959, Tony was asked back to take a picture of Princess Margaret herself. This was not the daring photograph of her head and bare shoulders that *The Crown* would have you believe was published in *The Times*, or something equally august. It was a perfectly respectable photograph of the princess half-turned towards the camera, showing a pearl choker and the merest hint of a well-covered shoulder. That, too, was well received. Soon after that, Tony was invited to dinner by Lady Elizabeth Cavendish, one of Margaret's ladies-in-waiting, and her husband the Poet Laureate John Betjeman. Princess Margaret was there, too.

The princess had been ringing Tony for occasional advice. Now, he became a regular visitor to Clarence House.

"They spent hours talking and comparing photographs," Payne wrote. "And many is the time I have watched Tony giving Margaret instructions and hints on the best way to take a certain picture."[10] When Christopher Warwick was preparing her official biography, she told him, "I enjoyed (Tony's) company very much, but I didn't take a lot of notice of him because I thought he was queer."[11]

Tony started returning in triumph to what Glenton called "The Room," with one discovery after another, many of them bought at bargain prices. There was, for instance, a badly sprung double divan bed that he picked up for nothing, threw a velvet coverlet over it, added a couple of cushions and made it look quite presentable. He bought a well-scrubbed table, a bit rocky, some basket chairs, and a huge eighteenth-century painting of a "vitriolic-looking" admiral on the deck of his ship. It was so tall it had to be cut down before it would even fit on a wall. There, the admiral stood in a great rage, no doubt casting a certain pall on the proceedings. Something had to be done. An upright piano did the trick; once pushed behind such a mighty bulk, the admiral retreated, glowering.

In those days, the flea markets of Petticoat Lane and Notting Hill Gate provided endless opportunities for the determined hunter of oddities, invariably cheap and usually with something really wrong with them. The birdcage fitted with a musical box that he displayed in triumph might long since have ceased to play anything. The china bowl with a bouquet of dusty flowers might have a chip in the rim that must be concealed; the seashell-encrusted picture frame might fall over and the Victorian plates retrieved with such care might have sold for real money if they had not been so faded. The china cows and the wooden box shaped like a book all went on proud (if battered) display. So did the daguerreotypes of some long-forgotten family that he rescued from a junk shop, adopted as his own and hung on the wall over the bed. Glenton thought that, taken together, Tony's magpie tastes seemed just right for background, given the raffish and faded state of the jeans and shirts he habitually wore.

Then Tony began to show off The Room to his friends. The arty Chelsea set naturally came first. They were followed by a slightly more upmarket crowd. For instance, his sudden Palace connections led to a request by the Poet Laureate Sir John Betjeman, to stay there for a couple of months. Tony's haphazard attire began to evolve into something more respectable and presentable, not to mention cleaner. There was only one bathroom in the house, which they all shared. It was furnished with the old-fashioned toilet first invented in the late nineteenth century, and which was still being installed in new houses in the 1930s. It had a separate reservoir up above, that one released by means of a long chain. One pulled it, and gravity did the rest. This one was old, rusty, and definitely temperamental. One never knew whether the pull would release a cascade that went everywhere or refuse to work at all. One day, Glenton discovered that the sensible toilet paper he always provided had gone. In its place was something violet, soft and inviting, with a smell that wafted through the room. Something was up.

In the days when they were at school together, Nicholas "Nicky" Haslam, the future interior designer, recalled that Tony was "small and neat, with pretty, slightly simian features."

"He was somewhat reserved and faintly mocking," Haslam said. "And I felt he was sizing me up."[12]

He fell in love and had an affair with Tony, as did Tom Parr, a family friend who wore elegant clothes and exuded worldly charm. But after a while, there were "other irons" in Tony's fire. One of his main girlfriends was a Chinese actress named Jacqui Chan, who had a flowerlike charm and went on to make movies including *The World of Suzie Wong*.[13]

Then one day, Tony turned up at one of the Queen Mother's formal lunch parties with much solid silver gilt in evidence, where everybody knew everybody, or almost. He was the one chatting with great brio to Princess Alexandra, and nobody knew who he was. He spoke with a soft, slightly high-pitched voice, and tended to illustrate his many anecdotes with sweeping gestures across the table. He laughed a lot—something more like a giggle, wrote John Payne, who was serving the guests that day. Once he broke into such a fit of giggling that the Princess, at the other end of the table, looked severely in his direction. The new arrival tended to look up with a smile at the footman whenever he was served. That, too, was the wrong thing to do, Payne observed—it just wasn't done.

"I never felt happy myself about the match," Payne continued.[14]

Townsend had a certain way of projecting determination and drive; Armstrong-Jones simply did not have it in him.

"I felt my Princess was wasting herself on this friendly, but unsuitable man."[15]

Just what kind of a person was he? Hugo Vickers, who liked him, said, "Tony was, of course, immensely talented and forever creating something new from a pair of spectacles to a special moving chair for the disabled. He was . . . very easy to talk to, good-humored and smiling (though clearly not always), and fun to be with. Full of jokes, very open. You could say anything to him. He was also mercurial, could be deceptive, and might pretend not to know something to see what you said—what you knew. I did not ever get the impression that he was laughing at me behind my back. He was more likely to explain a joke in front of you."[16]

By the time he was thirty, Tony Armstrong-Jones had mastered the camera's technical and artistic requirements and was launched on an exploration of its many latent possibilities. Rather than take a studied portrait, he was much more interested in what could be achieved in the fleeting moment, using a small format camera with a faster shutter speed. In the days when theaters typically used posed portraits for publicity, Tony took photographs at rehearsals.

"His method involved endless technical difficulties, and endless shots, but it produced some brilliant results," a critic from *The Washington Post* wrote. "Its actors looked alive."[17]

Not only had he mastered the split-second reactions required to capture the moment, but he pushed forward with some technical difficulties, often working into the night.

"He blew up segments of miniature negatives to a colossal size, emphasizing the grain," the same writer observed. "People had been toying with the device for years, but he made a hit with it."[18]

That is exactly what the hero of *Blow-Up* does five years later when he finds a suspicious object in one of his frames that, when repeatedly enlarged, turns out to be a murdered man.

Various examples show Jones's determination to get the shot despite the obstacles.

"The tale of how he got thrown out of the Opera House in Vienna, but returned in the wake of an armful of flowers delivered to the leading lady, is typical."[19]

He had an important coup during the general elections of 1959 when everyone was trying to get photos of the newly re-elected Prime Minister Sir Harold Macmillan, and he was turned away at the door of 10 Downing Street. Tony Armstrong-Jones badgered police until he was admitted. Then he took a photo of the prime minister watching television in his drawing room.[20] He sold it to the *Daily Express*, which blew up the photo across five columns on its front page.

The anonymous author of the article, who clearly knew both Margaret and Tony well, observed that they both disliked "stuffed shirts" and were gifted at mimicking them, although he was funnier than she was.

"At a deeper emotional level, both have disadvantages to overcome and have suffered setbacks . . . both have a touch of immaturity still" and while generally sociable, preferred each other's company. Their idea of the perfect evening was to sit on the floor with a drink or a plate of food, reading poetry and listening to Tony's new recording of "Irma la Douce." Just the two of them, secure in their secret hideout.

In Dockland, the reason for the arrival of the scented violet toilet paper began to leak out, bit by bit.

Tony's landlord wrote, "They could not just go out (for dinner) like other courting couples without risking the unwelcome attention of the press."[21]

They tried leaving Clarence House once—disguised in sports outfits and wearing dark glasses—and got away with it. They did not dare try it again because Clarence House was under the constant surveillance of suspicious eyes. The blissful alternative was the small room in Dockland. When Tony tried that in his Austin Mini, even smaller than a VW bug, and Margaret tied a scarf around her head, no one noticed. The novelty of no one watching her movements, a lumpy divan to sit on, boats sailing by the window, and cooking a meal was so outlandish as to be positively thrilling. She could go there whenever she liked and stay for as long as she liked. There was always a bottle of wine or something stronger. There was a piano to play. There were always ashtrays about, and Tony was rather a good cook, even if his repertoire was limited to steak and potatoes. They were alone together, and nobody was listening. At quiet moments, you could hear lapping water. Meantime, Glenton, who had puzzled over why Tony was being so secretive about this guest, was beginning to guess.

One evening, returning from an assignment, Glenton climbed the stairs just as Tony happened to open his door. There, "posed against the softly candlelit background was the unmistakable figure of my thoughts."[22] He and the princess met in due course. He stammered—what was he supposed to call her? Your Royal Highness? Princess Margaret? Ma'am? She relieved his agony by saying, "Tony has told me so much about you, and I've wanted to meet you for quite some time."

Her voice, he noticed, had a high pitch and that clipped, authoritative tone that denotes class and social status. A particular way of pronouncing "bad" to sound like "bed," "lost" to become "lawst," and vowels to be dropped, as in "secretary," compressed into "secret'ry."

As they got to know each other, the tone dropped, the staccato words softened, and the royal visitor's manner relaxed. He decided that this was just her way of making sure the newcomer did not take too much for granted. The couple were showing up more and more often in Tony's Mini, the princess well-bundled up in scarves and collars, looking like anybody.[23] Nobody realized what was going on and that had to do, at least in part, with The Room.

Her Royal Highness, Princess of the Realm, fell in love with an older divorced man when she was a teenager and, against all the odds, stayed in love. That love had certainly been tested, and every effort had been made to thwart it, first by her sister, head of the Church of England, and belatedly by a divorced prime minister and members of his cabinet who were divorced themselves. Even so, she fought on for some solution—any solution—that would keep them together. But by then Peter Townsend, who had endured every storm loyally and held onto her, had given up. Princess Margaret was now dealing with a twist of the knife in a deep emotional wound.

Peter was about to marry a lovely girl who (it was said) resembled her and was the same age, nineteen, when she had fallen in love with him. To that, one has to add the mores of her day. One of the reasons, no doubt, why girls of her class married so young was, perhaps, to ensure that they were still virgins. A girl who has had a long affair with someone and looks for a husband when she is thirty, is a different proposition. Is the word "shop soiled"? Or "old maid"? It hardly mattered. All she knew now was that the love of her life was marrying someone else.

By chance, one of her friends was a photographer, who was very personable, socially well-placed, with all kinds of friends in the arts. As she said, she always enjoyed talking to him but assumed he was gay. She admired his energy, determination, and his ingenious way of getting things done. No doubt he sympathized with the extent to which she, in her glass cage, had been frustrated, even maligned. If she was too often blocked, he was full of ingenious solutions. He would protect her: perhaps even give voice to all the things she couldn't say.

A few letters from her to Tony have been made public. These have a peculiar tone as if the princess is trying to persuade herself that she is madly in love and cannot quite make the switch, in a matter of months, from someone she has adored all her life to someone else. But if you are going to marry someone, people expect you to be "madly in love," and to answer that "you quite like them" is not going to be socially acceptable. Besides, only a few months separate Peter's announcement in November and the switch to a new candidate in January. This is the date given by William Shawcross, official biographer to the Queen Mother. His narrative includes friendly letters from Princess Margaret to Tony in the autumn of 1958 and spring of 1959 that warm in tone by the summer of that year.

In one of the letters to Tony in the summer of 1959, she referred to her "emotional turmoil"—easy to guess why—and how she felt after leaving him.

"You've made me happy. Are you pleased? I am . . . I left London tremendously NOT in turmoil. Are you aware how much that means to me—having traveled unhappily, bumping about."

Since then, she had had "golden dreams," and found herself "smiling unconsciously." She wanted him to write to her a lot, and send her "every detail, please."[24]

A week later, on her birthday (August 21), she wrote again to say "how peaceful and unworried" she was and thank him for being "so nice and gentle—very rare." By December 9, she loved him "passionately and peacefully," which some might consider a contradiction in terms.[25] They became engaged in January 1960, and the announcement was made a month later. Something had finally been settled, so no wonder she felt at peace at last. The Queen Mother and Queen Elizabeth II were almost embarrassingly relieved and grateful, for obvious reasons. Perhaps it was then that Princess Margaret remarked, "Everybody seems to like him." She was grateful too, since she could now face the public and not have the horrid feeling she was being seen as "cast aside." No doubt this is why she liked to say, in years to come, "At least I got in first." Even if she didn't.

The stage was set to have Mr. Jones looked over officially, and this was undertaken by the Queen Mother. This time, it was at the Royal Lodge for the weekend. When this test was successful, the next step was something formal, like a dance in their honor. As Tony Armstrong-Jones's suit seemed assured, this particular star of the new Bohemia relaxed his standards of acceptable behavior. Invited to spend a weekend at the Lodge, he was expected to arrive during the day on Friday but only appeared just before dinner. He knew that it involved a change into a dinner jacket, so he tossed a battered garment bag on his bed and went back downstairs for drinks.

Payne, who had been delegated to look after him, zipped the bag open and found everything in a jumble at the bottom: heavy boots, a pair of black patent leather evening shoes, a couple of ties, a rolled-up jacket, crumpled and stained, one much-used and evidently abandoned shirt, a toilet kit, and some equally haphazard underwear. Payne had less than an hour but was determined he was "not going to have his Princess" appear with someone who looked like *that*. He fished out what might turn out to be wearable and retired to the kitchen. Some heavy attention with a steam iron was given to the jacket and pants, and he did what he could with the well-worn shirt.

Like his future wife, Tony's habit was to stay up late and be ready for breakfast shortly before lunch. On his first visit, the princess was asked when she thought he would like to eat breakfast, and she guessed it might be around 11 a.m. Somehow the message did not get through, and at 9 a.m., the usual breakfast hour, there was a knock on his door. A footman arrived with a tray, which was set down beside the bed's occupant. No doubt said occupant protested weakly and went back to sleep. A couple of hours later, Mr. Jones awoke, sat up nude in bed, and asked for his breakfast. The cook sent back word that she was preparing lunch, and if he wished to eat breakfast, he should do it at the proper time.[26]

There was another thing: Tony never seemed to have any money. Payne recalled being gestured to one side while the visitor explained he was a bit short of cash and asked if he would lend Tony a few quid? Payne was then obliged to explain he was paid the miserly wage of an office clerk (about £5) and could not oblige. Mr. Jones then asked him to intercede with the household steward. Could the visitor get a check cashed? That never got anywhere either.

"Oh, dear me, no" was the usual response.

Payne had some sympathy for Tony's plight; after several late nights and some expensive wining and dining of the princess (in the days before credit cards), he was broke. Perhaps the princess never knew. She certainly knew about his chronic inability to be on time. Sometimes he even forgot about plans altogether. One night, when she invited him to dinner at Clarence House, he never showed up.

In 1960, Princess Margaret must have been seeing the light at the end of a very long tunnel. For years, after the end of World War II, a nation which should have been enjoying the fruits of victory was enduring the usual consequences for a nation that had been defeated. It was bankrupt. Rationing, i.e., for food, clothes, heating, went on as usual. The young were recruited to do two years of compulsory service, and only after that could they think about education. London, in particular, had been so massively bombed that the evidence was everywhere you looked. St. Paul's Cathedral, standing in a wasteland of broken masonry and weeds, was a kind of symbol of what had endured, despite all that had been done to break the human spirit. To add to the misery, pea-souper fogs rolled in with the seasons, foul smelling and obliterating the outlines of those gray, huddling buildings that remained.

Then the atmosphere cleared. It happened almost imperceptibly for her, and for everyone else as well. Bananas reappeared in the shops; toilet paper arrived, along with chocolate. Flowers bloomed in people's gardens. Paint and spackling came out to spruce up windows and doors. By the time she and her fiancé were preparing for their marriage in Westminster Abbey in May 1960, conscription had been abolished, food rationing was a receding memory, coupons for clothes and chocolate had been withdrawn, and one no longer had to wait six months to buy a new pair of shoes. The massive shortage of housing had begun to abate as the government built hundreds of thousands—then 1.5 million—"prefabricated" houses, meant to last for ten years, but which, as it happened, lasted for twenty in many cases. Bit by bit, London was transformed into a place where the young wanted to be: "a mood, a feeling, a geopolitical and social revolution," Dylan Jones wrote.

Perhaps the theater, with its plays of protest, had changed the mood. The highly respected Michael Caine, whose career as an actor on television and the radio and in the theater and movies is a model of consistent excellence, is a case in point. He was born in Rotherhithe, the area of the Docklands where

The Room was located. His mother was a cook and his father, a porter in the London fish market. Since he was 6'2" and exceptionally good looking, he was cast as an officer in a costume drama quite early in his career.

"That was the war," he explained in his film about London in the 1960s. "No director would have cast a Cockney boy in the role of an officer before the war. It just wouldn't have happened."

A new generation was offered the chance to become educated at grammar schools, paid for by the government and city councils, that taught foreign languages along with Latin and Greek, as well as a thorough grounding in the sciences. Such beneficence was unknown and began to remove barriers of caste that had seemed impenetrable for centuries. Young men like Ron Hall, the son of a builder, head boy of his school in Sheffield, felt he needed to lose his Midlands accent when he was accepted at Cambridge, one of Britain's exclusive universities. He finally arrived in London, joined the *Sunday Times* and became a top executive. He reflected ruefully, "I had to relearn my own accent because it was all the rage."[27] Another grammar school boy.

The Beatles, with their schoolboy charm and irresistible melodies, cut across borders of class and age to appeal to screaming audiences, not all of them teenagers. David Bailey, the poster child for young-man-makes-good, with his covers of Twiggy for *Vogue* and his elegant, sharp-edged and arresting portraits, and the "dolly birds" in their Mary Quant miniskirts twittering along Kings Road in Chelsea, dominated the headlines far from London itself.

"And even if you didn't hang out in Carnaby Street, have your clothes made by Mr. Fish or trip on acid or drive a Lotus Elan," one still felt freedom and revolt in the air.[28]

What was happening then was not just about breaking of caste barriers or better schools.

After Hiroshima, the atom bomb and the hydrogen bomb, the arrival of the Cold War, and (in 1962) the Cuban Missile Crisis, terror had a role to play in the sudden flash of youthful revolt. During Easter 1960, some sixty thousand people demonstrated against the build-up of nuclear weapons at Aldermaston. In Michael Caine's film, someone is heard to say, "If we have three minutes to live, we want to do everything *now*."

Enter the photographer as hero. The Italian director Michelangelo Antonioni, creator of *L'Avventura*, the haunting meditation about a young woman who disappears during a Mediterranean cruise, turned his poetic gaze to London in another masterful film, *Blow-Up* (1966). As the film opens, a rowdy crowd of students in clown costumes pile onto the back of a lorry and jump off in the middle of a deserted modern office piazza to interject some color and life into a dead world. They pelt through the streets, stopping here and there, and come upon Thomas, a scruffy-looking David Hemmings in stained clothes, who has just spent the night photographing some pitiful wrecks of men about to take showers in a shelter for the homeless.

He retrieves his luxurious convertible and returns to his studio, a warren of rooms painted dead white, while models as elaborately attired as flamingoes, passively wait to be told to do something. Thomas is the epitome of creative youth, with the vestige of a childlike gaze, taut and tousled, but all absurdist commands and calculated insults. To be sure we know how he feels about girls, he uses, then deliberately abuses, two vapid newcomers who are determined to be models and refuse to go away.

Then, jumping into his almost obscenely beautiful convertible, he rolls past streets with façades, one realizes, all painted red—this is, after all, a Surrealist vision.

He is in search of a small, remote park hidden behind a warren of streets, then discovers to his surprise that not only has he taken numerous photos of a couple, but, it would seem, documented a murder. What happens next is portrayed with the inconclusiveness, the feeling of fragmentary discovery—what is life about, anyway?—that permeates *Blow Up*. The hero or heroine, energetic, resourceful, and baffled, is in this case left watching an imaginary tennis game and listening to the back and forth of a ball being hit by unseen rackets.

Princess Margaret's own photographer, her fearless guide and matchless adventurer in the squalid back streets of London, appeared in her life. What she learned about the life Tony was leading must have been the most wonderful shock. Here was someone with boundless talent—after all, she had gifts of her own—who was free to do anything he wanted. Go to bed late, get up late, wear whatever clothes were on the floor, crash out of his house tearing down Rotherhithe on a motorbike, late as usual, demonstrating skill and professionalism all day and relaxing with bosom friends all night. Not giving a damn. He stood for escape, freedom, and autonomy. He went when and where he wanted on impulse, not decree. He was his own chauffeur.

One never sees a photograph of the princess driving a car. Perhaps she could and did, but perhaps it was one of the things she could not be *seen* doing. She is photographed after their marriage on a motorbike with Tony, and both are wearing identical, head-hugging cloth helmets. There is a certain bravado in her look as if to say she is "doing her own thing," like it or lump it. There is another undated photograph of her clinging for dear life to Tony as they hurtle down a roller coaster—perhaps her first one. He was the bad boy who did all the things she had longed to do all her life but had been prevented from doing. The Room he had restored in a notoriously grubby part of the city— did that, too, have its own role to play? Was it a symbol of the crucial decisions that were necessary if she was to shake off the back-breaking obligations she labored under, the endless timetables, the routines, the smiles, the excruciating boredom of it all? Where you had to live and what you had to become in order to be free? When she went from the door of his car to the front door of his house without a soul noticing, what had he given her?

When they returned from their leisurely honeymoon in the West Indies in the summer of 1960—sunning, swimming, and picnicking on shores so pristine it was as if they were the first human beings to have found them—the princess could not wait to describe them.

"You cannot imagine how wonderful it was," she told their landlord Bill, "Just to lie on those deserted beaches, without a single person, not even a sailor or native, in sight. Neither of us wanted to leave, and we would gladly have lived in a little grass hut."[29]

For her, it was a door opening onto a world she thought she could never be part of. For Tony Armstrong-Jones, one guesses it was the same. He was in a spotlight of massive public interest, the kind of recognition every young artist dreams of, and behind that came a fame and glory he could never have expected. A big position in the world. Perhaps it did not yet dawn on him that the freedom his anonymity had provided was gone forever, but his father reminded him. As soon as he was told, Tony's father said he was "too free a spirit to put up with the restrictions of royal life." One of his boyhood friends, Jocelyn Stevens, was even more pessimistic. He sent a telegram: "Never has there been a more ill-fated assignment." Noël Coward noted in his diary, "He (Tony) looks quite pretty but whether or not the marriage is entirely suitable remains to be seen."[30]

As for the princess, she could reasonably hope that being married would give her more freedom of action than she had experienced as a single eligible girl. Although, there was another aspect to the complication this particular marriage brought with it. Like it or not, it would be difficult, if not impossible, to taste the freedom she craved without abandoning the fact of her birthright and the deference and automatic status that came with it. She mattered because of her birth and that was why the rest of the world curtseyed and bowed its head. Without that, who was she? Anybody at all? As the playwright Alan Bennett put it in *The Madness of King George III*, to be heir to the throne, or even in line, "is not a position; it is a predicament."[31]

The announcement of their engagement came on February 26, 1960, and was made by the queen's secretary, Commander Richard Colville. He added that "Queen Elizabeth and her husband, Prince Philip, have said they are delighted because this is such an obviously happy match." This good feeling on the part of the prince was, if one is to believe the press, no longer in evidence a year later. Frederick Mullally, a columnist for a London paper, reported that the prince became irritated at the photographer's inability to be on time, his preference for art galleries rather than chopping logs and killing game, and the fact that, as a commoner, Armstrong-Jones had no business being in the royal family to start with. The prince may have derived some comfort from the fact that, as a commoner, said newcomer would have to walk two paces behind his wife and had already agreed to give up taking pictures. Of anybody.[32]

Billy Wallace, Margaret's longtime escort, who was periodically described as having been about to marry the princess himself, was more charitable. He said he "couldn't be happier" about the princess's engagement.

"You know, she's not had a very happy life. I've always hoped it would come out well. Now it has."

This generous assessment echoed far and wide on the forefront of public opinion and during the bride-to-be's subsequent appearances. Arriving in Liverpool in March to open a new school, she was almost carried off the platform when she began to give her set speech. *The Associated Press* reported that "well-wishers from the towns of Liverpool and Bootle jammed the streets along a six-mile route and repeatedly forced Margaret's car to a halt" while she waved and smiled. As a result, she was twenty minutes late. She was forgiven, of course.[33]

Her news stirred and reignited the considerable good will that had accompanied "a new Elizabethan age" after her sister ascended the throne and had carried their parents to new heights of popularity after victory in World War II. Perhaps it was meant to underline the approval most people felt when their princess tried to marry a Battle of Britain hero and was prevented from doing so. Everyone who was ordinary was happy she was happy at last—that was the fact.

Despite "all the appalling saccharine gush," as Drew Middleton wrote, the British loved the Royal Family, they respected and appreciated everything it stood for, and they wanted these young women to be happy. Besides, everybody loved to see the pomp and circumstance surrounding a royal wedding. Now, thanks to television, they could even watch in their own homes.[34]

Tony would move into the Palace. They could hardly let him go on sleeping in his basement studio on the Pimlico Road that was so small; by one account, he had constructed something resembling a bed on top of his capacious wardrobe. (He reached it by climbing up some shelving.)[35] He must have the best. So, he was moved into a four-room suite in Buckingham Palace, right next door to the queen's own apartment, that was often occupied by the Countess of Leicester, Lady of the Bedchamber, whenever she was on duty. The suite—consisting of living room, bedroom, dressing room, and bathroom—was sumptuous, naturally; it is described as high-ceilinged with ivory-colored walls and decorative carvings embellished with gold paint. To reach it, Tony's friends would be admitted through the privy purse door (there were numerous) and ushered to his new quarters by liveried footmen along red-carpeted corridors.[36]

Almost at once, the young photographer had his first experience of what it was going to be like to become the permanent escort of a working princess. They had spent a quiet weekend at the Royal Lodge in Windsor and were now being driven, suitably attired, to the Royal Opera House to attend a ballet performance by the great ballerina Dame Margot Fonteyn.

As the royal car crew up to the entrance, they found it dressed up like a stage set with cameramen, the brutal glare of TV arc lights and a jostling screaming crowd—most of them women and teenagers—in a constant scramble to get a better view. As soon as the car doors opened, the screaming developed into a roar and a barricade of police with ropes were trying desperately to prevent the crowd from breaking free. The princess was indeed a sight to see, in a jeweled satin evening gown, a white fur stole, and diamonds at her ears and around her neck.

There was one particular ring on her left finger.

The princess stepped out, flashing a smile, the epitome of serenity and confidence. Her fiancé looked blinded by the lights, aghast at the size of the crowd and white with disbelief. All he could do was numbly follow his princess, who gave him a reassuring smile as she swept through the doors to shouts of, "Good luck, Margaret!" and "Bless you both."[37] The Margaret and Tony show was off to a shaky start.

Not everyone, Prince Philip included, was full of such benevolent feeling. Tony's track record of boys as well as girls was well enough known to give birth to some calculated insults. Nicky Haslam was at the Waldorf Hotel with the Windsors in New York at the same moment as General de Gaulle, who called on the Duke to convey his congratulations about the forthcoming marriage using the name of Margaret Rose. The Duke thanked him and then explained that the princess was no longer using the name of "Rose." Haslam wrote, "From across the room, the duchess's usual drawl became a whiplash. . . . She's dropped the Rose and picked up the Pansy."[38]

Tony Armstrong-Jones asked Jeremy Fry, his close friend, to be best man at his wedding. On the surface, this would have seemed a logical choice. There were many admirable aspects to Fry, heir to a famous manufacturer of chocolate in Bristol (Fry's), now part of Cadbury's.

Jeremy, who served as a pilot during World War II, was a part-time race car driver, started his own engineering company, and was a generous patron of the arts. When he learned that the Theatre Royal, an eighteenth-century playhouse in nearby Bath, which had a distinguished history, was about to fall down, he bought it. Then he had it restored faithfully, and it is still in use for pre-London tryouts of new plays to this day.

Fry, his wife, and their two small sons decided to make their home in Bath and bought Widcombe Manor on its outskirts. This was another grand survivor from the eighteenth century, standing in its own grounds, but in much better condition than the theatre. They proceeded to have weekend parties, which became known for their unexpected mixture of guests, whether they were a Hindu guitarist, an owner of a bistro, or assorted models. There were reports of drink, drugs, and freewheeling sex of ingenious varieties.

The last of their children, Polly, was in her forties when she requested a DNA analysis for herself and Tony Armstrong-Jones. She had reason to believe that Tony was her biological father. Why should she do that? There had been constant rumors that Armstrong-Jones had vehemently denied. He continued to do so. Then the results came back. Indeed he was.

Why does it matter? It mattered for several reasons. In the first place, Camilla was in the final stages of her pregnancy with Polly at the moment when Tony was about to marry a princess in Westminster Abbey in May of 1960. Conception presumably took place while Tony was courting his princess in the autumn of 1959. Perhaps the most important part of this sorry affair was that he had taken his best friend's wife to bed and then lied about it. No doubt Jeremy believed, at the time, that he was Polly's father. His withdrawal from the role of best man came about ostensibly for another reason. In the days when there were still laws against it, Jeremy Fry had propositioned a stranger in a park, was taken to court, and paid a small fine. At the eleventh hour he withdrew and was replaced by Dr. Roger Gilliatt, a nerve specialist, who explained he was happy to step in even though he did not know the bridegroom very well.

In May of 1960, Tony had not only broken up with two girlfriends—in addition to Jacqui Chan, there was Gina Ward, a gorgeous debutante as well—had made his best friend's wife pregnant and, at a moment when she was about to give birth, was marrying someone else. The interesting part of all this has to do with his state of mind just then. It was leaked to the press that the Palace circle was becoming concerned about his health. He complained of pains in the shorter leg, and there was a worry that he might have to do too much standing during the marriage ceremony itself. Had the Palace guard known there was something else to worry about—his best friend's wife—the marriage might well have been postponed at the very least. But in the days before DNA testing, no doubt Mrs. Fry allowed the natural assumption to be made that it was her husband's child. But, in fact, despite Tony's sturdy denials, decades later the truth was revealed. He had let down two very important people in his life, betrayed them, in effect.

Princess Margaret married Tony Armstrong-Jones in blissful innocence. Since the truth did not come out until 2004, two years after her death, she never knew.

As soon as the engagement was announced, the prospective bridegroom did not quite arrive at Westminster Abbey with plans already drawn for staging the performance. But he took over one aspect in particular: just how he wanted his future wife to look. In the past, as we have seen, the princess was ready to indulge his creative talents and accept his judgments, in fact rather liked having him in charge, as she had done with Peter. So, when he said he designed clothes, she believed him. On close inspection it transpired that his only experience was to design a set of ski clothes that were bizarre to say the least. Knickerbockers of leather that would have become a clammy disaster after the first good fall in snow, tops in gaudy striped silks that were gathered from bosom to hip so that the wearer looked pregnant—even his titled mannequins, who did their best, could not make the resulting clothes look flattering. A writer for the *New York Times* observed, "Mr. Armstrong-Jones's designs made no impact whatsoever on the fashion industry, and he returned to work as a photographer."[39]

It is safe to say that royal gowns have been consistent for centuries, meant to display status and wealth—especially those designed for great occasions. Any young designer worth looking at is going to make a deliberate attempt to do the reverse. Perhaps he does not expect to get away with a short sleeveless, shapeless tunic that stops several inches above the knee (the "sack" actually did become the height of fashion a few years later), but he could do its daring equivalent. So, what Tony did, using miles of silk organza, was design a traditional silhouette fitted bodice and exuberant skirt and train—and leave out the rest. No appliqués, no elaborately embroidered initials. No pearls, rhinestones, diamonds, gold leaf, painstaking flower designs.

The result was layers and layers of fine silk piled on top of each other and held out by stiff hidden crinolines. He added a massive train and a transparently simple veil. Maybe a single row of pearls. She must have looked, as she walked down the aisle, like a perambulating powderpuff.

That was it. After the fashion press got over its shock, the word was out. How daring! How just right. How original! After all, the bride was at the height of her beauty. Nothing must compete.

Attention shifted to the coronet she wore, which was, from a design perspective at least, considerably more interesting. And she bought it herself.

Early in 1959, the Poltimore Tiara—named for one of its previous owners, wife of the second Baron Poltimore—came up for auction, and the princess promptly bought it. A photograph exists of the baroness in profile, head held as high as she dares before the magnificent object of diamonds, silver, and gold, slides off the back of her neck. This marvel of scroll-like flowers in diamonds is not only twice as big as the usual tiara but makes twice as big an impression; in fact, it looks like a small crown. It has the further refinement of being wearable as a necklace or even a considerable number of brooches—a cunning little screwdriver goes with it. There are no photographs of the princess wearing it in scattered bits and pieces but plenty showing it on her head. Its great distinction is its ability to look conjured up by an obliging fairy grandmother for a princess who has just been awakened from her enchanted sleep by an adoring prince. Its four-inch height was an advantage to someone who had been accused all her life of not measuring up. Include two-inch heels, and she has added six inches and can look down on anybody.

There were a few drawbacks, of course. When the moment came, on the fateful day, for her to enter the glass carriage for her journey to Westminster Abbey, between the tiara and her train, she was too tall and temporarily stuck in the doorway. (She was soon rescued.) The Poltimore Tiara continues to show up in her photographs. She wore it once in the nude. That was Tony's idea. The setting was the bathtub, and most of her was well covered by bubbles.

Thousands lined the route that May of 1960 to wave her onwards, and, if you can believe the papers, many millions more watched on TV as the drama unfolded. Prince Philip, in joking form and with a great pink flower in his lapel, had been delegated to give her away, and accompanied her in the carriage. We even know a bit about what they said to each other. This is because the *Sydney Daily Telegraph* in Australia sent two lip readers to decipher their conversation during the ceremony. This is always touch and go, but was particularly difficult, because the prince's remarks were hard to read against the dark background of his coat.

Nevertheless, the lip readers claimed to have interpreted what the prince was saying as he mounted the steps to the altar.

"I hope I keep in step."

That apparently passed without comment from the bride. Somewhat later, when he bent closer and said, "Chin up, old girl—it won't be long now," she responded with a grateful smile. When he pointed to the littlest of her eight bridesmaids (aged six to twelve) and asked, "How do you think she feels?" the bride stifled a laugh.[40] She knew from experience.

Another close observer, Cecil Beaton, was not only official photographer for the wedding but a guest at the queen's reception beforehand. He acknowledged a professional jealousy at this rising young photographer with direct access to the Royals, something he himself had cultivated for years. He also dismissed the news, when he heard it, with "Silly girl!" Whatever could she be thinking?

That month he wrote in his diary that "the man of her choice looked extremely nondescript, biscuit-complexioned, ratty and untidy. He fidgeted with his large hands as he held them behind his back, leant forward, and smiled a tired smile. The fact that this man is of little standing, that he is in no way romantic (even as Townsend was) makes no matter for he is the man the Princess has fallen in love with, and so all must be made perfect in the eyes of the world. The fact remains the young man is not worthy of this strange fluke fortune, or misfortune, and because he is likeable and may become unhappy makes one all the sorrier."

Whether Tony Armstrong-Jones knew it or not, he had already aroused the protective instincts of the one royal advisor who had done so much to destroy her marital plans the first time: Alan "Tommy" Lascelles. It goes without saying that his opinion would have been sought by the Queen Mother, and the queen herself, this time round. What Lascelles thought has been revealed in the diary of Harold Nicolson, who asked him the same question. Lascelles replied: "the boy Jones has led a very diversified and sometimes a wild life, and the danger of scandal and slander is never far off." In short, he saw this romance ending as badly as he claimed to have seen the reign of Edward VIII. He stopped that one from happening, but nothing could stop this one.

Kenneth Rose, considered one of the most astute observers of the postwar establishment, also happened to be at the wedding and in a ringside seat with a full view of the Queen Mother and the queen. Neither of them looked happy. He wrote, "the Queen Mother . . . like a great golden pussycat, (was) full of sad little smiles." The groom himself appeared to have "aged very much in the last few weeks," and his skin was a bad color. As for the queen herself, she wore "a sulking Queen Victoria face throughout the entire service—not a ghost of a smile."[41]

Queen Elizabeth, Queen Consort to King George VI (right) with Princesses Elizabeth (left) and Margaret Rose (center); 1930.

Princess Margaret Rose (left) and her older sister Princess Elizabeth (right) on the grounds of the Royal Lodge, Windsor; June 1936. Princess Margaret is holding one of their pet dogs, a Cairngorm terrier called Chu-Chu.

Princess Margaret Rose reading on the sofa at Windsor Castle accompanied by Jane the corgi; June 22, 1940.

Princesses Elizabeth (left) and Margaret Rose (right) wearing Girl Guide uniforms at Frogmore, Windsor, Berkshire; June 30, 1942.

Queen Elizabeth (far left) leads her family on a tour of Sandringham Park; August 1943. With the queen are (left to right): King George VI and Princesses Elizabeth and Margaret.

King George VI (center right), Queen Elizabeth (center left), and the Princesses Elizabeth (far left) and Margaret (far right) wave happily from the balcony of Buckingham Palace after Japan's unconditional surrender on V-J Day; August 15, 1945. The surrender brought World War II to an end.

Princess Margaret attending the premiere of the film *Captain Horatio Hornblower* at the Warner Theatre Leicester Square; April 12, 1951.

Queen Elizabeth II (right), her sister Princess Margaret (left), and the queen's baby daughter Princess Anne (center) on the grounds of Balmoral Castle, Scotland; August 21, 1951.

Princess Margaret and Peter Townsend on holiday in Scotland; August 23, 1951.

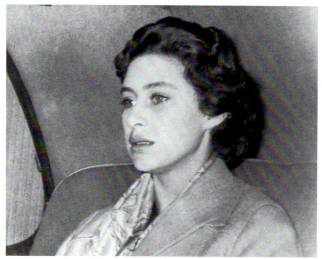

A troubled Princess Margaret returns to Clarence House after a weekend in the country where Group Captain Peter Townsend was also a guest; October 17, 1955. The decision not to marry Townsend was announced October 31, 1955.

Derek Berwin / Hulton Royals Collection via Getty Images

Princess Margaret and Antony Armstrong-Jones in the grounds of Royal Lodge after they announced their engagement; February 1, 1960.

President Lyndon B. Johnson dancing with Princess Margaret at a White House party given in honor of her husband Antony Armstrong-Jones and herself; November 17, 1965.

Princess Margaret and her husband Antony Armstrong-Jones (later Lord Snowdon) attend Badminton Horse Trials in Badminton, England; April 18, 1970.

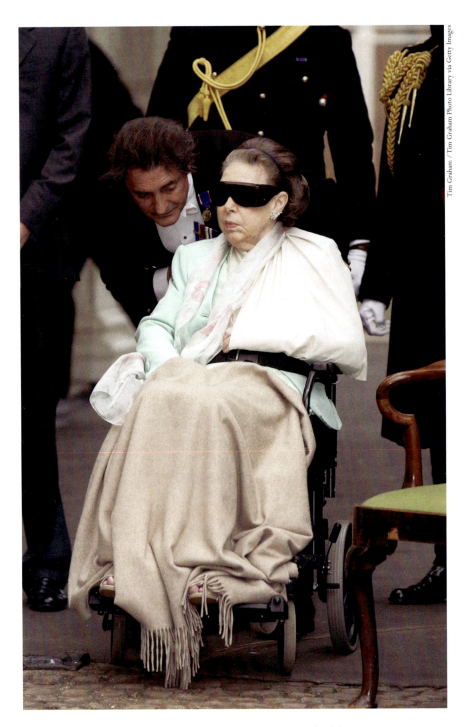

Princess Margaret at Clarence House in a wheelchair after suffering a number of strokes; August 4, 2001.

CHAPTER 10

HER SPECIAL ISLAND

> "Bali Ha'i will whisper on the wind of the sea
> Here am I, your special island. Come to me, come to me."
> —*South Pacific*

IN 1955 ON ONE OF her first trips to the West Indies, the princess landed in Barbados. It was a fine, fair morning in Bridgetown. Foghorns and sirens screamed her arrival. Flags, including her own standard, fluttered in the sunlight as she stepped off the royal yacht, wearing a dress in soft lilacs and a snappy pink hat. The island had assembled an amazing crowd, coming from all directions on bicycles and mules, estimated at thirty thousand. Wherever she looked, they were jammed into dozens of small ships jostling at anchor. One man, in this enthusiasm, fell off the pier. Another boat was so overloaded that it started to sink. But the real danger was on the pier, where the crowd, in constant slow motion like some vast amoeba, dipped and swayed, pressing against the barricades in an attempt to get closer, because, after all, nobody had seen a princess before.

As her open limousine made its stately progress through the massive crowds, people were making valiant efforts to touch the car because it was good luck. She was met by the governor, Sir Robert Arundell, in a white uniform and with a pith helmet sprouting extravagant plumes.

She made the obligatory inspection of the guard, walking up and down the rows and smiling a lot. All very routine. Still, the soft air, the crowd clapping, shouting and making wolf whistles, the atmosphere of festival and all those eager faces, gave the experience a special charm. Perhaps she thought it was rather like being smothered by a huge friendly dog who puts a paw on each shoulder, dislodges your hat, and smears your face with wet kisses. Given such a determined assault, formality is swept away in a spontaneous demonstration of affection.

The same thing happened wherever she went. By the time she was delegated to preside over the formalities accompanying Jamaica's independence, she had acquired a special bond with this former outpost of the British Empire, one that identified her as one of theirs. She would have been on easy terms with the music and dance one could find anywhere, a persistent reminder of the cultures African enslaved people brought with them. They might show traces of French court etiquette in the arrival of the dancers, their curtseys and bows, and the way they left the stage at the end.

The likenesses stopped there. These uninhibited leaps, jumps, hops, gyrations of hips and shoulders, accompanied by drums to the syncopated rhythms of steel bands, were one way of affirming their roots with an ancient culture despite everything; a defiant kind of self-expression with which someone like Princess Margaret could sympathize and identify. The dances were, in fact, so popular that they begin to influence ballroom dancing, which everybody did just then. Those relatively sedate quicksteps, slow quicksteps, waltzes, and tangos needed a new lease on life and were dressed up with new patterns of steps, sudden turns, hand claps, and even a skip or two. Margaret jumped and twirled and sang and drank along with everyone else. In one of her early tours, she stayed with Sir Hugh Foot, the governor of Jamaica, and his wife. He later revealed that, in a moment of exasperation, he had told his wife to turn the radio off, for goodness' sake. She explained that it was the princess, singing in her bath.[1] They were writing odes in her honor. She was their Calypso Princess.

Princess Margaret's unexpected popularity in this tucked-away corner of the world, now showing tourist potential, surprised people. She had performed with enough poise and diligence to please those who sent her, while diverging from the script in enough small ways to disarm those who had invited her. By now, she had made enough demanding trips on three continents to gain a comfortable familiarity with how you did what and when. A photograph of her taken in 1962, on the eve of Jamaica's independence, is indicative of her growing prominence. The photographer, standing behind her, records her right arm held stiffly by her side. Her left is bent to hold the regulation handbag. She is reviewing a very long line of soldiers some distance away. She is clearly a small, solitary figure with a very big responsibility.[2]

There was even a proposal that she should be made Governor of the Bahamas. The idea was first launched by the *Sunday Times* in 1955. Its owner, Lord Beaverbrook, proposed this following the collapse of her marriage plans with Townsend. The tone of the suggestion was in the order of "she's a natural—let's give her something by way of compensation."[3] Nothing came of that. But the year she married Tony, the idea surfaced again, this time as a rumor. Nothing came of that either.[4]

Margaret was a fine swimmer, and one of the attractions for her were the virginal beaches of the West Indies. There were few places in the British Isles where one could enjoy being beside the seaside. What one saw on a typical summer afternoon in Brighton, Lyme Regis, or Blackpool were miles of deck chairs in which holiday makers, bundled up in cardigans, have removed their shoes and rolled up their pant legs in the hope of testing the icy waters and going for a paddle. A few, brave and foolish, had stripped down to bathing suits and shivered their way through the breast-stroke. But when you retreated, there was nowhere to decently remove your wet suit and put on something dry, so you mostly didn't. Besides, it might rain.

The wealthy spent their summer holidays on the Riviera and the balmy climate of the Mediterranean. But that did not always mean they could go swimming. As late as 1970, the waters around Nice were contaminated by raw sewage being discharged directly into the waves. Once you had explored the exquisite glittering beaches of Trinidad and Barbados, where the pristine sands were molded, at the shoreline, with pretty water-born patterns and wading stirred up legions of tiny flashing fish, you never wanted to leave. She spent her honeymoon in an ecstasy of admiration, returning eventually to London "as brown as a berry" with a much-admired tan.

Despite the pleas of the princess for islanders to think of her and Tony as ordinary honeymooners and ignore them, there was always another ingenious infiltration, and elaborate precautions had to be taken. Roads leading to certain pretty beaches were cordoned off, and police were on hand to wave the cars away, along with the beachgoers. If the odd tourist was already swimming in the water, he or she would be politely asked to leave. Two weeks after their arrival, there was another threat. A twin-engine plane carrying a British journalist and some photographers was spotted cruising just above the trees on Tobago, looking, it seemed, for Tony and Margaret. This spying from above would become routine in the years to come, but was then an unpleasant aberration. (The plane was grounded for "flying too low.")[5]

These particular honeymooners arrived on the royal ship *Britannia*, always referred to as a yacht although it had long ceased to be one. Built in 1954, with the latest in modern equipment, including "stabilisers" to minimize its roll, it was the first such Royal boat designed to cross the oceans, which it did for more than forty years. The grand staircase, with its sweeping contours and gilt and black outlines, was clearly Art Deco in inspiration. To judge from contemporary photographs, the rest of the décor resembled nothing so much as a cozy living room in Glamis Castle, with its dowdy chintzes and unremarkable landscape paintings, right down to the fireplaces which one doubts were ever used. The Queen Mother probably felt right at home. There was even one in the master bedroom. To put it another way, when compared with the magnificent Cunard ocean liner, the *Queen Elizabeth* launched in 1938 as that queen's namesake, and the only thing the two ships had in common was furniture made of blond wood.

When Tony and Margaret went aboard, the *Britannia*, which after all was only five or six years old at the time, was smartened up with new blue paint and touches of red. The deck chairs on the sundeck repeated the theme, with a blue chair for Tony, no doubt designed to his specifications, and a chaise longue for Margaret painted red. A table for drinks had been thoughtfully provided. Tony showed up wearing a blue blazer with white pants, and Margaret all in red—sweater and skirt. No doubt it was an inside joke. Or perhaps he might have already been feeling too much a part of the furniture itself.[6]

Ship to shore communications being what they were, it is likely that neither had heard of a small commotion in London that had followed their departure. Apparently a certain "Mr. and Mrs. Armstrong-Jones" were offering a short let of their residence while they were abroad. The address was 51 Prince's Gate Mews, a very "Tony" part of Kensington. The flat itself had, or so the classified advertisement read, a "fine" first floor drawing room, an "elegant" dining room, two or three bedrooms, even a small den. What was more important than agreeing on the right rent was the suitability of the tenant, the same advertisement stated rather sniffily. That warning did not deter anyone, certainly not a busload of potential renters but also an avalanche of tourists, journalists, and photographers. It was quickly taken off the market because the property was "almost in a state of siege," the owner said. He was Ronald Armstrong-Jones, Tony's father.[7]

That understandable, perhaps mischievous, misunderstanding was soon cleared up. Another more puzzling incident at the same time has never been resolved. It concerned the exhibit of Princess Margaret and her new husband, Antony Armstrong-Jones, that had just been put on display at the famous Madame Tussaud's in London.

The honeymooners had hoped for a quiet homecoming that foggy morning on June 18, 1960, when *Britannia* hoved into view at Portsmouth Harbour, but it was not to be. At the first sight of the royal yacht, the coastal steamers, yachts, and dinghies already at anchor set up a barrage of sirens announcing the event and began to circle the boat. Tens of thousands of people already crowding the piers waved and cheered. The royal train, decked out with flowers, awaited their arrival and deposited them at Waterloo. More shouts, waves, and bouquets, more crowds in the station, and yet more on the pavements outside Clarence House. They escaped in due course to the weekend in the Royal Lodge at Windsor and some quiet at last. Presumably someone then told the groom what had happened, and he thought it was very funny.[8]

On the eve of their arrival, June 17, when Madame Tussaud's closed for the night, a newspaper seller said he saw three men carrying something bulky out of the back entrance. They loaded it into a Rolls Royce and sped away. Well, finding a very expensive, immediately recognizable car like that was tantamount to seeing one of the queen's coaches parked in an alley. So he noticed it.

Next morning, when Bernard Tussaud, the great-great-grandson of the founder, made his usual pre-opening inspection tour, he stopped dead in disbelief. In the Royal Family group, where a new display of Princess Margaret had been put on view to mark her marriage to Antony Armstrong-Jones, something was missing. It was Tony, dressed in white tie and tails. Not a sign of him anywhere. One of the staff said, "We were very cross about it."[9]

"Cross" is an understatement; they were, in fact, astounded. The famous museum, founded in 1802, never had a single waxwork stolen. A few odds and ends perhaps. The occasional piece of jewelry or even an actual finger, something you might slip into your pocket and not be missed. But never a waxwork, and certainly not this one. To begin with, it was 5'7" and weighed something like 160 pounds. Everything was gone: shoes, jacket, white tie, tails, the lot.

An immediate inspection was made of the premises. The men must have got in somewhere, but there was no evidence anywhere of a forced entry. That could only mean that the kidnappers had arrived while the museum was still open and then hid somehow until after it closed. (The staff pointed out that they could have been concealed in the chamber of horrors, where the lighting was dim.) Then the men simply let themselves out of the back door once the coast was clear. People found a certain significance in the fact that the figure captured and whisked away was him, not her. That was the strange part of it all. Why Tony?

For Bernard Tussaud, the immediate issue was replacing the missing man. Each year, a million visitors, paying four shillings each, came to marvel at such displays. Here was the actual death mask of Marie Antoinette. Here was a good guess at what William the Conqueror looked like. Here were the darling princes in the Tower, doomed for a horrible death, and here was everybody's favorite comedian, Peter Sellers.[10] It was going to take weeks to faithfully reproduce such a face, construct a convincing torso, fit him out with evening clothes, make the shoes, and fashion a lifelike wig of human hair. Such figures cost money. In 1960, the cost was £500. Nowadays it would be more like £10,000.

On the morning of June 19, a policeman making his usual early stroll along the Strand, made the discovery that one of the many red phone boxes seemed to have a drunken inhabitant. He was propped over the phone as if, in his inebriated state, he could neither make a phone call nor straighten up. He seemed to be paralyzed. The policeman opened the door and found he had discovered the missing exhibit from Tussaud's, much the worse for wear.

One paper reported that his handsome head was dented, as if it had been used as a bongo drum. His face was ashen and both hands had been broken off. His hair was all over the place. His white tie was similarly disarrayed. But perhaps the most interesting aspect was a green placard that had been tied around his neck. It said: WELCOME HOME.[11] It must be a joke. Or was it something else? Someone with a grudge? Getting even, perhaps. Someone with money. Could it have been his best man, the one whose wife he slept with? His best friend? The mystery remains.

No. 10 Kensington Palace is one of several handsome townhouses at the north end of the Palace grounds. Princess Margaret called it her "doll's house," but then, she would. Most newlyweds would consider a red brick, center hall Georgian townhouse with five bedrooms and five reception rooms, definitely on the grand side. It even had its own tiny walled garden. And the fact that it is contained within the precincts of a national treasure—the grounds surrounding Kensington Palace—would add to its special quality, since "every prospect pleases," as Jane Austen would have said.

These are listed as apartments, even though they are not. They were built as overflow housing, since there is a long tradition of accommodating Kings and Queens, Princes and Princesses, and their offspring for several centuries before the move to Buckingham Palace. Kensington existed as a stately home that housed an Earl originally and was expanded and embellished by Christopher Wren. He designed three-story pavilions at the four corners of the property, a *cour d'honneur* for its setting and marked its entrance with an archway containing its own clock tower. Satellite buildings like No. 10 came later; this was one of the most modest and right on the edge, adjoining the London Museum. From a certain vantage point, visitors to that museum can catch a glimpse of the comings and goings from No. 10. Visitors to the Palace itself—some of the grand rooms which once were frequented by Queen Victoria are now open to the public—can clearly see it from some of the windows. Inside the Palace, the apartments are lavish. The newlyweds wanted one of those instead.

In the meantime, the new husband, whose best ideas seemed to stem from distinctly unpromising projects, set to work. First it was white paint in the modern style for most of the interior, with pastels occasionally and special attention to certain stylistic flourishes where he liked the idea. He would attend to those himself. Empty walls clearly called out for shelving. He would do that. The challenge was exactly like The Room on a vastly larger scale and to make the best use of unpromising-looking spaces.

For instance, Princess Margaret had all kinds of novels, poetry, and biographies that had to go somewhere. She also had an even larger collection of recordings—jazz and also a whole section on ballet music. Their honeymoon was spent buying calypso and West Indian steel band music, and now there were forty more recordings that had to go somewhere. A well-designed cabinet would take care of all that. But there was nothing to be done about the wedding presents—all two thousand of them—so those stayed in storage, as did the bulk of Princess Margaret's massive wardrobe and all the hats, shoes, gloves, handbags, and coats that went with them. They went into storage as well.

There was only one reception room, and it was "so crowded with furniture that it looked as if an auction was about to take place," William Glenton wrote in *Tony's Room*.

"A grand piano took up a large part of the floor space, and the rest of the room was filled with a couple of roomy sofas, an armchair or two, several occasional tables and, wherever they could be squeezed in, some small upright chairs."[12]

Every table displayed silver-framed photographs of the princess's royal relatives. Almost as many, including she herself, stared down from the walls.

Glenton concluded that if more than two or three people were in the room, it would be a disaster. Not only were tiny tables everywhere, but the few that did not display pictures were laden with bowls of flowers, and it would take only one of Tony's expansive gestures for the whole thing to shatter and take cascades of water along with it. If they wanted to entertain, they had to corral their guests into the tiny dining room, where a buffet dinner would be set up, and there was only one long dinner table to clutter up the proceedings. Buffet dinners in which you served yourself! That must have been the first shock for Thomas Cronin, their new butler, when he arrived to command a skeleton staff.

While employed by Ambassador John Hay Whitney, Cronin had been in charge of a staff of thirty-seven. We know all about the splendor and lustre of his position after thirty or forty episodes of *Downton Abbey*. Within his precincts, the butler reigned supreme. That a royal household would serve buffet dinners was, no doubt, the first shock. The second was to discover the master of the household saying yes to his nos, taking charge of details he was not even supposed to know about, and patrolling the rooms with a hammer and slide rule. This would never do. He was hired in July and left a month later. So did Tony's personal valet and footman. What such staff need most of all is predictability and regular habits. They were not prepared for this whirlwind, who might want breakfast at noon and might never show up for dinner. Besides, the house resembled the same chaotic environment as The Room, with sawdust and paint brushes everywhere. Not to mention rolls of linoleum against the walls, chandeliers in plastic in the hallways, and new wall lights lying around for days on end.

No one really knows, but it seems likely that Princess Margaret endured the chaotic atmosphere with remarkable calm. One thinks back to the photograph of her in a limousine with a smile of sheer delight as Peter, her new fiancé, sat surrounded by papers organizing the next few hours and days. She clearly enjoyed a creative atmosphere in which anything could happen, secure in the knowledge that the person in charge is full of energy and determination. Tony could do anything. She stopped changing her hairstyles twice a week. She occasionally left her coat undone. She took to wearing skirts, sweaters, and sandals. She started make funny phone calls impersonating people and did such a good job that Glenton truly believed he was talking to Bea Lillie. Until he heard a familiar giggle.[13]

For Margaret, marriage to Tony represented a sharp division in her life, revealing vistas she could hardly have dared to imagine. Not only had she acquired, in her rigidly structured, claustrophobic world, a new status since she was now someone's wife, even if her husband was merely a freelance photographer. She had a house of her own. She was free at last from Clarence House and the tacit daily supervision that living a floor away from her mother implied. Not to mention all those unseen but watching eyes. Along with this came the freedom to comb her hair any which way, leave a button of her coat undone, and wear comfortable sandals instead of high heels.

"A sweet disorder in the dress/Kindles in clothes a wantoness," the poet Robert Herrick wrote in 1648.

Even more important, she could choose the company she preferred. She had never really taken to a world of horses, hounds, hunts, races, and all that was implied by marriage to one of the country's most eligible heirs of the great country estates. She was a born performer, with an instinctive gift that had helped her as she routinely mounted a platform to open something new day after day. Her world revolved around the theater. If she could not actually appear on a stage, she wanted to spend her life clinging to its edges. She sought the company of all those she admired and envied for their art, their awareness, their freewheeling approach to life, and the smell of greasepaint that lingered on their clothes. Tony had invented the kind of life she had always longed for. She wanted to stand as close to him as possible, become his shadow, be the Wendy to his Peter Pan. What she saw was the glow around him.

Tony's Room had given her the kind of heady experience that Audrey Hepburn, as a similarly hemmed-in European princess, had in *Roman Holiday* (1953) when she escaped from a hotel in Rome one night for life on the streets. She is rescued by a newspaperman who, thinking she is drunk (she was fed a sleeping pill), gives her a bed for the night. The next day, she goes wandering through the maze of streets around his Rome apartment, intoxicated by the novelty of drinking coffee in an outdoor café, buying an ice cream cone, and having her hair cut. He takes her for a ride on the back of a Vespa where she zips by the Coliseum, the Spanish Steps, the Fontana di Trevi—sights he sees every day—and experiences them anew through her amazed eyes. Gregory Peck, as her host, gradually realizes what a scoop her arrival represents and is all set to write about her. But the more he gets to know her, the more his reluctant sympathies are aroused. He ends by returning her to her hotel and the gilded straight jacket her position in life dictates. Rather than the accepted view of how desirable it is to be a princess, he realizes that he is the lucky one; he has learned enough.

In a curious parallel, William Glenton, who also earned a living as a freelance writer, could have betrayed the couple sheltering under his roof, and there was big money at stake. He did not write about it either until the story ended five years later. But by then, he knew just what this modest haven meant to them both.

After their marriage, he assumed they would not need it anymore and was astonished when they begged to be allowed to remain. Having The Room meant more than ever. Perhaps the princess shed a tear or two. of course they could stay. So, they went on visiting as usual, pulling up at the door in their "mini," the princess in dark glasses and muffled up with a large silk square over her hair. As usual. The marvel is that no one ever found out.[14]

One of the first people Her Royal Highness chose to invite to The Room was at the pinnacle of his fame as reigning grandee of the British theater: Noël Coward. This composer, actor, director, playwright, and solo performer had spent the war years in his own kind of war work. He moved to Paris to become an intelligence officer; a spy, in other words. He toured the camps entertaining the troops. He wrote and sometimes acted in films like *In Which We Serve* and *Brief Encounter*. One of the songs for which he is best remembered is a tender song about a little flower that was appearing everywhere in the bomb sites called London Pride. He saw it as the perfect symbol of the city's refusal to bend under assault and refuse to accept defeat. It was a metaphor for the resilience of a nation.

Coward had watched Margaret grow up and was well aware that her budding talents were soon likely to put her on a collision course with whatever fate awaited her. He saw it coming soon after she turned nineteen, in November 1949. It was during a dinner at the American Embassy.

"Princess Margaret obliged with songs at the piano," he wrote in his diary. "Surprisingly good. She has an impeccable ear, her piano playing is simple but has perfect rhythm, and her method of singing is really very funny."

The queen, whom he adored, "was sweet on account of being so genuinely proud of her chick."[15] Margaret's obvious talent had surprised everyone. Coward was much too diplomatic to give voice, even in a diary, to inner concerns.

In those years, his arrival anywhere, on or off the stage, was an occasion. He was so civilized, so funny, so poised and clever, and known in the profession for kindness, generosity, and as a dispenser of good sense. His solution was to sing duets with the princess whenever she wanted and do his best to help if and when an emotional storm hovered on the horizon. Just then he was working on *Sail Away*, a musical set on a luxury cruise liner that would become his most successful postwar musical. But there was a slight problem. Lots of people knew what he looked like, and even liked to mimic his clipped, staccato way of delivering a line. Now he was about to be smuggled into The Room.

Somehow Tony and Margaret, in their modest "mini," managed to shoehorn Noël, immaculately turned out in white tie and tails, along with his date for the evening—the actress Margaret Leighton, long-legged and a lanky 5'8"—into the back seat. She wore a full-length evening dress in a shade Glenton described as "peacock" brown. The princess, now pregnant, was demurely attired in something low-cut, turquoise, and loose around the middle.

Tony, too, wore white tie. The splendor of the outfits should have tipped off any observer. On the other hand, the two couples tore out of the car and into the doorway with such practiced ease that all anyone was likely to experience was a tinkle of laughter and the brief flash of a high-heeled ankle strapped in gold. In the dim entranceway, faces glimmered in the candlelight.

"What a simply charming smell," Margaret Leighton said suddenly. "Just like old rope!"[16]

They had arrived after dinner for conversation and music, swilled down with plenty of gin, scotch, and whatever else was in the house. The princess joined in. In those days, the newfangled idea that nicotine and alcohol might harm a developing baby was positively preposterous. Noël Coward, who grew up in the East End, said he had always wanted to work on a barge. Now that he was rich and famous, he was free to confess his modest, humdrum background, even take a certain pride in it. He particularly remembered his meandering crawls from one pub to the next and described in detail the ones that were no longer there. He was reciting the sad past history one night in a taxi. The driver, plainly moved, invited him back home and refreshed more of the great man's memories with generous glasses of gin.[17]

At this point, the princess sat down on the divan, her legs crossed under her in schoolgirl fashion and insisted on a full account of Coward's childhood. So, Coward began to reminisce about Battersea. As he did so, "his voice lost much of its familiar cabaret drawl"[18] and took on, according to Glenton's expert ear, the familiar vowels of someone who had grown up on the South Bank. Then Tony had an anecdote about a Battersea pub. It seems that, just after his engagement to the princess was announced, he was sitting in the pub, minding his own business, when a complete stranger sauntered in his direction and threw a glass of beer all over him. How annoying that the obnoxious stranger was so much bigger than he was. A friend came to the rescue. He pushed the offender outside and, Tony said with satisfaction, gave him "a jolly good thrashing."[19]

It was something of a Henry Higgins evening, come to that, the dialectician whose fame is forever celebrated in the undeniable fact that "an Englishman's way of speaking absolutely classifies him." The musical *My Fair Lady*—the famous offshoot Shaw's play, *Pygmalion*—was one of the princess's particular favorites. One of the funniest scenes is when Higgins tries out his new pupil Eliza at a tea party. By now, she can speak in ringing tones but, as yet, has no idea of subject matter. Then there is her shocking moment as she leaves and uses a swear word, "bloody." Princesses were not even supposed to *know* about such a word, much less throw it about. Her Royal Highness saw *My Fair Lady* to find out whether the word popped up. It did. How shocking! She saw the musical four times.

It was a bit shaming that Coward, the brightest of West End stars, should be reduced to using the world's most ancient piano, not to mention one that had not been tuned for eons under the watchful gaze of that fierce old sea captain, painted or not. He hammered away nevertheless. As the visitor reached crescendos, the room began to stir. China objects on shelves did a little jig. The floor heaved. Coward played on. Then, all at once, there was a huge crash over their heads. A door on the next floor up that had been hanging by a single hinge collapsed.

"I've always wanted to bring the house down," Coward said happily.[20] He went on playing and singing previews of *Sail Away*. Margaret chimed in. The landlord went to bed.

Once influential voices in and around the Royal Court learnt of the arrival of an heir in late autumn of 1961, something had to be done. That the new arrival was due to be named Mr. or Miss Armstrong-Jones could not possibly happen. It was "not ON," as the slang expression of the day would have had it. Margaret's new husband must be promoted, and the sooner the better. But what about the title? Somebody thought of the fact that he was Welsh in origin and what about that famous mountain in the picturesque northern and rural part of Wales? So it was fitting that he became Lord Snowdon. It sounded right.

To go from being an ignored and emotionally neglected boy living from hand-to-mouth in a basement in Pimlico to the consort of a princess, and just knighted, is a heady experience. This happy set of events coincided, in short order, with the news that they were to move to a twenty-room suite in Kensington Palace itself, which they rapidly tore out right down the Palace walls to his redesign at their leisure. The couple also explained that the new Earl would need a dark room for his photography. Done. Then, how about a workroom for his carpentry? He loved to design things. Done again.

The idea of his continuing as a photographer was something of a sore spot. Lord Snowdon had agreed when they married that he would no longer act as a photographer for hire. This complicated things because, like his competitor Cecil Beaton, he went on taking pictures of the Royals, including his own immediate family. Barely six months after their marriage, the *Sunday Pictorial* reported that he was "fighting tooth and nail to remain a professional photographer."

He had stoutly declared to "make himself useful," in his role as the consort of a princess. But then he turned down one job after another because "none of the ideas put forward by court officials has offered him any scope with a camera."[21] In this he was fiercely defended by his wife, who was very proud of his talent. They had opposite fighting skills. She tended to blurt out the first thing that came into her head, which could be a distinct disadvantage. He, on the other hand, worked with stealth, by indirection and subterfuge while smiling, which had problems of its own. At least you knew where you were with the princess. With her husband, you never knew.

Princess Margaret, by now, understood that someone like Tony, who grew up as an outsider in his own family, would gravitate to being an observer in a world at large, and the importance of the role in his emotional makeup. Those in charge had prevented her from developing her natural talents. They were not going to prevent Tony from doing the same. Her passionate support must have been soothing, if not reassuring, to her husband. With her behind him, how could he go wrong?

So when, in early 1960, the *Sunday Times* offered him a job as artistic advisor at its new magazine at the munificent annual salary of £10,000, he jumped at it. "Advisor" was actually a code word meaning that he would be taking pictures for them. In other words, a male member of the Royal Family was taking the unheard-of step of working for a salary. Senior royal males, who were well provided for by the public purse, always took *unpaid* jobs for worthwhile causes, proselytizing for orphanages or hospitals, or the welfare of the homeless. They did not *work* for anybody. The voices raised in opposition were loud and personal. Peregrine Worsthorne, a conservative commentator and royalist, wrote a blistering column published in the *New York Times*. It was a direct personal attack on him. The new Lord Snowdon was being compared unfavorably to people like the new Duchess of Kent.

"Because of their solid, respectable, propertied family backgrounds, their tastes and indeed their very appearance, they were somehow the right human raw material out of which princesses could be made," Worsthorne wrote of the Duchess. By contrast, Tony was upper-class in "quite the wrong sort of way—smart, rich, fashionable, without . . . any clear place in the traditional ordering of British society . . . Moreover, the rather raffish café-society life Tony Snowdon led before his marriage fitted into none of the traditional British class patterns." Could anyone see him as honorary colonel of a regiment? What a joke.[22]

Ignoring whatever assurances already made that he would no longer take pictures for a living, Snowdon's first assignment for the *Sunday Times* magazine was to take pictures of a ballet rehearsal in Covent Garden of Margot Fonteyn and Rudolph Nureyev shortly after the latter's defection from Russia, which would result in one of the great ballet partnerships of the times.[23]

"Who fixed it for Tony?"[24] the *Daily Mirror* wanted to know, concluding "The Royal Dicky Bird got the worm."

The other newspaper proprietors suspected "*La Reine le Veut*," which was true. Queen Elizabeth II did not see a problem.

The venerable *Sunday Observer*, in direct competition with the *Sunday Times*, was quick to feel the cold circulation winds of favoritism. Other papers like the *Evening Standard*, less directly affected, called the appointment a "bad blunder" and wrote that the Royal Family had fallen into a "booby trap."[25] Even Prime Minister Macmillan's government was obliged to answer the accusation that the prime minister had failed to bring the issue up with the queen on a recent visit to Sandringham.[26]

The disapproval that perhaps hurt the most came from the profession itself. The feeling seemed to be widespread that a struggling freelance photographer had seduced a princess so that he could corner every good assignment that was going, and they did not stand a chance. Such an objection to what looked like blatant favoritism was conveyed in a host of ways, which no doubt explained the incident of the glass of beer poured on the hapless Snowdon's head. He was described as talentless, a lightweight, a figure of fun. Having properly applied for and received a union card from the National Union of Journalists, Snowdon was faced, in the spring of 1962, with being "kicked out" of the journalists' union.

In the most ironic twist of all, Snowdon was now the hunted, and not just the hunter. Glenton observed that "it was especially difficult for him when he first came under fire from batteries of cameras."[27] To pose in a studio with the right lighting was one thing. Candid cameras could catch the kind of expression you should not be caught dead wearing, and there was nothing you could do about it.[28] Even he, whose skill at sliding away from confrontation was already pronounced, could not evade everyone; there were just too many of them. And they were out to get him.

"Poor Tony and Princess M. are really upset about their bad press," Coward wrote in his diary. "I tried to comfort them."[29]

Things were not all bad, though. Anthony "Tony" Wedgwood Benn, a distinguished Labour Party member of Parliament who began representing Bristol and Bath in 1950 and ended up as a Cabinet minister, was planning a lecture tour in 1961. The papers got it wrong—as usual, he noted wryly. One particularly egregious example was that of a college magazine, which announced that the MP was planning to appear, adding that he was "better known as Lord Snowdon." Benn sent the notice to Snowdon, with the comment, "My dear Snowdon, I thought you might be amused by this; they were very disappointed to find that I wasn't." Snowdon replied, "The press never says anything as nice about me as that, and I hope they keep it in their files."[30]

Once his son David Albert Charles was born early in November 1961, Tony turned again to discovering the miraculous in the very small that he found so absorbing earlier. This time there was a new subject perfectly willing to pose whenever he liked. Rather than be satisfied with a full-length picture of his wife holding their new baby, he focused on her head in close and intimate contact with their son's when the baby was perhaps just a month or two old.

Then Tony enlarged the image, cropped it, and enlarged it again. Finally, he had trimmed off enough, and what was left was enough to show the mother's smile, the baby's head, and the detail he had been working towards. In dead center were the curling, undulating fingers of the infant, looking like some delicately swaying plant left behind in a rocky pool at low tide. So fragile, and inexpressibly tender.

Chapter 11

A Slipper on the Lawn

"The one charm of marriage is that it makes a life
of deception absolutely necessary for both parties."
—Oscar Wilde

TONY SITS ON THE EDGE of the table aimlessly swinging his legs. He needs someone to relay his various complaints to the world and has fastened on Kenneth Rose. His onetime teacher at Eton has become a columnist for the *Daily Telegraph*, an establishment insider, and astute observer and sage, respected for his measured judgments. As a result, he is widely quoted. Tony's immediate issue is to find out what Rose's influential circle is saying about his new title as Earl of Snowdon. Rose is welcomed by the princess, now in the final stages of her pregnancy with baby David. She has provided afternoon gin and tonics, then discreetly left them alone.

Rose appreciates this. He notes in his journals that she has a tiresome habit of constantly interrupting her husband.[1]

At that particular moment, Rose seemed to find Tony an eminently more interesting and sympathetic figure than his wife. So did Milton Gendel, also a photographer with a definite Surrealist bent. Gendel, of Russian-Jewish extraction, grew up in New York and then embarked on a long and distinguished career as an American in Paris, London, or Rome without ever accepting the role of expatriate. When asked how long he intended to stay, he would always dismiss the question with "Oh, I am just passing through." And so it went on down the decades, his idea of a quiet joke. In fact, he did spend quite a lot of time in London after marrying Judy Montagu, one of Princess Margaret's bosom friends. Therefore, this quiet, funny, undeceived recorder of events is a reliable witness to the marriage of Tony and Margaret, which turned out to be such a bad idea.

He wrote in his diary, "Tony . . . is very attractive in an improbable way. The upper part of his face is pretty—curly blond hair, round blue eyes, pretty nose; the lower is big-jawed and masculine. His body is slight, but he has great muscular blond hairy forearms . . . (H)is character is . . . a curious mixture of masculine firmness and straightforwardness and feminine coquetry and occasional deviousness . . ."[2]

At the same time, Tony consulted Rose about his new title.

"I do hope people do not think I wanted the title for myself. The Queen wished me to have it, and it would have been arrogant of me to have refused," he told Rose defensively.

There were already murmurings about the astonishing way he and his wife had stripped the prestigious apartment 1A of the Palace—always called a "house," for reasons that are not clear—down to the bare walls. Just how much would it cost to rebuild? There were already murmurings of rebellion by senior politicians in both houses. But there, Tony had been very clever, Rose wrote in his journal. Before it was completely demolished, he had taken almost a hundred photographs of its interior. These showed that not only had it suffered from years of neglect, but was further subjected to serious bomb damage during the war. It had to be cheaper—certainly *simpler*—just to tear it all down and start again.

There was another reason for his indignation, since people were saying he was living off his wife. That was outrageous. As a matter of fact, he was supporting himself from his work as a photographer perfectly well. Compared to the "miserable hovel" they were living in—an oblique reference, apparently, to their five-bedroom townhouse—he had formerly lived in "great luxury." That was outrageous, but Tony, with a point to make, was a convincing liar.

What Rose knew then (but Tony did not) was the extent to which he was beginning to annoy other people, in this case the staff at Clarence House. The tradition of the Royal Family had always been to have doctors come to them, however radical the procedure, and George VI had stayed in Buckingham Palace even when an operation was performed on his lung. The Princess was slated for birth by C-section—a less serious operation than it was in the past—and that would be held at Clarence House, so back they went. Now Rose, with his fascinating connections, was getting the inside story from the Queen Mother's press secretary when that gentleman, Major John Griffin, came to dinner.

"The Household are very bored indeed with him," Griffin said. "When drinks are being poured out, (Tony) expects this to be done for him by the Household, and so on. And they are much shocked by his extraordinary dress." (Not explained, but they were probably referring to the usual scruffy check jacket, suede boots, and rumpled trousers.)[3] Rose learned, as Tony mentioned in an offhand kind of way, that he never read a book. Too busy, presumably.

Rose continued, "Part of the trouble of course, is that he is neither Royal or non-Royal, and never quite knows when to be either."

With his usual tact, Rose had managed to remain on good terms with this kaleidoscopic personality and was continually being consulted. A month later, Tony was about to give a speech at the annual dinner of the Royal Photographic Society and was in a new panic. Rose was summoned.

When the visitor arrived at the sitting room in Clarence House that Tony had been given while he wrestled with the Big Speech, Rose found every table littered with drafts of the opus in various versions. Rose sat down and went through them all. There were some good ideas tucked away between the paragraphs in which the author was plainly losing his argument. If you peeled away the dross, there was plenty worth saving, quite original and lively as well. You could do this, drop that . . . Rose set to work with a will. One imagines him cutting and pasting, inserts from A to T finding their way into the scheme, while Tony watched the master at work. At the end of a couple of hours, what had meandered about aimlessly was beginning to take shape. Tony began to perk up. It was rather good after all.

Tea arrived on a single enormous tray and cheered the author up even more.

"'Look,' says Tony, as excited as a little boy, 'a great meal, with knives and forks and buns and things,'" Rose wrote.

They made short work of the smoked salmon sandwiches and then set about demolishing the iced cake. After a short interval, another large tray, this time of whiskey and Malvern water, arrived to settle the matter.[4]

In those days, Princess Margaret was not only eager to praise her husband's ideas but would spring to his defense whenever she suspected he was being shabbily treated. Rose learned that, when it seemed the peerage patent would not be ready in time for one of his important official engagements, she went on the attack. How dared anyone treat him that way? They were being besieged, she said, at both ends of Kensington.

"At one end are the Press, at the other end the ban-the-bombers."
She threw in some scathing remarks about the plays of John Osborne for good measure.[5] Buoyed by her indignation, Tony was defiant. "I don't care what the public thinks," he said. "I want to be a real person, not a specially designed image for public consumption."[6]

His wife could have nailed it to her mast.

If, because of circumstances beyond her control, by her generation's standards, the Princess was now an old maid, she had redeemed herself in the eyes of the establishment at least. She had found someone who had not been married before. Even though he was a commoner, he was a very presentable one, since he had an upper-class background. He had attended Eton. That was big, since he had made the right contacts and acquired the right frames of reference. The pressure on her to marry and have children in order to continue the House of Windsor line must have been relentless. Was she marrying on the rebound? It was difficult not to think so. Never mind. She said she was in love, which was the main thing. After a year of marriage, Margaret was pregnant—with a boy, as it turned out. A baby girl would follow two years later. All was well.

Princess Margaret married and became a mother at an interesting historical moment. On the one hand, given the many millions who had died during World War II, there was an understandable effort to get young women married as soon as possible and start large families. One early postwar book (1947) that was widely read, *Modern Woman: The Lost Sex* (Lundberg and Farnham), argued that women were emasculating men by taking over their roles, at the same time rejecting their profoundest yearnings, which was to marry and have children. New manuals appeared giving detailed instructions on baby and child care, by Benjamin Spock in the United States and Penelope Leach in the United Kingdom, and became best sellers. They would suggest that many young women had followed such advice.

However, a second wave of feminism was making itself felt. One can trace such stirrings as far back as Virginia Woolf's plea for *A Room of One's Own*, (1929). Then there was an American novelist and poet with the unfortunate name of Olive Higgins Prouty, born at the end of the nineteenth century, whose writings were equally influential. Her most famous film, *Now Voyager* (1942), led the avant-garde with its argument that a girl's needs ought to be respected even if a psychiatrist was needed to make the transformation. That was the most shocking idea of all.

Many of the novels written by Olive Higgins Prouty were semi-autobiographical. One assumes this was her way of solving any inner hesitation by becoming a character in a book and then writing about herself at one remove. Something like that also seems to have happened with Doris Lessing when she committed herself in print to *The Golden Notebook* in 1962, just after Princess Margaret's son David was born. She had touched some kind of nerve—it was a sensation. All of this paled beside the sizable, educated majority of women who really did read books. Betty Friedan's *The Feminine Mystique* (in 1963) was a bombshell that had vast and long-lasting repercussions.

Did Her Royal Highness discover herself as a member of the "Lost Sex" and rededicate herself to her traditional role? Or experience the frisson of one whose expectations for her own life have just been turned upside down by *The Golden Notebook*? We shall never know.

She and Tony were completely taken up just then with the delicious problem of filling a big bare hole in Kensington Palace with four floors and twenty-two rooms. In this endeavor, they had the benign interest of Oliver Messel, Tony's uncle, the justly renowned and celebrated scene designer for theater and film. It was he who visited his nephew often when he was recovering from polio, encouraged his interest in design and construction and, when the time came, lent the Royal couple his principal assistant. Messel himself added some finishing touches, such as concocting a theatrically bright blue to one of the rooms that were otherwise weighted down by their delicate eighteenth-century furnishings. Margaret had a pale green, beige, and yellow bedroom this time but the same pink bathroom and pink wall-to-wall carpeting. Pink it should be, but never quite the pink one expects. That was Messel.[7]

Unlike Jackie Kennedy, who arrived at the White House in 1961 to do something drastic right away, Princess Margaret was very much the junior partner in the great Kensington Palace makeover. President Kennedy presumably looked on with a proud smile as his discriminating wife tossed out furniture that looked as if it had been won in a raffle and appealed to the country to restore the beautiful, now valuable original pieces that had somehow disappeared into other collections. She became an antiquarian, a historian, and the best possible spokesman for the concept that the nation's symbolic palace should look worthy of its role. Apartment 1A in Kensington Palace had a slightly different problem; an endless supply of exquisite furnishings was immediately available; what was needed was a kind of dash and flair. Tony, guided by his uncle, provided all that; his wife was relegated to sticking bits of things on other things, as she did when she was put to work gluing on mahogany panels to some rather plain doors. She is also credited with having discovered the right color of the kitchen units when, in a "eureka" moment, she scooped up the egg Tony was boiling, had it carefully wrapped, and sent to the paint manufacturer.[8]

On December 17, 1963, Kenneth Rose was invited to see the new quarters over breakfast.[9] They were served melon, haddock, and eggs in the dining room, which had apricot walls and pale-blue chairs. Then, they were taken through the drawing room with its white walls, rose curtains, and ingenious revolving bookcase, mostly containing beautifully bound presentation volumes that nobody was ever going to read. Including Tony.

Then Tony took his former teacher to his "very modern and elegant" study to admire the mahogany veneers of the doors—which Tony proudly said he had done himself, forgetting his helper—and a complicated piece of furniture to house not only a record player, tape recorder, and projector, but an elaborate system for broadcasting in every room. There were three paintings by Sidney Nolan, an Australian artist whom Snowdon much admired, hanging on the walls and three phones, all of them constantly ringing. The whole house, he wrote, had been "charmingly designed, with a pervading atmosphere of discreet wealth and civilized taste."[10]

Although Rose did not mention it, his former pupil must have boasted about his son, because he told everybody. The couple had agreed before their marriage that they did not want children. But then he changed his mind, and so, "[she] gave him two," she explained laconically. First David, then a daughter, Sarah.

"On her doctor's advice, she breast-fed her babies for the first few weeks of their lives and formed the fashionable 'bonding,'" Ingrid Seward wrote in her book, *Royal Children*. "If they started crying in the night, she would be the first up—*if* she had gone to bed."[11]

It was also becoming fashionable in the postwar years for young, educated mothers to start talking about early childhood education, and for the rich to hire those expensive but professionally guiding "Norland nannies" in Bath with their three years of training. Rather surprisingly, the princess chose one of the old-fashioned, no-nonsense kind she herself had experienced. A lady named Verona Sumner, whose origins are obscure, was put in charge of young David, then Sarah as well. The choice seems curious, particularly since she was not much liked, refused to talk to "lesser" beings in the household, turned up her nose at taxis instead of private cars, and must have made a formidable opponent whenever anything she decreed was challenged. She had, people explained, a grand manner, spoke with elaborate precision—which ought to have put her employer on guard right away—and acted "*plus royaliste que le roi*," as the French said.[12] There was the suspicion that she could be resentful and backbiting with other members of staff. Nevertheless, Nanny Sumner took over when, at the age of two months, David was left in her sole charge while his parents flew to Antigua for a three-week holiday. What her sister Queen Elizabeth had done without adverse comment when she left Prince Charles suddenly looked bad. Other times, other verdicts.

When the princess said she had not much wanted children, she no doubt had been truthful, which perhaps explains her apparent lack of interest in this all-important choice. Her husband took a closer look at what Nanny was saying and doing in her small kingdom and lively exception to it upon occasion—to judge from Anne de Courcy's account of the battles ahead. As for the princess, Glenton was amazed at her aplomb when, just two months after her first baby arrived, she acted as if nothing special had happened.

"If I had not offered them my congratulations, I do not think either of them would have mentioned it."[13]

Once the subject was officially recognized, the princess acted with commendable enthusiasm.

"He's a wonderful baby . . . hardly any trouble at all . . ." artlessly revealing just what constituted a "good" baby by her, and general, standards. This idealized notion of the smiling, cooing, rosy-cheeked infant who never seems to be hungry or teething or needs to be changed was reinforced from time to time by comments about how many teeth David had and how quickly—as if he were personally responsible; how fast he said "mummy" and "daddy"; how quickly he sat up, and so on. The really big news came when he graduated from his potty at eighteen months. What a paragon of goodness. No more diapers—or nappies, as they were called—at just eighteen months!

Glenton's wife Nenne was expecting a baby herself a few months later. The princess was full of the kind of reassurances that only a mother can give, who, having given birth by C-section, had not actually experienced labor pains herself. It was no trouble, in fact it "hardly hurt at all." Everything was so easy. The Glentons must have smiled politely. But they had no extra room, no money for a nanny or a maid or washing machine, let alone a clothes dryer. They didn't even have a backyard. All this mattered in the days when disposable diapers were a distant dream. What were they to do?

The one reliably warm area of the house, thanks to a new heater in the entry hall, was just inside the front door. The best possible place to dry laundry. So, in the manner of Neapolitan housewives who were used to hanging, unblushing, all the family's "smalls" for the world to see from one house to another across the street, Bill and Nenne did likewise inside the front door.

The solution could be disassembled quickly whenever guests were expected. The problem was, thanks to Tony's insistence on arriving late, or not at all, the Glentons could never plan ahead. As a result, a confrontation with wet diapers, whenever Tony and Margaret chose to arrive, was unavoidable. One imagines the door opening, the Glentons apologizing profusely while the visitors ducked and ran.[14]

Early in their marriage, there were plenty of occasions when the young couple arrived together. Whenever Margaret had an official appearance, she had to be accompanied by an escort—that was just the way it was—so that involved Tony, walking two decorous steps behind her. He tried it for a while. A photograph exists showing them at a UN meeting, in the act of listening to a speaker. The princess, dressed in full regalia, wearing a coronet, gives the proceedings her fierce attention, sitting ramrod straight on a bench. Tony, seated beside her, has given up all pretense of listening. He sits at right angles on the end of the bench, curled up in an agony of boredom.

Now that all the telephones were ringing all the time, Tony was busy. Too busy. So by autumn of 1962, someone else had taken over the escort job. He was a handsome major of the Coldstream Guards. His duty was to accompany the princess wherever she went, whether to Ascot or down a coal mine. Major Michael Patrick Mitchell was fine horseman, a smooth dancer, and a first-class shot, so he filled all the requirements. Perhaps he was even a good conversationalist. Nevertheless, for really important occasions, only the Earl of Snowdon would do.

Such a day came about when the island of Jamaica voted to secede from Britain and become a separate nation-state in 1962. It would still be part of the British Commonwealth, but its days as a colony were over. A member of the Royal Family was needed to preside over the formal proceedings, smilingly giving consent while the people clapped and cheered as the rule of Empire came to an end and the Royals were sent packing. Margaret was sent to represent the queen, along with Tony, all dressed up in formal attire, guiding her elbow and smiling from the sidelines.

The ceremonies were protracted: dinners, parades, singing, and dancing—it went on for a week and, that August of 1962, is minutely recorded in newsreels and glossy magazines. Even the United States was invited, at an occasion momentous enough to call for the presence of its then Vice President, Lyndon Johnson, and his wife Ladybird. The moment arrived when Princess Margaret was required to say, "My government in the United Kingdom has laid down its responsibilities and has ceased to have any authority in and over Jamaica, after more than 300 years . . ." This was a reference to the fact that

Britain had seized the island from Spain in 1655 and governed it ever since. The island she loved; it was too much. She did something unthinkable—that no princess ever dares to do. She burst into tears.

In those years, Margaret was often delegated to represent the queen, and she sometimes joined her husband on trips abroad as well. When Tony was sent on assignment to Uganda for the *Sunday Times*, she went with him, diligently taking notes for every shot so as to provide the essential captions.[15]

Tony, however, was not on the scene when, just as the renovations to their Kensington Palace apartment were almost finished, a spectacular fire broke out one day in January 1963. Flames thirty feet high shot up into the sky, and a hundred firefighters rushed to the scene to break holes in the roof and stop the blaze before too much damage had been done. It had begun in servants' quarters attached to an apartment occupied by Princess Marina, the Duchess of Kent, which adjoined their own. Margaret rushed to get her own camera, tied a huge scarf around her hair as camouflage, and proceeded to document the disaster herself. It took almost an hour to put the fire out. As usual, almost no one in the crowd noticed her. Apartment 1A escaped unharmed, and they moved in a month later.

It was a strange period in her life when near-disasters accompanied by lucky escapes arrived without warning.

She was shaken up (even if not injured) the summer before when she was in Ireland visiting Tony's sister Susan, now married to Lord de Vesci. Their host was driving the princess and her husband on a sightseeing tour of the local farms and village. Her Royal Highness was seated beside her host and not wearing a seatbelt, even though one had been provided—a police car followed behind. All went well until their car made a tight left-hand turn in County Tipperary and suddenly encountered a twenty-ton sound truck coming in the opposite direction; there was no room for them to pass. With great prescience, de Vesci braked sharply and swung the car up onto a grassy bank, missing the truck by inches. The princess grabbed the dashboard, and was hurled forward with a violent jolt. The car managed to skirt a hedge and carved a three-yard furrow in the grass but escaped damage with inches to spare. His passenger had somehow also escaped unharmed and "smiled reassuringly." The policeman in the car behind them had witnessed it all. It was nobody's fault; just one of those things, he said.[16]

The episode of tears at the Jamaican independence ceremony was not caught by the cameras. That must have been an accident because Her Royal Highness's commercial value continued to climb. By the early 1960s, it was said that she was right up there as one of the world's two most desirable photographic subjects, the other celebrity being Elizabeth Taylor. By then the queen had appealed to the Press Council that photographers had been persistently intruding on the "off-duty privacy" of the Royal Family. For instance, the *Sunday Express* and *The People* had both printed a group of bathing beauty photos a freelancer took of the princess getting in and out of rubber tops on their private beach. On another occasion, when she was preparing to waterski, two freelancers "were discovered hiding in the undergrowth, their lenses trained on a hut where Margaret was changing her clothes." The particular offender received "a sharp rap over the knuckles."[17] But then, anything that made pictures of a svelte princess harder to get made them more desirable than ever.

In 1964, the princess was involved with an even more newsworthy incident, which not only ended happily but which her own personal pack of paparazzi had not been able to record. Shortly after the birth of Sarah (May 1, 1964), she and Tony accepted an invitation from Prince Karim Aga Khan IV to spend three weeks in August on one of his vessels, in this case the *Amaloun*, a luxurious seventy-two-foot yacht valued at $200,000. They set off from Costa Smerelda, a new upmarket resort the Aga Khan was developing on the island of Sardinia, for three weeks of waterskiing, sunbathing, and snorkeling.

All went well at first. Then one day, as the *Amaloun* was skirting the shoreline of Mortorio and its protected coastline (it was a national park), there was a shudder, and the boat ground to a halt. It had hit a rocky slope, which gashed a hole in its side. Then it began to sink. Its passengers donned life jackets, climbed into a dinghy, and made it to the shore. The first thing the princess did was call her sister to say they were safe. The headlines were irresistible: PRINCESS IN SHIPWRECK! The paparazzi must have been gnashing its collective teeth.[18]

Princess Margaret was learning the hard lesson that the more prominent a person is, the more that person is considered a target, not only to be weighed and found wanting by anybody, but someone to be captured and paraded before the crowds as a trophy. That is, if there was a war to be won, and in Ireland, there always was. Despite the island's historic success in establishing most of its territory as a republic (by 1939), its Irish Republican Army would never be satisfied until its northern territories were also released into Irish hands. Anonymous telephone threats to find the princess and gun her down began to occur, one most notably in the summer of 1964 (in Stoke-on-Trent), but could be dismissed with the public's assurance that her guard would be increased.[19] Threats coming from Ireland, however, were a more serious matter, and it appeared that a guerilla war over Northern Ireland was about to begin with an announcement by the outlawed Irish Republican Army that any member of the British Royal Family who visited Ireland that January would be a target. Tony and Margaret were planning another visit to his sister Susan and her husband Lord de Vesci in their home, Abbeyleix House in central Eire. Whatever should they do? They went anyway.

They traveled by car, and as soon as they left Dublin, they discovered that trees had been felled across their route, anti-British pamphlets were strewn across the road, and there were "MAGGIE GO HOME" posters on village walls. That cold winter night in January, they had hardly gone to bed when a massive explosion shattered the windows in Abbeyleix House and sent people in the nearby small village running into the street.[20] People thought it was a bomb. It turned out that the IRA had thrown a heavy length of wire over a high voltage cable that supplied the house, causing the blast. Happily, no one was hurt. The subsequent trial confirmed the suspicion that it was all meant to make the British think twice about sending a princess into their midst. Nothing personal, of course.[21] All of a sudden, the accident that her host, de Vesci, had narrowly avoided three years before took on a sinister interpretation. At the very least, perhaps it taught the Princess to fasten her seatbelt.

"Mr. and Mrs. With It" as the *New York Times* called them, were perhaps safer in the wilds of Wyoming than driving around Eire that year. Tony, the new Lord Snowdon, had visited America before, but his wife never had. After King George VI and Queen Elizabeth's triumphant tour in 1939, it had been suggested that the princesses could take a train trip over there as well, suitably escorted, of course. Then World War II intervened, and any such idea was abandoned.

Visiting America was raised again in the 1960s to take advantage of the rave reviews for the Beatles, Mary Quant's sudden fashion innovations, and the extra added attraction of a visiting royal couple. It was a natural step. Everybody thought so, particularly the British export market. It is clear that the princess had abandoned the horsey set, if she was ever in it, and was being welcomed with open arms by the fashion manufacturers and the numerous worlds of performing and visual arts. Not to mention the film industry. She was a natural. People like Elizabeth Taylor and Richard Burton reigned supreme in Hollywood. James Mason and Stewart Granger had made the transition from Hampstead to Hollywood with hardly a misstep. Michael Caine was a sensation. The particular genius of such directors as Alfred Hitchcock and David Lean was being celebrated. And Tony and Margaret already had someone on the West Coast anxious and willing to welcome them. Why shouldn't they start there?

Their particular friend was Sharman Douglas, a slightly older, taller, and self-assured version of Margaret's friend Alathea from childhood, who possessed the kind of charm that inspires people to do things. Sharman had arrived in London in 1947, the daughter of Lewis W. Douglas, who had inherited some lucrative copper mines in Arizona and had served three times as Democratic Congressman from that state. Sharman felt as drawn to the high-spirited princess as Alathea had been. But whereas Alathea, the daughter of a Viscount, was easily deflated by the admonition that what she proposed "just wasn't done," Sharman, rather like the singer of "Don't Fence Me In" and cowboy defender of the wide-open spaces, would have scoffed at such a notion. If something had not been done yet, then "it was high time it was."

One can imagine the effect such an attitude of monumental impudence must have had on the princess. How to shock people and get away with it, must have sent her into gales of disbelieving laughter. Sharman was already experienced at organizing, and the idea of putting on a costume party for 250 people at the American Embassy would have presented no terrors. In July of 1949, Prince Philip could come as a waiter and the queen, a parlor maid. Then Sharman would organize a chorus line and get Danny Kaye, who was in London at the time, to whip them into shape. What about doing the can-can?

At that point, the origins of the notorious French dance went back at least a hundred years, and by the 1890s famous dancers like Jane Avril and La Goulue could be seen every night, along with a chorus line, at the Moulin Rouge in Paris. The can-can's shock value went back to several of its particular movements danced to the high-spirited melodies by Offenbach (for instance).

One of them was the high kick or battement, in which the dancers hold a knee up as high as it will go and do a twirl with their ankles—thought to be very sexy. Well-muscled dancers were needed to pull it off, along with all the other tricky parts of the can-can, like the flying jump and, most difficult of all, the finale in which everyone ends up doing a split after a running start.

Black stockings were the thing, ending at the upper thigh, which could be glimpsed glowing nakedly behind their suspenders. Even more shocking were the pantelettes, naughtily decked out in frills. As was the custom in those days of cumbersome skirts, these remained open at the crotch. A flash of this, a soupçon of that—in the days when even ankles were kept covered—it was no wonder that the can-can remained notorious. Princess Margaret wore a black silk dress, frilly underpants, and a red feather in her hat. The performance was greeted with acclaim and demands for an encore.[22] A proper audience at last.

One imagines that such sensational exploits were hatched in long, leisurely lunches, because no naughty double-entendres can be found in the letters

Princess Margaret wrote to Sharman after she and her father returned to the United States in 1950. In fact, they are almost boring, but that was probably deliberate, since both princesses were well-schooled in self-censoring any letters before they were sent: always finding something nice to say and never criticizing. The giggly tone is that of a teenager who admires this hearty, generous, take-charge sort of American girl, a kind of older sister. So, she put her small face up to be kissed, laughing and chattering, asking, as she so often did, "Do you like me? Do you really like me?"

Sharman had taken on a new public relations job in the movies, which meant she already knew everyone, so all was set up to begin in Hollywood on the West Coast when the Snowdons set off on their two-week trip across America in late autumn of 1965. If the celebrated pair wrote accounts of their trip, they have never been made public. But it is not difficult to guess what they felt after their plane touched down at the San Francisco airport following their trip of six thousand miles. The overwhelming experience for the English after becoming accustomed to their island's gentle undulations of hills and wooded valleys reached through two-lane roads and former shepherds' footpaths, is the monumental change of scale. The mountains and hills rival the Alps. The twelve-lane superhighways are frightening, and the cars that zoom past are as big as furniture vans. What is more, San Francisco faces a massive estuary onto the majestic Pacific and is spanned by bridges such marvels of engineering that they qualify for names like the Golden Gate.

Patrick O'Donovan, a talented British journalist who was following the royal entourage, also described San Francisco for the first time, calling it "the most beautiful, the sweetest, and most eccentric of American cities," whose "abrupt and startling hills" were reminders of the great 1906 earthquake that had once destroyed it. From clear sunny horizons, clouds were likely to roll in without warning, looking like "props in a baroque masque. One moment the water glitters dull silver and then . . . the mist rolls up over the water, laps round the bases of the bridges, muffles the towering apartments, and there is nothing to see but gray."[23]

The royal couple were received right away by the mayor and quickly moved on to a luncheon in their honor given by the English-Speaking Union, "the Anglo-Saxon underground," whose lady guests all wore hats because they thought it was expected of them, O'Donovan wrote. At cocktail hours, perhaps they investigated the concoctions being offered in the city's many celebrated hotels. One of them was the Fairmont, built by two daughters in memory of the father who had struck it rich in the silver mines of Nevada. In those days, you could imbibe your cocktail beside a wall-to-ceiling mural in memory of these men with their sudden vast fortunes and their peacock-preening evening attire. What about one in the foreground, with his whiskers, pocket watch, his polka-dot handkerchief, and his air of extravagant nonchalance, who dominates the proceedings? This must be him. But wait—isn't there something rather familiar about him? Could it be Walter Pidgeon, the movie star, in one of his most successful roles? An actor impersonating a millionaire—somehow, fantasy mingling with fact was appropriate for people whose lives embodied the impossible dream.

It was the biggest story ever, and the American press was there in force, big and small. Hedda Hopper elbowed out Betty Beale of the *Evening Star*, who was going mano-a-mano with Maxine Cheshire of the *Washington Post*, who was making mincemeat of Karl Meyer, Russell Baker, Art Buchwald, Drew Pearson, and Edward P. Morgan. Even a very junior reporter for the *New York Post*, Nora Ephron, the future screen writer, director, and all-round savant (according to her friends), practiced those sorts of keen observations that would make her so renowned. Most members of the press were desperate. What can you do when you cannot get anywhere near the reason for all the commotion, and all you get, as they rustle past, is a swift, dazzling smile? You are reduced to filing the news that Snowdon does not smoke English cigarettes but French ones (Gauloises), and Princess Margaret, wrapped in her silks and satins and alight with jewels, refuses to drink champagne. In sheer desperation, did anyone force the door of their hotel bedroom, to record the name of the lady's nail polish? Apparently not.

Things were looking up once Margaret arrived in Hollywood. As luck would have it, Hitchcock was filming what turned out to be a minor work, *The Torn Curtain*, and one of his stars was the English singer-actor, Julie Andrews. It also transpired that she did not have much of a role in this Cold War spy thriller. But it was better than nothing, and scores of people were allowed to watch, from a respectful distance.

"Mr. and Mrs. With It," as they entered, were welcomed with much ceremony and sat down to eat lunch on the set. The princess sat next to Gregory Peck, who had made such a splash in *Roman Holiday*.

It took someone like the star of the show, Paul Newman, as a double agent, to liven things up, which is what he did. Some twenty or thirty photographers took a minutely documented record of that afternoon in a series of photographs showing his triumphant progress through the crowd. One forgets that Newman is a model husband, father, and philanthropist—if one haunted by self-doubt and too much fondness for the bottle. That is because he plays a fool, a joker, and a con artist with such élan that, on the screen at least, he fools people over and over again. If you are in the audience, you forgive him, because you *want* to like him. It does not hurt that he is tall, slim, strongly built and, whatever his age, as close to physical perfection as most men get in this world.

They missed it. Not one of those camera-clicking, note-scribbling journalists looking for the front-page story even came close. How could they have missed that soft thud as the princess hit the floor and the mesmerized look in her eyes once she had been introduced to this paragon, the epitome of the handsome, joking, irresistible actor with the fabulous profile and a body to go with it. Did they not notice that, trance-like, she followed him around with slitty eyes, no more than a few feet away? That, when they sat down, she was the one who turned her chair sideways, so as not to miss a single pearl falling from those perfect lips? That she was always smiling, if not laughing? How about the way she would put her hand over her mouth and nose and bend at the waist so as to silently express the overwhelming funniness of what he had just said? Even Maxine Cheshire, who could get a secret out of a Tsar, missed the moment when Newman was called onto the stage, and Margaret's hand went up to his jacket to prevent him from leaving? What seemed a harmless gesture on one side of the Atlantic became an inexcusable faux pas on the other, where the rule for royalty in particular is look but *don't touch*. They all missed it, except Tony, of course. He revealed grumpily that the whole afternoon had been a sham show for their benefit, and the food was lousy.[24]

Acting on the theory that nothing was too good for the royal visitors, and not an hour of their two weeks could be wasted, Hollywood did what only it could do, i.e., turn grubby reality into fantasy. Faced with housing 1,700 guests, all of whom were paying $100 a seat to support a charity, and, since the only arena big enough was the ballroom in which Lawrence Welk and his band usually entertained the boogie-woogie crowd, the creative teams went to work. The Palladium's Art Deco style, built in the 1940s, was smartened up with twenty chandeliers, courtesy of the Warner Brothers movie lot. Flowers in vast urns distracted the eye, fresh or imitation, from the theater's shabby interior. The head table was covered with a massive 20-foot canopy studied with thousands of chrysanthemums and set with vermeil, sterling silver and bone china furnished by Tiffany's. Everything was done to distract the eye, short of importing Versailles itself; it cost $50,000. The principal guest, in a peacock blue outfit, unpacked her crown tiara and came fashionably late.

It was the event of the season, and the rumor spread that tickets that had cost a hundred dollars were changing hands for $1,000 each. Charlotte Curtis, women's editor for the *New York Times*, wrote that it was the most elaborate gala the city had ever known, and it made more money than it ever had before in aid of the World Adoption International Fund. Mrs. William Waif, president of the fund, waved away the superlatives.

"They're the best royalty we've ever had," she said. "We do so want them to enjoy themselves."[25]

By then, they had been so relentlessly entertained and had met Hollywood's own royalty so often that they probably ran out of movies to admire.

Among those studiously recording every cough and stumble was Curtis, a tireless member of the national's most distinguished society reporters, big-city reporters, and columnists expected, required even, to be up bright and clever and follow the princess wherever she and her consort chose to land. Their first chance to make up for jet lag was visiting Sharman Douglas and her family outside Tucson, Arizona. They could always talk about the scenery, even if the countryside around the Douglas ranch was flat and arid. The ranch itself turned out to be a long, low one-story building in the burnt adobe style with a spectacular view of the Catalina Mountains, familiar, Charlotte Curtis wrote, to readers of Willa Cather's books. The ranch interior, which the Douglases designed and built themselves, was a confused jumble of styles, English chintzes in their subdued flower patterns competing with Victorian furniture and bright Mexican pottery and paintings of the Virgin of Guadalupe.

A sitting room in the house in blue and white had been reserved for the princess; her husband had the room next door. But they were not staying there. They and their party were booked into a motel called the Lake Powell, after the lake which formed the main attraction for the small town of Page, Arizona. Their company took up all but two of the rooms, one supposes much like an early Howard Johnson's, with a neon sign over the roof and concrete walls. Very basic, in an anonymous sort of way, with its own air conditioning units. Where the press slept is not recorded, and a great deal of time was spent trying to fit everyone in somewhere. Charlotte explored the logistics involved in getting the couple from one stop to the next by means of planes, hired cars, and everything short of bicycles and long-distance runners. There was so much luggage, and everything had to be ready ahead of the main party, which consisted not only of chauffeurs and pilots but a lady-in-waiting, two secretaries, and maids that accompanied the couple. Fourteen people in all.

In the days when magazines like *Time* would only hire women as researchers, and big papers limited them to religion, education, and the society pages, Charlotte Curtis was an exception. The princess's arrival in Hollywood was certainly society page news, but more than that. It was a national event, and the *Times* sent her instead of the usual male reporter, and that had a great deal to do with her. She was clever, thorough, and relentless. She beat them all.

In person, she was about the last reporter one would expect to be capable of such effort. She was small and blond, a classic beauty with sharply etched features and the kind of figure that looks so right in simple, beautifully cut, expensive linen dresses worn with handmade Italian shoes. The proper heel height for walking, of course. She looked like a Junior League member who works hard on her volunteer projects from a sense of civic obligation. Her voice was surprisingly low, modulated, and unhurried, making one suspect elocution lessons.

For several years, she worked in her home town on the *Columbus Citizen* and became its society editor. She had a startling apartment in black and white— all spotless white carpeting and walls with all black furniture—which looked as stark as it sounds and made one suspect she saw life the same way. It would be truer to compare her with a winged goddess, a kind of nemesis, perfectly ready to be disliked in the cause of a noble goal, that is to say truth in reporting, then, as now, a somewhat exotic concept. In that respect, she paved the way for later writers like Tom Wolfe, who added ridicule to the mix. Charlotte never ridiculed anyone. One imagines her as the small girl who watches from the crowd and bravely points out that the king on the horse has no clothes. She might have flinched occasionally, but she never yielded. That true grit eventually had its just rewards when she was promoted to "Op Ed" page editor at the *Times* and became the first woman ever to grace its masthead.

One of the people to tangle with Charlotte turned out to be Lord Snowdon, ex–"Tony Armstrong-Jones" and now firmly ensconced with the Royal Family. In his days as a freelance photographer, Tony had used every inch of his considerable ingenuity to make ends meet when the money ran short. David John Payne recorded the times when he, as Princess Margaret's footman, had been pulled aside and begged for a loan. Then Tony the suitor became Tony the intended, and everything changed. Suddenly he had a valet to wash and brush his clothes two hours ahead and make him look presentable before dinner. He quickly understood the implications, and the magic vistas unrolling before him. He never had to pay again! He could order people about. So he did that, too, at Clarence House and rubbed its staff the wrong way. Why were they pouring drinks for someone who could do that perfectly well for himself? Now he was on a big trip, all expenses paid. Or so he thought.

It is useful to bear in mind that the dollar in 1965 bought a great deal more than it does now. The average salary for an office worker in those days was around $55 a week, or $2,860 a year. A $20 bill could buy a week's groceries for a family of three. Charlotte Curtis's instincts told her it might be interesting to discover just how much it had cost the tiny town in the vast open deserts of Arizona to entertain the royal couple and their entourage for a long weekend. By the time you added in the costs of room and board, drinks, flowers, security personnel, boats to take them out on the lake, a special boat so that Lord Snowdon could water ski and the like, it added up to $1,414. That is to say, half a year's salary for some people.

Those costs did not include the fleet of cars that took the Douglases and their guests from one place to another. They also did not take into account the labor for such eventualities as not having a big enough dining table one night and having to haul one across the mesa from the house of Mrs. Earl Johnson, daughter of owner of Canyon Tours, Art Greene.

"When we read that Tiffany did the table in Los Angeles, we thought the princess might be disappointed here," she explained. "We don't have anything very fancy."

Another part of the bill was a bit delicate. It seemed that one cold, clear day, Snowdon, in a black suede jacket, black ski pants, and hiking boots, and the actor Roddy McDowall, who was visiting them, stopped off at the Waterdog, a back-country general store in Page. The store carried everything from groceries, fishing tackle, and sheepskin coats to California wines. But what they were looking at were the Western boots everyone was wearing. Snowdon tried on three or four pairs, taking them on and off, and finally settled on two pairs, one a high-heeled pair in black with pointed toes ($17) and another pair in tan with crepe soles ($24). Then he walked out with both pairs under his arm. The princess had already chosen a pair for herself in black with high heels ($16), and made off with them, too. The storekeeper Grant Jones, who had put on a shirt and bow tie for the occasion, was left holding a bill of $57. He explained to Charlotte Curtis with some emphasis that he had no intention of giving away three pairs of boots.

The article, with its careful list of costs, subsequently appeared in the *New York Times* and received an indignant response from the former Ambassador. Sharman Douglas said the article was in error and asked for an apology. Meantime, the couple went riding in their new boots and when a big picture session followed, the princess stood with her back to a hand-hewn fence, while her husband sat on the railing above her, proudly displaying his free pair of black boots with pointed toes. The pictures went all over the world.[26]

What has not reached the history books is that Snowdon was *on time*, sometimes to the second, and that they smiled their way through sixty functions of one sort or another, from news conferences, fashion shows, civic receptions, and visits to museums, schools, hospitals, and sundry displays of British goods.[27] They had also taken a trip on a cable car in San Francisco, lunched at a movie set in Hollywood, skied in Arizona, viewed the Grand Canyon by plane and, in short, done everything that had been expected of them, with the exception of occasional exhaustion.

Once in Washington, and appearing at the British Embassy, the elite press of the two big newspapers had a go at them. Betty Beale, columnist for the *Star*, who was not always polite, was surprised. She wrote, "The girl who has been sometimes described as headstrong, quick-tempered, impish, restless and . . . spoiled, has been utterly charming, cooperative, delightful, sweet, and as royally deliberate as her royal sister."[28]

Her surprised reaction was echoed elsewhere, in such eminent journals as the *New York Times*, which called her "dazzling."[29] She had "stirred a cross-country commotion," and not being invited to one of the parties spawned "an irate society of the uninvited." A committee woman in Los Angeles said they had "never seen such scratching and clawing."[30]

"THE BRITISH RE-TAKE WASHINGTON," ran a headline in the *New York Journal-American*[31] above photographs of the princess "looking radiant." Hedda Hopper, Hollywood columnist, declared that "Princess Margaret Ruled this Town."[32] The hunt was on in Washington for suitably "with it" guests to amuse this star-studded couple. There was a problem, as Scottie Lanahan, daughter of F. Scott Fitzgerald and Zelda, who was freelancing for newspapers, pointed out. That came after Nicholas Katzenbach, the attorney general, and his wife Lydia, were delegated to provide an evening party. The hostess had given notice that the guests were to be "young and amusing." They were no such thing, as Lanahan wrote.

"It is well known that Washington is essentially a stuffy city . . . There is no jet set here . . . most people go to bed early so that [they] can get up next morning."[33] No argument there.

There was a different kind of problem with the White House dinner. That date happened to fall on President Johnson and his wife's wedding anniversary, which was not going to stifle the yawns. Fast forward to *The Crown* series decades later. Try as they might, the writers of this series could not find a titillating incident to add to their series of quasi-accurate, mostly fictional retellings. The most that can be said of the facts is that *Life* magazine subsequently used as its cover a picture of the tall president looking down a bit too fondly on his dancing partner a good foot below. What could they do? Writers were reduced to pretending that the president and his royal guest swapped dirty stories at dinner, and she ended up very drunk and dancing on top of the table. None of that was true, but viewers wanted to believe it anyway. Adding insult to injury, a magazine article published in 2019 asserted that the couple had so many "epic hangovers" on their trip that Parliament banned them from returning to the United States for the next ten years. Parliament was not happy, but not for that reason. A cursory investigation of the facts discloses the couple were back three years later and regularly after that. Facts are so tedious.[34]

What did not need much embellishment was the dance party at the Katzenbachs, who were in their early forties, given at their sprawling house in Cleveland Park that November night in 1965. Art Buchwald, everyone's favorite funnyman, made fun of the faux pas that the hostess had so thoughtlessly unleashed when she dismissed all those members of the Washington elite who were also on the wrong side of forty, Buchwald included. He was able to mock the irony of it all across several columns and was still making fun of it when he was delegated to give a running commentary on what was happening to the press, who were cooped up outside in the garden behind a secure fence.

The party started at 10 p.m., but for once the royals arrived rather late, showing up at shortly after 11 o'clock. By then the seventy guests were all assembled. Buchwald stepped outside occasionally to amuse the shivering press, who had nothing much to do but observe the arrivals and look for some signs of life behind the windows with their tightly drawn blinds. What Nora Ephron liked to call any sign of "life, wit or drama." No such luck.

Inside, the hostess had taken the step of asking each guest to provide her with a snapshot of him/herself as a tot, so as to provide a fun presentation volume to the royals. After she found out that at official functions Snowdon never knew whether to wear a black tie or jeans, she decided to remedy that dilemma. She hand-knitted a giant black sweater studded with black ties, a kind of "one outfit fits all." The guest of honor agreed to model the uproarious result, which came down below his knees, causing much merriment at the party. Someone suggested inviting American writer Walter Lippmann on the grounds that even though he was seventy-six, he was younger in spirit and funnier than anyone else. But he was blacklisted. Buchwald went out to let the press know that two guests had been found who were not young or funny.

"They are talking about pushing them into the pool."

Russell Baker, another columnist famous for his sense of humor, was asked upon leaving how he had enjoyed the party. "The fun was intense," he said.[35]

The trip finally came to an end in New York, where some high-profile hostesses took them on another whirl of sightseeing: obligatory inspections

A Slipper on the Lawn

of high-priced British goods just right for Christmas, intimate little lunches and grand balls in the Waldorf Astoria, and the top of the Empire State Building. No doubt they staggered back onto a plane at the end. Hardly any of the London papers noted their return. The usual Labour Party Members of Parliament did and clamored to see the balance sheets so they could storm about the exorbitant costs involved. Back in the United States, those who had not been invited to the Katzenbach party were chagrined to find themselves socially shunned, while those on the inside were able to dine out for weeks on what he and she said and how they said it. What had happened at midnight? No one was sure, but it must have been wonderful. A cartoonist for the *Washington Post* summed it up for them all. A man had knocked at the door of the Katzenbach house and was answered by the housekeeper. He wished to convey a message to Lydia Katzenbach. Please inform her, he told the maid, that "a glass slipper" had been found on the lawn.[36]

CHAPTER 12

PORTRAIT OF A LADY

> "Every roof is agreeable to the eye, until it is lifted;
> then we find tragedy and moaning women, and
> hard-eyed husbands."
> —Ralph Waldo Emerson, "Experience"

IN THE AUTUMN OF 1965, the couple were heralded as "the most original royals ever to come out of Britain." They even outdid Uncle David (for news value, according to *The New York Times*), in their ability to glide between "the official world of stifling protocol," and the creative milieu of artists, designers, composers, and the stars of stage and screen.[1] As trendsetters and patrons, they worked hard, played hard, were willing to go anywhere, and relished their roles as makers and shakers of a new culture for the young, or at least young*ish*. (In 1965 they were both thirty-five.) So it was said.

Princess Margaret had reached the pinnacle, in 1966, of being named one of the "most admired women in the world," right up there with Mrs. John F. Kennedy, Mrs. Lyndon Johnson, and people like Clare Booth Luce, Marian Anderson, and Pearl S. Buck.[2] Those who saw her in terms of her height and dismissed her were in the minority. Others, such as the popular author Godfrey Winn, who excelled in the soothing phrase, thought she had "the minute perfection of a Dresden figurine." He continued, "She has the same shiny neatness, the same unruffled self-possession, the same beautifully shaped hands and feet. Only her mouth seems to belong to someone of larger clay, her eyes to the close-up of a film star." She was exquisite.[3] When she visited Hong Kong for a week to promote British goods, some twenty-five thousand school children were on hand to provide "a cheering, flag-waving welcome."[4] As one anonymous onlooker commented, watching her triumphant entry into New York, she deserved the ultimate accolade that a street-hardened New Yorker can give: "She is a doll."

Given the princess's love for the West Indies and her immediate rapport with its native inhabitants, it seemed like a very good idea to give her some kind of roving ambassador role within the Commonwealth. But then, presumably, no one could figure out how to do that, and perhaps its new governments argued against it. Another idea was to invest her as Governor General of Australia or perhaps New Zealand, and one that was being seriously considered, according to Tony's landlord William Glenton.[5] Nothing came of that either. In 1957, someone in Scotland floated the idea that she should reign as their queen.

According to a report in the *Baltimore Sun*, "enthusiasm reigned high among the patriots who have complained for years, with virtually no chance of success, for some role north of the English border."[6]

Since her own sister was also Queen of Scotland and she would be in the position of deposing her, that idea went nowhere, along with all the others.

Her charm, outgoing nature, and gift for the significant gesture seemed to make her the perfect symbol, rather like a female figurehead of ships—a kind of mascot braving the waves and guaranteeing safe arrival on some distant shore. Making her first trip to America, her triumphs, the way crowds had flocked to see her, the compliments and flowers thrown at her feet—she was a natural. It was clear that she had not only represented her Royal Family with aplomb but was managing to steer herself skillfully into the worlds of art, architecture, and the performing arts that her new husband inhabited. Somehow, she had made it all happen.

Her portrait had been painted twice. The first was by Pietro Annigoni, the Italian master whose startling portrait of the young Queen Elizabeth II invested her with not only hauteur: bare-headed, in a sylvan landscape and wearing a fabulous robe, she attained an almost mythical stature. Then Annigoni painted Margaret; the portrait was predictable, perfectly acceptable, and dull beyond words.

In 1970, Bryan Organ, a rising young portrait painter, received an assignment to paint Princess Margaret. He was just thirty-five and had already attracted considerable praise for his interpretations in oils of such characters as Prince Charles, Princess Diana, and Mary Quant. He seemed to have pleased his sitters while, at the same time, showing them in a fresh and perceptive light, which is harder than it seems. Since any portrait of Princess Margaret was deemed important, the work had its first viewing at the National Portrait Gallery in London. The reaction was negative, to put it mildly: "grim," "ghostly," even "disastrous."

One could call the result offbeat and something of a riddle. The artist suspended his sitter's head, wearing its four-inch tiara, against a background so murky and bleak that one cannot make out whether the railings in the background behind her are indeed railings, or prison bars. She has no neck. Has her head been put on the chopping block? Is she alive or dying? Half of her features are sketched in behind a gauzy surface; the left eye shimmers and hovers. Only on the right half of her face do her features appear with any clarity. They are expressionless.

Organ was ready for the objections, having seen them coming. He explained that his sitter was a very private person, too private to be invaded by him. One must respect her privacy. No metaphors here.

But in fact, this is exactly what Organ *was* doing. The princess is lost, and the darkness is so all-pervasive and impenetrable, one must paint her that way. How else was the artist to convey the bleakness of a forlorn and stumbling soul? A few viewers thought that these kinds of insights were being demonstrated, calling the paradoxical non-portrait "most successful," and even "inspiring." The princess said she liked it.

Such reviews could have been even more admiring had they known about the handicap under which this unhappy woman conceivably labored all her life, groping blindly. But judging from the symptoms, the princess's health and developing personality matched what is known of its effects to a remarkable degree. Not only was her height directly affected, along with her clear difficulty in learning, but her scatter-shot approach to strangers was in common with other children with the condition. She was also gifted, another point in common, responding to sound and musically precocious, as has been noted. She was, like others with the same syndrome, emotionally insecure and physically fragile, suffering from headaches, stomach pains, and digestive upsets, and had rapid changes of mood. If frustrated, such children might scratch or bite themselves and pull out their hair. Nowadays they would be called special needs children.

Waves of sudden anger could engulf them. Liz Kulp described how such feelings began in her toes. They began to travel and once they reached her knees, and "she could not stop herself."[7] She explained, "The process is overwhelming . . . if someone is accusing me of something I didn't do, calling out a mistake in public, or being demeaning, I can still get mad too quickly . . . Then I say things I wish I could take back." The only way to deal with the feeling was to keep telling herself she really was a worthwhile person, no matter what others said.

Even so, the light switch that did not turn on, the mislaid pen, the dreaded phone call, a leaf floating in the swimming pool . . . The slightest affront to the rightness of things, the *absolute necessity* of perfection at all times, would inspire an immediate revolt, if not actual self-mutilation. Author and leading expert on fetal alcohol syndrome, Diane Malbin, wrote that such a child is "often like a firecracker, filled to bursting with pain, frustration, and rage."

Another kind of problem, Malbin found, was trying to convince parents and teachers that such children are not being naughty and defiant but had special problems they did not know about. Or are being wrongly diagnosed, since the syndrome is often mistaken for ADHD (Attention Deficit/Hyperactivity Disorder).[8]

Although warnings about the effects of alcohol on the growing fetus go back to antiquity, it was not until 1973 that pediatricians in France and the United States sounded the alarm about the poisonous effects on the developing baby of any amount of alcohol imbibed by the mother beginning three weeks after conception, when many women did not even know yet that they were pregnant. Before that, doctors assured pregnant women that the unborn baby's placenta protected him or her from harm. The bad news was slow to travel, particularly in Scotland, where the culture of drinking was a social assumption, if not a necessity. Families spiked their numerous cups of tea with Scotch whiskey because it made you feel better. So "a wee dram" must be good for you, as Kenneth Rose discovered when he arrived at Clarence House for tea and found trays of spirituous liquor awaiting him before and after the meal. His hostess was, after all, a Scot, known for her free and easy drinking ways. And in Scotland, the fact was that its population had among the highest intake of alcohol in the world. The World Health Organization estimated at the time that this was 40 percent more than Americans.

Children who are in some way affected and have some aspect of fetal alcohol syndrome that their parents do not know about are surprisingly common, according to further studies. It is known as the "invisible disability." For instance, in a hard-drinking family like the Bowes-Lyons, the fact that five daughters, either direct cousins of the Queen Mother or near relatives, were virtually disabled, was put down to "bad genes." That there might be a connection with the way their mothers drank has never been raised. We know little about their lives except that they seem to have been shunted from one barely adequate facility to another and their existence kept secret. When it appeared (in 1987) that the five girls had been abandoned and buried in pauper's graves, there was public outrage.

In 2022, the National Health Service in Scotland estimated that some fifty-three thousand children in Scottish schools, or 7.5 percent of the total, were at risk, having trouble with motor skills, cognition, language, academic progress, memory, attention spans, impulse control, and hyperactivity. The same Health Service estimated that many of these children were probably afflicted with fetal alcohol spectrum disorder. The counties of Ayshire and Arran opened the first clinic in Scotland dealing directly with fetal alcohol syndrome a few years ago. Its free pamphlet, "Understanding Fetal Alcohol Spectrum Disorder" is sixty pages long.[9] When a child has this invisible handicap, far too often he or she is considered spoilt, rebellious, and defiant. Everyone thought that when Princess Margaret was growing up. The makers of manners in Buckingham Palace tried to reform her. So did her nursery staff, her parents, her older sister, her church and, inevitably, an even bigger chorus of self-appointed critics pounding away at the theme of the Rebel Princess. They all just knew they were right, and nobody knew they were blaming the victim. And that was her tragedy.

One of the reasons why the princess probably never became a roving ambassador had to do with the way she would blurt out the truth, or what she believed to be true. Could she have been at the mental age of nine or ten? She certainly had not reached the stage when the idea that one needed to be careful about what one said even occurred to her. If it ever did. The complication comes from the Royal Family's own pleasure in practical jokes, Papa being the expert. Wasn't he fond of making apple pie beds and balancing books on top of a door just before someone else is going to open it? Wasn't it the biggest joke when he gave Crawfie a matchbox containing a green writhing mass, and she recoiled in horror? Didn't they all have a good laugh about that? And when the time came for getting even with her older sister, wasn't it great fun to throw one of her corgis into the nearest stream and watch the frightened animal swim back to shore while Princess Elizabeth screamed revenge?[10] Getting even, that was the thing, especially if you had a grudge, or even when you didn't.

A case in point was the always perilous matter of an appearance in Ireland, particularly during the Troubles—hadn't she already had an attempt made on her life? No wonder that one evening at dinner she was said to have claimed that "the Irish were pigs." The off-the-cuff remark was made to the Mayor of Chicago, Jane Byrne, who happened to be Irish herself. Naturally, she was not amused. Somehow the press found out, and the remark made headlines in the *New York Post*, as well as a lot of other places.[11]

Once, when a "British Week" was in the planning stages, bound for Hong Kong, and the British fashion industry was gearing up for a big event, someone asked the princess why only two Chinese models had been included. She artlessly explained that was because so many Chinese girls were bow-legged. The press had fun with that one, too. Then there was the time when the decision came down in 1958 that the annual presentation of debutantes was to be discontinued. It was getting bigger and bigger, and successful businessmen were presenting their daughters as well. The official version was no doubt polite. Princess Margaret was more direct. It had to stop because "every tart in London was getting in."[12] Said, no doubt, with relish. Whatever would she say next?

The fact that the princess might, all unknowing, antagonize a whole culture was one thing. What was more worrying was the princess's inability, like many others afflicted with fetal alcohol syndrome, to recognize actual physical danger. Leading expert Diane Malbin cited several examples of children who seemed unable to understand danger and avoid it in time. In one of her books, she cites the example of a father in Nome, Alaska, who is watching his daughter as she is sled down a hill. The little girl had begun her descent when her father realized that a truck was about to cross her path. He waved at her in horror. She waved back happily and headed straight for the truck. By some miracle, she sailed right under its wheels and emerged unscathed.[13]

Perhaps as a result, Princess Margaret did not see the point of a safety harness in a car, even though one was offered when de Vesci, her host in Ireland, took her for a drive in 1962. She was then expecting her second child, Sarah, but waved away his concerns and almost hit the windshield when the sand truck appeared over the top of the hill. Only de Vesci's fast actions saved their lives. Was she shaken? Not at all. She smiled, reassuring everyone and seemed perfectly at ease. Just like the little girl who had sailed under the truck.

Then there was the time when her hair caught on fire. Major Colin Burgess, equerry to the Queen Mother, was witness to this event that might also have had serious consequences. It happened during a family dinner one Christmas at Sandringham. The princess reached across the table at one point to get something, and her hair brushed past a candle. Her hair began to smolder and then burst into flame. Others saw the danger before she did and beat out the flames with their bare hands. She seemed more surprised than scared. What puzzled the major, who subsequently recorded the incident in his memoir *Behind Palace Doors*,[14] was that the princess had not noticed the strong, acrid smell of burning hair.

Perhaps the most puzzling incident of all has been described by Nicholas Haslam in his autobiography, *Redeeming Features*. Haslam, a close friend of Snowdon's, is known for his retentive memory, and there is no reason to doubt the accuracy of something he witnessed himself. The account is undated but seems to have taken place at a moment when the marriage was beginning to unravel. He states that the couple were at a party, seated fairly close together, when Snowdon began to light matches and throw them at his wife. She protested; he was going to set fire to her dress. He had never liked the material. Haslam wrote, "The Princess . . . stiffened. 'We call it stuff,' she said."[15] Such an incident is most puzzling of all. When your husband throws lit matches at you, why are you still sitting there? Why are you not insisting he stop? Why are you quibbling about his vocabulary? The conclusion is unavoidable.

Tony Armstrong-Jones's marriage and rapid escalation to the peerage as the first Lord Snowdon must have been a heady experience. All at once he had been picked up, as if by a giant hand, from the scruffy little basement apartment in Pimlico where he managed, somehow, to work and sleep, and set down in the rarefied confines of a prince of the realm, being treated accordingly. There was no further need to argue himself into No. 10 Downing Street or impersonate a delivery service at some stage door. He was now a very big Somebody himself. He had contracted for £10,000 a year with the weekend magazine of a big national newspaper, and, as a sign of their deep resentment of his new status, his former colleagues, all those photographers jockeying for five-column exposures themselves, tried to expel him from their ranks. Not that it mattered. They had been outmaneuvered and outclassed. He managed not only to make this astonishing leap, but even sweet talk his way out of the humbling experience of, say, a Prince Philip, forever trailing along two steps behind his wife publicly (even if Philip ruled the roost behind the scenes). That was perhaps the biggest victory of all. For the time being.

He established himself as the creative mind inside the Royal enclosure. The idea caught on, and from an unexpected direction. In 1960–61, he was asked to set his fertile mind to work on the new London Zoo. It seems the Zoo was looking for someone to design an exhibit for its collection of birds with the minimum constraints for them and the maximum enjoyment of the visitors. Snowdon came up with an outdoor exhibit, a vast and freewheeling wire cage that put people in mind of the sweep of a bird's wing, and one that visitors could enter. To ask someone like Snowdon was, in fact, inspired. He might be voluntarily entering an enclosed world, but it was under the freest of all terms. The new Zoo responded enthusiastically, and when it opened in 1964, his "bird cage," as he called it, became Snowdon Aviary.

That was Snowdon, the inventor. Snowdon as photographer was even more germane. He was quickly signed up for glossy magazines like *Vogue* and *Vanity Fair* to tackle such enduring subjects as Marlene Dietrich, Iris Murdoch, Elizabeth Taylor, and David Hockney along with intellectual heavyweights like Vladimir Nabokov, Tom Stoppard, and J. R. R. Tolkien. Perhaps the most interesting and ambitious project was to publish a book about the London art world. It was called *Private View*—as in many such titles, the implication was ironic. It would be a compendium not just of the prominent painters and sculptors of the day but gallery owners, authors, art critics—everyone in the 1960s who counted. It was the moment, as the book's authors—John Russell, art critic, and Bryan Robertson, curator—saw it to assert that London was now on a par with Paris and New York as a world center for art.

The choice of ultimate authority might once have revolved around the name of a famous artist or sculptor. Now it had become the photographer who symbolically represented the New Age. Now he was the person at the helm of a new generation of restless, exploring souls who abandoned the old formulas and shock the bourgeoisie with their daring forays into forbidden worlds: sex, for instance. The new safe sex, fueled by drugs and drink, demolished yet another social taboo. Although it must be added that women were not included. A new name had been invented for those sweet young things Alan Clark called "succulent"; they were "birds." Although, if the truth were known, the kinds of girls who arrived on the scene looked to be pre-pubescent, in their Size Six shapes, their small-framed Twiggy outlines, their pathetic little knees and bangs that reached their eyelashes, their wide-eyed stares. They were now "the birds." Attired as schoolgirls, they twittered feebly at the strong, silent boys, begging to be bedded by the Lords of the Universe.

Allen Jones, the pop artist and sculptor, who appears in *Private View*, was the first to see the opportunities presented by the new sex games: women as objects. Although Jones denied it, his fiberglass sculptures of women with their sado-masochistic implications, gave the game away. One of his most successful achievements was a group of three fiberglass figures which he made in many variations titled "Hatstand, Table and Chair." Three girls, dressed up in high heels, black hose, thigh-high boots, thongs, and with bare breasts, stare vacantly into space as they, respectively, act as a hatstand, a stool, and a coffee table. The result was heavily criticized but also very popular. One of the typical variations sold for $2.8 million.

Jones, one of the subjects in *Private View*, recalled the day he sat for his photograph in this massively handsome book, which, incidentally, reproduced one of his easel paintings but not his experiments in sculpture. The only problem was that Snowdon was at a loss to think of a way for him to pose. He was all for Allen stripping to the waist but had already used that idea for De Kooning, and the artist was against it.

"Certainly not!" Jones exclaimed.

He did not, however, mind looking like a male peacock. They settled for his choice of a poster-paint yellow jacket with a bright red tie. That did not make the book either but is now at the National Portrait Gallery in London.

Private View, with its documentation of the painters, sculptors, critics, even the pubs—in their worlds of home, studio, classrooms, and family—is perhaps the most exhaustive evidence of the kind of work Snowdon could do. Going from extreme close-ups to views of an artist teaching a class, as seen from four flights up, Snowdon incidentally provides evidence of the ingenious ways he found to illustrate the same theme. There are so many photos in the book it must have absorbed all his time and attention for a year at least.

In the film *Blow-Up*, Antonioni's hero is never satisfied. As portrayed by the young actor David Hemmings, he is tireless as he develops picture after picture, barely taking time to eat or sleep as he searches for something—he hardly knows what—that is just out of reach. One can sense that same patience for the exactly right moment that those photographs of *Private View* represent. The book was published in January 1965, running neck and neck with *Blow-Up*, Antonioni's imaginative version of swinging London some two years later (in December 1966). The moment when Sidney Nolan, for instance, stick in hand, is seen plodding across a muddy sand that the sea has just revealed and is juxtaposed besides his rhapsody in blues, "Greek Bay," is beautifully delineated.[16] Or there is the portrait of David Jones, soberly dressed in rough gray wool and with a plain wool tie, and living in a one-room flat in Hendon, which captures an unforgettable expression of agonized self-doubt.

Another equally compelling work shows Robyn Denny pausing for just a second; he has lit a cigarette, and his crossed arms indicate both doubt and amused acquiescence. Or there is Jon Hoyland, along with his son Jeremy, cavorting on a bunk bed to make a triangular unity of form and mood. Then there is the exquisite moment when Brett Whiteley's wife Queenie pulls her husband's head to her breast in an intimate, telling, poetic gesture. The book is full of such gentle revelations.

Like Snowdon, Antonioni's hero spent his spare time posing models for big magazines when not haunting doss houses in which the sad naked figures of derelicts are taking a shower, posed against almost obscenely squalid backgrounds. Perhaps the Italian master's instinct for art imitating life caused him to equip his hero with a very expensive convertible that also had a built-in walkie talkie. It happens that in the summer of 1965, no doubt as the film was being conceived, Lord Snowdon bought himself an Aston Martin, perhaps the fastest car in the world, capable of 150 miles an hour, for the staggering price of $13,232.[17] If so, one rather doubts whether Snowdon ever pulled up beside the curb of a grimy street, jumped out, and walked away as the hero does in *Blow-Up*. Dared one park the world's most expensive car with the same nonchalance? And if not, what good was it?

The arrival of the "With It" couple into the public spotlight could have been predicted. For a time, at least, they had an enormous sway over public attention, what the author and aphorist Logan Pearsall Smith once called a "swimgloat," a word he invented to describe people suddenly in the public eye. If they showed up at a theater to see a new play, opera, or ballet, the performances immediately sold out. If they frequented a pub or a restaurant, everyone wanted to be seen there. If Princess Margaret was reported as having worn black tights with beetles appliqued, these sold out the next morning. If she dropped in at a morning rehearsal to watch Rudolf Nureyev work out, the photographers were waiting. Sometimes help was needed to make their escape without actual bodily harm. They made the mistake of going to the Piccadilly premiere of the Beatles' movie, *A Hard Day's Night*, during which the huge crowds attending were in such a state of mind that dozens, mostly teenagers, had to be treated for injuries and exhaustion. The royal couple escaped harm by being escorted through a back alley to John Lennon's dressing room, where they sat around debating the precise meaning of the Beatles' favorite word: "Grotty."[18] (Usually, it's translated as "wretchedly shabby" if not "filthy and gross.")

An anonymous critic was quoted as saying that "their effect on the public taste cannot be overestimated . . . If they take up a new singer, a new artist or a new restaurant, they're automatically made."

Knowing dockland as well as they did, they were perfectly likely to appear at the opening there of some small avant-garde show.

"It's all very informal when they show up," one young artist explained. "No advance trumpets, a few drinks, some jokes. The Princess talks very well about modern art. Tony has taught her a lot."[19]

Once at an outdoor market, when Snowdon came upon a painting of a Spanish village scene, he asked permission to take it home for his wife's approval before buying it. He explained, "They are her walls too."

The butler returned in a few hours with the payment of $50. They were assiduous buyers "at the flea markets on Portobello Road, and often found things they liked. But then the Princess might turn down a 1740 Georgian teapot, 'I'm afraid it's too dear for me.'" Her husband usually had better luck, bringing home a Georgian mustard pot for the lordly sum of $3.50.

"I knocked down the price for him," the dealer said. "He's a very good sort for an Earl."

They particularly enjoyed the novel experience of slipping in and out of crowds unnoticed. On one visit to Ireland, they managed to insinuate themselves into a pub and began heartily singing Irish ballads with the customers. On another occasion, during a quiet weekend at Sandringham, they gave the family the slip and ran off to a local country fair. There they rode the roller coaster. (It must be added that some photographer tracked them down and took a photograph of a frightened and delighted princess.) After a couple of hours, a palace equerry pounced and escorted them home. Princess Margaret's set had been replaced by Tony's friends: journalists, critics, actors, playwrights, film stars, art dealers, those who had won great renown and others climbing their way up. Princess Margaret said approvingly, "I never knew there were so many interesting people in the world."

Special friends were usually invited, in due course, to dine at Kensington Palace, often after the theater. These dinners usually took the form of lavish buffets accompanied by wines selected by the host from the wine cellar he had built himself. Then the guests would carry their plates out to the sink and stack them themselves. Dancing would often follow to some early Sinatra ballads to Rolling Stones in the princess's collection, or her husband might turn on his newest gadget, called a Mellotron, from which any amateur could produce the effect of a full orchestra. Sharman Douglas brought Shirley MacLaine to one of the Snowdon parties when her film *The Yellow Rolls Royce* was showing in London. An early arrival might find Tony, in black tie, hanging floodlights, or the princess setting up the bar.

The actor Laurence Harvey, who was frequently invited, said, "The Princess is completely captivating. But she enjoys being a Princess, and she never lets you forget it. No one can leave a party before she does. If you're due on the set at six a.m. and the Princess decides to dance until dawn, you dance. She's a superb dancer—and tireless."

If they were in the right mood, the hosts might take turns performing. Snowdon once greeted his guests dressed up, in the days before his marriage, convincingly attired as his own landlady. On another occasion, this time as a guest, he appeared in a white shirt, clutching a security blanket, and pushed about in a pram—one wonders from what recesses of his unconscious mind such a slip of the subconscious had arrived.

Peter Sellers was a particular favorite, not just because he was so funny, but because he loved dressing up as much as they did. His fertile imagination was forever coming up with stunts to catch a guest unawares. Once, when invited to a black-tie dinner at Kensington Palace, he came up with the jolly idea that male guests should just wear the tie and be naked to their waistlines. Margaret thought it was hilarious. Peter adored them both and showered Tony with every kind of photographic equipment, from the most advanced models of cameras to the latest lenses. Once when Tony lavishly admired Peter's new Italian Riviera speedboat, the actor gave it to him.

Perhaps Peter's most lavish gift was to produce a home movie to celebrate the birthday of Queen Elizabeth II, who would be thirty-nine years old on April 21, 1965. Everybody would have a chance to dress up. Peter's wife Britt Ekland would appear as a Hollywood vamp. Tony, whose bout of polio had left him with a limp, would play a golfer with one leg hopping down the freeway. Peter would, part of the time, reprise his Indian doctor role for which he was famous. At the climax of the film, Peter would become a magician who turned himself into somebody else. At the pivotal moment, he would duck behind a screen, there would be a mad scuffle, clothes would fly up and out, and he would appear, minutes later as . . . Princess Margaret! It was, of course, really she herself, a bit shy, curtseying, smiling, and disappearing.

The resulting movie was shown on the queen's birthday at a theater—one assumes it was a small, invited audience. Before the show began, Peter planted his former *Goon Show* star Spike Milligan in the audience, and they launched themselves on an impromptu skit involving a lady's knickers and Prince Philip's suspenders while the hapless victims had to sit and watch. This bawdy birthday salute had all the earmarks of perennial jokes on greeting cards of the 1930s from Blackpool, which always involved enormously fat ladies and tiresome double entendres about the size of their bottoms. And on just about the same level. Surprisingly enough, the film was not very funny either.

Shortly after the couple were married in 1960, Allen Jones went to a large party being given in a Holland Park mansion bordering a wooded area, the trees of which, Jones observed, "reeked" of cannabis before one even got inside. In addition, there were police cars parked everywhere to indicate Royalty was expected. The reception rooms were already jammed except for the basement, where Jones found a solitary figure, watching homemade pornographic films, who turned out to be an eminent philosopher.

Lord Snowdon subsequently appeared at the entrance wearing a snappy Nehru jacket and waving friendly hellos. Then the princess also arrived, seemingly surprised to find her husband in the crowd. Jones began thinking, *Don't these people ever talk to each other?* But then his attention was transfixed by the dress the princess was wearing, in the very latest style, and what appeared to be curtain material that draped rather badly. It was the moment for the sheath, a tubular item that had the appearance of a sack and hardly suited anyone over the age of fourteen. This looked particularly awkward on women with curvy shapes that went in and out instead of up and down. The style was abandoned fairly soon by the A-line, which got wider as you went down and was easier to wear.[20]

No doubt the dress the princess was wearing that night was an idea of her new husband's, who was all for the very latest in fashion and trends. He persuaded his wife to try very short, expertly cut Vidal Sassoon hair styles that, again, you had to be very young to wear and looked like nothing much on anyone over thirty. He also decreed no jewelry, or not much. There is a photograph of Princess Margaret in the world's plainest dress, a child on each arm, with no jewelry and flat shoes. All of which meant she went through a distinctly ordinary looking period. She smoked for years, delicately extracting each cigarette from a tiny silver case she carried and lighting each one with her gold-plated lighter. But then, in 1964, came the first news that smoking and lung cancer were probably connected, and Tony went off cigarettes, switching to small cigars. Margaret might have done well to follow his example but did not.

Everybody knew that however undistinguished Lord Snowdon's status might be really, at home he was the boss. Bill Glenton could verify that whenever they were occupying Tony's Room, the princess, modestly dressed in a sweater and skirt, was very much subordinate to Tony's dictates. She would be sent upstairs to borrow a tablespoon of this or a pinch of that, to complete the recipe, and apologize for being such a perfect nuisance. Again. At the end of the evening, everything was cleared away and put away by the conscientious wife before they quietly disappeared into the night. The point being that Tony thought of everything, directed everything, and had the best ideas.

He had the rare gift of turning what looked like a problem into an asset. It turned out that a gravel pit, no longer in use, had become a kind of lake not far from the Windsor Royal Lodge in Berkshire. No one knew what to do with it. It was too small for sailing. But wait, what about water skiing? In short order, Tony had bought himself skis, figured out how to ski, hired a motorboat, and was off to the gravel pit. He returned some time later with big smiles. "I only fell off twice," he said. Pretty soon Margaret wanted to try it, and before long they were making use of what had begun as an eyesore. That was Tony.

It took someone like Tony to imagine a twenty-room apartment in Kensington Palace when there was nothing to be seen except bare walls and a long drop to the foundations below. He tackled emerging problems and went mano-a-mano with their nanny when she tried to pull precedence on him. He was ready for any kind of fight. When the new butler Thomas Cronin arrived to take over the household shortly after their marriage, he came from the former household of the U.S. Ambassador John Hay Whitney. It was August of 1960, and he set about putting things to rights, as he saw it, although the small number of servants taking care of the new royal couple represented a distinct step down the ladder in his eyes. Cronin must have thought this role was his domain, and his commands were not to be questioned. His new employer disagreed. In the butler's opinion, this interference on his employer's part represented an intolerable meddling. He resigned a month later and was observed by the taxi driver who came to collect him leaving from the back door of Kensington Palace one night and taken to a common rooming house.[21] It upset the proper order of things, in the cab driver's view. But that was Tony.

They still showed up quite often in The Room that they had been visiting regularly for almost five years and which, by some miracle, had never been discovered by the press. But something dreadful was about to happen. After threatening that its long-term goal was to tear down those unsightly old houses and put a nice river walk in its stead, the London County Council was ready to start. Strangely enough, after a brutal war that had demolished far too many inner-city areas, the new cadre of British architects were all for pulling down some more in the magical transformations predicted by Le Corbusier. His futuristic vision was in the ascendant: straight roads, high-rise buildings and the triumph of the automobile. Those miserable little hovels were in the way. They had to go.

After a few hundred years, the houses had developed dry rot, and the London County Council had a winning argument. Old houses everywhere in Britain faced the same problem: too much moisture and the right temperature encouraged harmful forms of fungi. Once established, these would go to work, and the wood became weak and brittle. To remove the damage and start again had to be reserved for historically valuable houses; these were not. Having successfully hid their visits to Tony's Room for years, they could hardly reveal their secret connection now. Each of them pulled as many strings as they dared, but in vain. With a deadline looming, the princess began to spend days in The Room by herself, usually playing the piano. She was there, according to her landlord, for hours and hours at a time, playing as if she were on the deck of the Titanic.[22]

Then the day arrived that everything was loaded on a van to be moved to Buckingham Palace. They packed the rusting bird cages, the fierce glowering captain, the lumpy mattress, the shabby velvet throws, the odd glasses and mismatched china, the pots and pans, and all those precious knick-knacks and tchotchkes that Tony rescued from street markets all over the city and brought back with such pride. Along with his photos of a phantom family, the one he chose himself. The princess wrapped them lovingly one by one.

Their grief united them. She said of The Room, "I'll never forget it." He said, "I don't know how I am going to live without it." Perhaps they were in tears. It took quite a long time and "every half hour or so Tony would stop and sigh, and glance around the increasingly bare walls or the view from the windows."[23] Whether Tony and Margaret returned to watch the building be torn down is not known, but not likely. Glenton and his wife rallied. They went in search of another house similarly situated on the banks of a river, found it somewhere in Ireland, and settled in. The royal couple never did.

What The Room represented for Princess Margaret seemed to be a kind of dollhouse for grown-ups, a fantasy play time where she could come and go like other people and do whatever she liked. For Tony, it became an essential part of himself. It was his secret, jealously guarded, protecting him from that other world which essentially required him to play a subordinate role, in a world of watchers, for the rest of his life. Writing in 1974, the well-known biographer Stephen Birmingham observed that "for generations the British royal family has been trained to think of itself as a breed superior to all others, with standards of behavior that are absolutely unimpeachable. The side must never be let down."[24]

Even if the princess's husband was now excused from routine escort duty, there were still far too many occasions he must attend in the cause of not letting the side down. He must then walk two steps behind her, be in constant attendance to her needs, eat when she did, leave when she was ready to leave, and remain with her when she was not. What actually constituted basic royal etiquette translated as her precedence over him. He did what she did, and his own needs did not count.

James Lees-Milne, author and architectural historian, caught sight of Snowdon one night in obligatory attendance at a Queen's party in Windsor Castle. He was wearing scarlet household livery and had a chest full of medals, presumably unearned. Lees-Milne wrote that he looked "like a Ruritanian prince . . . something out of the 'Desert Song.'"[25] This was to be the sad fate of a son whose mother had not wanted him, often could not remember him even when he was there, and had never visited him when he spent months in a hospital. It must have been unbearable. On the other hand, he was now in an identical situation, again ignored in the middle of a crowd.

What did it feel like? Didn't his late, beloved father try to warn him? He had seen clearly enough that his son "was too free a spirit to put up with the restrictions of royal life." In one of his most provocative plays, *Dear Brutus*, J. M. Barrie explores what most people ask themselves at some point in their lives, i.e., what would have happened if they had taken a different path? In the play, his characters have a chance to find out. One of the couples in the group, who were childless, were allowed to become parents of a little girl, for a time, at least. In the play, the couple reluctantly decide to go back to their other life. The little girl finds out and begs them to stay. She says, "Oh Daddy, I don't want to be a might-have-been!"

Tony, faced with the prospect of a hemmed-in existence, began to rebel. In a small way at first. He had always used the safety valve pressure-of-work excuse to get out of dates he did not want to keep. Even before their marriage, he never arrived at a dinner the princess had planned and left her exasperated and powerless. Well, he was an artist and that was all there was to it. He could not always be on time. He tried it on the queen herself. He actually did not turn up for an important dinner at Buckingham Palace, definitely a scandal. The queen made her displeasure known, but he seemed to have survived a serious social gaffe. The queen merely let it be known that she was not amused.

Bit by bit, he started to show his contempt for the family into which he had married with his eyes wide open. Perhaps that was the moment when the princess, sensing all was not as it should be, began to make demands herself. She was one of the few royals who could use HRH before her name. These initials, an abbreviation of Her Royal Highness, constitute a fairly nonsensical term. Nevertheless, it was her due, and she made her growing children use it when speaking of her to anybody else.

The princess had always, no matter how intimate her friendship, required and got a deep curtsey. The day came when one of her ladies-in-waiting, out shopping in Bond Street, her arms full of parcels, suddenly came upon the princess and had to make a deep curtsey, parcels, handbag, and all.[26] No matter how genuine your friendship, you must never, ever, refer to "your sister" or anyone else in the Royal Family. Her sudden sharp retort, "You must mean the Queen?" was designed to sting, and did. You learned there were hidden reefs if you wished to stay on good terms with this imperious little person. You misjudged her at your peril.

Tony knew how vulnerable she was. Torn between love and hate, he launched himself on a campaign of getting even and used it against her. Being calculated and clever, he knew how to do that.

Stephen Birmingham tells the story about an anonymous London architect, an old friend of Tony's, who wanted to give a small dinner for the royal couple and invite a few artists, writers, and actors they might find congenial. Did the princess like Chinese food? Tony said she loved it. All was arranged, and the carefully chosen guests sat down to eat. The princess "hardly touched her food." Her hosts were distraught. What was wrong? The story ends there, and the reader is left wondering whether the guest of honor did not feel like eating that night, or whether her husband deliberately named the kind of food she detested.[27] Whether by accident or design, Tony had made her look small.

What seemed to gall Snowdon the most was the requirement that he constantly dance attendance on her. During one weekend stay at the home of a nobleman, a dinner dance was given in their honor.

"I went [to] enormous trouble to produce the kind of thing they like," their host recalled. "I invited a collection of the so-called young . . . I bought the newest pop records; I had the big drawing room cleared for dancing.

"Around midnight the first evening, Tony and I left the others and went to the library—he said he needed my advice on a work problem. But hardly had he broached the matter when Margaret appeared . . . demanding that he return to the party because she wanted to dance.

"This seemed to me utterly unreasonable—and somewhat rude . . . But any sympathy I had for him . . . vanished when he turned and said, 'Oh go away, you bore me!'"

That incredible retort was widely circulated.[28] On the other hand, the princess had refined her own version of getting back at him. One evening when friends had gathered at their Kensington Palace apartment and Tony was showing one of them some photographs, a stack of negatives in his lap, the princess appeared. She was carrying a cup of coffee. Without a word, she poured the whole cup on his lap, ruining his negatives. Then she left. Birmingham wrote, "He was not heard from for four days."

A London hostess said, "They've become impossible to entertain. The hate between them is almost tangible—the cold insulting looks and the little knife-edged innuendos. A lot of married people don't get on, but at least they have the good taste to stay apart from each other at parties . . . Margaret follows him around like a jealous cat."[29]

A certain game began to develop among their friends having to do with who was most to blame, the husband or the wife. Once Margaret realized that Tony was going to make a point of defying her in public and decided he must be brought to heel, the stage was set for angry battles. It was true that a once-compliant and understanding husband was now looking for ways to "show her up" as opinionated and ignorant, and the only wonder is they did not resort to blows. Perhaps they did. Once upon a time he had not bought a painting until his wife had approved of it, because, "these were her walls too."

A writer by the name of Antonia Chatsworth (surely a pseudonym) told the story about their visit to a London art gallery during which Snowdon wanted to buy one of the paintings, a slightly pornographic male nude. What did Margaret think? She looked at it doubtfully.

"Isn't it a bit . . . *much?*" Chatworth wrote. "Her comment was reasonable, but it seemed to enrage Snowdon. He turned and barked, 'A bit much indeed! What in hell do you know about art anyway?'"[30]

One evening, Milton Gendel and his wife Judy were dinner guests at Kensington Palace. Tony arrived shortly afterwards from Rome. They heard the sound of the lock in the front door and thumps as bags and cases were deposited in the hall. He had just returned from a fashion shoot with Carlo Ponti, the producer, and Sophia Loren, his wife, who were their friends. The princess asked about his trip with every appearance of genuine interest. Then Gendel wrote in his diary, "Snowdon began to get at her, snubbing her enthusiastic questions. She looked as if he had hit her in the face; and when he asked if he could have a drink—meaning whether she would get him one—she wouldn't move."[31] What she had asked was whether he had given Sophia and Carlo her love. His reply was, "No, of course not. I wasn't dropping names; I was on a job." Gendel wrote, "I couldn't help saying, when I saw her crushed expression, 'You mean, they didn't know you were married?'" It was too bad. It was devilish of him. A couple of times that evening, and to relieve the strain, Gendel said, "Tony is the devil."[32]

Another friend, whose sympathies were with Margaret, believed it would have been easier for her to marry Peter Townsend if she had had other brothers and sisters "behind whom she could hide." Townsend's marriage to Marie-Luce Jamagne, his Belgian wife, had been a great success, he had found work in public relations, and they had had three children.

"We were all wrong about that in 1955," the same friend said sadly. "She *should* have married Peter, and she *could* have married him. His divorce need not have mattered all that much . . . But the Queen always looks to others for advice, and at the time all Margaret's friends advised against it. We were wrong."[33]

Years later, Harold Brooks-Baker, publishing director of Burke's Peerage, in a comment made on the death of Peter Townsend in 1995, said: "In my opinion this was the turning point to disaster for the royal family. After Princess Margaret was denied marriage, it backfired and more or less ruined Margaret's life."[34] What was never said (but was implied) was that she, at almost thirty, was under pressure to marry somebody because she was an old maid by the standards of the day. As her marriage to Tony underwent great strain, she was overheard exclaiming, "I wish I had never married at all. I'm sure I'd be much happier."[35]

Stephen Birmingham observed that "Not long ago (1968) when Princess was vacationing—alone—in the Caribbean, a friend brought up the subject of the marriage between Jacqueline Kennedy and Aristotle Onassis. 'It's the scandal of the century!' said the friend. 'No,' said Princess Margaret sweetly, 'Tony and I are the scandal of the century.'"[36]

Chapter 13

Dr. Kenneth Jones

"It's not that she *won't*," Dr. Claire Coles explained.
"She *can't*."
[To author]

THE "INVISIBLE DISABILITY" FROM WHICH Princess Margaret suffered all her life was first identified fifty years ago. In 1973, two U.S. pediatricians published a revolutionary paper in *The Lancet*, the British medical journal that takes note of particularly important studies. They were the young Dr. Kenneth Lyons Jones and his mentor Dr. David Weyhe Smith, pediatricians at the University of Washington's medical school. The study made the then-outrageous assertion that women who drank large amounts of alcohol during pregnancy could cause serious harm to their developing babies, and the more they drank, the worse the effects. But, any amount of alcohol was harmful. What had been considered a cautionary tale for centuries, the doctors, who specialized in dysmorphology or developmental anomalies commonly called birth defects, had demonstrated these effects in their clinical trials. The study of fetal alcohol syndrome had begun.

Since those days, Dr. Jones, now aged eighty-three, has become the world's leading expert on the subject of the connection between alcohol and its irreversible effects on the baby, and particularly a child's developing brain, effects that linger for a lifetime. He has given testimony at trials, lectured around the world, and believes he has examined something like a thousand children. He said, speaking of drugs: "You can take all of the illicit drugs you can think of—heroin, methamphetamine, marijuana, cocaine—you can wrap them up in a single bag, and they don't hold a candle to alcohol in terms of its effects on the developing baby."[1] What alcohol destroys in the process can never be replaced. It leaves the brain looking, as one wit put it, "like a wedge of Swiss cheese."

Smith and Jones were the first to publish a paper in English, but similar conclusions were made five years before by Dr. Paul Lemoine, a pediatrician in Nantes, who published his own findings in 1968. These findings, in France as well as the United States, were greeted with derision. Dr. Jones said that when he gave his first lecture on the subject in 1973 to the American Academy of Pediatrics, a member of the audience said, "You are crazy. This has nothing to do with alcohol." In those days, one did not warn a pregnant mother to abstain because everyone knew that the placenta prevented alcohol from being transmitted into the baby's blood stream. We now know that this is not true. In fact, the growth of the fetus begins very early after conception, long before the mother-to-be even knows she is pregnant, and inadvertent damage to the young life can begin then.

Dr. Jones explained that the medical school staff had based their study on eight children with delayed developmental problems. To their astonishment, four of them, completely unrelated, looked exactly alike. They all had small eyes, spaced far apart, a thin upper lip, and where in most people there are two skin ridges between mouth and nose, the skin was smooth. They were all low birthweight babies and showed remarkably similar emotional problems. In fact, since it is often impossible to determine whether or not a mother drinks, let alone how much, a professional diagnosis has to rely on patterns of behavior in her child. And if a baby looks like any other healthy child, that does not mean he or she has escaped. As Dr. Jones explained, "Nine out of ten babies who are affected look perfectly normal." The problems begin to show up when the toddler reaches the age of three or four.

Even though Margaret lacked the facial characteristics associated with fetal alcohol syndrome, Dr. Jones believes that the princess has a great many behaviors and physical characteristics in common with other afflicted children (including short stature, another indicator). This form of fetal alcohol syndrome is called an alcohol-related neurodevelopmental disorder (ARND), which doesn't necessarily inhibit growth or include specific facial features consistent with fetal alcohol syndrome. Such disorders have often been misdiagnosed as ADHD or even autism. Because there is so much guilt attached to the idea that any mother has unwittingly damaged her own child, Dr. Jones says that fetal alcohol syndrome will be the last thing any pediatrician will suggest. They look perfectly normal. They are, however, slow to develop mentally and physically and tend to be short. The princess was fully grown at five feet and faced a lifetime of being called a "midget" as a result. To this day such a child will, as she was, be considered stubborn and willful, and "in need of a good hard slap," as one courtier actually said of the young princess. They look perfectly normal, as she did. Nevertheless, "they have a medical problem that needs to be addressed," Dr. Jones said. So does Dr. Claire Coles, a neuropsychologist and professor in the Department of Psychology and Behavioral Sciences at Emory University. Dr. Coles works with such children in a development program run by the University in Atlanta, Georgia.

She said the theory about the bad child is remarkably common among parents, and such children are often punished for a disability that is no fault of their own. She explained, "It's not that she *won't*. She *can't*." Special techniques are needed because the problem never goes away; in fact, it gets worse. An attempt was made recently in Ukraine to find out whether a special diet could help such a child. A year-long study of vitamin supplements was conducted but failed to produce any results.[2]

A recent study by the National Institutes of Health involving six thousand children found that between one and five percent of first graders suffered to some degree, like the princess, from ARND. For many parents, the discovery is an unwelcome surprise. "It is nevertheless quite common," Dr. Jones remarked. Since no one knew the effects of alcohol on a developing baby in Margaret's day, it is no wonder she herself was misdiagnosed, even by her clever governess Marion Crawford. No one has ever known.[3]

At Kensington Palace, what began as sniping had developed into constant daily disagreements and undisguised sneers. Once upon a time, the princess became ill with rage if she suspected that the government was dragging its feet and denying Tony his rightful title as the new Earl of Snowdon. She suspected, rightly or wrongly, that her new husband was being made the target of their secret disdain. She might have thought that what they had succeeded in doing with Peter they were now trying to do with Tony. However, once Tony launched his campaign to turn opinion against her, her stout defense of him withered away and died.

Suddenly, he was plotting and scheming to make her look bad. Or that was how it must have seemed. He worked by stealth. His biographer, Anne de Courcy, described the way he would insert little "I hate you" notes, in various permutations, among her gloves and underwear, to give her, at unsuspecting moments, a nasty jolt. She was no match for him, however much she flew into a temper or resorted to screams of rage.

She was being outclassed by Tony, who was capable of smiling in secret satisfaction as he waited for her to fall into another carefully designed trap, followed by screams of frustration. Sudden moods she could not control; such was the legacy of her invisible disability, whether directed at Tony or anyone else. Another pounding headache or gastric upset: she could never win.

Once Gendel realized the extent to which Tony was doing his best to humiliate his wife and destroy not just her fragile self-assurance but her very sense of herself, as was evident from her little-girl-lost look, his instinct was to protect her.

Two summers later, in 1973, he and his wife were boating along the Italian coastline as guests of Queen Juliana of the Netherlands and her husband Prince Bernhard among a select group of guests. Tony behaved particularly badly that day. As his wife looked on, he was "pinching bottoms and going after girls in the most embarrassing way," Gendel wrote in his diary.[4] Later that day, after returning to the shore and sitting around a terrace, the princess appeared. She asked her husband, "Why are you rude to me?" Tony, momentarily embarrassed, fumbled for a cigarette and began to edge away. He looked at a loss for words. Then, Gendel added, "he suddenly snarled at me, 'You sycophantic courtier.'"[5]

Tony enraged was capable of anything. Two summers before, in 1971, both were invited to a party in London being given by Henry J. "Jack" Heinz, heir to the Heinz foods empire, and his British wife Drue. Peter Cazalet, trainer of the queen's horses, was dancing with the Countess of Westmoreland when he felt a tap on his shoulder. The Earl of Snowdon was about to "cut in on" Cazalet. The latter, immediately offended, snapped, "This is not America," and kept on dancing. Snowdon promptly threw a glass of white wine over Cazalet's shirt front. What happened then is not reported. Snowdon returned to his table and his wife on the edge of the dance floor. As Cazalet waltzed by with the countess, Snowdon promptly picked up another glass, this time filled with red wine, and threw that at Cazalet's shirt front as well. This open act of hostility, presumably made for the princess's benefit, ought to have led to a fist fight, but Cazalet mopped himself up and waltzed on. *Associated Press* learned of the affair and transmitted it far and wide. Without, however, any pictures.[6]

As for the princess, social events were always difficult because Tony used them to stage yet another of his public demonstrations of rebellion whenever she asked him to do what every other royal escort had accepted as his role towards a socially superior wife. Nigel Dempster, once London's best-known and most reliable gossip columnist, reported a particularly egregious example that took place during a charity ball for the Red Cross at a prominent hotel in Barbados called the Sandy Lane in Christmas of 1971. Dempster reported that the night of the ball, she suffered from a migraine headache but appeared anyway. She danced and smiled bravely but by about midnight she was ready to go to her room. Tony was nowhere to be found. The Scotland Yard detective Inspector Falconer and Jonathan Aitken, the future Conservative member of the Cabinet, then a journalist, who was seated at her table, went looking for him.

A determined search finally found Tony.

"He was literally under a table giggling with a pretty girl who worked in the hotel boutique," Aitken said. "I told him Princess Margaret was desperate to go, and he replied, 'Fuck off, arselicker.' So Falconer and I reached under the table, grabbed him by the armpits and propelled him towards Princess Margaret. He wasn't best pleased."[7]

Something similar happened to the architectural historian and diarist James Lees-Milne at a private party, on Christmas Day of 1973. Princess Margaret was there, looking "small and slight." So was Snowdon, recovering from a recent operation for hemorrhoids.

"He looks gray, his hand shakes, and he chain-smokes one cigarette after another," Lees-Milne wrote. It was time for them both to leave. Knowing that none of the other guests could leave before the princess did, Lees-Milne heard Tony tell his wife that he was not ready to go because he had not finished his drink. By now, it was "the same old business" endlessly repeated.

"No, you must hurry along," Lees-Milne said.

"I won't be hurried," Tony retorted.

Princess Margaret replied, "Then I shall have to walk home by myself," and left the room.[8] The princess gave up the uneven fight. Whoever was going to replace Tony?

In the autumn of 1967, the princess had an extended interlude with Robin Douglas-Home, a Scottish aristocrat a couple years her junior. He was in the category of "suitable, almost to a fault" as a lover, or even husband material, being related, on his father's side, to the 13th Earl of Home (as a grandson) and on his mother's, as a grandson of Charles, the 6th Earl Spencer. As if that were not enough to ensure his staggering suitability, he was a relative of Sir Alec Douglas-Home, one of Britain's prime ministers. Yet another relative, the editor of the *Times*, would have inspired awe and dread all by itself. Given such illustrious connections and a recent divorce to round out his sterling qualifications, Robin Douglas-Home did not need looks as well and did not have any. As a hopeful adolescent, he had a goofy, toothy smile, in the great tradition of Lord Peter Wimsey, who, as everyone knows (because his creator Dorothy Sayers keeps telling us) was irretrievably plain. Or even better, the equally celebrated Bertie Wooster, who is on bun-throwing terms with his aristocratic fellow members of the Drones Club. Bertie is forever inventing ingenious ways to liven up his staid existence, which always ends disastrously, at which point he is rescued by his imperturbable butler named Jeeves.

Unlike Bertie, Robin Douglas-Home did not have a butler to save him from himself, much less a comfortable fortune. By day he wrote copy for an advertising agency and received a slightly better salary after hours playing jazz piano at nightclubs. His talent as a writer was marked. He soon published four novels and a biography of one of his pals, Frank Sinatra. In his twenties, he had succumbed to the charms of Princess Margaretha, sister of King Carl XVI Gustaf of Sweden and a great granddaughter of Queen Victoria. Various competing explanations are given for the fact that the union never took place. The first was that she did not want to marry him, and the second was that her relatives would not let her.

Nothing daunted, Douglas-Home turned his attentions to Sandra Clair Paul, an adorable eighteen-year-old model, who was just beginning her career. They met because she showed up one day at his advertising agency proposing to become the new face of Dove soap and got the job. They were married in the summer of 1959 when he was twenty-seven and had a baby boy three years later named Sholto. Sandra Paul was soon in the seen-everywhere category of high-priced faces. All would have gone well had not her husband made the invariably careless mistake of taking somebody else's wife to bed and then getting her pregnant. She was Nico, the Marquess of Londonderry. Her husband, in the manner of Jeremy Fry, naturally assumed the girl was one of his. No more was said until DNA came along, and the grown-up daughter, Lady Cosimo Somerset, found out who her biological father was. But in the interim Sandra found out somehow.

Pretty soon Douglas-Home was divorced and fancy free, still pounding away at the piano, writing novels, and looking for love. Then another Margaret appeared in his life. His son Sholto, in an interview many years later, believed his father was less motivated by constant conquest, in the manner of Tony Armstrong-Jones, and more like someone in search of an impossible ideal. What he wanted was the romance of it all. He appeared in Princess Margaret's life just as she had jettisoned her last scrap of consideration and thoughtfulness, when faced day after day by her husband's vengeful reality.

Put another way, both she and Tony had deeply felt needs that the other was unwilling or unable to satisfy. He was away for longer and longer periods. Margaret began to smoke in her teens, using an elegant turtleshell holder her father gave her, presumably on the discredited theory that this was the solution for nicotine's harmful effects, and used it from then on. A holder had a certain cachet. One could wave it around to indicate silent agreement or dismiss someone else's comment without a word. Nowadays she lit up another almost immediately with ominous implications: some sixty cigarettes a day.

One gathers that the princess, like her mother, took small but frequent drinks all day long, beginning in late morning. As we have learned, a tray containing orange juice and glasses was refreshed each morning and, it was explained, might even contain a bottle of gin as well, depending on the princess's mood. As time went on, James Lees-Milne thought her rounds of Scotch and water were being served in larger and larger glasses.[9] He described an evening he spent with the princess and her husband, along with the queen, Prince Charles, and some others following a premier performance of a new film. For dinner, they went to an upstairs room in Rule's, Maiden Lane. Prince Charles, politely and with a smile, went around the table shaking hands. Princess Margaret looked as attractive as ever but was not as charming. In fact, "she is cross, exacting, too sophisticated and sharp," he wrote.

After the meal, Prince Charles needed to leave early, so his mother went downstairs with him to see him off.

The queen had taken her shoes off during dinner. As a reproof, perhaps, princess Margaret picked them up and put them on her plate. That was unlucky, Tony said; he didn't like it. So, the princess transferred the offending objects to the queen's chair instead. Then she walked to the window and stood there looking out, in an angry mood. It was time to go.[10] Lees-Milne thought the princess looked "trussed-up," which could have meant well-corseted. The princess had gained weight—some reports put this at twenty pounds—and developed not only her mother's expansive bust but similar pads of fat had settled around her former small waistline, of which she had always been so proud. Perhaps Tony's sharp comments required physical barriers as well as a mental one.

"It's a damn bore being married to one person," Tony said, and took a bachelor pad in London for his escapist and capricious fantasies. Margaret remarked that she could not stand to be in the same room with him. Then she said, "I wish I had never married at all," and poured some more vodka into her tea.[11]

On that ill-fated trip to Barbados in 1971, when they were still together, Jonathan Aitken recalled a remarkably candid moment when he and the princess were sunbathing on a raft a few yards offshore. The beach was private and in a setting where they could not be overheard.

Aitken said that the princess knew very few people on Barbados, so he, being a single man, was invited everywhere and became a witness to her husband's rough treatment: crawling under tables, refusing to get her drinks, or be sent on small errands, and frequently calling her "fat" in front of everyone. That particular day, Tony was being "very snappy over lunch." The princess was getting "really upset, in a rather touching way, obviously helpless to defend herself." So, when she suggested the two of them swim out to the raft, and Aitken accepted, she was clearly grateful. The conversation turned to Tony and how beastly he was being.

"I said, 'Well, why did you marry him, Ma'am?' It sounded a bit forward of me, but we were getting on very well, and we'd had a bit too much to drink at lunch and were very relaxed."

She answered, "Well to tell you the real story, I hadn't got any plans to marry him." She was still "head over heels" in love with Peter Townsend. That is, until she received his letter saying he was engaged to someone else. Perhaps it is true that she and Peter had agreed, as she claimed, that if they could not marry each other, they would never marry anyone else.

This could account for the bitter letter she wrote to him, as attested to by the biographer Anne Edwards, who read it. She reported that the princess accused him of betraying their great love. She asked him to burn her letters.[12] Edwards recalled the moment in Paris when Townsend ". . . told her that he was afraid he might carry some guilt about the princess to his grave." Townsend's actual words were, "She believed I had betrayed her." It was a point of wounded pride for Margaret just then, a desperate, last-ditch effort not to seem, to the public eye, like a woman spurned. She was ready to marry anybody. And there was Tony.

Aitken said, "I felt sorry for her. I remember tears welling up in my eyes. She'd told the story in a defiant way, yet an upset way. And I did something that was rather forward—I gave her hand a great squeeze."[13]

For Townsend the outcome was a happy one. He and Marie-Luce married quietly, had three children, and stayed together until the end of their days. Did the princess ever recover from the determined onslaught by Crown, church, and state to prevent her from marrying this clearly sane, sensible, and kind man? Did she ever recover emotionally? It seems that Aitken must have been too polite to ask.

It turns out that both Tony and Margaret had begun affairs with other people, and this could have been the motive for particularly outrageous insults.

Elsewhere and at length, Tony made strenuous allowances for his own flirtations, along with a refusal to allow his wife the same license. No doubt he reasoned that an unhappy husband had the right to find solace elsewhere. An unhappy wife, however, was not allowed to. Those were the rules. Just the thought of her in someone else's bed was humiliating. She had promised to obey and now she hadn't. She had made him into some sort of cuckold. So now he began publicly humiliating *her*, and how did she like that? He must have felt badly hurt.

Snowdon might have been thinking of a recent scandal surrounding George Henry Hubert Lascelles, 7th Earl of Harewood, first cousin of Princess Margaret's and the queen's. After seeing action during World War II, he was wounded, taken prisoner, and held in Colditz until the Germans surrendered. He took his seat in the House of Lords in 1956 and began devoting his life to his two main enthusiasms: football and the support of grand opera. All was thoroughly honorable and commendable. But then he caused a scandal in 1967 by divorcing the wife who had given him three sons. What made the divorce so awkward was that, by then, his mistress Patricia ("Bambi") Tuckwell, had given birth to yet another son. To have impregnated one woman while being married to another was the most awful breach of etiquette, to say the least, and the couple were ostracized for years. When you are the queen's cousin, it is rather difficult to avoid having anybody know. The Earl of Snowdon, whose mistress had given birth while he was marrying someone else, was fortunate enough to have someone else believe she was his daughter. But you never knew. Meantime, Snowdon could virtuously protest that his wife was making a joke of their marriage while he, behind the scenes, was doing exactly the same. It had its ironic aspects.

The first girl on the list was Lucy Lindsay-Hogg, the wealthy daughter of a flourishing Irish clothing manufacturer. They had met on a film set and fallen for each other. Then he offered her a job as his assistant, and she took over. She was tall, gorgeous, gentle, compliant, and perfectly prepared to submit to his dictates and the doubtful thrill of riding pillion on the back of his motorbike. It was back to the old days of Tony's Room and a girl, ever submissive and admiring, in the shadowy background.

Angelic as Lucy was, one adventure was never enough to slake his ravenous thirst. On to the next, this time a semi-permanent mistress. She was a journalist named Ann Hills, who had received an assignment to interview him. She swore before she even arrived that she would get him into bed. This probably turned out to be easier than she expected—and she stayed on for the next twenty years. She survived the upheaval that took place in Tony's life when he and the princess separated in 1976, divorcing two years later, and then the further shock to his menage when Lucy Lindsay-Hogg got pregnant. This time Tony did not have to pretend because his wife obliged by moving up the date so the baby could be born to properly married parents in the summer of 1979. Ann soldiered on as a sometime partner for a decade or so and then faced yet another beauty in Tony's life, another sensational girl, Jacqueline Rufus-Isaacs, even more distinguished because her grandfather had been viceroy of India. It was only a matter of time before Lucy Lindsay-Hogg, now Lady Snowdon, found out he had made yet another girl pregnant. So she divorced him.

By the time twenty years had rolled around, Anne de Courcy wrote that her subject saw Ann as an old friend, but she had much warmer feelings for him—in fact, he was the closest man in her life. On Christmas 1997, she wanted to be with him but understood he would need to be with his family. She rang as she had so often done before, asking him to call her back. Whether she actually heard his reply is not known. It only said that he would love to see her but that he was tied up over Christmas and New Year's. He added, "Chin up!" which, under the circumstances, seems ironic.

On New Year's Eve of December 1996, the fifty-five-year-old, dressed in black and stiletto heels, ascended her Marylebone house to its chilly rooftop garden, lay down, took an overdose of Paracetamol and tranquilizers, washed down with a bottle of Moet et Chandon, and died.[14] She left a suicide note saying that she had always loved Tony and always would. When he heard the news, Snowdon "put his hand up to his face and said . . . 'I certainly wouldn't dream of talking about her in any way except that she was a friend and it's a very, very sad incident that has happened.'"[15]

The joke was, "if it moves, he'll have it," apparently coined by a friend and often repeated.[16] After all, when a man is commuting between his wife, his mistress, and a couple of affairs on the side, one can only wonder however he finds the time, even on a motorbike. He himself liked to toss off such comments as, "I didn't fall in love with boys—but a few men have been in love with me." This was probably true. If his dance card was about full, there was always room for one more jive around the room as long as it did not take too long. Michael Findlay, the long-time director of the Acquavella Gallery in New York and himself a distinguished author, said that he met the royal pair in the 1960s when he was working for Michael Feigen, a prominent New York dealer. He said, "Tony's manner was restrained, polite and gently mocking. He was not 'out' exactly but I got a very strong 'gay' vibe."[17]

Tony's restless need for the constant reassurance that he was sexually desirable was also known in certain circles that were less select. According to the grapevine at Elizabeth Arden's in Bond Street, whose expert hairdressers used to know all the rumors, Tony was always looking for action in the early 1970s. According to them, his secret apartment was just off Kings Road in Chelsea. He was often seen in the early evening climbing into a Volkswagen bug with blackened windows. Pretty soon he would be cruising along the Kings Road, close to the pavement, looking for single men.[18]

Princess Margaret met Robin Douglas-Home in the autumn of 1967 at the Casanova Club, where he was performing, and the attraction was immediate. In theory, the coupling of someone like Robin, who loved Frank Sinatra, read poetry, wrote books, and moved in Margaret's worlds, would be tailor-made. From this moment in time, it is impossible to know how much of Douglas-Homes's natural good manners and sense of fun were part of the attraction, and what part of the equation had to do with a new admirer who wanted her, and her need to get even for all those times when Tony lunged for another woman—any woman—while she watched. How satisfying to think that the word would get out fairly fast that she had a besotted admirer. What did it matter if, behind the scenery was the undoubted fact that Robin always thought he had found the great love of his life at last, only to be disenchanted two weeks later when he found out he had not. Again. What if he drank too much and smoked too much or even did drugs? So did everybody else. What, in fact, if he was a compulsive gambler and therefore always broke? A princess could afford him. That was when certain newspapers at home and abroad started speculating that Tony and Margaret were about to get a divorce.

Robin and Margaret's relationship was in full flower by Christmas of 1966 and ended two or three months later.

Snowdon, who happened to be in New York in February of 1967, was asked about the rumors by the New York press. He faced them with an easy smile.

"It's news to me, and I would be the first to know," he joked.[19]

Snowdon and Margaret were planning a reunion in March in the Caribbean.

Meantime, his wife was writing a series of heartfelt letters to her new amour explaining why she could not see him again. At least for a while. Something could have happened between herself and Tony. One does not know what, but it is possible that he reassured her fervently that he did not want to break up and could not bear the idea. Would she please stop seeing Robin? Was he on his knees? Did it matter? She was convinced and her pride satisfied. It only remained to write Robin hearts and flowers Valentines, emphasizing over and over how wonderful his letters were, redolent of "new mown grass and lilies" (her phrase). She would love him forever and ever. Perhaps he believed it.

We know this because one of Douglas-Home's friends was Noel Botham, a Damon Runyonesque character who inhabited Fleet Street with the same kind of impudence and flamboyance that Runyon exhibited in his glory days on Broadway. In the latter's case, that meant writing in the vernacular and inventing the kind of raffish characters who inhabited such masterpieces as *Guys and Dolls*. Both men sported shirts, ties, jackets, and fedoras with (no doubt) cards printed "PRESS" stuck in the hatbands, instead of today's baseball caps and running shoes. They used typewriters, two-finger style, wrote scruffy notes—only a few had shorthand—and, like Botham, worked for tabloids all over London. And whatever they did not remember, they made up.

One of the characters Botham might have created (but didn't) was "Hooray Harry," a loud-mouthed, upper-class twit in London society whom everyone loved to pillory, whether he ever existed or not. As for Botham, he ended his life where he should have started, running his own pub in Soho. There the chances of slaking his own thirst were built-in, and constant delectable rumor and innuendo was always on offer. It was at this pub that Botham first won Douglas-Home's friendship and then was handed a number of letters from the princess designed to let her new conquest down gently. Botham then started to write *Margaret: The Untold Story*[20] and quoted the handwritten letters to show how shockingly she had treated this sweet, loving, adorable suitor, as well as what other overlooked revelations the author had tucked away in his back pocket.

The book was a great success. Botham was always an entertaining, if unreliable, guide. For instance, whenever a drinking pal decided to go on the wagon, Botham was there to steady his elbow, soothe his addled reasoning, and talk him out of it. Botham later wrote a book arguing that Princess Diana had been murdered, along with almost two hundred conspiracy theorists, all of whom were discounted. His argument that Princess Margaret, by her heartlessness, brought about Douglas-Home's suicide, has been more generally accepted.[21]

What was not known at the time, according to Douglas-Home's son Sholto, was that, following his affair with the princess, his father began writing a very long novel (seven hundred pages) about a love affair between a married man and a famous woman. Only she was not the princess. She was Jacqueline Kennedy Onassis.

Sholto explains that his father's friendship with the First Lady began in 1962 as a result of his connection with his brother Alec, who was then the British foreign secretary. Robin was invited to the White House and subsequent functions. Given his invariable reaction to ladies of distinction, his immediate attraction to the First Lady was a foregone conclusion.

"The definitive face," he called her. An introduction led to frequent invitations and then a friendship. When the First Lady and her sister Lee Radziwill took a holiday to Ravello in the summer of 1962, Robin joined them. He later alluded to confidences expressed in leisurely late-night conversations. After the horrifying assassination of November 1963, Jacqueline continued the contact, and the two took another holiday together the following summer.

Once their friendship became common knowledge, Douglas-Home was offered a handsome sum by *Queen Magazine* to write about it. Being broke, as usual, he accepted. A ten thousand–word profile was subsequently published by that magazine. One editor for the magazine told his son that Douglas-Home never said he had had an affair with his subject, but implied it. He finished the book in the months before his death, then put it into storage, and it was not discovered until after he died. What particularly disturbed Sholto was the novel's conclusion: A man "who sounded very much like my father" committed suicide. Was Douglas-Home predicting his own death? It was almost too painful to think about.

On October 15, 1968, Douglas-Home recorded a message: "There comes a time when one comes to the conclusion that continuing to live is pointless."

He mixed a lethal cocktail of alcohol and sodium amytal, a sedative, and lay down. Then he closed his eyes. He was only thirty-six. How much did the suicide have to do with a novel about the First Lady? That is the better question.[22]

"Journalists are the enemies," Margaret said.[23]

In the early 1970s, London, that focus of massive wrath by the initiators and losers of World War II, had become, if not a Garden of Eden, then something pretty like it. Everywhere one looked the aspect, as Jane Austen wrote, was pleasing. Bone-chilling winters wreathed in sleet and fog had given way to the first tiny evidence of snowdrops and crocuses pushing through the frozen soil, not just in the city's many parks but also those oases provided by the old builders, who had grouped their quadrangles of townhouses around secret, secluded gardens, their equivalents of bosky dells.

By late March, daffodils established themselves into great rolling waves of dancing yellow, sweeping into Hyde Park and St. James's, with no horrid little signs telling people to "KEEP OFF." Parliament Square developed wide edges, delineated by red and yellow tulips and enhanced by vast banks of flowering azaleas. Tubs of pansies appeared outside doorways, and window boxes brightened walls far and wide, spilling out wallflowers, tulips, primula, geraniums, and delicate, trailing vines. This vast, sprawling city reflected a delirium, not just of hope but renewed enthusiasm for the future. All would be well.

That May of 1970, Princess Margaret and her husband celebrated their tenth wedding anniversary with a host of new family photographs to mark the occasion. One in particular showed them seated in a convertible with their children, David Albert Charles, Viscount Linley, aged eight, and Lady Sarah Armstrong-Jones, aged five, in the passenger seats. The gossip about divorce three years before had been explained away as the normal ups-and-downs of any marriage. Their reunion in the Caribbean had apparently been a success. The children were apparently being well cared for in their own quarters in Kensington Palace, and one assumes their parents were on their best behavior whenever they did get together. David, for a time, was sixth in line to the throne and had been enrolled in Ashdown House in Sussex, a select, all-male boarding school in a wooded setting. There, he was subject before breakfast to ten minutes of outdoor "marching and breathing" exercises first thing. A hearty breakfast of sausages or kippers was followed by a fairly indigestible menu that might include Latin, French, Scripture, and mathematics.[24]

Although the article in an American paper did not mention it, and neither did the headmaster of Ashdown House, the safety of young David was uppermost in the spring of 1970. A rumor went around that he might be kidnapped. The notorious Kray twins, Ronald and Reginald, the most famous gangsters in London, had received thirty-year sentences for their part in a murder, and each was incarcerated in a separate, high security prison. The story was that David was about to be whisked away and held in order to force the release of the Krays. Somehow David must be protected, so presumably scouts were set up in the woods and traffic blocks placed along the roads. His father boasted to Milton Gendel during a dinner at Kensington Palace that he made sure his son knew nothing about it, and all the pupils at Ashdown had been sworn to silence. Gendel thought that to pretend it was not happening was foolish and risky: "Much better to tell the child, as he is bound to find out anyway."[25]

After two disastrous wars, the British Empire broke off and fell away, and the king, as has been noted, lost the title of emperor he had inherited from Queen Victoria. So did the power of the public schools, once dedicated to "building" the characters as rulers, and opened the way for a different kind of school. One of them was Bedales.

This private boarding school just outside the market town of Petersfield in Hampshire was established in 1893 in reaction to the rigidity of much Victorian education. It broke another tradition soon after by accepting girls as well. Founded on Montessori principles, its mission was to find out what each child's talents were and then encourage him or her to pursue them. Naturally, enough, when David (born November 1961) and Sarah (May 1, 1964) showed artistic talent, Bedales was just the place.

David, who was growing up to look very like his father with the same impish grin, shared his creative abilities and began building; first, furniture and then the fiendish demands of marquetry. Before long he and a friend started a furniture company. He graduated to the arts generally, and, by 2002, the new Viscount Linley became chairman of Christie's UK. His sister Lady Sarah went to art school after Bedales and began to experiment in oils and fastidious watercolors of haunting beauty and delicacy. On a trip to India, she met Daniel Chatto, an up-and-coming actor, and married him. Both children went on to have families and long and stable marriages. Their mother was overheard to murmur, "Well, at least I did something right." Or words to that effect.

At the age of forty, Margaret was very much involved in public duties.

"In my own sort of humble way I have always tried to take some . . . of the burden off my sister," she explained stiffly. "She can't do it all, you know." [26]

In 1971, she told Milton Gendel she had racked up 177 appearances, visiting hospitals, speaking in schools, opening exhibitions, and the like. She was always ready for an evening's festivities. After a ball the night before, she couldn't wait to talk it all over with Milton. She rang him up next morning. Gendel wrote:

> "Spoke to Pss M. 'Wasn't it a lovely ball? What a good time she had had . . . And Tony found it boring. Would I believe it, but she was still in evening dress? What, from the ball? No, no, I'm glad we haven't a television phone because it's too funny. But we had to be up early this morning for the opening of Parliament and I had to put on my tiara and dress for it. On the way back, we dropped in on my mum's and found her in the middle of a large party for the governor of South Carolina, who must have been amazed to see us got up this way.'" [27]

Although she and Tony were still being seen together at big events, the distance between them was not just because of the strain it was being together—when summoned against his will, Tony also spent the evening complaining—but because their interests were diverging. She had always been subject to migraine headaches when under stress. These began occurring more often. She still drank and smoked all day long.

The New Statesman, a serious-minded, leftist publication observed, "Like Elizabeth, (Margaret) was never allowed to acquire the mental disciplines of an academic education, but unlike her, this gap has not been filled by the practical disciplines of office."

As a result, the princess became "restless, spasmodic—though often intense—in her interests; easily bored," the New York Times reported. "Unlike Elizabeth II, she [was] deeply emotional and [oscillated] easily between elation and gloom. She [devoured] magazines, modish books, delights in fashionable West End musicals . . . 'good' jazz and the latest semi-intellectual cultural interests from America. There is a certain brittle superficiality about her mind, an inability to concentrate for long, which sometimes disturbs her elders."[28]

Since we now know that the princess suffered from a neurodevelopmental disorder (ARND), there is a way to understand her seeming lapses, i.e., her lack of ability to concentrate, rapid mood changes, and childlike reactions. In other words, her actions can be seen as much more than just rebelling against the role she was destined to play and her apparent character flaws. Those who did know about the family history of the Bowes-Lyons and the five little girls, cousins of Queen Elizabeth II and Princess Margaret who had to be institutionalized, thought they had a secret understanding of the problem. It was all about Margaret's genes.

There was yet another problem, in that she who was being misunderstood was, ironically, not very good at understanding others herself. She tended to take people at face value. We now know that her husband, in many ways a kind and generous man, had an unfortunate tendency to dissemble and maintain a fake façade against all the odds. He undertook about as public an act as anyone can ever make, i.e., a marriage in Westminster Abbey before millions of viewers, while being aware that his best friend's wife was in the final stages of giving birth to his baby. What is more, the baby was born while he was on his honeymoon. Had any hint of the truth come to light, this marriage would certainly never have taken place. But he squeaked through. It was said that he could be "tricky." Perhaps the future Lord Snowdon even *enjoyed* living on the edge. Getting away with it. But in doing so, he betrayed his best friend and his new wife as well. "WELCOME HOME" indeed, the placard, tied around the neck of his look-alike, mockingly said after he returned from his honeymoon in 1960. *Somebody* knew. It must have made for a very uncomfortable inner life. The odds are good that the princess never knew or even suspected.

In light of the princess's many blind spots, it is no surprise that she picked up an acquaintance with someone she almost met on the street. (Actually, they met at a dinner first.) He was Ned Ryan, born in a country town in Tipperary, who had moved to London to find fame and fortune. He eventually did, but it took a while. When he and the princess first met, he had settled on the role of small antiques dealer in one of the many street markets she and Tony formerly explored together. Now Tony was on to more important things, and she, accompanied by one of her ladies-in-waiting and with the usual detective in the background, continued her explorations of ephemera. Questions led to conversations, and all of a sudden, Ned Ryan was in her life. He stayed there for thirty years.

By the time he got there, Ryan was a somewhat overweight, beaming figure, already balding, his remaining hair forming a scraggly fringe and his open-necked shirts arranged to reveal the gold neckline chains he affected. He had already gravitated from one improbable occupation to the next. He started out as a ticket taker and dispenser on one of London's double-decker buses. He discovered quickly enough that running up the stairs to the upper deck all day (at one time they were actually on the *outside* of the bus) was not only dangerous but quite tiring. So he stopped bothering. It was not long before someone found out that half his passengers were riding without paying. So that was the end of that.

Nothing daunted, he transferred his natural talent for talking himself into anything and became a buyer for the Army and Navy stores. Before long, they were sending him overseas. There was a yearly conference abroad, so he always went to that. One year, the conference was canceled, but he went through the motions of going anyway and then submitted a report from previous years. He was found out then, too. Sacked again.

By the time the princess met him, he sold silverware, some of it bought at West End shops and improbably sold for more on the back streets of London. He was well known in Bermondsey as a bit of a character, a bustling, joking presence, a kind of factotum of the jumble sales. It is said that one morning, it being rather muddy around his table, Ned Ryan threw down his own coat with a fine disregard for the consequences so that the princess would not get her dainty feet wet. One could not help thinking of Sir Walter Raleigh and Queen Elizabeth I in the days when men wore cloaks and puddles were swamps. Naturally, everyone at the market then knew what kind of clientele the seller of silver had at his table, and his reputation was made.

If he had been a sharp operator, Ryan could have easily taken advantage of his new connections, Artful Dodger fashion. Happily, he did not. He seems to have been a benign presence in her life, a kind of twentieth-century version of Mr. Pickwick. His gold chains jangling, he would greet her in his goodhearted, well-meaning sort of way and help her organize her life. One of his first tips was to recommend that the princess be at the market by 5:30 a.m. to get the best deals. The idea that the girl who did not go to bed until 3 should be up and about two hours later is almost preposterous. But she did, and Ned was waiting for her. He continued to dispense more and more good advice as the years rolled by, whether escorting her to lunch at Walton's restaurant in Chelsea, shouldering her through rock concerts, or driving her into the country for the fun of hunting down even more treasure at bargain-basement prices. He had a gift.

Bit by bit, Ned insinuated his way into royal affairs. The queen, who never addressed anyone by their first name, called him Ned. The Queen Mother allowed him to twirl her around on the dance floor. He was awfully good at arranging charity balls. He had a knack for keeping guests busy and happy at country house weekends along with the virtue of never tipping off the press. He was a sympathetic and kindly presence in her increasingly fragmented world.[29]

As more and more bad news about the Margaret-and-Tony battles began to make headlines, along with more and more unflattering comments, whatever favorable reports there were about the princess herself dwindled and disappeared. Not surprisingly, escaping from the drumbeat of constant criticism began to acquire an irresistible allure. If you are far enough away and rich enough, the odds get better that less and less newspaper barons will be willing to spend the money to snoop. If you are vacationing on your own special island, the odds get positively delightful.

Such was the case with Colin Tennant, Lord Glenconner, the very rich and disturbingly eccentric husband of Anne Glenconner, the princess's devoted lady-in-waiting and author of a best-selling memoir. He was the one who had made a devoted servant his only heir and cut out his five children and wife of fifty years. Nobody, including his wife, believed he would do something as cruelly unfair as that. But by then, everyone, including her, had learnt to expect the nastily unexpected. The first night after their wedding he ushered his bride into a tenement where a nude couple was engaging in sex so as to demonstrate what was now expected of her. That was predictable, along with screaming tantrums, such as the time when he did not get the seat he expected on a plane and immediately lay down in the aisle and had a major meltdown. He was, at such moments, capable of anything, including biting.

The irony is that the handsome Glenconner was brilliant in business, tremendously capable, a born showman and impresario, as generous as he was tiresome and with an emotional age of about eight. He, too, sought out and bought a remote, neglected island in the Caribbean for a derisory sum and then put up the equivalent of a "No Trespassing" sign. Since his need to keep people out exactly matched the princess's, when asked in 1960 what she wanted as a wedding present, she promptly asked for a building site on his island. A few years later, she asked if a house came with it? He obliged. All at once, a dazzling island somewhere in distant seas was tantalizing her imagination, irresistibly desirable.

"Mustique is not yet quite part of the modern world," British author David Pryce Jones wrote of this particular island in 1970. "About half of it has become as tidy as any plantation ever was, and perhaps the whole island will go that way, but for the time being there is still some of the untamed Caribbean left—of scrub and coral and coconuts, and the sea beating against empty shores."[30] He might have added an original plague of mosquitoes, accounting for its sparse inhabitants when Glenconner bought it back in 1959. He told himself he would buy it only if there was a fresh water spring on the island. There was none, but he bought it anyway. He vowed to turn this modest little ledge in a vast ocean—only three miles long, and containing nothing but a few scattered shops, a modest café, and a ramshackle jetty—into a jet-set playground. That he finally did, and starting off with a princess was an inspired idea.

The site chosen was a particularly choice spot on its own headland with a steep drop all round. At its base were sandy coves and lagoons. At such a commanding height, what one would see from the house itself was an endless expanse of glittering waves on every side. The house itself would seem to be "hanging mysteriously in a blue dimensional dream," as Patrick Leigh Fermor wrote. She would call it *"Les Jolies Eaux."* It would be her replacement for that tiny secret room in a London backwater she had shared with Tony, where nobody had ever thought to look. Better yet, it would be hers alone, and the first house she had ever owned—everything else belonged to the Crown. Tony would have nothing to say about it.

Tony tried hard to change her mind. He spent much of his childhood in Old House, a house in Sussex owned by his grandparents, and memories of boyhood were everywhere among the hand-painted china, the display cabinets full of toy soldiers, the Jacobean bed and heavy oak table where visitors had carved their initials. It was now derelict, and he was all for taking it on as his next big project, but the princess could not be persuaded.

Her husband, in turn, did not like Mustique; it was too far away. He poured scorn on the idea.

This gift, Gendel wrote in his diary, showed the "amiable and generous side of Colin. But Tony wouldn't have . . . that—it was all calculation. He would be using PM [Princess Margaret] for publicizing his miserable island," and more of the same. Gendel dismissed the remarks as "petty spleen—the smaller, irrational side of Tony."[31] Irrational was the right word, because Oliver Messel, the brilliant stage designer who was his uncle, knew just what Princess Margaret needed and how to give it to her. One climbed into a jeep and made one's way along a rutted track up a hillside, arriving at a courtyard fringed by palms and tropical flowers.

The neo-Georgian house, U-shaped, married quiet elegance with the merest suggestion of walls, set at frequent intervals with glassed-in French doors or expansive windows. Such was his solution to the real reason for being there, i.e., the view. The girl who had lived in glass houses all her life, to be poked, prodded, and jeered at, like a specimen behind glass, had built another display case. Only this time the display was on the outside, and she was hidden safely behind it. Let Tony immerse himself in his past; she faced a happier future. Then she met Roddy.

Chapter 14

Arrows of Desire

> "AND I
> Am the arrow,
> The dew that flies
> Suicidal, at one with the drive
> Into the red
> Eye, the cauldron of morning."
> —Sylvia Plath, "Ariel," 1962

"Roddy," otherwise known as Sir Roderic Victor Llewellyn, 5th Baronet, then aged twenty-five, was described by Christopher Warwick, Princess Margaret's official biographer, as "a spontaneous and exuberant character" who wore a gold earring in one ear. That idea had been urged upon him by Nicholas Haslam who had already met and housed for a year this "bashful imp," "golden-skinned, auburn-mopped . . . His nose wrinkled whenever he laughed, and long lashes would sweep down over his oriel gaze with appealing diffidence."[1]

Roddy arrived in Princess Margaret's life more or less by accident. It was high summer of 1973, the Glenconners were planning a huge party at the family seat, the Glen, outside Edinburgh, and the princess had forsaken Mustique so as to be there. At the eleventh hour, a male guest dropped out, and they were frantic for a replacement. In desperation, Lady Glenconner was told to try someone she knew about but had never actually met. Would Sir Roderic be free for dinner at short notice? He would be delighted. Her husband would meet his train in Edinburgh. The princess would go, too. When the car eventually returned, Lady Glenconner was surprised to find the princess and the new arrival together in the back seat, practically holding hands. She said to her husband, "Gosh, what have we done?"[2]

From then on, they were more or less inseparable. At the Glen party, they stayed up late after dinner, "sitting at one of the card tables in the drawing room after an evening of playing bridge or canasta. They remained very close to each other, their heads almost touching."[3] They had fallen in love and would remain together for the next eight years.

Roddy, at 5'9", had a boyish charm that reminded some people of her husband's, from whom she was separated in all but name at that point—a legal separation took three more years to achieve (1976) and yet another two years before there was a divorce (1978). Like Snowdon, Roddy was equally slim and several inches taller, with a handsome mien, similarly buoyant movements and a mop of auburn-tinted hair. Also Welsh, of course. He was a nonstop chatterer with a fund of jokes, including ones he couldn't bear to abandon, such as "What did one cuff say to the other? I'm afraid."[4] The princess laughed every time. Roddy would sit beside her at the piano, watching with admiration her hands fly about, and turning the pages for her at the right moment. He plainly adored her. When he praised her eyes to Anne Glenconner, she sensibly replied, "Why don't you tell her?" So he did. Her escorts had told her that for years, and she usually had a tart response, but not this time.

"Their days were spent walking through the estate, taking in the wonderful early autumn hues, picnicking beside the lake, and swimming in the steaming pool."[5] When she pulled out a cigarette, he rushed to light it for her. When she began playing "Me and My Gal," he would chime in with "The bells are ringing/For me and my gal." Anne Glenconner wrote that his arrival made "all the difference to Princess Margaret, who, by the time they met, had endured several years of unhappiness with Tony."[6]

This bright light in a shadowed world could not have arrived at a better moment. Roddy had already begun to publish books on landscape design, which began, after all, with a spade. This naturally led to the press's crowing with glee as if a new Lady Chatterley and her brawny lover had suddenly materialized. In the eye of observers for whom the princess had long since provided ample opportunity for exclamations of lascivious alarm, Roddy was a new target.

The prevailing view was that an old man with enough money could play around with battalions of curvaceous twenty-year-olds. But if an older woman took a young man to bed, it was something to sneer at or condemn. She was obviously keeping him, and that was unmanly, against the natural order of things. The sobriquet "toyboy" was freely used, with its predatory implications. A revealing program by *FRONTLINE* revealed the financial benefits of this shocking encounter. The *Daily Mail* and *Daily Express* were in a circulation war with no holds barred. Such a naked confrontation had unleashed "a new, more raucous kind of press voyeurism," which combined "the snobbish, the coy and the explicitly sexual." Before long, you could buy "RODDY FOR PM" t-shirts at vendors outside the big tube stations, designed to cash in on the news. (Incidentally, PM can denote the prime minister, but it also refers to the initials "PM" that he used when referring to his new girlfriend.)

While savoring every detail of the royal antics, the tabloid tone was sanctimonious shock over the queen's assumed embarrassment, along with nudging the reader towards the costs to the taxpayer as noted in the Civil List. A reliable poll of April 1978 showed how much damage the princess had inflicted on royal status itself. By the time obituaries were published in 2002, the shock and disapproval had been replaced by a generalized contempt. One writer observed, "The only constants in the blindingly mediocre life of Princess Margaret would appear to be privilege, illness and lashings of alcohol." Another commented, "She looks what she is, a bitter, unhappy, selfish old woman."[7]

Her critics are still at work and waiting to pounce. The book *99 Glimpses of Princess Margaret* was written by a well-known satirist, Craig Brown, who amused himself by wondering what it would be like if the princess had ended up in a semi-detached with Peter Townsend, or married Picasso, interspersed by diaries of others who bowed to her in public and vented their spleen on paper behind the scenes. That book came out in 2017, fifteen years after her death. The poll of 1978 also revealed that this particular royal representative had been pilloried with a venom unmatched by any other period of the twentieth century.

The royal divorce of 1978 also released yet another wave of ridicule and fault-finding, this time with respect to her relationship with Roddy Llewellyn. In 1979, the satirical British weekly *Private Eye* published a cartoon of the pair in the nude on its cover. The caption was "The Picture they Tried to Ban."[8] Perhaps this was the moment that the queen made her comment, often quoted, to her sister's "guttersnipe life."[9]

Or perhaps the queen was referring to something else, an earlier episode in the life of her sister. Two or three years before meeting Roddy, all unsuspecting, the princess had made a new friend on the beach in Mustique. He was John Bindon, already known for a couple of walk-on roles in films, and well-established as a bouncer at London restaurants and pubs—someone you did not want to tangle with if you knew what was good for you. Only someone with an invisible disability could possibly think he was a friend worth having.

She was always going to be, in emotional terms, a little girl running through life and putting her hand into that of the first smiling stranger. And, as an intriguing newcomer, Bindon was very interesting indeed. In Bindon's obituary, Philip Hoare described him as "the archetypal actor-villain . . . all-round 'good geezer' with such a story-telling gift that he could make a horse laugh."[10] He had shown up in Mustique because his steady girlfriend Vicki Hodge, herself a sometime actress and model, was also the daughter of a baronet. The fact that Bindon had grown up in Fulham, then a working-class part of London, and was the son of a taxi driver, had a certain allure for young aristocrats who were curious about working-class boys and kept them as pets.

Bindon also had a unique parlor trick that he was ready and willing to show at the least provocation, rather like a kid with a new toy. He would proudly unzip his pants to exhibit his penis, which, when erect, could carry five half-pint beer mugs by the handles. Childlike, looking for praise. It was all a bit embarrassing to everyone except, apparently, the gullible princess. She appeared to take a special performance, just for her, in her stride, and in due course invited Bindon to spend three weeks as a guest at *"Les Jolies Eaux."* What was one to think? It must have seemed pretty obvious to Vicki Hodge.

The same edition of *Private Eye* had a paragraph or two tucked away inside that made a glancing reference to what was, in the early days, standard practice on the deserted beaches of Mustique. Given general agreement, the by-then well-oiled guests, ever prepared to abandon formality, cheerfully ripped off their brief bikinis and billowing bottoms, throwing modesty to the tropical winds and cavorting in their all-togethers.[11] One thing led to another, and suspicions of sex in the sand dunes came next. Sensing a sensational windfall, the hunt was on for some really brilliant circulation boosters, if the tabloids could get their hands on some pictures. The story went around that Charlie Glenconner, Colin and Anne's eldest, was a heroin addict, therefore always in need of money, therefore malleable. Who could tell what he might have found? The whisper was that he had put his hands on something worth having: the princess and Mr. Bindon in a close encounter.

This delicious prize never did hit Page One. The best anyone could come up with was an out-of-focus photograph of the principal actors, fully dressed and seated beside each other out of doors—the princess with her arm seemingly on Bindon's chair. Never mind, there was more to be had somewhere, perhaps in a safety box buried in the vaults of Lloyds Bank, Baker Street branch. And, in fact, in September of 1971, a professional gang decided to tunnel its way under London to reach the vaults of that very bank and rifle the 268 safety boxes in residence there. The date is curiously apt, but whether the gang's motive was that particular prize, or had more to do with the valuables inside the other 267, is more to the point. The story gets muddled up, if only because the sequel some seventeen years later was a film, *The Bank Job*, modeled on its real-life predecessor, that actually did include a search for that particular stash. Perhaps such evidence existed. No doubt something like eight hundred pieces of information about the 1971 heist now in the National Archives will tell all. But they are sealed until January 2071.

Pictures of Roddy with the princess were marginally less desirable perhaps. If so, it was because he was not turning out to be the strutting "stud muffin" everyone was expecting. He was the kind of person who knows about plants, hates bullies, is happiest when at work in a garden, gets traffic tickets like the rest of us, occasionally worries about his sexuality, and sometimes thinks of ending it all or at least boarding a train to take him far, far away, he doesn't care where. Someone who was given a poor hand by fate, just as the princess had herself. This was Nigel Dempster's view in *HRH The Princess Margaret* in 1981. Roddy was never going to attack her in public or fall into a fury. When expected, as routine protocol required, he would publicly bow in her direction. Roddy was always going to look up to her, tell her funny stories, pass the salt, and act as the ad hoc host to however many guests she had invited with politeness and a smile. In public, he attended to her needs and comforted her in private, the way Peter Townsend had done.

As for the Princess, there was a level of protectiveness on her part as well. If Roddy needed guidance and reassurance, it was freshly offered. She called him her "Darling Angel." When he decided to buy a small flat, she offered whatever insight she had learnt at Kensington Palace and combed the department store Peter Jones, looking for nice things to adorn it. Friends began to see a warmer, happier person in Her Royal Highness and noticed she was losing weight. Perhaps she confided in him and told him about the time when Tony tried to set her dress alight, or the time when she was frantic to sleep and he made sure she could not by roaring around in his car outside her window, blowing his horn.[12] Roddy might have talked about his father, who had been a famous show jumper and won an Olympics medal, and how both parents concentrated on advancing his career to the exclusion of everything else, including their children. Perhaps he explained to her that he thought of his father as a kind of god, and how frightened he was of him. Perhaps he talked about the times when he had almost committed suicide and how his father's mount *Foxhunter* was a magical mount, and people wanted to touch him because he was a national treasure.[13,14]

Now Roddy was caught up in Surrendell, a kind of upper-class hippy encampment near Hullavington and the Cotswolds. This ancient settlement's western border was still the Old Fosse Way, built by the Romans, straight ahead on the march to the barbarians in the north of England. Sarah Ponsonby, the artist daughter of the Earl of Bessborough, relocated a group headed by Shakespearian actors, with Helen Mirren in the lead, from a small village outside Stratford-on-Avon to Surrendell in 1975. What had been an artists' commune of actors, photographers, musicians, and the like was about to take up the back-to-the-land movement, complete with livestock and an extensive garden which would supply a restaurant located in the pricey part of Bath. The idea was to give the locale a taste of what organic food was all about.

Roddy would be head gardener, and all of them would be distributed among eleven barns and a Jacobean stone farm house that was 350 years old. Unfortunately, the previous tenant, who was renting the place out, had used the house for grain storage and, for the moment, no one could sleep there. So, they made do with caravans or slept in their cars. Roddy happened to have a Ford transit van. In a photograph taken at the time, the buildings look unpromising—the word "dilapidated" comes to mind—and a goat, apparently leashed, looks around a corner of a building. In the months to come, there would be many more animals, including cows, geese, chickens (even the occasional lion). Roddy had his pet pig with the improbable name of "Mah-Jong" and was to be seen in situ, "stripped to the waist, swearing at the goats for eating all his strawberries, or moving his pet sow from one part of the garden to another."

The princess came to visit quite often. For her, it was the new version of Tony's Room, a place to escape in a bandana, mackintosh, and wellies, just like any other person. Her clothes were nondescript. She looked ordinary, too, like a farmer's wife, according to the locals. Everybody had to "muck in," and she did it without complaint, almost as if she relished the demands being made on her. We don't know exactly what she did at Surrendell, but something can be gathered from the way she behaved whenever she visited Lady Anne Glenconner's flint stone farmhouse in Norfolk, where she came prepared to be useful. She would arrive there similarly attired in camouflage and with her own kettle, because she liked to make a cup of tea in the early morning and take it back to bed.[15] Then she would happily tackle the fireplaces in the house, a messy job, and lay them afresh in the manner of, as she said, "I was a Girl Guide, leave it to me." Her idea of fun was a long and lengthy weeding of the garden. She explained to the queen, "No one has any money—it's all share and share alike." The queen thought she should help, so she sent along a dozen brace of pheasants.[16]

The adventure was almost too big, needing too many willing helpers full time, considering all that acreage to plant, weed, and harvest. Then there were all those animals to care for, workers to feed, barns to sweep out, major repairs to a house that had been a granary. Then one day the police found that a crop of cannabis was about to be harvested. That did it. The restaurant, quaintly named Parseen Sally on Milsom Street, was closed, turned into a Café Rouge, and a few years later the valiant pioneers had scattered far and wide.[17]

But before that happened, rumors were circulating that whenever the weather permitted, a flash of pink bottoms could be glimpsed on the grounds of what was clearly becoming a nudist colony. This led to a lively neighborhood interest in just what was going on inside this pile of deserted and ancient buildings. Surrendell was becoming a tourist attraction just as, in 1978, her two years of waiting were up for the princess, and she could legally be released from her self-righteous and very vengeful spouse. A sudden ripple of alarm went through certain echelons of society who had visions of similar encampments within the sylvan acres of the noble Palace itself. Something must be done. All at once, the princess was interpreted as saying she would give up seeing Roddy. Or not. Then Roddy himself put out a statement saying he was certainly not going to get married. He hoped they would all go away and stop bothering him. Or polite words to that effect. Then the princess was ill with symptoms that looked like flu. Soon after that, she had gastritis. Roddy also took to his bed, with "a bleeding stomach condition." Were arms being twisted behind the scenes? The journalists were on the case.[18]

Once the panic died down, the couple went on with their close relationship for the next two or three years. Then Roddy fell in love with someone the princess's junior who liked the idea of having children as much as he did. They married in 1982, had a family, and lived happily ever after. The machinations surrounding the royal divorce are nevertheless instructive for revealing the force of the opposition mounted against them. Their joint reactions are significant, too, in that they both retreated to their beds with symptoms fancied, or real. In the case of the princess, they were no doubt real. She was fragile, not just emotionally, but physically as well.

Nowadays to see the princess's life through the prism of her invisible disability is long overdue. Many others have done so with their own. Daniel

Radcliffe, the irresistible, ever youthful hero of eight *Harry Potter* films, began when he was twelve and became one of the world's highest paid actors. Like the princess, he never grew very tall—he is 5'5", and also like her, he had problems with writing and could not tie his shoes, although he did not find out why until he was nineteen.

Jim Carrey, a prominent actor and comedian, told the *Hollywood Reporter* in 2018, "My mom was addicted to pain medication. She was very sick in a lot of ways. She was lovely, too, but she was a child of alcoholics"—so she was born with problems of her own, he implied. He has joint deformities, involuntary facial contortions, and sporadic seizures that have been traced to fetal alcohol syndrome.

Another victim of a mother who drank, Reese Witherspoon, has won an Academy Award, a British Academy Film Award, a Primetime Emmy Award, and two Golden Globe Awards. As Princess Margaret did, Witherspoon stopped growing at 5'1". She is now a tireless advocate for the education of pregnant mothers. As fate would have it, Witherspoon starred in *Walk the Line*, the famous film about the life of Johnny Cash. The role of Johnny was played by another fetal alcohol syndrome sufferer, Joaquin Phoenix, a victim of the same malaise. There are many others in the performing arts including Oprah, Madonna, and Morgan Fawcett. Senator Bernie Sanders, the well-known independent from Vermont who campaigned to be president in the 2016 and 2020 U.S. elections, has never actually said that he was a victim of fetal alcohol syndrome, but he has lectured often in his state to bring about growing awareness of the dangers. All of them are people with a mission. They know how big the stakes are.

Princess Margaret is a poster child for all the children who grow up and whose behavior is put down to laziness, defiance, stubbornness, and refusal to learn. Nowadays, special programs can help to guide such children. It is well understood that their intelligence is normal but that they have an impaired mental functioning caused by brain damage that is permanent and irreversible. Many who turn out to be dropouts have trouble with the law, are addicted to alcohol, nicotine, and drugs, have the same undiagnosed issues, what is also described as a "central nervous system dysfunction." The neurobehavioral deficits in children have been well studied.

What is not yet well known, for obvious reasons, is what happens to older men and women past the age of thirty. A report in the National Institute of Health is tentative, but the agreements are not in doubt. People laboring under this handicap actually do get more depressed, for obvious reasons. They actually do consider suicide, and some succeed. They have poor reasoning and judgment skills. They have learning disabilities and hyperactive behavior. They are obsessive compulsive. They drink too much and smoke nonstop. The list is long and growing of all the ailments that could afflict them in later life, based on animal studies: hypertension, diabetes, immune deficiencies, autoimmune diseases, cardiovascular diseases, and cancer.

They do poorly in close personal relationships, and the miracle is that the princess managed to sustain a happy relationship with Roddy for as long as she did; eight years is the length of many marriages. She joked that she was glad she and Roddy were breaking up, because "she couldn't afford him" any more. But photographs show otherwise. One taken in a car as they separated shows him in profile, looking forward with optimism. She sits beside him, looking downwards, and her face is bloated, even battered, like the loser in a prize fight. It was one more example of the extra handicap she suffered, being on such constant display and under the kinds of pressures most of us never have to endure. Nobody understood. The princess, with all those mattresses, who woke up black and blue, was no longer sleeping on a pea, but a bed of rocks.[19]

Could the queen also have been affected in some way? Given the letter her mother sent to her father in 1925 when she was pregnant with her firstborn, a stubborn attack of morning sickness caused her to wail that she was never going to recover her drinking powers. Obviously she did at some point, but the subsequent lack of these sorts of symptoms in the young Elizabeth suggests that the Queen Mother was alcohol-free for the duration of that pregnancy, at least. Given that Princess Elizabeth was fretting about what to do with Margaret when she was only twelve, it is instructive to conclude that this was an old, old problem for the grown-ups—she included herself—that had no answer.

Sarah Bradford, biographer of Queen Elizabeth II, whose study is a model of insights, has described someone who learned fast to put her emotions aside and the more challenging task of not showing them. She must have concluded a long time ago that she did not know what to do. Faced with similar issues, Anne Glenconner was told to "get on with it," and that was that. She, the queen, had learned the hard way. Why couldn't Margaret? After all, they had the same parents. Margaret and Elizabeth had seen their parents go through a terrible war, as models of steady determination, and witnessed the tumultuous response from the British people when it all turned out right.

She, Elizabeth, had worn a uniform and dedicated herself to the task of representing a great nation for the rest of her life. She was, in all ways, a remarkable woman, but she had her limitations. Did she ever become a real mother? She never had time. Did she really understand her children's needs?

Three out of four ended up divorced. What could she do to make Margaret feel better? There is no doubt she listened to Margaret and sympathized, but she was getting a bit tired of the constant effort involved. Bradford tells a now-famous story of the final limit of the queen's patience. One day the lady-in-waiting rang to say that the princess was about to throw herself from her bedroom window. What should she do?

"Which floor was it?" the queen asked, in her practical way.

"It was the ground floor, your highness."

"Well, she won't kill herself," the queen replied briskly and turned to other matters.

Perhaps the queen was spared from a first-hand view of the appalling battles between her sister and Snowdon, literally trying to tear each other apart. Their friends were horrified. Lord Rupert Nevill, a friend of Princess Margaret, was so concerned that he managed to tape one of their battles and asked for the help of Mark Collins, a Harley Street psychiatrist. The response was, "This lady needs help, and she needs it soon." The possibility is that she was finally persuaded to see this psychiatrist for a couple of sessions, but no more. As for the queen, she was clearly out of her depth.[20]

On the other hand, how close did this particular family want to be? Given that members of the House of Windsor were never going to be allowed to leave—they were doomed to be united forever—one might need to erect a certain reserve if only in self-defense.

"They are a very odd family," an anonymous relation observed. "They're not welcoming and cozy. They'll never ask how you are or what sort of day you've had. They're probably the least close-knit family that I have ever come across."

While she was still alive, the Queen Mother tried hard to keep them all in touch with each other. The same observer wondered whether "one half was ever pleased to see the other half."[21]

As Edith Wharton wrote, "In reality they all lived in a kind of hieroglyphic world, where the real thing was never said or done or even thought, but only represented by a set of arbitrary signs."[22]

The late Christopher Warwick, who became Princess Margaret's official biographer, came to her attention in the most gradual and unobtrusive of ways. When they met in 1980, he was working as a junior assistant to British publisher Weidenfeld and Nicolson of London, who were publishing a new gardening book by Sir Roderick Llewellyn. Warwick was in the team of editors, very much behind the scenes. It took a year before they all had lunch together in 1981. Warwick remembered that well. He said that the princess's concluding words were, "I expect before you met me you thought I was the person the press say I am. Well, now you know I'm not."

He was captivated by her beauty, the directness of her blue eyes and her outward confidence. She seemed taller than she was, which could have had something to do with her platform shoes, but also the way she held herself, that indefinable something that commands the eye. Only later did he discover that her height was a sore point, one people noticed even when she tried to ignore it herself. People forgot that when crowds came to see her, she could often overhear comments. Once in Wales, she overheard a woman say, "Isn't she quaint!" It still rankled.

"She looked at me and said, 'I'm not quaint, am I?'" Warwick wrote.[23]

At the time, Warwick was a budding author, and it was a great thrill when the princess chose him to be her biographer. Part of that, he learnt, had to do with her ability to dictate what he could say and what he couldn't. He couldn't write about her childhood, for instance. None of that "childhood stuff." Neither could he describe the Peter Townsend saga from her perspective. That was all over and done with. His book, *Princess Margaret: A Life of Contrasts,* with its carefully non-judgmental title, was published by Weidenfeld and Nicolson in 1983 and reprinted several times since.

Warwick wrote that "she could be difficult and could pull rank to the point of rudeness. In answer to those who say she could also be very 'grand,' Anne Glenconner once said to me, 'Of course she could be "grand" because she *was* grand, she was the daughter of a king-emperor.' But while there are those who . . . milk the negative side, she was for the most part the opposite. She was very good to be with, was very thoughtful, generous and actually very kind. She was also genuinely dedicated to her work. There was a lot about her to like."[24]

In the days when the young Elizabeth and Margaret were being closely attended by nannies, governesses, and servants—tutors would follow—there were numerous reasons for concern. Apart from the smallpox vaccine, which had eradicated that scourge after fifty years, there were no vaccines to prevent the childhood epidemics—ones that we now take for granted. All but one are postwar: pertussis (1939), influenza (1946), tetanus (late 1940s), polio (1960), measles (1963), and so on. Both princesses had their share of problems, but Margaret, for reasons that must have been unclear at the time, was always the least able to throw them off. As she grew older, migraine headaches came and went. She had appendicitis as the war ended and an immediate operation.[25] She came down with measles at eighteen. There was a constant parade of minor worries: "gastric chills," "feverish" colds, gastric upsets, two attacks of influenza (1961), laryngitis (1962), and so on. Her lungs seemed particularly vulnerable, so one wonders why she was not warned about all that smoking? Perhaps her doctors tried. At the end of her marriage to Tony, she was deeply depressed and smoked more than ever. It is rumored that she had a nervous breakdown, and there were threats of suicide. She came down with hepatitis and had a mild stroke.

Then, in 1985, she was rushed to hospital for an emergency operation on her lung. A mass had been discovered. Happily for her, it turned out to be benign. But after a slow recovery, she was warned of danger and stopped smoking. It is said that nicotine is one of the hardest drugs to live without. After a month she was back smoking again, at not quite the same rate: thirty a day, instead of sixty. For a while, at least.[26]

While the princess continued to decline, Christopher Warwick kept in touch. She needed help with her library, and by then he was a familiar face at Kensington Palace and came and went whenever he had the time. He said that after Tony had been persuaded to leave—to the tune of 100,000 pounds sterling—Princess Margaret reclaimed his all-white study, more like an operating theater than a room, and turned it into a library for herself.

"I'd been interested in the 'library' project since 1980," Warwick wrote, and saw the transformation take place. The room now had "leaf-green, drag-painted walls, swagged drapes of orange roses on a cream background at the pair of tall windows, and . . . white painted book cases." It became an elegant room, country-house fashion, styled in what was called *Style Anglaise*.[27] The stark contrast between the two personalities could not be more succinct.

By then, her biographer was aware that she was losing friends. As Marina Vaizey observed, she was used to spending her day getting ready to go out. When most people were coming home from work, she was going out to dinner, the theater, and the night club, smoking and drinking until the small hours. Those were the good old days. Now, old friends had moved on. They wanted to be in bed by eleven and knew, from sad experience, that they could not leave any party until the princess did, and she always wanted one more drink. Her children had grown up and left home. Her looks changed as well. She always had an appealing, heart-shaped face with a delicate and perfectly formed chin. When she gained weight, some of that stayed around her chin. After she slimmed down, somehow that particular feature vanished, to be replaced by something ponderous, settling around a wider and thinner mouth. Where once a half-smile seemed to play, now there was something else; she looked sterner, less approachable. And if she actually disapproved, she could freeze you with a look.

Warwick thought that she was basically insecure. It would have taken a very strong ego to withstand the multiplicity of forces arrayed against her once she had decided upon Peter Townsend, a mere equerry. Particularly someone of the ferocious power and influence of Sir Alan Lascelles, whose nickname was "Crusty," a courtier capable of hoping the Duke of Windsor, whom he once served, would fall off a horse and break his neck. As luck would have it, he, too, lived in Kensington Palace, but she would pass him by without a word. She told everyone, "He ruined my life." When faced at the age of thirty with being relegated to the ranks of spinster (for which one can nowadays appreciate this meant "unwanted"), she fell back on an unpredictable and mercurial photographer whom she knew from first-hand experience would quite likely forget to come to dinner. Predictably, in due course he would "forget" to come to a banquet the queen had arranged, an unforgivable insult. After the marriage ceased to work very well, she was subjected to a barrage of vindictiveness no one should have to endure. It also takes heroic self-confidence to survive the battering of the Establishment, the jeering of the press, and the subtle putdowns of people who exercised every soupçon of protocol and precedence they might have over her. People who became friendly were puzzled by her insistence on being correctly addressed, not understanding that being a king's daughter and a queen's sister was all she had. She also had eight years with a man she loved. Until he left her.

It is hardly surprising that she lost whatever sense of self-worth she had. And that, whenever she felt threatened, she lashed back, using the retorts, the cutting remarks that she had endured. There were so many of them.

Early one evening, Christopher Warwick stopped by the library to check that all was in order. The library adjoined the drawing room, and as he passed by, he saw the princess sitting and watching television. That particular evening, he noticed that the butler, the late John Leishman, was nearby and watching the program, too. It transpired that, since protocol decreed he could not sit in her presence, the butler was there to keep her company. That is when Christopher realized just how lonely she was.[28]

Then there was the fate of *"Les Jolies Eaux,"* where she went twice a year, spring and fall, for years and years after it was built. How could she forget her untamed Caribbean island of scrub and coral and coconuts, where the sea broke on empty shores and her lovely house was "hanging mysteriously in a blue dimensional dream." It was her refuge, her sanctuary. She could do anything she wanted there, in her private, special hideaway. No one could enter unless specifically invited.

In the early days, the Island's social life revolved around Colin, its owner and impresario, and Anne, who had become the princess's own special lady-in-waiting and never stopped being. In those halcyon days one could strip off one's swimsuit and plunge naked into the breaking surf. Or visit the swimming pools of strangers, do a length, jump out, and run off laughing. Or, at the end of a party, it was a done thing to drive off in the nearest car and sort it out the next morning.

She and Anne would then have lunch on the beach, which is elsewhere described as a full-dress affair with tablecloths, butlers, silverware, and lots and lots to drink. Then they might go hunting for shells in the afternoon and, when the hint of dusk began to appear, one might repair to Basil's Bar for a sundowner before returning one's special indoor-outdoor kind of house. Anne recalled one conversation in which the Princess spoke readily, and at some length, about her first love, Peter Townsend, and how they fell madly in love on the tour of South Africa in 1947. Lady Glenconner was a witness to the fact that they met again in 1993 one day at Kensington Palace. Peter was in London, so he came to lunch.

"I watched him from the window, now a very old man, making his way slowly to the house," she wrote.

She did not witness the luncheon, but later she asked the princess how it had gone and learnt they never stopped talking. "He hasn't changed at all," the princess said.[29] (Note: he died two years later at age eighty.)

Visitors to Mustique knew about Colin's collection of trunks, which anyone could investigate, full of a vast collection of fancy dress outfits. The range was infinite, and you could be anything you wanted: perhaps a pirate, or a Grand Duke, or a ballerina, anything at all, and step out into life as somebody else. The parties Colin threw in those fabulous, no-holds-barred, spare-no-expense days, were the stuff of legend. In 1976 he threw himself a 50th birthday. Being the Midas that he was, the theme he chose was Gold. He designed his own outfit, of course: a shirt top and matching pants in white silk embroidered with massive rows of gold stars; there was a hat to match as well. The trees were painted gold. The grass was sprayed with gold. Even the beach received its carpet of gold glitter. The birthday boy then hired as decorative objects young men who, once stripped and liberally provided with alcoholic sustenance, were encouraged to mingle clad only in a few strategically placed coconuts. Painted gold, of course. By then, Mick Jagger had been persuaded to buy a modest house in Mustique, and the throngs of other celebrities grew to include the queen herself, along with Prince Philip, mingling in the swirling crowd.

At another of Colin's birthday parties, Anne Glenconner observed, "Bianca Jagger stepped out of a great ball of glitter." At yet another ball Colin bought "reams of silk clothes from India and arranged them on a yacht offshore so everyone could take their pick."[30] When Princess Margaret was presented with a dress made all in gold, she exclaimed, "For the first time, I feel like a real princess."[31] So many times in those years Lady Glenconner would see her in her favorite place, standing on the cliffs outside her house, a small, unmoving figure, looking silently out to sea.[32]

After Lord Glenconner sold Mustique in the 1980s, he and his wife would return as guests and always stayed at *"Les Jolies Eaux."* They saw the princess often and became concerned about her declining state. They could not have known that because of her invisible handicap she was aging faster than others in her generation. But, given her dependence on alcohol and nicotine as well as her tendency to be depressed by setbacks others could shake off, her threats of suicide—all of them cited as common to sufferers of ARND—to see her as fragile, emotionally and physically, was natural enough. Besides, the major lung operation in January 1985 had also done its debilitating work.

In 1998, they were all at dinner one evening with their mutual friends, the Harding-Lawrences, when halfway through the meal the princess gasped and slumped onto the table. She had had a stroke. Anne Glenconner observed, "there were no obvious lasting effects—her speech wasn't slurred, her muscles hadn't stopped working—but she became gradually slower."[33]

However, by then the princess had already made the painful decision that the time had come to pass her magical house along to the younger generation. Her son David and his new wife Serena accepted the gift as a delayed wedding present in 1996. All went well, but maintaining property at a long distance is always something of a challenge. Before long, the young couple were renting out the place—as most people did on the island. Then, after two or three years, they put the house up for sale. That was in early 1999. Before it was sold, the princess was invited for one last, precious visit. As luck would have it, that was the day that a property agent had booked an inspection tour for some interested buyers. The princess was subjected to the agony of enduring other people walking through her most precious possession while she sat and watched. She was, Nicholas Courtney wrote, "upset."[34] That had to be an understatement. Surely that was the cruelest cut of all. The very next morning, she had a serious accident.

In Elizabeth Arden's Bond Street days, one of the select group of hairdressers often attended Princess Margaret. His name was Glenn Irving. He explained that the salon offered steam treatments, actual individual cabinets in which one sat down, doors closed, and one's body was encased in steam—all except one's head, which was not involved. Irving explained, "The whole point of the exercise was to sweat." He thought the princess had fluid retention problems, probably caused by alcohol, and seemed to benefit from the experience. She came often. But afterwards, the escaping steam had "wrecked her hair," so he was summoned to repair the damage.

At home, she used the same idea. First, she had a leisurely breakfast in bed. Then she would take a steam bath. After that, the lady-in-waiting that day would help her dress. That particular morning, the duty fell to "Janie" Stevens, another longtime lady-in-waiting and personal friend. Lady Stevens knew that there was no central hot water system at "*Les Jolies Eaux*," but a system of hot water heaters in the kitchen and bathrooms known as geysers. In the bathrooms each was suspended over the tub, with its own controls. Quite what happened is not clear. Perhaps a cut-off valve malfunctioned, and the water just kept getting hotter and hotter. There are all kinds of versions for what happened next, which is what makes Janie Stevens's version so crucial, since she was actually there. She said, "I was sitting outside on the terrace waiting for the Princess to come and get me," she said. But time went by, and she did not appear. "So I thought I had better take a look." More and more steam was escaping around the door and into the hallway. One version, that the door was locked, was not true. But she knocked, nothing happened, and finally opened it to be confronted with a wall of steam. There was the princess, seated on the side of the bath at the deep end of the tub, with both legs in scalding water. So why did she not call for help? The logical conclusion is that she was in a state of shock, that is to say, confusion and disorientation. And how long she had been seated there, as if transfixed, is another troubling question. Perhaps she herself turned the wrong button, making the water even hotter. Perhaps she was too befuddled to know what she was doing. Lady Stevens learned later that the princess sat down, put in a foot, and realized the water was painfully hot. She tried to pull the foot out, and it was stuck to the bottom. She stood up, trying to get enough traction to step away, and put another foot into the water. That immediately stuck as well.

As Anne Glenconner wrote in *Lady in Waiting*, Janie Stevens and the resident detective managed to pull the princess out, but her feet were so badly burned that after the water drained away, bits of skin could be seen sticking to the side of the bath. The princess took to her bed, insisting that the room be kept dark while the lengthy repair of these massive burns began with her ladies-in-waiting in constant attendance; Lady Glenconner moved into the room. After two weeks, she was urged to fly to London for advanced treatment but refused. The queen insisted. So she was put on a stretcher and transported to the specialists in a London burn unit. The burns healed agonizingly slowly, and her convalescence was prolonged. Lady Stevens said, "She recovered to some degree but never really walked again."[35]

One suspects that all her life, Princess Margaret used the excuse of a tummy ache or a cold to avoid being dragooned into doing something she did not want to do, perhaps from childhood. But there were plenty of times when ill health lurked for someone with her invisible malady, despite being carefully isolated from catching childhood diseases like measles, which only meant you caught them when you grew up. Appendicitis could happen to anyone. So could hepatitis, tonsilitis, mumps, and a host of other diseases. Then there were emotional crises, when she would shut herself in her room and refuse to eat. Her big sister had managed somehow to discipline her own emotions and reached the stage when she could successfully conceal them, at least when other people were around. No doubt this was an idea which had long since taken over and come to dominate the way Princess Margaret behaved. When her close friend Lady Glenconner was yelled at by her boorish husband because she had not opened the door for him fast enough, and tears came to her eyes, Princess Margaret jumped on her. She said, "Stop that at once, Anne. It's absolutely no use." By which she probably meant, "Don't let him get to you." But she could also have been thinking, "You can't win so you might as well give up." As she describes in her new book *What Happens Next?,* Lady Glenconner chose to interpret the advice as that she should "stiffen her spine and get on with it." This advice was not much help when her husband, in a fit of ungovernable rage, tried to kill her. There was yet another possible response, and that was to protest the poor treatment and, if it continued, to leave and take the children. That she finally did.

Burning her own feet, coming as it did just after Princess Margaret was forced to witness people touring her house as a prelude to buying it, is too shocking and at the same time puzzling to pass without comment. Maybe there is no connection. It was all an accident, just that. Or perhaps, if you cannot even show how much this has hurt you, and you are helpless to change things, the only solution is despair and self-mutilation.

Months and months of devoted care came and went. The princess, dressed in a spring green dress, jacket, and hat, was pushed around the Chelsea Flower Show in May 2000 and attended a memorial service for the founder of the Royal Ballet in Westminster Abbey a few months later. She could have walked a bit using a cane but did not. The little girl who had once been prevented from walking and imprisoned in a baby carriage had become the old lady who refused to walk. Her appetite, always under draconian control, was erratic. When they all moved to Sandringham over Christmas 2001, she was refusing to eat again. Anne, who was attending her just then, was gently persistent at tea time. A bit later on, she met the queen in the hall, who asked how things were going. Anne replied that the princess had managed to eat a jam tart.

"A jam tart!" The queen was suitably impressed.[36]

After lunching with the princess the previous summer (May 2001), Lord Glenconner gave an interview to blast away at her family for not seeing the state the princess was in. His biographer said the tone of the criticism was scathing. They had refused to see how ill she was and how her mental state was declining by the day.[37] He was voicing the increasing alarm of her old friends.

Lady Prudence Penn, who had known her since she was sixteen, was shocked and saddened.

"I used to go and read to her but she seemed unable to take it in," she said. The next time they met was a week before the princess died.[38] By then, she had lost the use of her left side, so that "her face had fallen down and she couldn't talk properly."[39]

Since fetal alcohol syndrome and its related neurological damage (ARND) was identified in 1973, this new field of study has become widely accepted. It is known that women alcoholics, who tend to be binge drinkers, do the most damage to the developing baby's mind and body. But what lesser amount is still too much is an open question. Public authorities have come up with the warning that any amount is too much. What complicates the issue is the fact that only seventeen days after conception—that is, before the mother-to-be has missed her first period—an infant's face is starting to form. The other problem is the difficulty of getting the new mother to confess; naturally enough, nobody wants to believe they have harmed their child, so they will say they didn't drink even when they did.

In 2016, Scottish hospitals began testing just-born babies and found that their mothers had lied and said they had not been drinking when they had. As many as 40 percent of mothers drank during pregnancy and 15 percent admitted to drinking more than one or two small glasses of wine per week.[40] Naturally enough, there are no double-blind studies.

Not much is known about the puberty of girls, apart from the fact that it comes much earlier—about age 8 instead of 11, and that it stunts their growth (Margaret, at 5', was petite). Boys have been better studied, and at least one, Nikolas Cruz in particular, was responsible for the horrific murder of 17 school children and staff, and wounding 17 others in February 2018. The attack took place in the Margery Stoneman Douglas High School in Fort Lauderdale, Florida. His mother Brenda Woodard was a sex worker and alcoholic, and he was adopted as a baby by an older couple. Brenda denied she ever drank, but it did not take long for his new parents to realize he had severe problems. At just two years old he began to behave in bizarre and troubling ways and could become violent. They took him to numerous specialists but did not know that he was a victim of fetal alcohol syndrome. Dr. Jones believed the youngster was misdiagnosed.

He had a troubled childhood. At the age of five, he saw his father collapse and die in front of him. His teenage years were dominated by an older brother who bullied him, and a trusted friend sexually molested him when he was 12. Another death, this time of his mother, the only one he had ever had, came when he was 19. This might have explained the school attacks, since they followed shortly after he purchased—legally—an AR-15 style semi-automatic rifle and began to plan one of the deadliest massacres of U.S. history. He started to carry around a dead cat in a bag and tell everyone that he, Nick, would be the next school shooter. Nobody listened.

In the subsequent trial, which took four months, Dr. Kenneth Jones testified on behalf of Nikolas Cruz. Dr. Jones said his birth mother had the worst case of binge drinking he had ever encountered, and that her baby had suffered distress, along with severe damage, as a result. She had also taken drugs, but he discounted these and suggested the effects of alcohol were far worse.

Nobody realized what was wrong with Nick until it was too late. Someone could, conceivably, have understood what was wrong with Princess Margaret, this well-known public figure, but never did, perhaps because she lacked the tell-tale signs, such as the widely spaced eyes and a missing philtrum between nose and lip. She must be normal. She was not. Nobody knew. There are lots more children like her today, perhaps one in seven, with unknown disabilities resembling hers. Particularly in Scotland, where alcohol consumption is, according to the World Health Organization, the highest in the world. Speaking to Alistair Jamieson of NBC News, an eighteen-year-old girl said, "Drinking is a joke in Scotland, something to be proud of, and that's a problem. We have to do something about it."[41]

The last public appearance of the princess came after that final physical blow that actually turned her into someone no one recognized. This was made very clear when she made an appearance for the Queen Mother's 101st birthday at Windsor on August 7, 2001. Strapped into a wheelchair, wearing wraparound sunglasses that obscured most of her swollen face, with her limp left arm in a sling and what could be seen of another crumpled hand, all one could see was a single gold earring and a lipsticked, tightly pursed mouth. Was she biting back pain? Or was it a sign of the determination it took even to be there at all? Could she have been showing to the world, as she was paraded before all those pairs of eyes, just what had become of her? An implied reproach, perhaps? The photo appeared in all the Sunday papers, Kenneth Rose observed in his diary: "Oh, the pity of it."[42]

One night in the winter of 2002, it seemed as if the end must be near. She was transferred to King Edward Hospital, and her children, David and Sarah, went with her. What has been revealed only recently is that in those final hours she was also attended by the Archbishop of Canterbury. He was no longer Geoffrey Fisher, the cleric who had exerted all his power and authority to prevent her from marrying the divorced Peter Townsend. When, in 1955, she dutifully complied, giving as her explanation that "mindful of the church's teaching," a marriage was indissoluble, the then Archbishop did not actually do a victory dance, but he came close.

"What a wonderful person the Holy Spirit is!" he purred.[43]

The present Archbishop of Canterbury George Carey seemed much more interested in the human cost when he entered quietly to sit at her bedside, and listened to the dying woman's halting words. She wanted to talk about her emotions, and how, even then, she was desperately sad at having had to give Peter up.

"Here was a woman who longed for love and commitment, and the love of her life was forbidden," he commented later.

He talked to her quietly for a while, said a prayer, then anointed her with oil.

She died soon after that, on February 9, 2002. The Archbishop also commented that "there were lessons to be learnt" from what had happened. He did not elaborate.[44]

Whenever she was in Mustique, the princess could usually be found on the beach, looking for shells, and usually with Anne. They would take their great heaps back up the hillside to *"Les Jolies Eaux"* and dry them in the sun. Once ready for display, these mute testaments to the bounty of the sea would be displayed inside glass lamps in the drawing room. Or, perhaps, singled out laboriously to make interesting table tops. Even more rare and exotic ones were put in glass cases, lit from behind, in Kensington Palace and part of any apartment tour. Some of those came from Japan and were much admired, but then, the Emperor turned her over to that country's leading expert so that a princess might acquire nothing but the best. Perhaps when she was alone, she would carefully extract one of these exquisitely molded carapaces which had contained something vulnerable and precious. Perhaps she had special favorites and would hold each one to her ear. And there, wherever she was, if she listened very carefully, she would be able to hear the eternal roar of the sea.

ENDNOTES

Chapter 1: Pomp and Circumstance
1. Marion Crawford, *The Little Princesses*, (St. Martin's Press, 1950), 72.
2. Barbara W. Tuchman, *A Distant Mirror*, (Alfred A. Knopf, 1978), 13.
3. Leslie Parris, *The Pre-Raphaelites*, (Tate Gallery, 1999), 140.
4. Alan Allport, *Britain at Bay*, (Alfred A. Knopf, 2020), 55.
5. Hugo Vickers, *Coronation*, (The Dovecote Press, 2013), 11.
6. *The New York Times*, 5/13/1937.
7. Idem.
8. Creation, Idem, 11.
9. *The New York Times*, 5/30/1937.
10. *The New York Times*, idem.
11. Marion Crawford, idem, 47.

Chapter 2: The Ghosts of Glamis
1. Mike Dash, (*Smithsonian Magazine*, 2/1/2012).
2. *Smithsonian*, Ibid.
3. *The New York Times*, 7/8/1928.
4. William Shawcross, *The Queen Mother*, (Alfred A. Knopf, 2009), 79–80.
5. *The New York Times*, 8/21/1930.
6. *The New York Times*, Ibid.
7. *The New York Times*, 7/8/1928.
8. William Shawcross, *The Selected Letters of Queen Elizabeth, the Queen Mother*, (Farrar, Straus and Giroux, 2012), 143.
9. Major Colin Burgess, *Behind Palace Doors*, (John Blake, 2006), 53.
10. *The Selected Letters*, Ibid, 177.
11. *Associated Press*, 8/17/1930.
12. *The New York Times*, 8/22/1930.
13. *The New York Times*, Ibid.

14 Ibid.
15 *The Little Princesses*, Ibid, 20.
16 *Selected Letters*, Ibid, 8/27/1930, 178.
17 *The New York Times*, 4/2/1928 and 7/8/1928.
18 *Associated Press*, 2/12/1927.
19 *The New York Times*, 2/12/1927.
20 *The New York Times*, 3/12/1927.
21 Robert Lacey, *A Brief Life of Queen Elizabeth 2*, (Duckworth, 2019), 57.
22 *The Washington Post*, 6/27/1927.
23 Ibid.
24 *The New York Times*, 4/22/1930.
25 Shawcross, Ibid, 319.
26 Ibid, 318.
27 Ibid, 316.
28 *The New York Times*, 12/20/1936.
29 Shawcross, 319.
30 *Selected Letters*, 181.
31 Crawford, Ibid, 24.
32 Liz Kulp, *The Best I Can Be*, (betterendings.org, 2013), 9.
33 Shawcross, Ibid, 332.
34 Ibid, 332.
35 Ibid, 576.
36 Ibid, 679.
37 Ibid, 680.
38 Sarah Bradford, *Elizabeth*, (Farrar, Straus and Giroux, 1996), 33.
39 Liz Kulp, Ibid, 29.
40 Crawford, Ibid, 46.
41 Ibid, 39.
42 Liz Kulp, Ibid, 37.
43 Ibid, 37.
44 Ibid, 43.
45 Ibid
46 Jeremy Paxman, *On Royalty*, (Penguin Books, 2007), 62–63.

Chapter 3: Too Strict: Too Lax
1 *The New York Times*, 10/21/1930.
2 Ben Pimlott, *The Queen: A Biography of Queen Elizabeth II*, (Harper Collins, 1997).
3 Ibid, 5/3/1927.
4 *The New York Herald Tribune*, 3/8/1932.
5 *The Sunday Express*, Associated Press, 8/18/1934.
6 Crawford, Ibid, 26.
7 Anne Glenconner, *Lady in Waiting*, (Hachette, 2020).

Chapter 4: Odd Girl Out
1 In homage to *Odd Man Out*, 1947, by Carol Reed, starring James Mason. "One of the Great British Films."

Endnotes

2. Marion Crawford, Ibid, 3.
3. Philip Whitwell Wilson, *The New York Times*, 7/8/1928.
4. *Selected Letters*, Ibid, 208.
5. Marion Crawford, Ibid, 20.
6. Ibid, 30.
7. Ibid, 31.
8. Ibid, 27.
9. Margaret Rhodes, *The Final Curtsey*, (Birlinn Ltd. and Umbria Press, 2012), 9.
10. Anne Glenconner, Interview with the author.
11. F. J. Corbitt, *My Twenty Years in Buckingham Palace*, (David McKay Company, Inc., 1956), 88, 102.
12. Ibid, 37.
13. Crawford, Ibid, 38.
14. Ibid, 52.
15. Ibid, 52.
16. Dennis Friedman, *Inheritance*, (Sidgwick & Jackson, 1993), 136.
17. Idem, 136.
18. Crawford, Ibid, 29.
19. Crawford, Ibid, 64.
20. Crawford, Ibid, 64.
21. Ibid, 81.
22. Vere Connaught, "The Royal Chambermaids," (*Cosmopolitan,* January 1961), 41–45.
23. Crawford, Ibid, 71.
24. David Cannadine, *The Decline and Fall of the British Aristocracy*, (Vintage Books, 1999), 246–249.
25. Sir Lionel Cust, *King Edward VII and His Court*, (E. P. Dutton, 1930), 223.
26. F. J. Corbitt, *My Twenty Years in Buckingham Palace*, Ibid, 10.
27. Crawford, Ibid, 81.
28. *Selected Letters*, Ibid.
29. Jane Ridley, *The Heir Apparent*, (Random House, 2012), 13.
30. *The Heir Apparent*, 22.
31. Crawford, Ibid, 49.
32. Ibid, 87.
33. Ibid, 30.
34. *The New York Times*, 12/20/1936.
35. Robert Coughlan, "Britain's National Deb," (*Life Magazine,* 10/31/1949), 96–113.
36. Ibid.
37. Ibid.
38. Ibid.
39. Ibid.
40. Crawford, Ibid, 39.

Chapter 5: The Glass Curtain

1. F. J. Corbitt, Ibid, 10.
2. Idem, 21–22.
3. Liz Kulp, *The Best I Can Be*, Ibid.

4   Ibid, 17, 19, 43.
5   Sarah Bradford, *George VI*, Ibid, 419.
6   Diane Malbin, *Syndrome Effects*, (Hazelden, 1993), 16.
7   Diane Malbin, *Trying Differently Rather Than Harder*, (FASCETS, Inc., 2017), 26.
8   Jeremy Paxman, *On Royalty*, Ibid, 13.
9   Alan Alport, *Britain at Bay*, Ibid, 29–30.
10 *Selected Letters*, Ibid, 217–218.
11 Louie Stride, *Memoirs of a Street Urchin*, (Bath University Press, no date), 13.
12 Ibid, 13.
13 Ibid, 18.
14 Ibid, 8.
15 Anne Glenconner, *Lady in Waiting*, Ibid, 41.
16 Kelcy Wilson-Lee, *Daughters of Chivalry: The Forgotten Children of King Edward Longshanks*, (Pegasus Books, 2019), 178.
17 *The New York Times*, 2/6/1997.
18 John Mortimer, *Clinging to the Wreckage*, (Penguin, 1982), 10.
19 Stanley Baldwin, (*The Guardian*, 2/4/2018).
20 "Bright Young Things: David Cannadine," *The Decline and Fall of the British Aristocracy*, Ibid, 351–352.
21 *Chips: The Diaries of Sir Henry Channon*, (Weidenfeld and Nicolson, 1967), 23.
22 F. J. Corbitt, Ibid, 214.
23 Ibid, 214.
24 Ibid, 215.
25 Sir Alan "Tommy" Lascelles, *King's Counsellor*, (Weidenfeld & Nicolson, 2006), 104.
26 Idem.
27 Paxman, Ibid, 10.
28 Channon, Ibid, 6/3/1937.
29 James Pope-Hennessy, *The Quest for Queen Mary*, ed. Hugo Vickers, (Hodder & Stouton/Zuleika, 2018), 231–232.
30 Janet Flanner, *London Was Yesterday*, (Viking Press, 1975), 21.
31 Janet Flanner, Ibid, 39.
32 William Shawcross, Ibid, 311.
33 William Shawcross, Ibid, 334.
34 Ibid, 335.
35 Janet Flanner, *Paris Was Yesterday*, (Viking Press, 1972), 185.
36 Janet Flanner, Ibid, 185–186.
37 Edward F. Folliard, *The Washington Post*, 6/7/1939.
38 *Selected Letters*, Ibid, 71.
39 *The Baltimore Sun*, 6/11/1939.
40 *The New York Times*, 5/28/1939.
41 Inez Robb, International News Service, *The Washington Post*, 6/14/1939.

Chapter 6: The King Will Never Leave
1   *Bournemouth Echo*, 9/20/2016.
2   *The Guardian*, 9/15/2010.
3   Idem.

Endnotes

4 William Shirer, *The Rise and Fall of the Third Reich*, (Simon and Schuster, 1960), 785–792.
5 *The Washington Post, Associated Press*, 2/9/1941.
6 Shawcross, Idem, 517; H. V. Morton, *In Search of London*, (Dodd, Mead & Co., 1951), 243.
7 William Shawcross, Idem, 522.
8 Margaret Rhodes, *The Final Curtsey*, Ibid, 70.
9 Philip Zieger, *London at War*, (Mandarin, 1991), 121.
10 Shawcross, Ibid, 524.
11 Joseph Kennedy, letter to his wife Rose, 9/10/1940, *Hostage to Fortune*, (Penguin Books, 2001), 466.
12 Joseph Kennedy, Ibid, 239.
13 Ibid, 252–253.
14 Ibid, 326.
15 Ibid, 352.
16 Ibid, 466.
17 Marion Crawford, Ibid, 120.
18 Margaret Rhodes, Ibid, 68.
19 Crawford, 124–125.
20 Rhodes, Ibid.
21 Rhodes, Ibid.
22 Crawford, Ibid, 127.
23 Letters of Princess Margaret to Queen Mary: By permission of the Royal Archives.
24 *The Washington Post*, 2/9/1941.
25 Rhodes, Ibid, 171.
26 Rhodes, Ibid, 71.
27 Ibid, 73.
28 Ibid, 37–38.
29 Isabella Naylor-Leyland, preface to *The Windsor Diaries*, (Hodder & Stoughton, 2020), Letters of Alathea Fitzalan Howard, page X.
30 Alathea, Ibid, 35.
31 Ibid, 41.
32 Ibid, 54.
33 Ibid, 85.
34 Ibid, 186.
35 Ibid, 85.
36 Ibid, 9.
37 Ibid, 43.
38 Ibid, 66.
39 Ibid, 80.
40 Ibid, 118.
41 Alathea, Ibid, 147–148.
42 Ibid, 100.
43 Ibid, 96.
44 Ibid, 144.
45 Ibid, 96.
46 A. J. Liebling, *The Road Back to Paris*, (The Modern Library, 1997), 123.
47 Liebling, Ibid, 322.

48 Ibid, 323.
49 Memoir by the author.
50 Mollie Panter-Downes, *The New Yorker*, 5/19/1945.
51 Alan "Tommy" Lascelles, *King's Counsellor*, Ibid, 322.
52 BBC-1 TV Program, "VE Day Remembered" with Princess Margaret, May 1995.
53 Margaret Rhodes, Ibid, 83.
54 Ibid, 83.
55 Mollie Panter-Downes, Ibid.
56 Margaret Rhodes, Ibid, 83–84.

Chapter 7: A Pawn in the Game
1 Dennis Friedman, *Inheritance*, Ibid, 134.
2 Ibid.
3 Ibid, 133.
4 Ibid, 136.
5 Nigel Balchin, *Look Magazine*, 6/29/54.
6 Ibid, 27.
7 *Daily Mail*, 9/13/1948.
8 Letter, Princess Margaret to Queen Mary, 5/20/1949.
9 Letter, Princess Margaret to George VI, 5/3/1949.
10 Ibid.
11 Ibid, 5/8/1949.
12 Ibid, 5/16/1949.
13 Ibid.
14 *The Washington Post*, 11/15/1945.
15 Summary of article by J. Bryan III, *McCall's*, Feb. 1949.
16 Alice Munro, "To Reach Japan," *Dear Life*, (McLelland & Stewart, 2012), 6.
17 *Look*, 6/19/1954.
18 Ibid.
19 *The Baltimore Sun*, 8/21/1955.
20 *The Baltimore Sun*, 12/3/1940.
21 *The New York Times*, 12/10/1950.
22 Ibid.
23 *Life Magazine*, 10/31/1949.
24 Chips Channon in 1948, Ibid, 478.
25 Idem.
26 Idem.
27 *Australian Women's Weekly*, 7/15/1950.
28 Noël Coward in *Lord of the Isle* by Nicholas Courtney, (Bene Factum Publishing, 2012), 47.
29 Ibid.
30 William Shawcross, Ibid.
31 Chips Channon in 1942, Ibid, 927.
32 Courtney, Ibid, 49.
33 Sarah Bradford, Ibid, 287.
34 F. J. Corbitt, Ibid, 229.

Endnotes

35 Ibid, 230.
36 Peter Townsend, *Time and Chance*, (Fontana/Collins, 1979) 116.
37 Norman Barrymaine, *The Peter Townsend Story*, (E. P. Dutton, 1958), 50.
38 Peter Townsend, Ibid, Prologue, 9–11.
39 Townsend, Ibid.
40 Norman Barrymaine, Ibid, 41.
41 Probably many more; this was the total for the period as commander of No. 85 Squadron from May 1940 to June 1941, BBC.com.
42 Peter Townsend, Ibid, 115.
43 Townsend, Ibid, 116–117.
44 Townsend, Ibid, 115.
45 Townsend, Ibid, 120.
46 Ibid, 120.
47 Ibid, 120.
48 Barrymaine, Ibid, 51.
49 Townsend, Ibid, 120.
50 *Life Magazine*, 10/10/1955.
51 *McCall's*, 2/59, 145.
52 Kenneth Rose, *Journals, Vol. I*, 1944, 443.
53 Idem, 107.
54 Townsend, Idem, 181.
55 Ibid, 181.
56 Ibid, 181.
57 Ibid, 186.
58 Ibid, 189.
59 Ibid, 189.
60 Bradford, Ibid, 416.
61 Idem, 459.
62 Compiled from Bradford and *McCall's*, Feb. 1959.
63 Bradford, Ibid, 171.
64 Bradford, Ibid.
65 J. Bryan II and Bradford, Ibid.
66 Bradford, Ibid, 171.
67 J. Bryan III, Ibid.
68 Princess Margaret, Letter to her father, 3/14/1947.
69 Letter, Princess Margaret to father, 8/23/1951.
70 Chips Channon diaries, Ibid, 802.
71 *Life Magazine*, 10/10/1951, 138.
72 Barrymaine, Ibid, 93.
73 *Maclean's*, 4/12/1952.
74 Townsend, Ibid, 187.
75 Ibid.
76 *McCall's*, Ibid.
77 Townsend, Ibid, 188.
78 Ibid.
79 Townsend, Ibid, 197.

80 Chips Channon diaries, Ibid, 846–847.
81 *The Baltimore Sun*, 7/16/1953.
82 Chips Channon diaries, Ibid, 1048.
83 Ibid, 12/1/1936, 88.
84 *McCall's*, 2/9/59.
85 Lord Moran, *Churchill*, taken from the Diaries (Houghton Mifflin, 1966), 402.
86 *The Times*, 12/17/2021.
87 Townsend, Ibid, 211.
88 Derek Brown, *The Guardian*, 3/14/2001.
89 Keith Kyle, *Suez 1956: the Crisis and its Consequences*, (Oxford, 199: Scholarship on Line).
90 Lord Moran diaries, Ibid, 622.
91 *McCall's*, Ibid.
92 *The Baltimore Sun*, 3/7/1955.
93 *Sunday Dispatch*, Associated Press, 3/6/1955.
94 *The People*, 3/6/1955.
95 *The Baltimore Sun*, Associated Press.
96 *Manchester Guardian*, 10/14/1955.
97 *The New York Times*, 10/15/1955.
98 Ibid.
99 *New York Daily News*, 10/15/1955.
100 *The Baltimore Sun*, 10/16/1955.
101 *Manchester Guardian*, 10/14/1955.
102 Christopher Warwick, *Princess Margaret: A Life of Contrasts*, (Andre Deutsch, 2002), 184.
103 Townsend, 183.
104 *The New York Times*, United Press, Reuters, 4/18–20/1958.
105 Secret file in National Archives about events of 1955 not made public for 50 years that would have allowed them to marry.
106 *Marie Claire*, 12/31/1969.
107 Bradford, Ibid, 287.

Chapter 8: Margaret Learns to Lie
1   *Associated Press*, 11/3/1955.
2   *Associated Press*, 12/24/1955.
3   Cecil Beaton, *The Unexpurgated Beaton*, (Alfred Knopf, 2002), 66–67.
4   Letters, Ibid, 489.
5   Ibid.
6   *McCall's Magazine*, Feb. 1959, 149.
7   Peter Townsend, *Time and Chance*, Ibid, 235.
8   Ibid, 235.
9   Ibid.
10 Ibid.
11 Ibid.
12 *Associated Press*, 7/10/1956.
13 *Associated Press*, 7/15/1956.
14 David Payne, *My Life with Princess Margaret*, (Gold Medal Books, 1961), 35.
15 Ibid, 26–27.

Endnotes

16 Ibid, 27.
17 Ibid, 198.
18 Ibid, 198.
19 Ibid, 39.
20 Ibid, 50.
21 *The Washington Post*, 6/8/1958.
22 Hugo Vickers, *A Biography of Cecil Beaton* (Little, Brown, and Company, 1985), 435.
23 David Payne, Ibid, 57–58.
24 *Evening Standard*, 8/21/1957.
25 *The Baltimore Sun*, 8/22/1957.
26 *The New York Times*, 7/20/1958.
27 UPI, 8/1/1958.
28 *The New York Times*, 7/19/1958.
29 *The Baltimore Sun*, 10/22/1956.
30 *The New York Times*, 10/15/1956.
31 *The Baltimore Sun*, 3/30/1958.
32 *The Baltimore Sun*, 11/23/1957; *The Washington Post*, 11/25/1957.
33 *The Baltimore Sun*, 9/11/1957.
34 Barrymaine, Ibid, 227.
35 Ibid, 229.
36 *The Baltimore Sun*, 8/15/1958.
37 *Associated Press*, 11/16/1958.
38 *Daily Mail*, 10/21/2016.
39 Payne, Ibid, 95.
40 *Daily Mail*, 10/21/2016.

Chapter 9: Everybody Likes Him

1   William Glenton, "A Room on the London Docks," *McCall's Magazine*, October 1965, 116–117.
2   Nicholas Haslam, *Redeeming Features*, (Knopf, 2009), 83.
3   Anne de Courcy, *Snowden, The Biography*, (Weidenfeld & Nicolson, 2008), 4.
4   Kenneth Rose, *The Journals of Kenneth Rose, Vol I*, (Weidenfeld & Nicolson), xv.
5   De Courcy, Ibid, 18–19.
6   William Glenton, Ibid, 117.
7   Ibid, 118.
8   Ibid, 118.
9   Ibid.
10 Payne, Ibid, 45.
11 Ibid.
12 Haslam, Ibid, 77.
13 Ibid, 103.
14 Payne, Ibid, 134.
15 Ibid.
16 Hugo Vickers to author, 2/12/2022.
17 *The Washington Post*, 5/1/1960.
18 Ibid.

19 Ibid.
20 Ibid.
21 Glenton, Ibid, 178.
22 Ibid, 178.
23 Ibid.
24 The Queen Mother's Letters, Ibid, 726–729.
25 Ibid, 729.
26 *Cosmopolitan Magazine*, 1/9/1961; Payne, Ibid, 168–169.
27 To author.
28 *The Guardian*, 3/10/2017.
29 *McCall's*, Ibid, 184.
30 Anne de Courcy, Ibid, 84.
31 Jeremy Paxman, *On Royalty*, (Penguin Books, 2007), 60.
32 *The Baltimore Sun*, 2/27/1960; *The Washington Post*, 3/20/1960.
33 *The Baltimore Sun*, 3/18/1960.
34 Drew Middleton, *The New York Times*, 2/26/1960.
35 *The Washington Post*, 3/13/1960.
36 *New York Daily News Service*, 3/7/1960.
37 *Associated Press*, 3/1/1960.
38 Nicholas Haslam, Ibid, 193.
39 *The New York Times*, 2/29/1960.
40 *The Washington Post*, 5/16/1960.
41 Kenneth Rose, Ibid, 161.

Chapter 10: Her Special Island
1 *The Washington Post*, 6/15/1955.
2 AP wire photo, *The New York Times*, 8/5/1962.
3 *Sunday Express*, 12/11/1955.
4 *The Washington Post*, 12/28/1960.
5 *The Washington Post*, 5/21/1960.
6 *The New York Times*, 5/8/1960.
7 *The Washington Post*, 5/19/1960.
8 *The Washington Post*, 6/21/1960.
9 *The New York Times*, 6/18/1960.
10 *The New York Times*, Ibid.
11 *The Sun*, London, 6/20/1960.
12 William Glenton, Ibid, 83.
13 Anne Coleridge, *The Washington Post*, 9/11/1960; Glenton, Ibid, 7.
14 William Glenton, Ibid, 95.
15 Noël Coward, *The Noël Coward Diaries*, (Little, Brown, and Company, 1982), 136.
16 Glenton, Ibid, 119.
17 Ibid, 121.
18 Ibid, 121.
19 Ibid, 122.
20 Ibid, 120.
21 *The Washington Post*, 11/7/1960.

22 Peregrine Worsthorne, *The New York Times*, 2/1/1962.
23 *The New York Times*, 2/23/1962.
24 *Daily Mirror*, 2/1/1962.
25 *The Washington Post*, 1/17/1962.
26 *The Washington Post*, 1/15/1962.
27 William Glenton, Ibid, 163.
28 Ibid.
29 Noël Coward, Ibid, 4/26/1963.
30 Anthony "Tony" Wedgewood Benn, *Years of Hope*, (Hutchinson, London, 1988), 419.

Chapter 11: A Slipper on the Lawn
1   Kenneth Rose, Vol. 1, Ibid, 189.
2   Milton Gendel, *Just Passing Through*, (Farrar, Straus and Giroux, 2022), 119.
3   Rose, Ibid, 201–202.
4   Rose, Ibid, 204.
5   Ibid, 200.
6   Ibid, 200.
7   Anne de Courcy, Ibid, 107.
8   Ibid, 107.
9   Ibid, 264.
10 Ibid, 264.
11 Ingrid Seward, *Royal Children*, (St. Martin's Press, 1993), 214–215.
12 Christopher Warwick, Ibid, 271.
13 William Glenton, Ibid, 147.
14 Ibid, 128.
15 Marie McNair, *The Washington Post*, 11/2/1965.
16 *The Baltimore Sun*, 8/24/1962.
17 *The Baltimore Sun*, 12/10/1964.
18 *The New York Times, The Sun*, 8/26/1964.
19 *Reuters*, 7/2/1965.
20 UPI, 1/18/1965.
21 *The Baltimore Sun*, 1/8/1964.
22 *Daily Express*, 7/25/1949; *The Chronicle*, Adelaide, 7/25/1949.
23 *The Washington Post*, 11/7/1965.
24 Maxine Cheshire, *The Washington Post*, 11/10/1965.
25 *The New York Times*, 11/9/1965.
26 Charlotte Curtis, *The New York Times*, 11/12-15/1965.
27 *The Washington Post*, 12/28/1965.
28 Betty Beale, 11/17/1965.
29 *The New York Times*, 11/21/1965.
30 *Newsweek*, 11/15/1965.
31 *New York Journal American*, 11/17/1965.
32 Hedda Hopper, *The Washington Post*, 11/10/1965.
33 Scottie Lanahan, *The New York Times*, 10/31/1965.
34 *Vanity Fair*, 2/2019.
35 Russell Baker, *The New York Post*, 11/17/1965.

36 The Washington Post, 11/20/1965.

Chapter 12: Portrait of a Lady
1   The New York Times, 10/31/1965.
2   Gallup Poll, Sunday, 12/28/1966.
3   Godfrey Winn, The Baltimore Sun, 12/31/1950.
4   The Washington Post, 3/8/1966.
5   William Glenton, Ibid, 176.
6   The Baltimore Sun, 1/18/1957.
7   Liz Kulp, Ibid, 4.
8   Diane Malbin, Fetal Alcohol Syndrome and Fetal Alcohol Effects, (Hazelden, 1993), 29.
9   National Improvement Hub, 7/11/2022.
10 McCall's Magazine, April 1974, 76.
11 The Baltimore Sun, 10/18/1979.
12 Fiona MacCarthy, Last Curtsey, Independent, U.S. Edition, 10/22/2006.
13 Diane Malbin, Ibid, 16–17.
14 Major Colin Burgess, Behind Palace Doors, (John Blake, 2006), 154.
15 Nicolas Haslam, Ibid, 235.
16 "Greek Bay" by Sidney Nolan, Robertson/Russell/Snowden, Private View (Thomas Nelson and Sons, 1965), 70, David Jones, 190, Robyn Denny, 241, Jon Hyland, 273, and Brett Whitely, 260.
17 The Baltimore Sun, 7/1/1965.
18 Ladies Home Journal, 9/1965, 114.
19 Idem.
20 Allen Jones, Interview with the author.
21 The New York Times, 8/5/1960.
22 Glenton, The Washington Post, 10/2/1965.
23 Glenton, Ibid, 181.
24 Stephen Birmingham, McCall's Magazine, Ibid, 78.
25 James Lees-Milne, Ancient as the Hills, (John Murray, 1997), 511.
26 Lady Davina Alexander, Interview with the author.
27 Stephen Birmingham, Ibid, 73.
28 Ladies Home Journal, 8/1970, 114.
29 Ibid, 76.
30 Ladies Home Journal, Ibid.
31 Milton Gendel, Ibid. 77.
32 Ibid, 79.
33 Anonymous, Ibid, 78.
34 The New York Times, 6/21/1995.
35 McCall's, Ibid.
36 Ibid, 72.

Chapter 13: Dr. Kenneth Jones
1   Independent, 9/15/2022.
2   Dr. Claire Coles, Interview with the author, 3/9/2023.
3   Dr. Kenneth Jones, Interview with the author, 3/9/2023.

Endnotes

4 Milton Gendel, Ibid, 149.
5 Ibid, 151, (July 1973).
6 *Associated Press*, Ibid, 7/12/1971.
7 Nigel Dempster, *HRH Princess Margaret*, (Quartet Books, 1983), 83–84.
8 James Lees-Milne, Ibid, 116.
9 Lees-Milne, Ibid.
10 James Lees-Milne, Ibid, 6/3/72, 60–61.
11 Stephen Birmingham, Ibid.
12 Tim Heald, *Princess Margaret: A Life Unraveled*, (Weidenfeld & Nicolson, 2007), 268.
13 *Daily Mail*, 10/22/2016.
14 *Daily Mirror*, 7/28/1996.
15 Anne de Courcy, Ibid, 319.
16 Wikipedia.
17 Michael Findlay, Interview with the author.
18 Anonymous, Interview with the author.
19 *The Baltimore Sun*, 2/2/1967.
20 Noel Botham, *Margaret: The Untold Story*, (Blake Publishing, 1994), 248 ff.
21 *The Guardian*, 2/12/2012.
22 *Daily Mail Sunday*, 5/22/2005.
23 Kenneth Rose, *The Journals of Kenneth Rose, Vol. 2*, p. 139.
24 *The Baltimore Sun*, 9/15/1969.
25 Milton Gendel, Ibid, 4/30/1970, p. 65.
26 *The New York Times*, 8/21/1970.
27 Milton Gendel, Ibid, 675.
28 *The New York Times*, 8/31/1970.
29 *Irish Independent*, 7/16/2020.
30 David Pryce-Jones, *Architectural Digest*, October 1979, p. 112.
31 Milton Gendel, Ibid, 9/14/1971.

Chapter 14: Arrows of Desire

1 Nicholas Haslam, Ibid, 260.
2 Anne Glenconner, *Lady in Waiting*, (Hachette Books, 2020), 171.
3 Ibid, 172.
4 Nicholas Courtney, *Lord of the Isle: The Extravagant Life & Times of Colin Tennant*, (Bebe Factum Publishing, 2012), 131.
5 Nigel Dempster, Ibid, 97.
6 Anne Glenconner, Ibid, 72.
7 *Guardian*, 2/9/2002.
8 *Private Eye*, cover, 3/16/1979.
9 Christopher Warwick, Ibid, 268.
10 Philip Hoare, *Independent*, 11/6/1993.
11 Nicholas Courtney, Ibid, 153.
12 Anne Glenconner, 175.
13 "Lady Macbeth and the Princess" by Catch Themes, *Utopia Britannica*, no date; Victoria Moore, "Queen of the Hippies," *Daily Mail*, 3/2/2007.

14 Sir Roderic Victor Llewellyn interviewed by the People's Collection for Wales, No. 387260.
15 "Queen of the Hippies," Ibid.
16 *People*, 4/26/2006.
17 Date not known.
18 April–May 1978.
19 "Fetal Alcohol Syndrome in Adults," New Jersey Rehab/Detox Center, 2015.
20 Sarah Bradford, *Elizabeth*, (Farrar, Straus and Giroux, 1996), 405.
21 Ibid, 443.
22 Edith Wharton, *Age of Innocence*, (Collier Books, 1968), 44.
23 Letter from Christopher Warwick to author, 9/19/2021.
24 Christopher Warwick, Ibid.
25 November 11, 1945.
26 *Guardian*, 2/9/2002.
27 Christopher Warwick to author, 9/19/2021.
28 Christopher Warwick, letter to author, Ibid.
29 Anne Glenconner, Ibid, 274–275.
30 Anne Glenconner, *Telegraph Magazine*, 11/2/2020.
31 Ibid.
32 Anne Glenconner, *Lady in Waiting*, Ibid, 288.
33 Ibid, 277.
34 Nicholas Courtney, Ibid, 211.
35 Janie Stevens, Interview with the author, 3/24/2022.
36 Anne Glenconner, Ibid, 285.
37 Ibid, 212.
38 Lady Prudence Penn, Interview with the author, 8/20/2022.
39 Ibid.
40 Allan Little, "Scotland and Britain 'Cannot Be Mistaken for Each Other,'" BBC News, June 6, 2018, sec. Scotland, https://www.bbc.com/news/uk-scotland-36168729.
41 5/1/2018.
42 Kenneth Rose, Vol. 2, Ibid, 357.
43 William Shawcross, biography, Ibid, 699.
44 *Daily Mail*, 4/11/2023.